Jorge Juan, Antonio de Ulloa

**A Voyage to South America**

Describing at large, the Spanish cities, towns, provinces, etc. on that extensive

continent. Vol. 2

Jorge Juan, Antonio de Ulloa

**A Voyage to South America**
*Describing at large, the Spanish cities, towns, provinces, etc. on that extensive continent. Vol. 2*

ISBN/EAN: 9783337409272

Printed in Europe, USA, Canada, Australia, Japan

Cover: Foto ©Andreas Hilbeck / pixelio.de

More available books at **www.hansebooks.com**

# A VOYAGE TO SOUTH AMERICA:

DESCRIBING AT LARGE,

The SPANISH CITIES, TOWNS, PROVINCES, &c. on that extenfive CONTINENT.

INTERSPERSED THROUGHOUT

With REFLEXIONS on whatever is peculiar in the RELIGION and CIVIL POLICY; in the GENIUS, CUSTOMS, MANNERS, DRESS, &c. &c. of the feveral Inhabitants; whether NATIVES, SPANIARDS, CREOLES, INDIANS, MULATTOES, or NEGROES.

TOGETHER WITH

The NATURAL as well as COMMERCIAL HISTORY of the Country.

And an Account of their GOLD and SILVER MINES.

Undertaken by Command of the KING of SPAIN,

By Don GEORGE JUAN, and Don ANTONIO DE ULLOA,

Both Captains of the SPANISH NAVY; and Members of the ROYAL SOCIETIES of LONDON and BERLIN; and of the ROYAL ACADEMY at PARIS.

Tranflated from the Original Spanifh.

Illuftrated with Copper Plates.

VOL. II.

# CONTENTS

OF

## VOLUME the SECOND.

### BOOK I.

Chap. 1. *Journey from* Quito *to* Truxillo. page 1

Chap. 2. *Arrival at* Truxillo. *Description of that city, continuation of our journey to* Lima. p. 19

Chap. 3. *Account of* Lima. p. 29

Chap. 4. *Of the public entrance,* &c. *of the Vice-roy.* p. 46

Chap. 5. *Of the inhabitants of* Lima. p. 52

Chap. 6. *Of the climate; and of the whole country of* Valles. *Divisions of the seasons.* p. 64

Chap. 7. *Inconveniences, distempers, and evils to which the city of* Lima *is subject.* p. 78

Chap. 8. *Fertility of the territories of* Lima. p. 93

Chap. 9. *Provisions at* Lima. p. 102

Chap. 10. *Trade and commerce of* Lima. p. 106

Chap. 11. *Jurisdiction of the Vice-roy of* Peru: *of the audiences; and diocesses of that kingdom.* p. 112

Chap. 12. *Of the provinces in the diocesses of* Truxillo, Guamanga, Cusco, *and* Arequipa. p. 120

Chap. 13. *Of the audience of* Charcas; *the jurisdictions and bishops fees in that archbishopric.* p. 141

Chap. 14. *Account of the three diocesses of* La Pas, Santa Cruz de la Sierra, *and* Tucuman, *and of their respective provinces.* p. 156

Chap. 15. *Account of* Paraguay *and* Buenos Ayres. *Missions of the Jesuits established in the former, their government and police.* p. 168

### BOOK II.

Chap. 1. *Voyage from* Callao *to* Paita, *thence to* Guayaquil, *and to* Quito. *Description of* Paita. p. 189

Chap.

## CONTENTS.

Chap. 2. *Tranfactions at* Quito. *Unhappy occafion of our fudden return to* Guayaquil. *Second journey to* Lima. p. 195
Chap. 3. *Voyage to* Juan Fernandes. *Account of the feas and winds in that Paffage.* p. 206
Chap. 4. *Account of* Juan Fernandes. *Voyage to* Santa Maria. *Thence to the bay of* Conception. *Nautical remarks.* p. 217
Chap. 5. *Defcription of the city of* Conception, *in the kingdom of* Chili ; *ravages it has fuffered from the* Indians ; *its commerce and fertility.* p. 232
Chap. 6. *Defcription of* Conception *bay; its roads or harbours, fifh,* &c. *fingular mines of fhells in its neighbourhood.* p. 246
Chap. 7. *Defcription of the city of* Santiago. p. 253
Chap. 8. *Account of that part of the kingdom of* Chili *within the jurifdiction of the audience of* Santiago. p. 258
Chap. 9. *Commerce of* Chili. *Account of the wild* Indians *there.* p. 268
Chap. 10. *Voyage to the iflands of* Juan Fernandes, *and thence to* Valparaifo. p. 279
Chap. 11. *Voyage to* Callao. *Second return to* Quito, *third journey to* Lima. p. 285

## BOOK III.

Chap. 1. *Departure from* Callao. *Arrival at* Conception. *Voyage from thence to the ifland of* Fernando de Norona. p. 293
Chap. 2. *Nautical obfervations in the Voyage round* Cape Horn. *Currents and winds commonly met with in that paffage. A table of the variations of the needle obferved in failing from* Conception *to* Fernando de Norona. p. 306
Chap. 3. *Defcription of that ifland.* p. 317
Chap. 4. *Voyage from* Fernando de Norona. *Engagement with two* Englifh *privateers.* p. 326
Chap. 5. *Voyage of the* Delivrance *to* Louifbourg, *where fhe was taken. Nautical remarks on the paffage.* p. 335
Chap. 6. Don George Juan's *Voyage from* La Conception *to* Guarico ; *thence to* Breft. *His return to* Madrid. p. 347
Chap. 7. *Account of the harbour and town of* Louifbourg, *and of its being taken by the* Englifh. *Of the* French *fifhery, and the trade carried on there.* p. 363
Chap. 8. *The colony of* Bofton ; *its rife, progrefs, and other particulars.* p. 380
Chap. 9. *Voyage from* Louifbourg *to* Newfoundland; *account of that ifland and the Cod-fifhery. Voyage to* England. p. 389

A

# A VOYAGE TO SOUTH AMERICA.

## BOOK I.

*Account of our Journey to* LIMA; *with a Description of the* TOWNS *and* SETTLEMENTS *on the Road, and of the City of* LIMA.

### CHAP. I.

*Journey from* QUITO, *to* TRUXILLO.

THE accidents to which human enterprizes and attempts are generally exposed, direct, with an inconstant, but wonderful harmony, the series of our actions and adventures, and introduce among them a great variety of alterations and changes. It is this variety, which, in vegetation embellishes nature, and equally displays the glory and wisdom of the supreme creator in the political and rational world; where we admire the surprizing diversity of events; the infinity of human actions, and the

the different schemes and consequences in politics, the succeffive chain of which, renders hiftory fo delightful, and, to a reflecting mind, fo inftructive. The inconftancy, fo often feen in things the moft folid and ftable, is generally one of the moft powerful obftacles, to the advantages which might otherwife be derived from works of any duration. However great they are, either in reality, or idea, the perfection of them is not only impeded by the viciffitudes of time, and the inconftancy of things, but they even decline, and fall into ruins. Some, thro' want of proper fupport and incouragement; while others, from the mind being wearied out by delays, difficulties, and a thoufand embarraffements, are abandoned; the imagination being no longer able to purfue its magnificent fcheme.

To meafure fome degrees of the Meridian near the equator, the principal intention of our voyage, if confidered only in idea, and abftractedly from the difficulties which attended its execution, muft appear eafy, and as requiring no great length of time; but experience convinced us, that a work of fuch importance to the improvement of fcience, and the intereft of all nations, was not to be performed without delays, difficulties and dangers; which demanded attention, accuracy, and perfeverance. Befides the difficulties neceffarily attending the requifite accuracy of thefe obfervations, the delays we were obliged to make in order to take them in the moft favourable feafons, the intervening clouds, the Paramos, and difpofition of the ground were fo many obftacles to our making any tolerable difpatch; and thefe delays, filled us with apprehenfions, that if any other accidents fhould happen, the whole defign would be rendered abortive, or at leaft, fuffer a long interruption.

It has already been obferved * that while we were at Cuenca, finifhing our aftronomical obfervations in that

* Vol. 1. Chap. II. Book V.

that extremity of the arch of the Meridian, we unexpectedly received a letter from the marquis de Villa Garcia, vice-roy of Peru, defiring us to come, with all fpeed to his capital, any delay on our part might have been improper; and we were folicitous not to merit an accufation of the leaft remiffnefs in his majefty's fervice. Thus we were under a neceffity of fufpending our obfervations for fome time; though all that remained was the fecond aftronomical obfervation, northward, where the feries of our triangles terminated.

The occafion of this delay, arofe from an account, received by the vice-roy, that war being declared between Spain and England, the latter was fending a confiderable fleet on fome fecret defigns into thofe feas. Several precautions had been taken to defeat any attempt; and the vice-roy, being pleafed to conceive that we might be of fome ufe to him in acquiting himfelf with honour on this occafion, committed to us the execution of fome of his meafures; giving us to underftand, that the choice he made of us, was the moft convincing proof of the high opinion he entertain'd of our abilities; and indeed our obligations were the greater, as the diftance of four hundred leagues had not obliterated us from his remembrance, of which he now gave us fo honourable a proof.

On the 24th of September 1740, the vice-roy's letter was delivered to us, and we immediately repaired to Quito, in order to furnifh ourfelves with neceffaries for the journey.

Every thing being performed, we fet out from that city on the 30th of October, and determined to go by Guaranda and Guayaquil; for tho' there is a road by land thro' Cuenca and Loja, yet the other feemed to us the moft expeditious, as the ways are neither fo bad, nor mules and other beafts of carriage fo difficult to be met with. The long ftays in villages were here also little to be apprehended, which are frequently rendered necessary in the other road by inundations, rivers, and precipices.

On the 30th of October we reached the Bodegas, or warehouses, of Babayoho, where taking a canoo we went down the river to Guayaquil; and embarking on board a small ship bound for Puna, we anchored in that port November the 3d. At this place we hired a large balza, which brought us thro' the gulph to Machala. For tho' the usual rout is by the Salto de Tumbez, we were obliged to alter our course, the pilot not being well acquainted with the entrance of a creek, thro' which you pass to the Salto.

On the 5th in the morning our balza landed us on the coast of Machala, from whence we travelled by land to the town, the distance being about two short leagues. The next day we sent away our baggage in a large canoo to the Salto de Tumbez; going myself in the same canoo, being disabled by a fall the preceding day. Don George Juan, with the servants followed on horseback: the whole country being level, is every where full of salt marshes, and overflows at high water, so that the track is not sufficient for two to go a breast.

The Salto where I arrived on the 7th at night, is a place which serves as a kind of harbour for boats and small vessels. It is situated at the head of some creeks, particularly that of Jambeli, between fourteen and sixteen leagues from the coast, but intirely destitute of inhabitants, no fresh water being found in any part of the adjacent country; so that it only serves for landing goods consigned to Tumbez, where they are carried on mules, kept there for this purpose; and in this its whole trade consists. The Salto is uninhabited; nor does it afford the least shelter, all the goods brought thither being deposited in a small square; and, as rain is seldom or never known here,
there

there is little danger of their receiving any damage before they are carried to Tumbez.

Here, as along the sides of all the creeks, the mangrove trees stand very thick, with their roots, and branches so interwoven as to be absolutely impenetrable; tho' the swarms of moschetos are alone sufficient to discourage any one from going among them. The only defence against these insects is, to pitch a tent, till the beasts are loaded, and you again move forward. The more inland parts, where the tides do not reach, are covered with forests of smaller trees, and contain great quantities of deer; but at the same time are infested with tigers; so that if the continual stinging of the moschetos deprives travellers of their rest, it also prevents their being surprized by the tigers, of the fury of which there are many melancholy examples.

On the 9th in the morning I arrived at the town of Tumbez, situated seven leagues from the Salto; the whole country thro' which the road lies is intirely waste, part of it being overflowed by the tides, and the other part dead sands, which reflect the rays of the sun so intensely, as to render it necessary in general to perform this journey in the night; for travelling seven leagues thither, and as many back without either water or fodder, is much too laborious for the mules to undergo in the day time. A drove of mules therefore never sets out from Tumbez for the Salto, till an account arrives, generally by one of the sailors belonging to the vessel, of the goods being landed, and every thing in readiness; as it would otherwise be lost labour, it being impossible that the mules should make any stay there.

Don George Juan had reached Tumbez on the 8th, and tho' he did every thing in his power to provide mules for continuing our journey, we were obliged to wait there some time longer. Nor could we make any advantage of our stay here, except to observe obferve the latitude, which we did on the ninth with a quadrant, and found it to be 3° 13ʹ 16ʺ fouth.

NEAR Tumbez, is a river of the fame name, which difcharges itfelf into the bay of Guayaquil, almoft oppofite to the ifland of St. Clare. Barks, boats, balzas, and canoos may go up and down this river, being three fathom deep, and twenty-five broad; but it is dangerous going up it in the winter feafon, the impetuofity of its current being then increafed by torrents from the mountains. At a little diftance from the cordillera, on one fide of the banks of the river, ftands the town of Tumbez in a very fandy plain, interfperfed with fome fmall eminences. The town confifts only of feventy houfes, built of cane, and thatched, fcattered up and down without any order or fymetry. In thefe houfes are about one hundred and fifty families of Meftizos, Indians, Mulattoes, and a few Spaniards. There are befides thefe other families living along the banks of the river, who having the conveniency of watering their grounds, continually imploy themfelves in rural occupations.

THE heat is exceffive; nor have they here any rain for feveral years fucceffively; but when it begins to fall, it continues during the winter. The whole country from the town of Tumbez, to Lima, contained between the foot of the Cordillera and the fea, is known by the name of Valles, which we mention here, as it will often occur in the remaining parts of this narrative.

TUMBEZ was the place where in the year 1526, the Spaniards firft landed in thefe parts of South America, under the command of Don Francifco Pizarro; and where he entered into feveral friendly conferences with the princes of the country, but vaffals to the Yncas. If the Indians were furprized at the fight of the Spaniards, the latter were equally fo at the prodigious riches which they every where faw, and the largenefs of the palaces, caftles, and temples:

temples; of all of which, tho' built of stone, no vestiges are now remaining.

Along the delightful banks of this river, as far as the water is conveyed, maize, and all other fruits and vegetables that are natives of a hot climate, are produced in the greatest plenty. And in the more distant parts, which are destitute of this advantage, grows a kind of leguminous tree, called algarrobale, producing a bean, which serves as food for all kinds of cattle. It resembles almost that known in Spain by the name of Valencia; its pod being about five or six inches long, and only four lines broad, of a whitish colour, intermixed with veins of a faint yellow. It proves a very strengthening food to beasts of labour, and is used in fattening those for the slaughter, which hence acquire a taste remarkably delicious.

On the 14th, I arrived at the town of Piura, where I was obliged to wait some time for Don George Juan, during which I entirely recovered from the indisposition I before laboured under from my fall.

Here I experienced the efficacy of the calaguala; which I happily found not to fall short of the great reputation it has acquired in several parts of Europe.

From the town of Tumbez, to the city of Piura, is 62 leagues, which we performed in 54 hours, exclusive of those we rested; so that the mules, which always travel one constant pace, go something above a league an hour. To the town of Amotape, the only inhabited place in the whole road, is 48 leagues, the remainining part is one continued desart. At leaving Tumbez, its river is crossed in Balzas; after which for about two leagues the road lies thro' thickets of Algarrobal, and other trees, at the end of which the road runs along the sea coast, to Mancora, 24 leagues from Tumbez. In order to travel this road, an opportunity at low-water must be taken for crossing a place called Malpasso, about six leagues from Tumbez; for being a high steep rock, washed by the sea during the flood, and the top of it impassable from the many chasms and precipices, there is a necessity of passing between the sea and its basis, which is about half a league in length. And this must be done before the flood returns, which soon covers this narrow way, tho' it is very safe at low-water. During the remainder of this journey, it is equally necessary to consult the tide, for the whole country being sandy, the mules would, from their sinking so deep in it, be tired the first league or two. Accordingly travellers generally keep along the shore, which being washed by the breaking of the waves, the sand is more compact and firm; and consequently much easier to the beasts. During the winter, there runs thro' Mancora a small rivulet of fresh water, to the great relief of the mules; but in summer the little remaining in its course is so brackish, that nothing but absolute necessity can render it tolerable. The banks of this rivulet are so fertile by its water, that it produces such numbers of large Algarrobales, as to form a shady forest.

FROM Mancora, the road for fourteen leagues runs between barren mountains, at some distance from the coast, with very troublesome ascents and declivities, as far as the breach of Parinnas; where the same cautions are to be observed as at Mancora, and is the second stage; from whence the road lies over a sandy plain, ten leagues in length, to the town of Amotape, and at some distance from the coast.

This town, which stands in 4° 51' 43" South latitude, is an appendix to the Parish of Tumbez, belonging to its lieutenancy, and in the jurisdiction of Piura. The houses are about 30 in number, and composed of the same materials with those of Tumbez; but the inhabitants are only Indians and Mestizos. A quarter of a league from it is a river of the same fame name, and whofe waters are of fuch prodigious ufe to the country, that it is every where cultivated, and divided into fields, producing plenty of the feveral grains, efculent vegetables, and fruits, natural to a hot climate; but like Tumbez, is infefted with Mofchitos. This river in fummer may be forded; but in winter when the torrents defcend from the mountains it muft be croffed in a balza, the rapidity of its current being then confiderably increafed. There is a neceffity for paffing it in going to Piura, and after this for about four leagues the road lies thro' woods of lofty Algarrobales. Thefe woods terminate on a fandy plain, where even the moft experienced drivers and Indians fometimes lofe their way, the wind leveling thofe hills of fand, which ferved as marks, and effacing all the tracks formerly made: fo that in travelling this country, the only direction is the fun in the day time, and the ftars in the night; and the Indians being little acquainted with the fituation of thefe objects, are often bewildered, and expofed to the greateft hardfhips, before they can again find their way.

From what has been faid the difficulties of traveling this road may be conceived. Befides as far as Amotape, not only all kinds of provifions muft be carried, but even water, and the requifites for kindling a fire, unlefs your provifion confifts of cold meat. In this laft ftage is a mine of cope, a kind of mineral tar, great quantities of which are carried to Callao, and other ports, being ufed in fhips inftead of naphtha, but has the ill quality of burning the cordage; its cheapnefs however induces them to ufe it mixed with naphtha.

The city of Piura, which is at prefent the capital of its jurifdiction, was the firft Spanifh fettlement in Peru. It was founded in the year 1531 by Don Francifco Pizarro, who alfo built the firft church in it. This city was originally called San Miguel de Piura, and ftood in the valley of Targa-
fala,

fala, from whence on account of the badnefs of the air it was removed to its prefent fituation, which is on a fandy plain. The latitude of it is 5° 11' 1" South, and the variation of the needle we obferved to be 8° 13' Eafterly. The houfes are either of bricks dried in the fun, or a kind of reeds called Quinchas, and few of them have any ftory. Here the Corregidor refides, whofe jurifdiction extends on one fide along Valles, and on the other among the mountains. Here is an office for the royal revenue, under an accomptant or treafurer, who relieve each other every fix months, one refiding at the port of Paita, and the oth r in this place: At the former for receiving the duties on imports for goods landed there, and alfo for preventing a contraband trade; and at the latter for receiving the revenues and merchandizes on goods configned from the mountains to Loja; or going from Tumbez to Lima.

This city contains near fifteen hundred inhabitants; and among thefe fome families of rank, befides other Spaniards, Meftizos, Indians, and Mulattoes. The climate is hot and very dry, rains being feldomer known here than at Tumbez: notwithftanding which it is very healthy. It has a river of great advantage to the inhabitants as well as the adjacent country, the foil of which is fandy, and therefore eafier penetrated by the water; and being level the water is conveyed to different parts by canals. But in the fummer the river is abfolutely deftitute of water, the little which defcends from the mountains being abforbed before it reaches the city; fo that the inhabitants have no other method of procuring water, but by digging wells in the bed of the river, the depth of which muft be proportioned to the length of time the drought has continued.

Piura has a hofpital under the care of the Bethlemites; and tho' patients afflicted with all kinds of
diftempers

distempers are admitted, it is particularly famous for the cure of the French disease, which is not a little forwarded by the nature of the climate. Accordingly there is here a great resort of persons infected with that infamous distemper; and are restored to their former health by a less quantity of the specific than is used in other countries, and also with greater ease and expedition.

As the whole territory of this jurisdiction within Valles produces only the Algarroba, maize, cotton, grain, a few fruits and esculent vegetables, most of the inhabitants apply themselves to the breeding of goats, great numbers of which are continually sold for slaughter, and from their fat they make soap, for which they are sure of a good market at Lima, Quito, and Panama; their skins are dressed into leather called Cordovan, and for which there is also a great demand at the above cities. Another branch of its commerce is the Cabuya, or Pita, a kind of plant from whence a very fine and strong thread is made; and which abounds in the mountainous parts of its jurisdiction. Great advantages are also made from their mules, as all the goods sent from Quito to Lima, and also those coming from Spain, and landed at the port of Paita, cannot be forwarded to the places they are consigned to but by the mules of this province; and from the immense quantity of goods coming from all parts, some idea may be formed of the number of beasts employed in this trade, which continues more or less throughout the year; but is prodigious when the rivers are shallow.

Don George Juan being arrived at Piura, every thing was got ready with the utmost dispatch, and on the 21st we continued our journey. The next day we reached the town of Sechura, ten leagues distant from Piura, according to the time we were travelling it. The whole country between thefe two places is a level fandy defart.

Though the badnefs and danger of the roads in Peru fcarce admit of any other method of travelling than on mules, yet from Piura to Lima there is a conveniency of going in litters. Thefe inftead of poles are fufpended on two large canes, like thofe of Guayaquil, and are hung in fuch a manner as not to touch the water in fording rivers, nor ftrike againft the rocks in the afcents or defcents of difficult roads.

As the mules hired at Piura perform the whole journey to Lima, without being relieved, and in this great diftance, are many long defarts to be croffed, the natural fatigue of the diftance, increafed by the fandinefs of the roads, render fome intervals of reft abfolutely neceffary, efpecially at Sechura, becaufe on leaving that town we enter the great defart of the fame name. We tarried here two days: during which we obferved the latitude, and found it $5° \ 32' \ 33\frac{1}{2}''$ S.

The original fituation of this town was contiguous to the fea, at a fmall diftance from a point called Aguja; but being deftroyed by an inundation, it was thought proper to build the prefent town of Sechura about a league diftance from the coaft, near a river of the fame name, and which is fubject to the fame alterations as that of Piura; for at the time we croffed it no water was to be feen; whereas from the months of February or March till Auguft or September, its water is fo deep and the current fo ftrong, as to be paffed only in balzas; as we found in our fecond and third journey to Lima. When the river is dry the inhabitants make ufe of the above mentioned expedient of digging wells in its beds, where they indeed find water but very thick and brackifh. Sechura contains about 200 houfes of cane, and a large and handfome brick church; the inhabitants

are

are all Indians, and confift of near 400 families, who are all employed either as drivers of the mules or fifhermen. The houfes of all thefe towns are quite fimple; the walls confifting only of common canes and reeds, fixed a little way in the ground, with flat roofs of the fame materials, rain being hardly ever known here; fo that they have fufficient light and air, both the rays of the fun and wind eafily finding a paffage. The Indian inhabitants of this place ufe a different language from that common in the other towns both of Quito and Peru; and this is frequently the cafe in great part of Valles. Nor is it only their language which diftinguifhes them, but even their accent; for befides their enunciation which is a kind of melancholy finging, they contract half of their laft words, as if they wanted breath to pronounce them.

THE drefs of the Indian women in thefe parts, confifts only of an Anaco, like that of the women of Quito, except its being of fuch a length as to trail upon the ground. It is alfo much larger, but without fleeves, nor is it tied round them with a girdle. In walking they take it up a little, and hold it under their arms. Their head drefs confifts of cotton cloth laced or embroidered with different colours; but the widows wear black. The condition of every one may be known by their manner of dreffing their hair, maids and widows dividing it into two platted locks, one hanging on each fhoulder, whilft married women braid all their hair in one. They are very induftrious, and ufually employed in weaving napkins of cotton and the like. The men drefs in the Spanifh manner; and confequently wear fhoes; but the women none. They are naturally haughty, of very good underftandings, and differ in fome cuftoms from thofe of Quito. They are a proof of what has been obferved (Book VI. Chap. VI. vol. 1.) with regard to the great improvement they

receive

receive from a knowledge of the Spanish language; and accordingly it is spoken here as fluently as their own. They have genius, and generally succeed in whatever they apply themselves to. They are neither so superstitious, nor so excessively given to vice as the others; so that except in their colour and other natural appearances, they may be said to differ greatly from them; and even in their propensity to intemperance, and other popular customs of the Indians, a certain moderation and love of order is conspicuous among these. But to avoid tedious repetitions, I shall conclude with observing that all the Indians of Valles from Tumbez to Lima are industrious, intelligent, and civilized beyond what is generally imagined.

The town of Sechura is the last in the jurisdiction of Piura, and its inhabitants not only refuse to furnish passengers with mules, but also will not suffer any person of whatever rank, to continue his journey, without producing the Corregidor's passport. The intention of this strictness is to suppress all abuses in trade; for there being besides this road which leads to the desart, only one other called the Rodeo; one of them must be taken; if that of the desart, mules must be hired at Sechura for carrying water for the use of the loaded mules when they have performed half their journey. This water is put into large callebashes, or skins, and for every four loaded mules one mule loaded with water is allowed, and also one for the two mules carrying the litter. When they travel on horseback, the riders carry their water in large bags or wallets made for that purpose; and every one of the passengers, whether in the litter or on horseback, provides himself with what quantity he thinks sufficient, as during the whole journey nothing is seen but sand and hills of it formed by the wind, and here and there, masses

ſes of ſalt: but neither ſprig, herb, flower, or any other verdure.

On the 24th we left Sechura, and croſſed the deſart, making only ſome ſhort ſtops for the eaſe of our beaſts, ſo that we arrived the next day at five in the evening at the town of Morrope, 28 or 30 leagues diſtance from Sechura, tho' falſly computed more by the natives. The extent and uniform aſpect of this plan, together with the continual motion of the ſand which ſoon effaces all tracks, often bewilders the moſt experienced guides, who however ſhew their ſkill in ſoon recovering the right way; for which they make uſe of two expedients: 1ſt, to obſerve to keep the wind directly in their face; and the reverſe upon their return; for the ſouth winds being conſtant here, this rule cannot deceive them: 2d, to take up a handful of ſand at different diſtances, and ſmell to it; for as the excrements of the mules impregnate the ſand more or leſs, they determine which is the true road by the ſcent of it. Thoſe who are not well acquainted with theſe parts, expoſe themſelves to great danger, by ſtopping to reſt or ſleep; for when they again ſet forward, they find themſelves unable to determine the right road; and when they once have loſt the true direction, it is a remarkable inſtance of providence if they do not periſh with fatigue or diſtreſs, of which there are many melancholy inſtances.

The town of Morrope conſiſts of between 70 and 80 houſes, built like thoſe in the preceeding towns; and contains about 160 families, all Indians. Near it runs a river called Pozuelos, ſubject to the ſame changes as thoſe above-mentioned; tho' the lands bordering on its banks are cultivated, and adorned with trees. The inſtinct of the beaſts uſed to this road is really ſurprizing; for, even at the diſtance of four leagues, they ſmell its water, and become ſo impatient that it would be difficulty to ſtop them; accordingly

cordingly they purſue themſelves the ſhorteſt road, and perform the remainder of the journey with remarkable chearfulneſs and diſpatch.

On the 26th we left Morrope, and arrived at Lambayeque, four leagues from it: and being obliged to continue there all the 27th, we obſerved its latitude, and found it 6° 41' 37" S. This place conſiſts of about 1500 houſes, built ſome of bricks, others of bajareques, the middle of the walls being of cane, and plaiſtered over, both on the inſide and outſide with clay: the meaneſt conſiſts entirely of cane, and are the habitations of the Indians. The number of inhabitants amount to about 3000, and among them, ſome conſiderable and opulent families; but the generality are poor Spaniards, Mulattoes, Meſtizos, and Indians. The pariſh church is built of ſtone, large and beautiful, and the ornaments ſplendid. It has four chapels called Ramos, with an equal number of prieſts, who take care of the ſpiritual concerns of the Indians, and alſo attend, by turns, on the other inhabitants.

The reaſon why this town is ſo populous is, that the families which formerly inhabited the city of Sana, on its being ſacked in 1685, by Edward Davis, an Engliſh adventurer, removed hither; being under a farther neceſſity of changing their dwelling from a ſudden inundation of the river of the ſame name, by which every thing that had eſcaped the ravages of the Engliſh, was deſtroyed. It is the reſidence of a Corregidor, having under his juriſdiction, beſides many other towns, that of Morrope. One of the two officers of the revenue appointed for Truxillo, reſides here. A river called alſo Lambayeque, waſhes this place; which, when the waters are high, as they were when we arrived here, is croſſed over a wooden bridge; but at other times may be forded, and often is quite dry.

The neighbourhood of Lambayeque, as far as the induſtry

industry of its inhabitants have improved it, by canals cut from the river, abounds in several kinds of vegetables and fruits; some of the same kind with those known in Europe, and others of the Creole kind, being European fruits planted there, but which have undergone considerable alterations from the climate. About ten leagues from it are espaliers of vines, from the grapes of which they make wine, but neither so good, nor in such plenty as in other parts of Peru. Many of the poor people here, employ themselves in works of cotton, as embroidered handkerchiefs, quilts, mantelets, and the like.

On the 28th, we left Lambayeque, and having passed thro' the town of Monsefu, about four or five leagues distant from it, we halted near the sea coast, at a place called Las Lagunas, or the Fens; these containing fresh water left in them by the overflowings of the River Sana. On the 29th we forded the river Xequetepeque, leaving the town of that name, at the distance of about a quarter of a league, and in the evening arrived at the town of St. Pedro, twenty leagues from Lambayeque, and the last place in its jurisdiction. By observation we found its latitude to be 7° 25′ 49″ S.

St. Pedro consists of about 130 baxaraque houses, and is inhabited by 120 Indian families, 30 of whites and Mestizos, and 12 of Mulattoes. Here is a convent of Augustines, tho' it seldom consists of above three persons, the prior, the priest of the town, and his curate. Its river is called Pacasmayo, and all its territories produce grain and fruits in abundance. A great part of the road from Lambayeque to St. Pedro, lies along the shore, not indeed at an equal, but never at a great distance from it.

On the 30th of November, we passed through the town of Payjan, which is the first in the jurisdiction of Truxillo, and on the first of December we reached that of Chocope, 13 or 14 leagues distant from

St. Pedro. We found its latitude to be 7° 46′ 40″ S. The adjacent country being watered by the river called Chicama, diftributed to it by canals, produces the greateft plenty of fugar canes, grapes, fruits of different kinds, both European and Creole: and particularly maize, which is the general grain ufed in all Valles. From the banks of the river Lambayeque to this place, fugar canes flourifh near all the other rivers, but none of them equal, either in goodnefs or quantity, thofe near the river Chicama.

CHOCOPE confifts of betwixt 80 and 90 baxareque houfes, covered with earth. The inhabitants, who are between 60 and 70 families, are chiefly Spaniards, with fome of the other cafts; but not above 20 or 25 of Indians. Its church is built of bricks, and both large and decent They report here, as fomething very remarkable, that in the year 1726, there was a continual rain of 40 nights, beginning conftantly at four or five in the evening, and ceafing at the fame hour next morning, the fky being clear all the reft of the day. This unexpected event, intirely ruined the houfes, and even the brick church, fo that only fome fragments of its walls remained. What greatly aftonifhed the inhabitants was, that during the whole time the foutherly winds, not only continued the fame, but blew with fo much force, that they raifed the fand, tho' thoroughly wet. Two years after a like phænomenon was feen for about eleven or twelve days, but was not attended with the fame deftructive violence as the former. Since which time nothing of this kind has happened, nor had any thing like it been remembered for many years before.

CHAP.

## CHAP. II.

*Our arrival at* Truxillo; *a Description of that City, and the Continuance of our Journey to* Lima.

WITHOUT staying any longer at Chocope than is usual for resting the beasts, we continued our journey, and arrived at the city of Truxillo, 11 leagues distant, and according to our observations, in 8° 6′ 3″ S. latitude. This city was built in the Year 1535, by Don Francisco Pizarro, in the valley of Chimo. Its situation is pleasant, notwithstanding the sandy soil, the universal defect of all the towns in Valles. It is surrounded by a brick wall, and its circuit entitles it to be classed among cities of the third order. It stands about half a league from the sea, and two leagues to the northward of it is the port of Guanchaco, the channel of its maritime commerce. The houses make a creditable appearance. The generality are of bricks, decorated with stately balconies, and superb porticos; but the other of baxareques. Both are however low, on account of the frequent earthquakes; few have so much as one story. The corregidor of the whole department resides in this city; and also a bishop (whose diocese begins at Tumbez) with a chapter consisting of three dignitaries, namely, the dean, arch-deacon, and chanter; four canons, and two prebendaries. Here is an office of revenue, conducted by an accomptant and treasurer; one of whom, as I have already observed, resides at Lambayeque. Convents of several orders are established here; a college of Jesuits, an hospital of our lady of Bethlehem, and two nunneries, one of the order of St. Clare, and the other of St. Teresa.

The inhabitants consist of Spaniards, Indians, and

all the other cafts. Among the former are several very rich and diftinguifhed families. All in general are very civil and friendly, and regular in their conduct. The women in their drefs and cuftoms follow nearly thofe of Lima, an account of which will be given in the fequel. Great number of chaifes are feen here, there not being a family of any credit without one; as the fandy foil is very troublefome in walking.

IN this climate, there is a fenfible difference between winter and fummer, the former being attended with cold, and the latter with exceffive heat. The country of this whole valley is extreamly fruitful, abounding with fugar canes, maize, fruits, and garden ftuff; and with vineyards and olive yards. The parts of the country neareft the mountains produce wheat, barley, and other grain; fo that the inhabitants enjoy not only a plenty of all kinds of provifions, but alfo make confiderable exports to Panama, efpecially of wheat and fugars. This remarkable fertility, has been improved to the great embellifhment of the country; fo that the city is furrounded by feveral groves, and delightful walks of trees. The gardens alfo are well cultivated, and make a very beautiful appearance; which with a continual ferene fky, prove not lefs agreeable to travellers than to the inhabitants.

ABOUT a league from the city is a river whofe waters are conducted by various canals, through this delightful country. We forded it on the 14th when we left Truxillo; and, on the 5th after paffing thro' Moche, we came to Biru, ten leagues from Truxillo. The pafs of the corregidor of Truxillo muft be produced to the alcalde of Moche, for without this, as before at Sechura, no perfon would be admitted to continue his journey.

BIRU, which lies in $8° 24' 59''$ S. latitude, confifts of 50 baxareque houfes, inhabited by 70 families of Spaniards, Indians, Mulattoes and Meftizos.

About

About half a league to the northward of it, is a rivulet, from which are cut several trenches, for watering the grounds. Accordingly the lands are equally fertile with those of Truxillo, and the same may be said of the other settlements farther up the river. This place we left the same day, travelling sometimes along the shoar, sometimes at a league distance from it.

On the 6th we halted in a desart place called Tambo de Chao, and afterwards came to the banks of the river Santa; which having passed by means of the Chimbadores, we entered the town of the same name, which lies at about a quarter of a league from it, and 15 from Biru. The road being chiefly over vast sandy plains, intercepted between two hills.

The river Santa, at the place where it is usually forded, is near a quarter of a league in breadth, forming five principal streams, which run during the whole year with great rapidity. It is always forded, and for this purpose persons make it their business to attend with very high horses, trained up to stem the current, which is always very strong. They are called Chimbadores; and must have an exact knowledge of the fords, in order to guide the loaded mules in their passage, as otherwise the fording this river would be scarce practicable, the floods often shifting the beds of the river; so that even the Chimbadores themselves are not always safe: for the fords being suddenly changed in one of the streams, they are carried out of their depth by the current, and irretrievably lost. During the winter season, in the mountains, it often swells to such a height, as not to be forded for several days, and the passengers are obliged to wait the fall of the waters, especially if they have with them any goods; for those who travel without baggage may, by going six or eight leagues above the town, pass over it on balzas made of calabashes; tho' even here not without danger, for if the balze happens to meet any ftrong current, it is fwept away by its rapidity, and carried into the fea. When we forded it, the waters were very low, notwithftanding which, we found from three feveral experiments made on its banks, that the velocity of the current was 35 toifes in 29½ feconds; fo that the current runs 4271 toifes, or a league and an half in an hour. This velocity does not indeed equal what M. de la Condamine mentions in the narrative of his voyage down the river Maragnon, or that of the Amazones, at the Pango, or ftreight of Manceriche. But doubtlefs, when the river of Santa is at its ufual height, it exceeds even the celerity of the Pango; at the time of making our obfervations, it was at its loweft.

The latitude of the town of Santa Miria de la Parrilla, for fo it is alfo called, we determined by an obfervation of fome ftars, not having an opportunity of doing it by the fun, and found it 8° 57' 36" S. It was firft built on the fea coaft, from which it is now fomething above half a league diftant. It was large, populous, the refidence of a Corregidor, and had feveral convents. But in 1685, being pillaged and deftroyed by the above-mentioned Englifh adventurer, its inhabitants abandoned it, and fuch as were not able to remove to a place of greater fecurity, fettled in the place where it now ftands. The whole number of houfes in it at prefent does not exceed thirty; and of thefe the beft are only of baxareque, and the others of ftraw. Thefe houfes are inhabited with about 50 poor families confifting of Indians, Mulattoes, and Meftizos.

During our obfervations we were entertained with a fight of a large ignited exhalation, or globe of fire in the air, like that mentioned in the firft volume of this work, tho' not fo large, and lefs effulgent. Its direction was continued for a confiderable time towards the weft, till having reached the fea coaft, it difappeared with an explofion like that of a cannon. Thofe

who

who had not seen it were alarmed, and imagining it to be a cannon fired by some ship arrived in the port, ran to arms, and hastened on horseback to the shore, in order to oppose the landing of the enemy. But finding all quiet, they returned to the town, only leaving some centinels to send advice, if any thing extraordinary should happen. These igneous phænomena are so far from being uncommon all over Valles, that they are seen at all times of the night, and some of them remarkably large, luminous, and continuing a considerable time.

THIS town and its neighbourhood are terribly infested with Moschitos. There are indeed some parts of the year when their numbers decrease, and sometimes, tho' very seldom, none are to be seen; but they generally continue during the whole year. The country from Piura upwards is free from this troublesome insect, except some particular towns, situated near rivers; but they swarm no where in such intolerable numbers as at Santa.

LEAVING this town on the 8th, we proceeded to Guaca-Tambo, a plantation so called, eight leagues distance from Santa, and contiguous to it is the Tambo, an inn built by the Yncas for the use of travellers. It has a shed for the convenience of passengers, and a rivulet running near it.

ON the 9th we came to another plantation known by the name of Manchan, within a league of which we passed through a village called Casma la Baxa, having a church, with not more than ten or twelve houses. Half way betwixt this and Manchan is another rivulet. The latter plantation is about eight leagues distant from the former. From Manchan on the tenth we travelled over those stony hills called the Culebras, extremely troublesome, particularly to the litters, and on the following day being the 11th, we entered Guarmey, 16 leagues from Manchan; and after travelling about three leagues further we reached the Pascana, or resting place, erected instead of a Tambo or inn, and called the Tambo de Culebras. The town of Guarmey is but small and inconsiderable, consisting only of 40 houses, and these no better than the preceding. They are inhabited by about 70 families, few of which are Spaniards. Its latitude is 10° 3' 53" S. The corregidor has obtained leave to reside here continually, probably to be free from the intolerable plague of the Moschitos at Santa, where formerly was his residence.

On the 13th we proceeded from hence to a place called Callejones, travelling over 13 leagues of very bad road, being either sandy plains, or craggy eminences. Among the latter is one, not a little dangerous, called Salto del Frayle, or the Friar's leap. It is an entire rock, very high, and, towards the sea, almost perpendicular. There is however no other way, tho' the precipice cannot be viewed without horror; and even the mules themselves seem afraid of it by the great caution with which they take their steps. On the following day we reached Guamanmayo, a hamlet at some distance from the river Barranca, and belonging to the town of Pativirca, about eight leagues from the Callejones. This town is the last in the jurisdiction of Santa or Guarmey.

PATAVIRCA consists only of 50 or 60 houses, and a proportional number of inhabitants; among whom are some Spanish families, but very few Indians. Near the sea coast, which is about three quarters of a league from Guamanmago, are still remaining some huge walls of unburnt bricks; being the ruins of an ancient Indian structure; and its magnitude confirms the tradition of the natives, that it was one of the palaces of the ancient caseques, or princes; and doubtless its situation is excellently adapted to that purpose, having on one side a most fertile and delightful country, and on the other, the refreshing prospect of the sea.

ON

On the 15th we proceeded to the banks of the river Barranca, about a quarter of a league diftant. We eafily forded it, under the direction of Chimbadores. It was now very low, and divided into three branches, but being full of ftones is always dangerous. About a league further is the town of Barranca, where the jurifdiction of Guaura begins. The town is populous, and many of its inhabitants Spaniards, tho' the houfes do not exceed 60 or 70. The fame day we reached Guaura, which from Guamanmayo, makes a diftance of nine leagues.

This town confifts only of one fingle ftreet, about a quarter of a league in length, and contains about 150 or 200 houfes; fome of which are of bricks, others of baxareques; befides a few Indian huts.

This town has a parifh church, and a convent of Francifcans. Near it you pafs by a plantation, extending above a league on each fide of the road, which is every where extremely delightful; the country eaftward, as far as the eye can reach, being covered with fugar-canes, and weftward divided into fields of corn, maize, and other fpecies of grain. Nor are thefe elegant improvements confined to the neighbourhood of the town, but the whole valley, which is very large, makes the fame beautiful appearance.

At the South-end of the town of Guaura, ftands a large tower, with a gate, and over it, a kind of redoubt. This tower is erected before a ftone bridge, under which runs Guaura river; and fo near to the town that it wafhes the foundations of the houfes, but without any damage, being a rock. From the river is a fuburb which extends above half a league, but the houfes are not contiguous to each other; and the groves and gardens with which they are intermixed, render the road very pleafant. By a folar obfervation, we found the latitude of Guaura to be 11° 3' 36" S. The fky is clear, and the temperature

perature of the air healthy and regular. For though it is not without a fenfible difference in the feafons, yet the cold of the winter, and the heats of fummer are both eafily fupportable.

In proceeding on our journey from Guarmey we met with a great many remains of the edifices of the Yncas. Some were the walls of palaces; others, as it were large dykes, by the fides of fpacious highways; and others fortreffes, or caftles, properly fituated for checking the inroads of enemies. One of the latter monuments ftands about 2 or 3 leagues North of Pativirca, not far from a river. It is the ruins of a fort, and fituated on the top of an eminence at a fmall diftance from the fea; but the veftiges only of the walls are now remaining.

From Guaura we came to the town of Chancay; and though the diftance between this is reckoned only twelve leagues, we concluded, by the time we were travelling it to be at leaft fourteen. From an obfervation we found its latitude $11° 33' 47''$ S. The town confifts of about 300 houfes, and Indian huts; is very populous, and among other inhabitants can boaft of many Spanifh families, and fome of diftinguifhed rank. Befides its parifh church, here is a convent of the order of St. Francis, and a hofpital chiefly fupported by the benevolence of the inhabitants. It is the capital of the jurifdiction of its name, and belongs to that of Guaura. The Corregidor, whofe ufual refidence is at Chancay, appoints a deputy for Guaura. The adjacent country is naturally very fertile, and every where well watered by canals cut from the river Paffamayo, which runs about a league and a half to the Southward of the town. Thefe parts are every where fowed with maize, for the purpofe of fattening hogs, in which article is carried on a very confiderable trade; the city of Lima being furnifhed from hence.

We left Chancay the 17th; and after travelling

a league beyond the river Paſſamayo, which we forded, arrived at the Tambo of the ſame name, ſituated at the foot of a mountain of ſand, exceeding troubleſome, both on account of its length, ſteepneſs, and difficulty in walking; ſo that it is generally paſſed in the night, the ſoil not being then ſo fatiguing.

FROM thence on the 18th we reached Tambo de Ynca, and after travelling 12 leagues from the town of Chancay, we had at length the pleaſure of entering the city of Lima.

FROM the diſtances careful'y ſet down during the whole courſe of the journey, it appears that from Tumbez to Piura is 62 leagues; from Piura to Truxillo 89, and from Truxillo to Lima 113; in all 264 leagues. The greateſt part of this long journey is generally performed by night; for the whole country being one continued ſand, the reflection of the ſun's rays, is ſo violent, that the mules would be overcome by the heat; beſides the want of water, herbage, and the like. Accordingly the road all along, is rather diſtinguiſhed by the bones of the mules, which have ſunk under their burdens, than by any track or path. For notwithſtanding they are continually paſſing and re-paſſing throughout the whole year, the winds quickly efface all the prints of their feet. This country is alſo ſo bare, that when a ſmall herb or ſpring happens to be diſcovered, it is a ſure ſign of being in the neighbourhood of houſes. For theſe ſtand near rivers, the moiſture of which fertilizes theſe arid waſtes, ſo that they produce that verdure not to be ſeen in the uninhabited parts, as they are ſuch, merely from their being deſtitute of water; without which no creature can ſubſiſt, nor any lands be improved.

IN the towns we met with plenty of all neceſſary proviſions; as fleſh, fowl, bread, fruits, and wine; all extreamly good, and at a reaſonable price; but

the

the traveller is obliged to drefs his meat himfelf, if he has not fervants of his own to do it for him; for in the greateft parts of the towns he will not meet with any one, inclinable to do him that piece of fervice, except in the larger cities where the mafters of inns furnifh the table. In the little towns, the inns, or rather lodging-houfes, afford nothing but fhelter; fo that travellers are not only put to the inconvenience of carrying water, wood and provifions from one town to another, but alfo all kinds of kitchen utenfils. Befides tame fowl, pigeons, peacocks and geefe, which are to be purchafed in the meaneft towns, all cultivated parts of this country abound in turtle doves, which live intirely on maize and the feeds of trees, and multiply exceedingly; fo that fhooting them, is the ufual diverfion of travellers while they continue in any town; but except thefe, and fome fpecies of fmall birds, no others are to be had during the whole journey. On the other hand, no ravenous beafts, or venomous reptiles are found here.

THE diftribution of waters by means of canals, which extend the benefit of the rivers to diftant parts of the country, owes its origin to the royal care and attention of the Yncas; who among other marks of their zeal for promoting the happinefs of their fubjects, taught them by this method, to procure from the earth, whatever was neceffary either for their fubfiftance, or pleafure. Among thefe rivers, many are entirely dry or very low, when the waters ceafe to flow from the mountains; but others, as thofe of Santa Baranca, Guaura, Paffamayo, and others, continue to run with a full ftream during the greateft drought.

THE ufual time when the water begins to increafe in thefe rivers is the beginning of January or February, and continues till June, which is the winter among the mountains; and, on the contrary, the

fummer

summer in Valles; in the former it rains, while in the latter the sun darts a violent heat, and the south winds are scarce felt. From June the waters begin to decrease, and in November or December the rivers are at their lowest ebb, or quite dry; and this is the winter seasons in Valles, and the summer in the mountains. So remarkable a difference is there in the temperature of the air, tho' at so small a distance.

## CHAP. III.

*Account of the City of* LIMA, *the Capital of* PERU.

FORTUITOUS events may sometimes, by their happy consequences, be classed among premeditated designs. Such was the unforeseen cause which called us to Peru; for otherwise the history of our voyage would have been deprived of a great many remarkable and instructive particulars; as our observations would have been limited to the province of Quito. But by this invitation of the vice-roy of Peru, we are now enabled to lead the reader into that large and luxuriant field, the fertile province of Lima, and the splendid city of that name, so justly made the capital of Peru, and the queen of all the cities in South America. It will also appear that our work would have suffered a great imperfection, and the reader consequently disappointed in finding no account of those magnificent particulars, which his curiosity had doubtless promised itself, from a description of this famous city, and an accurate knowledge of the capital province. Nor would it have been any small mortification to ourselves, to have lost the opportunity of contemplating those noble objects, which so greatly increase the value of our work, tho' already enriched with such astronomical

observations

obfervations and nautical remarks, as we hope will prove agreeable to the intelligent reader. At the fame time it opens a method of extending our refearches into the other more diftant countries, for the farther utility and ornament of this voyage; which, as it was founded on the moft noble principles, fhould be conducted and clofed with an uniform dignity.

My defign however is not to reprefent Lima in its prefent fituation, as I fhould then, inftead of noble and magnificent objects, introduce the moft melancholy and fhocking fcenes; ruinated palaces, churches, towers, and other ftately works of art, together with the inferior buildings of which this opulent city confifted, now thrown into ruin and confufion; by the tremendous earthquake of October the 28th 1746; the affecting account of which reached Europe with the fwiftnefs which ufually attends unfortunate advices, and concerning which, we fhall be more particular in another place. I fhall not therefore defcribe Lima, as wafted by this terrible convulfion of nature; but as the emporium of this part of *America*, and endeavour to give the reader an idea of its former glory, magnificence, opulence, and other particulars which rendered it fo famous in the world, before it fuffered under this fatal cataftrophe; the recollection of which cannot fail of being painful to every lover of his country, and every perfon of humanity.

THE city of Lima, or as it is alfo called the city of the kings, was, according to Garcilafo, in his hiftory of the Yncas, founded by Don Francifco Pizarro, on the feaft of the Epiphany, 1535; tho' others affirm that the firft ftone was not laid till the 18th of January that year; and the latter opinion is confirmed by the act, or record of its foundation, ftill preferved in the archives of that city. It is fituated in the fpacious and delightful valley of Rimac, an Indian Word, and the true name of the city itfelf, from a corrupt pronounciation of which word the Spaniards

have

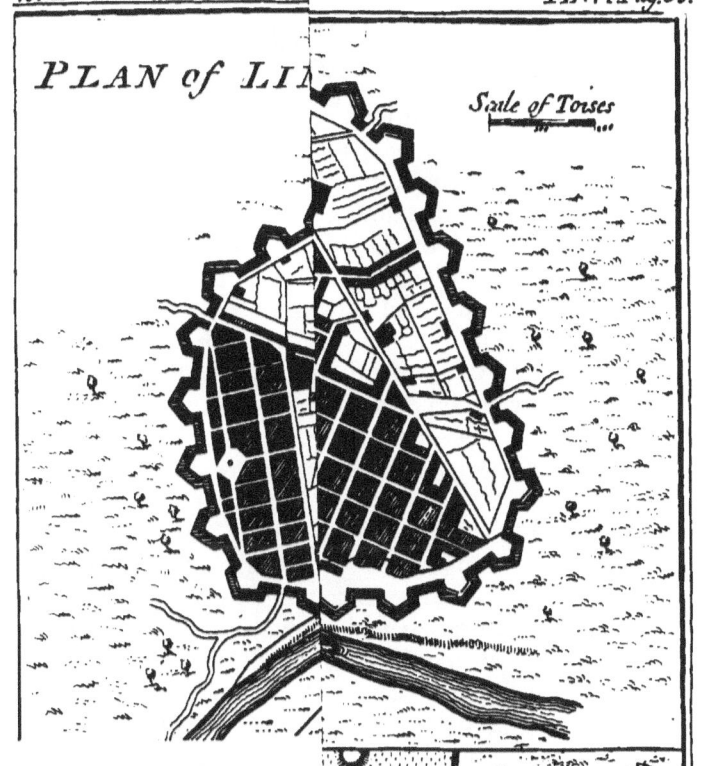

observations and nautical remarks, as we hope will prove agreeable to the intelligent reader. At the same time it opens a method of extending our researches into the other more distant countries, for the farther utility and ornament of this voyage; which, as it was founded on the most noble principles, should be conducted and closed with an uniform dignity.

My design however is not to represent Lima in its present situation, as I should then, instead of noble and magnificent objects, introduce the most melancholy and shocking scenes; ruinated palaces, churches, towers, and other stately works of art, together with the inferior buildings of which this opulent city consisted, now thrown into ruin and confusion; by the tremendous earthquake of October the 28th 1746; the affecting account of which reached Europe with the swiftness which usually attends unfortunate advices, and concerning which, we shall be more particular in another place. I shall not therefore describe Lima, as wasted by this terrible convulsion of nature; but as the emporium of this part of *America*, and endeavour to give the reader an idea of its former glory, magnificence, opulence, and other particulars which rendered it so famous in the world, before it suffered under this fatal catastrophe; the recollection of which cannot fail of being painful to every lover of his country, and every person of humanity.

The city of Lima, or as it is also called the city of the kings, was, according to Garcilaso, in his history of the Yncas, founded by Don Francisco Pizarro, on the feast of the Epiphany, 1535; tho' others affirm that the first stone was not laid till the 18th of January that year; and the latter opinion is confirmed by the act, or record of its foundation, still preserved in the archives of that city. It is situated in the spacious and delightful valley of Rimac, an Indian word, and the true name of the city itself, from a corrupt pronounciation of which word the Spaniards have

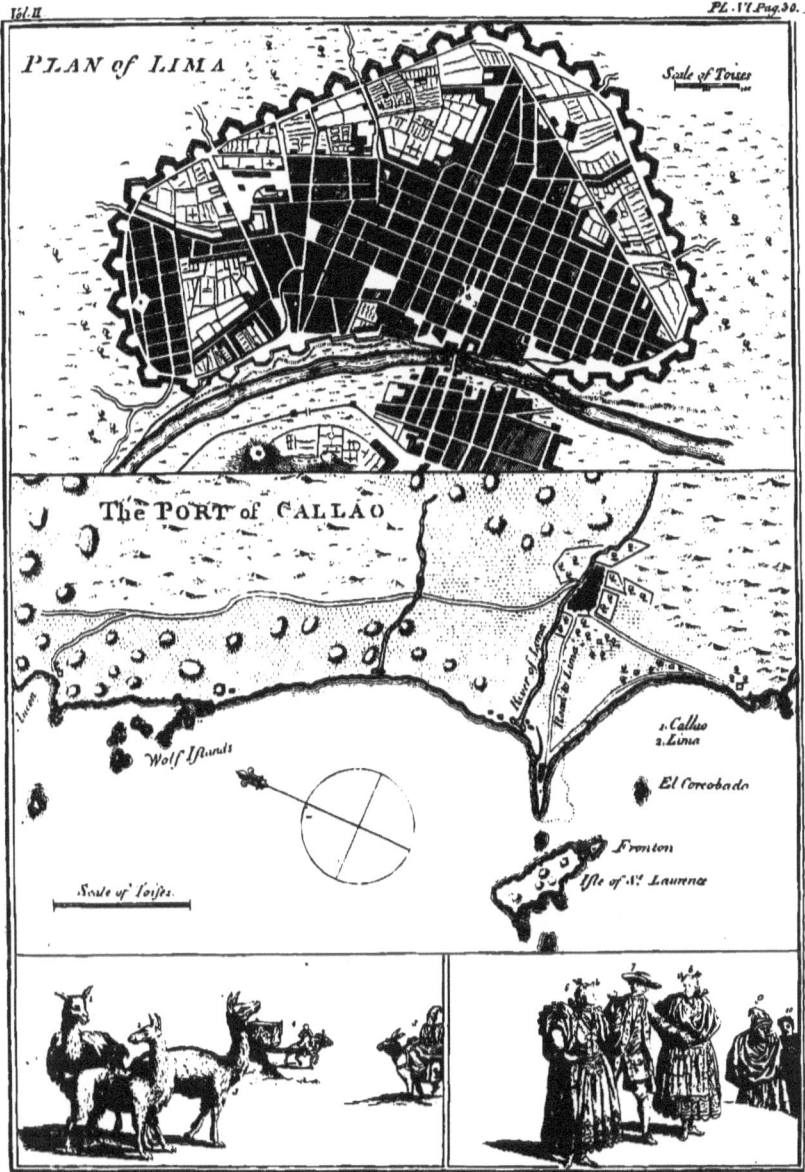

1. The Llama or Peruvian Sheep.  4. The Calash used at Lima.  7. A Spaniard in the Peruvian dress.
2. Vicogn.                       5. A Mestizo woman on horseback. 8. A Lady of Lima in a riding dress.
3. The Huanoco.                  6. A Lady of Lima.               9. A Mulatto woman. 10. A Negro servant.

have derived Lima. Rimac is the name by which both the valley and the river are still called. This appellation is derived from an idol to which the native Indians used to offer sacrifice, as did also the Yncas, after they had extended their empire hither; and as it was supposed to return answer to the prayers addressed to it, they called it by way of distinction Rimac, or, he who speaks. Lima, according to several observations we made for that purpose, stands in the latitude of $12° 2' 31''$ S. and its longitude from the meridian of Teneriffe is $299° 27' 7\frac{2}{3}''$. The variation of the needle is $9° 2' 30''$ easterly.

Its situation is one of the most advantageous that can be imagined; for being in the center of that spacious valley, it commands the whole without any difficulty. Northward, tho' at a considerable distance, is the cordillera, or chain of the Andes; from whence some hills project into the valley, the nearest of which to the city are those of St. Christopher, and Amancaes. The perpendicular height of the former, according to a geometrical mensuration performed by Don George Juan, and M. de la Condamine in 1737, is 134 toises; but father Fevilleé, makes it 136 toises and one foot, which difference doubtless proceeds from not having measured with equal exactness, the base on which both founded their calculations. The height of the Amancaes, is little less than the former, and situated about a quarter of a league from the city.

The river, which is of the same name, washes the walls of Lima, and when not increased by the torrents from the mountains is easily forded; but at other times, besides the increase of its breadth, its depth and rapidity, render fording impossible; and accordingly a very elegant and spacious stone bridge is built over it, having at one end a gate, the beautiful architecture of which is equal to the other parts of this useful structure. This gate forms the entrance into the city, and leads to the grand square, which

which is very large and finely ornamented. In the center is a fountain, equally remarkable for its grandeur and capacity. In the center is a bronze ſtatue of fame, and on the angles are four ſmall baſons. The water is ejected through the trumpet of the ſtatue, and alſo through the mouths of eight lions which ſurround it, and greatly heighten the beauty of this work. The eaſt ſide of the ſquare is filled by the cathedral and the archiepiſcopal palace, whoſe height ſurpaſſes the other buildings in the city. Its principal foundations, and the baſes of its columns and pilaſters, together with the capital front which faces the weſt, are of free-ſtone; the inſide reſembles that of Seville, but not ſo large. The outſide is adorned with a very magnificent facade or frontiſpiece, riſing into two lofty towers, and in the center is the grand portal. Round the whole runs a grand gallery, with a baluſtrade of wood, reſembling braſs, in colour, and at proper diſtances are ſeveral pyramids which greatly augment the magnificence of the ſtructure. In the north ſide of the ſquare is the vice-roy's palace, in which are the ſeveral courts of juſtice, together with the officers of revenue, and the ſtate priſon. This was formerly a very remarkable building both with regard to its largeneſs and architecture, but the greateſt part of it being thrown down by the dreadful earthquake with which the city was viſited, Oct. 20th, 1687, it now conſiſts only of ſome of the lower apartments erected on a terras, and is uſed as the reſidence of the vice-roy and his family.

On the Weſt ſide which faces the cathedral, is the council-houſe, and the city priſon; the South ſide is filled with private houſes, having only one ſtory; but the fronts being of ſtone, their uniformity, porticoes, and elegance, are a great embelliſhment to the ſquare, each ſide of which is 80 toiſes.

The form of the city is triangular, the baſe, or longeſt ſide, extending along the banks of the river.

Its

Its length is 1920 toises, or exactly two thirds of a league. Its greatest breadth from N. to S. that is, from the bridge to the angle opposite to the base, is 1080 toises, or two fifths of a league. It is surrounded with a brick wall, which answers its original intention, but is without any manner of regularity. This work was begun and finished by the duke de la Palata in the year 1685. It is flanked with 34 bastions, but without platforms or embrasures; the intention of it being merely to inclose the city, and render it capable of sustaining any sudden attack of the Indians. It has, in its whole circumference, seven gates, and three posterns.

On the side of the river opposite to the city is a suburb, called St. Lazaro, which has, within these few years, greatly increased. All the streets of this suburb, like those of the city, are broad, parallel, or at right-angles, some running from N. to S. and others from E. to W. forming squares of houses, each 150 yards in front, the usual dimensions of all these quadras or squares in this country, whereas those of Quito are only 100. The streets are paved, and along them run streams of water, conducted from the river a little above the city; and being arched over contribute to its cleanliness, without the least inconveniency.

The houses, though for the most part low, are commodious, and make a good appearance. They are all of Baxareque, and Quincha. They appear indeed to be composed of more solid materials, both with regard to the thickness of the principal walls, and the imitation of cornices on them; and that they may the better support themselves under the shocks of earthquakes, of which this city has had so many dreadful instances, the principal parts are of wood, mortised into the rafters of the roof, and those which serve for walls are lined both within and without with wild canes, and chaglias or others; so that the timber work is totally inclosed. These others are plaſtered over with clay, and white waſhed, but the fronts painted in imitation of free-ſtone. They afterwards add cornices and porticos which are alſo painted of a ſtone colour. Thus the whole front impoſes on the ſight, and ſtrangers ſuppoſe them to be built of thoſe materials which they only imitate. The roofs are flat, and covered only ſo far as is neceſſary to keep out the wind and intercept the rays of the ſun. The pieces of timber, of which the roofs are formed, and which on the inſide are decorated with elegant mouldings and other ornaments, are covered with clay to preſerve them from the ſun. This ſlender covering is ſufficient as no violent rains are ever known here. Thus the houſes are in leſs danger than if built of more compact materials; for the whole building yields to the motions of the earthquakes, and the foundations which are connected with the ſeveral parts of the building follow the ſame motion; and by that means are not ſo eaſily thrown down.

The wild canes, which ſerve for the inner parts of the walls, reſemble in length and bigneſs, thoſe known in Europe, but without any cavity. The wood of them is very ſolid, and little ſubject to rot. The chaglla is alſo a kind of ſhrub growing wild in the foreſts and on the banks of rivers. It is ſtrong and flexible like the oſier. Theſe are the materials of which the houſes in all the towns of Valles mentioned in the preceding chapter, are built.

Towards the eaſt, and weſt parts of the city, but within the walls, are a great many fruit and kitchen gardens; and moſt of the principal houſes have gardens for entertainments, being continually refreſhed with water by means of the canals.

The whole city is divided into the five following pariſhes. 1. Sagrario, which has three prieſts. 2. St. Ann, and 3. St. Sebaſtian, each having two prieſts. 4. St. Marcelo, and 5. St. Lazaro, each of which has one prieſt only. The pariſh of the latter extends it-

ſelf

self five leagues, namely to the valley of Caraballlo, and to it belong the many large plantations in that space; chapels are therefore erected for celebrating mass on days of precept, that the people may perform their duty without the fatigue and trouble of travelling to Lima. Here are also two chapels of ease, that of St. Salvador in the parish of St. Ann; and that of the orphans, in the Sagrario. There is also in the Cercado, one of the quarters of the town, a parish of Indians, under the care of the Jesuits.

The convents here are very numerous; four Dominicans, viz. La Casa grande, Recolleccion de la Magdalena, the college of St. Thomas, appropriated to literature, and Santa Rosa. Three of Francifcans, viz. Casa grande, Recoletos de nuestra Senora de los Angeles, or Guadalupe, and Los Descalzos de San Diego, the latter is in the suburb of San Lazaro. Three of the order of Auguftin, namely Casa grande; the Seminary of San Ildefonso, a literary college; and the noviciate at Nuestra Senora de Guia. Three also belong to the order of Mercy, namely, the Casa principal, the college of St. Pedro Nolasco, and a Recolleccion, called Bethlehem.

The Jesuits have six colleges or houses, which are those of St. Paul, their principal college; St. Martin, a college for secular students; St. Anthony, a noviciate; the house of possession, or desamparados, under the invocation of Nuestra Senora de los Dolores; a college in the Circado, where the Indians are instructed in the precepts of religion; and that of the Chacarilla, appointed for the exercises of St. Ignatius; and accordingly all seculars on their desire to perform them are admitted. They are also allowed the liberty of beginning when most convenient for themselves, and are handsomely entained by the college during the eight days of their continuance. But it must be observed, that of all these convents, the Casas grandes, are now the most
con-

confiderable; the others, befides being fmall, have but few members, and fmall revenues.

BESIDES the preceding nineteen convents and colleges, here are alfo an oratory of St. Philip Neri; a monaftery of the order of St. Benedict, with the title of Nueftra Senora de Monferrat, the abbey of which is commonly the only member, and fent from Spain; and though this foundation is one of the moft ancient in the whole city, its revenue is hardly fufficient to fupport any more: a convent called Nueftra Senora de la Buena Muerte, or the order of that name, generally known by the name of Agonizantes. This order founded a hofpital in the city, in 1715, under the particular direction of the fathers Juan Mugnos, and Juan Fernandez, who with a lay brother of the fame order having in 1736, obtained a licenfe from the council of the Indians, went from Spain and founded a convent of community in every form. In the fuburb of St. Lazaro is alfo a convent of St. Francis de Paula, a modern foundation, under the name of Nueftro Senora del Scorro.

THERE are alfo in Lima three other charitable foundations, namely St. Juan de Dios, ferved by the religious of that order, and appropriated to the relief of perfons recovering from ficknefs; and two of Bethlemites; one of which, being the Cafa grande, is without the city, and founded for the relief of fick Indians, who are taken care of in Santa Ana; and the other within the city, called that of the incurables, being appropriated to perfons labouring under difeafes of that nature. The latter, as we have already obferved,\* was founded fo early as the year 1671. This opulent city has alfo nine other hofpitals, each appropriated to fome peculiar charity.

1. San Andres, a royal foundation, admitting only Spaniards.

\* Chap. IV. Lib. V. Vol. I.

2. San Pedro, for poor ecclefiaftics.

3. El Efpiritu Santo, for mariners, and fupported by the fhips belonging to thefe feas, their crews being properly affeffed for that purpofe.

4. San Bartholome, for the negroes.

5. Senora Santa Ana, for the Indians.

6. San Pedro de Alcantara for women.

7. Another for that ufe, under the care of the Bethlemite fathers, erected before their Cafa grande.

8. La Caridad alfo for women.

9. San Lazaro, for the lepers, which with thofe already enumerated, make twelve.

Here are alfo 14 nunneries, the number of perfons in which would be fufficient to people a fmall town. The 5 firft are regulars, and the other 9 recollects.

1. La Encarnation. 2. La Conception. 3. Santa Cathalina. 4. Santa Clara. 5. La Trinidad. 6. El Carmen. 7. Santa Terefa, ò El Carmen baxo. 8. Las Defcalzas de San Jofeph. 9. Las capuchinas. 10. Las Nazarenas. 11. Las Mercidarias. 12. Santa Rofa. 13. Las Trinitarias Defcalzas. 14. Las Monjas del Prado.

Laftly, here are four other conventual houfes, where fome few of the fifters are not reclufes, tho' moft of them obferve that rule. Thefe houfes are:

1. Santa Rofa de Viterbo. 2. Nueftra Senora del Patrocinio. 3. Nueftra Senora de Capacabana, for Indian ladies. 4. San Jofeph.

The laft is a retreat for women who defire to be divorced from their hufbands. There is alfo a houfe conftituted in the manner of convents, for poor women, and under the direction of an ecclefiaftic appointed by the archbifhop, who is alfo their chaplain.

The moft numerous of all thefe nunneries, are the Incarnation, Conception, Santa Clara, and Santa Cathalina. The others are indeed not fo large; but the Recollects in the rectitude and aufterity of their lives, are an example to the whole city.

HERE is also an orphan-house, divided into two colleges, one for the boys, and the other for the girls: besides several chapels, in different parts of the city; but the following list will shew at once, the parishes, hospitals, churches and monasteries of Lima; which was always no less conspicuous with regard to a zeal for religion than for splendor.

LIST of the parishes, convents of each order, hospitals, nunneries, and conventual houses in Lima.

Parishes 6.
CONVENTS of San Domingo, 4. Of San Frances, 3. Of San Augustin, 3. Of la Merced, 3.
COLLEGES of Jesuits, 6.
ORATORY of St. Philip Neri, 1.
MONASTERY of Benedictins, 1. Of San Francisco de Paula, 1. Of Agonizantes, 1. Of San Juan de Dios, 1. Of Bethlemites, 2.
NUNNERIES of Regulars, 5. Of Recollets, 9.
CONVENTUAL houses, 4. House for poor women, 1. Orphan house, 1. Hospitals, 12.

ALL the churches, both conventual and parochial, and also the chapels, are large, constructed partly of stone, and adorned with paintings and other decorations of great value; particularly the cathedral, the churches of St. Dominic, St. Francis, St. Augustin, the fathers of Mercy, and that of the Jesuits, are so splendidly decorated, as to surpass description; an idea being only to be formed by the sight. The riches and pomp of this city, especially on solemn festivals, is astonishing. The altars, from their very bases to the borders of the paintings, are covered with massive silver, wrought into various kinds of ornaments. The walls also of the churches are hung with velvet, or tapestry of equal value, adorned with gold and silver fringes: all which in this country, is remarkably dear; and on these are splendid pieces of plate in various figures. If the eye be directed from the

the pillars, walls and ceiling, to the lower part of the church, it is equally dazzled with glittering objects, presenting themselves on all sides; among which are candlesticks of massive silver, six or seven feet high, placed in two rows along the nave of the church; embossed tables of the same metal, supporting smaller candlesticks; and in the intervals betwixt them pedestals on which stand the statues of angels. In fine the whole church is covered with plate, or something equal to it in value; so that divine service, in these churches, is performed with a magnificence scarce to be imagined; and the ornaments, even on common days, with regard to their quantity, and richness, exceed those which many cities of Europe pride themselves with displaying on the most common occasions.

If such immense riches are bestowed on the body of the church, how can imagination itself form an idea of those more immediately used in divine worship, such as the sacred vessels, the chalices, ostensoriums, &c. in the richness of which there is a sort of emulation between the several churches. In these the gold is covered with diamonds, pearls, and precious stones, so as to dazzle the eye of the spectator. The gold and silver stuff for vestments and other decorations, are always of the richest and most valuable among those brought over by the register ships. In fine, whatever is employed in ornamenting the churches, is always the richest of the kind possible to be procured.

The principal convents are very large, with convenient and airy apartments. Some parts of them, as the outward walls which inclose them, are of unburnt bricks; but the building itself of quinchas or baxareques. The roofs of many are arched with brick, others only with quinchas; but of such curious architecture as entirely to conceal the materials; so that the frontispieces, and principal gates have a majestic appearance. The columns, freizes, statues and cornices are of wood, finely carved, but so nearly imitating the colour and appearance of stone, as only to be discovered by the touch. This ingenious imitation does not proceed from parsimony, but necessity; in order to avoid as much as possible the dreadful devastations of earthquakes, which will not admit of structures built with ponderous materials.

The churches are decorated with small cupolas of a very pretty appearance; and though they are all of wood, the sight cannot distinguish them from stone. The towers are of stone from the foundation the height of a toise and a half, or two toises, and from thence to the roof of the church of brick, but the remainder of wood painted of a free-stone colour, terminating in a statue, or image alluding to the name of the church. The height of these may be nearly known from that of St. Dominic, which by a geometrical mensuration we found to be between 50 and 60 yards; a height which tho' small in proportion to the largeness of the structure, is a necessary caution both with regard to the shocks of earthquakes, and the weight of the bells, which in size and number exceed those of Spain, and on a general ringing produce a very agreeable harmony.

All the convents are furnished with water from the city, though not from that of the rivulets, which, as we before observed, run through the streets in covered channels; but brought from a spring by means of pipes. While on the other hand, both the monasteries and nunneries are each obliged to maintain a fountain in the street, for the public use of poor people, who have not the conveniency of water in their houses.

The vice-roys whose power extends over all Peru, usually reside at Lima; but the province and audience of Quito has been lately detached from it; as we have observed in our account of that province. This government is triennial, though at the expiration
of

of that term the sovereign may prolong it. This office is of such importance, that the vice-roy enjoys all the privileges of royalty. He is absolute in all affairs, whether political, military, civil, criminal, or relating to the revenue, having under him offices and tribunals for executing the several branches of government; so that the grandeur of this employment is in every particular equal to the title. For the safety of his person and the dignity of his office, he has two bodies of guards; one of horse, consisting of 160 private men, a captain, and a lieutenant: Their uniform is blue, turn'd up with red, and laced with silver. This troop consists entirely of picked men, and all Spaniards. The captain's post is esteemed very honourable. These do duty at the principal gate of the palace; and when the vice-roy goes abroad, he is attended by a piquet guard consisting of eight of these troopers. The 2d is that of the halbadiers, consisting of 50 men, all Spaniards; dressed in a blue uniform, and crimson velvet waistcoats laced with gold. These do duty in the rooms leading to the chamber of audience, and private apartments. They also attend the vice-roy when he appears in public, or visits the offices, and tribunals. The only officer of this body is a captain, whose post is also reckoned very eminent. Both captains are nominated by the vice-roy. Besides these there is another guard within the palace, consisting of 100 private men, a captain, lieutenant and sub-lieutenant; being a detachment from the garrison of Callao. These are occasionally employed in executing the governour's orders, and the decrees of the tribunals, after they have received the sanction of his assent.

THE vice-roy, besides assisting at the courts of justice, and the councils relating both to the finances and war, gives every day public audience to all sorts of persons; for which purpose there are in the palace, three very grand and spacious rooms. In the first,

firſt, which is adorned with the portraits of all the vice-roys, he receives the Indians and other caſts. In the ſecond, he gives audience to the Spaniards; and in the third, where, under a rich canopy are placed the pictures of the king and queen then reigning, he receives thoſe ladies who deſire to ſpeak to him in private without being known.

The affairs relating to the government are expedited by a ſecretary of ſtate, with an aſſiſtant, properly qualified for ſuch an arduous poſt. From this office are iſſued the orders for paſſports which muſt be had from every Corregidor in his juriſdiction. The ſecretary has alſo the power of filling all juridical employments as they become vacant, for the term of two years; as alſo thoſe of the magiſtracy, who at the expiration of their term, have not been replaced by others of his majeſty's nomination. In a word this office may be ſaid to be the channel by which all affairs relating both to war and government are tranſacted.

All cauſes relating to juſtice, are tried in the court called the *Audiencia*, from the decrees of which there is no appeal to the ſupreme council of the Indies, unleſs after notorious injuſtice or a ſecond trial; as the vice-roy himſelf preſides in it. The Audiencia which is the chief court at Lima, is compoſed of 8 auditors or judges, and a fiſcal, for civil cauſes. This court is held in the vice-roy's palace, in the 3 ſaloons appropriated to it. In one the deliberations are held, and in the other two, the cauſes are tried either publickly or privately, the ſenior judge always preſiding. Criminal cauſes are tried in a 4th apartment, the judges being 4 Alcaldes of the court, and a criminal fiſcal. There is alſo a fiſcal protector of the Indians, and ſome ſupernumeraries.

Next to the tribunal of audience, is the chamber of accounts, conſiſting of a commiſſioner, five chief accomptants, two receivers, and two directors, with other

other inferior officers belonging to each clafs. Here all Corregidors, intrufted to collect the revenue, pafs their accounts. Here alfo the diftributions and managements of the royal revenue are regulated.

Lastly, the royal treafury, under a treafurer, accomptant, and agent, who have the fuperintendance of all his majefty's revenue of what kind foever; fince whatever revenue arifes from the other parts of this province is remitted to Lima as the capital of the kingdom.

The corporation of Lima, confifts of regidores or aldermen, an alferez real, or fheriff; and two alcaldes, or royal judges; all being noblemen of the firft diftinction in the city. Thefe have the direction of the police, and the ordinary adminiftration of juftice. The alcaldes prefide alternately every month; for by a particular privilege of this city, the jurifdiction of its corregidor extends only to the Indians.

Here is a court for the effects of deceafed perfons, which takes cognizance of the goods of thofe dying inteftate, and without lawful heir; and likewife of thofe entrufted with the effects of other perfons. It confifts of a judge, who is generally one of the auditors, a counfellor, and an accomptant.

The next tribunal is that of commerce, or the Confulado. Its principal officers are a prefident and two confuls. All who are entered in the lift of merchants are members of it, and have a vote in the choice of thefe officers, who, with an affeffor, decide all commercial difputes and proceffes, by the fame rules as the confulados at Cadiz and Bilboa.

Lima has alfo a corregidor, whofe jurifdiction extends to all Indians both within the city and five leagues round it. The principal places in this jurifdiction are Surco, Los Chorrillos, Miraflores, la Magdalena, Lurigancho, Late, Pachacama, and Lurin, together with the Indian inhabitants of the two fuburbs of Callao, called new and old Pitipiti. The
infinite

infinite number of Indians who inhabited this valley before and at the time of the conqueſt, are now reduced to the few inhabitants of the abovementioned places; and have only two Caſiques, namely thoſe of Miraflures and Sureo, and theſe in ſuch low circumſtances as to teach muſic at Lima for ſubſiſtence.

THE cathedral chapter, beſides the archbiſhop, conſiſts of the dean, archdeacon, chanter, treaſurer, and rector, four canons by ſuffrage, five by preſentation, ſix prebendaries, and ſix ſemi-prebendaries; but the eccleſiaſtical tribunal conſiſts only of the archbiſhop and his chancellor. His ſuffragans are the biſhops of Panama, Quito, Truxillo, Guamanga, Arequipa, Cuzco, St. Jago, and Conception; the two laſt are in the kingdom of Chili.

THE tribunal of inquiſition conſiſts of two inquiſitors, and a fiſcal, who like the ſubordinate officers, are nominated by the inquiſitor general; and in caſe of a vacancy, filled up by the ſupreme council of the inquiſition.

THE tribunal of the Cruzada, is conducted by a ſub-deligate commiſſary, an accomptant, and treaſurer, with other inferior officers. But the dean, or ſenior judge of the audience, generally aſſiſts at its deliberations.

LASTLY, here is alſo a mint with its proper officers, where the gold and ſilver are coined.

IN the univerſity and colleges, the happy geniuſes of the natives are improved by divine and human learning, and as we ſhall ſhew in the ſequel, ſoon give elegant ſpecimens of their future acquiſitions. They are in this much more indebted to nature than either to art or their own application; and if they do not equally diſtinguiſh themſelves in other ſtudies, it is not from want of talents, but of proper perſons to inſtruct them in the neceſſary elements. For by their ready comprehenſion of whatever is taught them, we may conclude, that their abilities

are

are equal to other improvements. The chief of thefe feminaries is the univerfity of St. Mark, and the colleges of St. Toribio, St. Martin, and St. Philip. In the former are chairs for all the fciences, and filled by fuffrage; a method always favourable for perfons of learning and underftanding. Some of thefe profeffors, have, notwithftanding the vaft diftance, gained the applaufe of the literati of Europe.

The univerfity makes a ftately appearance without, and its infide is decorated with fuitable ornaments. It has a large fquare court, with a handfome vaulted piazza round it. Along the fides are the halls, where lectures are read; and in one of its angles is the theatre for the public acts, adorned with the portraits of the feveral great men who had their education in this feat of learning, in frames finely ornamented with fculpture, and richly gilded; as are alfo the two rows of feats which extend entirely round the theatre.

FROM what has been faid it fufficiently appears, that Lima is not only large, magnificent, and diftinguifhed, as the capital of the kingdom, by the refidence of the vice-roy, and the fuperior courts and offices, but alfo that it has an acknowledged fuperiority over the other cities in thefe parts, from the public nurferies erected for the advancement of learning and the fciences.

THE richnefs of the churches, and the fplendor with which divine fervice is performed, we have already defcribed. The magnificence of its inhabitants and of its public folemnities are proportional, and difplayed with a dignity peculiar to minds inflamed with a defire of honour, and who value themfelves on celebrating the principal folemnities in a manner, which diftinguifhes Lima from the other cities of its kingdom: Tho' the latter are not wanting in their endeavours to vie with their capital.

OF all the folemnities obferved in America, the
public

public entrance of the vice-roy, is the moſt ſplendid; and in which the amazing pomp of Lima is particularly diſplayed. Nothing is ſeen but rich coaches and calaſhes, laces, jewels, and ſplendid equipages, in which the nobility, carry their emulation to an aſtoniſhing height. In a word this ceremony is ſo remarkable, that I flatter myſelf the reader will not be diſpleaſed at the deſcription.

## CHAP. IV.

*Of the public Entrance of the Vice-Roy at* LIMA; *his Reception, and the chief annual Solemnities.*

ON the landing of the vice-roy at Paita, two hundred and four leagues from Lima, he ſends a perſon of great diſtinction, generally ſome officer of his retinue, to Lima, with the character of an ambaſſador; and, by a memoir, informs his predeceſſor of his arrival, in conformity to his majeſty's orders, who had been pleaſed to confer on him the government of that kingdom. On this Ambaſſador's arrival at Lima, the late vice-roy ſends a meſſenger to compliment him on his ſafe arrival; and on diſmiſſing the ambaſſador, preſents him with ſome jewel of great value, and a juriſdiction or two which happen at that time to be vacant, together with an indulgence of officiating by deputy, if moſt agreeable to him. The corregidor of Piura receives the new vice-roy at Paita, and provides litters, mules, and every other neceſſary for the vice roy and his retinue, as far as the next juriſdiction. He alſo orders booths to be built at the halting places in the deſarts; attends him in perſon, and defrays all the expences, till relieved by the next corregidor. Being at length arrived at Lima, he proceeds, as it were incognito

through

CH. IV.   SOUTH AMERICA.   47

through the city to Callao, about two leagues and a half diftant. In this place he is received and acknowledged by one of the ordinary alcaldes of Lima, appointed for that purpofe, and alfo by the military officers. He is lodged in the vice-roy's palace, which, on this occafion, is adorned with aftonifhing magnificence. The next day, all the courts, fecular and ecclefiaftical, wait on him from Lima, and he receives them under a canopy in the following order. The audiencia, the chamber of accounts, the cathedral chapter, the magiftracy, the confulado, the inquifition, the tribunal de Cruzada, the fuperiors of the religious orders, the colleges, and other perfons of eminence. On this day the judges attend the vice-roy to an entertainment given by the Alcalde; and all perfons of note take a pride in doing the like to his attendants. At night there is a play, to which the ladies are admitted veiled, and in their ufual drefs, to fee the new vice-roy.

THE fecond day after his arrival at Callao, he goes in a coach provided for him by the city, to the chapel de la Legua, fo called from its being about half-way between Callao and Lima, where he is met by the late vice-roy, and both alighting from their coaches, the latter delivers to him a truncheon as the enfign of the government of the kingdom. After this, and the ufual compliments, they feparate.

IF the new vice-roy intends to make his public entry into Lima, in a few days he returns to Callao, where he ftays till the day appointed; but as a longer fpace is generally allowed for the many preparatives neceffary to fuch a ceremony, he continues his journey to Lima, and takes up his refidence in his palace, the fitting up of which on this occafion, is committed to the junior auditor, and the ordinary alcalde.

ON the day of public entry, the ftreets are cleaned, and hung with tapeftry, and magnificent triumphal arches erected at proper diftances. At two in the
afternoon

afternoon the vice-roy goes privately to the church belonging to the monaſtery of Monſerrat, which is ſeparated by an arch and a gate from the ſtreet, where the cavalcade is to begin. As ſoon as all who are to aſſiſt in the proceſſion are aſſembled, the vice-roy and his retinue mount on horſes, provided by the city for this ceremony, and the gates being thrown open, the proceſſion begins in the following order.

The militia; the colleges; the univerſity with the profeſſors in their proper habits; the chamber of accompts; the audience on horſes with trappings; the magiſtracy, in crimſon velvet robes, lined with brocade of the ſame colour, and a particular kind of caps on their heads, a dreſs only uſed on this occaſion. Some members of the corporation who walk on foot, ſupport the canopy over the vice-roy, and the two ordinary alcaldes, which are in the ſame dreſs, and walk in the proceſſion, act as equerries, holding the bridle of his horſe. This part of the ceremony, tho' prohibited by the laws of the Indians, is ſtill performed in the manner I have deſcribed; for the cuſtom being of great antiquity, the magiſtrates have not thought proper to alter it, that the reſpect to the vice-roy might not ſuffer any diminution, and no perſon has yet ventured to be the firſt in refuſing to comply with it.

This proceſſion is of conſiderable length, the vice-roy paſſing through ſeveral ſtreets till he comes to the great ſquare, in which the whole company draw up facing the cathedral, where he alights, and is received by the archbiſhop and chapter. Te Deum is then ſung before the vice-roy, and the officers placed in their reſpective ſeats; after which he again mounts his horſe and proceeds to the palace-gate, where he is received by the Audiencia, and conducted to an apartment in which a ſplendid collation is provided, as are alſo others for the nobility in the anti-chambers.

On the morning of the following day, he returns

to the cathedral in his coach, with the retinue and pomp ufual on folemn feftivals, and public ceremonies. He is preceded by the whole troop of horfe-guards, the members of the feveral tribunals in their coaches, and after them the vice-roy himfelf with his family, the company of halbadiers bringing up the rear. On this occafion all the riches and ornaments of the church are difplayed, the archbifhop celebrates in his pontifical robes, the mafs of thankfgiving; and the fermon is preached by one of the beft orators of the chapter. From hence the vice-roy returns to the palace attended by all the nobility, who omit nothing to make a fplendid figure on thefe occafions. In the evening of this, and the two following days, the collations are repeated, with all the plenty and delicacy imaginable. To increafe the feftivity, all women of credit have free accefs to the halls, galleries, and gardens of the palace, when they are fond of fhewing the difpofitions of their genius, either by the vivacity of repartees, or fpirited converfations, in which they often filence ftrangers of a very ready wit.

This fhew and ceremony is fucceeded by bull feafts at the city's expence, which continue five days. The three firft for the vice-roy, and the two latter in compliment to the ambaffador who brought advice of his arrival, and the great honour conferred on him by the fovereign in the government of this kingdom.

This ambaffador, who, as I before obferved, is always a perfon of eminent quality, makes alfo a public entrance into Lima on horfeback on the day of his arrival, and the nobility being informed of his approach, go out to receive and conduct him to the palace, from whence they carry him to the lodgings prepared for him. This ceremony ufed to be immediately followed by feafts and public diverfions; but in order to avoid that inconvenience, juft when the city is every where bufied in preparing for the reception of the vice-roy, they are deferred, and given at one and the same time as above recited.

The bull-feasts are succeeded by that ceremony, in which the university, the colleges, the convents and nunneries acknowledge him as their vice-royal protector. This is also accompanied with great splendor; and valuable prizes are bestowed on those who make the most ingenious compositions in his praise. These ceremonies, which greatly heighten the magnificence of this city, are so little known in Europe, that I shall be excused for enlarging on them.

They are begun by the university, and the rector prepares a poetical contest, adapted to display either the wit or learning of the competitors. After publishing the themes, and the prizes to be given to those who best handle the subject they have chosen, he waits on the vice-roy to know when he will be pleased to honour the university with his presence; and, the time being fixed, every part of the principal court is adorned with the utmost magnificence. The prizes which are placed in order distinguish themselves by their richness, while the pillars and columns are hung with emblematical devices, or pertinent apothegms on polished shields, surrounded by the most beautiful mouldings.

The reception is in the following order. On the vice-roy's entering the court he is conducted to the rectoral chair, which, on this occasion, glitters with the magnificence of an eastern throne. Opposite to it sits the rector, or, in his absence, one of the most eminent members of that learned body, who makes a speech, in which he expresses the satisfaction the whole university feels 'in such a patron. After this the vice-roy returns to his palace, where, the day following, the rector presents him with a book, containing the poetical contest, bound in velvet, and plated at the corners with gold, accompanied with some elegant piece of furniture, whose value is never less than eight hundred or a thousand crowns.

The

The principal end of the univerſity in this ceremony being to ingratiate itſelf with the vice-roy and his family, the rector contrives that the poetical pieces which gain the prizes, be made in the name of the principal perſons of his family, and accordingly the moſt diſtinguiſhed prizes are preſented to them; and there being 12 ſubjects in the conteſt, there are three prizes for each, of which the two inferior fall to thoſe members, whoſe compoſitions are moſt approved of. Theſe prizes are pieces of plate, valuable both for their weight and workmanſhip.

The univerſity is followed by the colleges of St. Philip and St. Martin, with the ſame ceremonies, except the poetical conteſt.

Next follow the religious orders, according to the antiquity of their foundation in the Indies. Theſe preſent to the vice-roy the beſt theſes maintained by ſtudents at the public acts.

The vice-roy is preſent at them all, and each diſputant pays him ſome elegant compliment, before he enters on his ſubject.

The ſuperiors of the nunneries ſend him their congratulatory compliments, and when he is pleaſed in return to viſit them, they entertain him with a very fine concert of muſick, of which the vocal parts are truly charming; and at his retiring they preſent him with ſome of the chief curioſities which their reſpective inſtitutes allow to be made by them.

Besides theſe feſtivities and ceremonies, which are indeed the moſt remarkable; there are alſo others, ſome of which are annual, in which the riches and liberality of the inhabitants are no leſs conſpicuous. Particularly on New Year's Day, at the election of Alcaldes, who being afterwards confirmed by the vice-roy, appear publickly on horſe-back the ſame evening, and ride on each ſide of him, in very magnificent habits ornamented with jewels, and the furniture of their horſes perfectly anſwerable. This cavalcade

cavalcade is very pompous, being preceded by the two companies of horſe-guards, the halbadiers, followed by the members of the tribunals in their coaches, the vice-roy's retinue, and the nobility of both ſexes.

ON twelfth day in the morning, and the preceding evening, the vice-roy rides on horſeback thro' the town, with the royal ſtandard carried in great pomp before him. This is performed in commemoration of the building of the city, which, as we have already obſerved, was begun on this day; ſolemn veſpers are ſung in the cathedral, and a maſs celebrated; and the ceremony is concluded with a cavalcade, like that on new year's day.

THE Alcaldes choſen for the current year, give public entertainments in their houſes, each three nights ſucceſſively; but that the feaſts of one might not interfere with thoſe of another, and occaſion reſentments, they agree for one to hold his feaſts the three days immediately ſucceeding the election, and the other on twelfth day and the two following. Thus each has a greater number of gueſts, and the entertainments are more ſplendid and ſumptuous. The other feaſts in the courſe of the year, are not inferior to theſe either with regard to numbers or expence; at leaſt the number of them muſt excite a high idea of the wealth and magnificence of Lima.

---

CHAP. V.

*Of the Inhabitants of* LIMA.

HAVING, in our accounts of ſeveral towns thro' which we paſſed to Lima, included alſo the inhabitants, we ſhall obſerve the ſame rule with regard to Lima; for though amidſt ſuch an infinite variety of cuſtoms, there is always ſome reſemblance

between

between those of neighbouring people, yet the difference is also considerable, and no where more so than on this continent, where it doubtless arises from the great distance between the several towns; and, consequently, I may say, from the different genius's and dispositions of the people. And though Lima is the capital of the country, it will appear that it is not a model to other places, with regard to dress, customs, and manner of living.

The inhabitants of Lima are composed of whites, or Spaniards, Negroes, Indians, Mestizos, and other casts, proceeding from the mixture of all three.

The Spanish families are very numerous; Lima according to the lowest computation, containing sixteen or eighteen thousand whites. Among these are reckoned a third or fourth part of the most distinguished nobility of Peru; and many of these dignified with the stile of ancient or modern Castilians, among which are no less than 45 counts and marquises. The number of knights belonging to the several military orders is also very considerable. Besides these are many families no less respectable and living in equal splendor; particularly 24 gentlemen of large estates, but without titles, tho' most of them have ancient seats, a proof of the antiquity of their families. One of these traces, with undeniable certainty, his descent from the Yncas. The name of this family is Ampuero, so called from one of the Spanish commanders at the conquest of this country, who married a Coya, or daughter of the Ynca. To this family the kings of Spain have been pleased to grant several distinguishing honours and privileges, as marks of its great quality: and many of the most eminent families in the city have desired intermarriages with it. All those families live in a manner becoming their rank, having estates equal to their generous dispositions, keeping a great number of slaves and

and other domestics, and those who affect making the greatest figure, have coaches, while others content themselves with calashes or chaises, which are here so common, that no family of any substance is without one. It must be owned that these carriages are more necessary here than in other cities, on account of the numberless droves of mules which continually pass thro' Lima, and cover the streets with their dung, which being soon dried by the sun and the wind, turns to a nauseous dust, scarce supportable to those who walk on foot. These chaises, which are drawn by a mule, and guided by a driver, have only two wheels, with two seats opposite to each other, so that on occasion they will hold four persons. They are very slight and airy; but on account of the gildings and other decorations, sometimes cost eight hundred or a thousand crowns. The number of them is said to amount to 5 or 6000; and that of coaches is also very considerable, tho' not equal to the former. The funds to support these expences, which in other parts would ruin families, are their large estates and plantations, civil and military employments or commerce, which is here accounted no derogation to families of the greatest distinction; but by this commerce is not to be understood the buying and selling by retail, or in shops, every one trading proportional to his character and substance. Hence families are preserved from those disasters too common in Spain, where titles are frequently found without a fortune capable of supporting their dignity. Commerce is so far from being considered as a disgrace at Lima, that the greatest fortunes have been raised by it; those, on the contrary, being rather despised, who not being blessed with a sufficient estate, through indolence, neglect to have recourse to it for improving their fortunes. This custom, or resource, which was established there without any determinate end, being introduced by a vain desire of the first

Spaniards

Spaniards to acquire wealth, is now the real support of that splendor in which those families live; and whatever repugnance these military gentlemen might originally have to commerce, it was immediately removed by a royal proclamation, by which it was declared that commerce in the Indies should not exclude from nobility or the military orders; a very wise measure, and of which Spain would be still more sensible, were it extended to all its dependencies.

At Lima, as at Quito, and all Spanish America, some of the eminent families have been long since settled there, whilst the prosperity of others is of a later date; for being the center of the whole commerce of Peru, a greater number of Europeans resort to it, than to any other city; some for trade, and others, from being invested in Spain with considerable employments: among both are persons of the greatest merit; and tho' many after they have finished their respective affairs, return home, yet the major part, induced by the fertility of the soil, and goodness of the climate, remain at Lima, and marry young ladies remarkable equally for the gifts of fortune as those of nature; and thus new families are continually settled.

The Negroes, Mulattoes, and their descendants, form the greater number of the inhabitants; and of these are the greatest part of the mechanics; tho' here the Europeans also follow the same occupations, which are not at Lima reckoned disgraceful to them, as they are at Quito; for gain being here the universal passion, the inhabitants pursue it by means of any trade, without regard to its being followed by Mulattoes, interest here preponderating against any other consideration.

The third, and last class of inhabitants are the Indians and Mestizos, but these are very small in proportion to the largeness of the city, and the multitudes of the second class. They are employed in

agri-

agriculture, in making earthen ware, and bringing all kinds of provisions to market, domeſtick ſervices being performed by Negroes and Mulattoes, either ſlaves or free, though generally by the former.

The uſual dreſs of the men differs very little from that worn in Spain, nor is the diſtinction between the ſeveral claſſes very great; for the uſe of all ſorts of cloth being allowed, every one wears what he can purchaſe. So that it is not uncommon to ſee a Mulatto, or any other mechanic dreſſed in a tiſſue, equal to any thing that can be worn by a more opulent perſon. They all greatly affect fine cloaths, and it may be ſaid without exaggeration, that the fineſt ſtuffs made in countries, where induſtry is always inventing ſomething new, are more generally ſeen at Lima than in any other place; vanity and oſtentation not being reſtrained by cuſtom or law. Thus the great quantities brought in the galleons and regiſter ſhips, notwithſtanding they ſell here prodigiouſly above their prime coſt in Europe, the richeſt of them are uſed as cloaths, and worn with a careleſneſs little ſuitable to their extravagant price; but in this article the men are greatly exceeded by the women, whoſe paſſion for dreſs is ſuch as to deſerve a more particular account.

In the choice of laces, the women carry their taſte to a prodigious exceſs; nor is this an emulation confin'd to perſons of quality, but has ſpread thro' all ranks, except the loweſt claſs of negroes. The laces are ſewed to their linen, which is of the fineſt ſort, though very little of it is ſeen, the greateſt part of it, eſpecially in ſome dreſſes, being always covered with lace; ſo that the little which appears ſeems rather for ornament than uſe. Theſe laces too muſt be all of Flanders manufacture, no woman of rank condeſcending to look on any other.

Their dreſs is very different from the European, which the cuſtom of the country alone can render
excuſable;

excufable; indeed to Spaniards at their firft coming over it appears extreamly indecent. Their drefs confifts of a pair of fhoes, a fhift, a petticoat of dimity, an open petticoat, and a jacket, which in fummer, is of linen, in winter of ftuff. To this fome add a mantelette, that the former may hang loofe. The difference between this drefs and that worn at Quito, though confifting of the fame pieces is, that at Lima it is much fhorter, the petticoat which is ufually tied below the waift, not reaching lower than the calf of the leg, from whence, nearly to the ancle, hangs a border of very fine lace, fewed to the bottom of the under petticoat; through which the ends of their garters are difcovered, embroidered with gold or filver, and fometimes fet with pearls; but the latter is not common. The upper petticoat, which is of velvet, or fome rich ftuff, is fringed all round, and not lefs crowded with ornaments, than thofe defcribed in the firft volume of this work. But be the ornaments what they will, whether of fringe, lace, or ribbands, they are always exquifitely fine. The fhift fleeves, which are a yard and a half in length, and two yards in width, when worn for ornament, are covered with rolls of laces, variegated in fuch a manner as to render the whole truly elegant. Over the fhift is worn the jacket, the fleeves of which are exceffively large, of a circular figure, and confift of rows of lace, or flips of cambrick or lawn, with lace difpofed betwixt each, as are alfo the fhift fleeves, even of thofe who do not affect extraordinary ornament. The body of the jacket is tied on the fhoulders with ribbands faftened to the back of their ftays; and the round fleeves of it being tucked up to the fhoulders, are fo difpofed together with thofe of the fhift, as to form what may be term'd four wings. If the jacket be not buttoned or clafped before; it is agreeably faftened on the fhoulders; and indeed the whole drefs makes

2                        a moft

a moſt elegant figure. They who uſe a cloſe veſt, faſten it with claſps, but wear over it the looſe jacket, already deſcribed. In the ſummer they have a kind of veil, the ſtuff and faſhion of which is like that of the ſhift and body of the veſt, of the fineſt cambrick or lawn, richly laced: But in winter the veil worn in their houſes is of bays; when they go abroad full dreſſed, it is adorned like the ſleeves. They alſo uſe brown bays, finely laced and fringed, and bordered with ſlips of black velvet. Over the petticoat is an apron of the ſame ſtuff as the ſleeves of the jacket, hanging down to the bottom of it. From hence ſome idea may be formed of the expence of a dreſs, where the much greater part of the ſtuff is merely for ornament; nor will it appear ſtrange, that the marriage ſhift ſhould coſt a thouſand crowns, and ſometimes more.

ONE particular on which the women here extreamly value themſelves, is the ſize of their feet, a ſmall foot being eſteemed one of the chief beauties; and this is the principal fault they find with the Spaniſh ladies, who have much larger feet than thoſe of Lima. From their infancy they are accuſtomed to wear ſtreight ſhoes, that their feet may not grow beyond the ſize of which they eſteem beautiful; ſome of them do not exceed five inches and a half, or ſix inches in length, and in women of a ſmall ſtature they are ſtill leſs. Their ſhoes have little or no ſole, one piece of Cordovan ſerving both for that and the upper leather, and of an equal breadth and roundneſs at the toe and heel, ſo as to form a ſort of long figure of eight; but the foot not complying with this figure, brings it to a greater regularity. Theſe ſhoes are always faſtened with diamond buckles, or ſomething very brilliant in proportion to the ability of the wearer, being worn leſs for uſe than ornament; for the ſhoes are made in ſuch a manner, that they never looſen of themſelves, nor do the

buckles

buckles hinder their being taking off. It is unufual to fet thefe buckles with pearls, a particular to be accounted for, only from their being fo lavifh of them in the other ornaments of drefs, as to confider them as of too little value. The fhoemakers, who are no ftrangers to the foible of the fex, take great care to make them in a manner very little calculated for fervice The ufual price is three half crowns a pair; thofe embroidered with gold or filver coft from eight to ten crowns. The latter. however, are but little worn, the encumbrance of embroidery being fuited rather to enlarge than diminifh the appearance of a fmall foot.

They are fond of white filk ftockings, made extreamly thin, that the leg may appear the more fhapely; the greateft part of which is expofed to view. Thefe trifles often afford very fprightly fallies of wit in their animadverfions on the drefs of others.

Hitherto we have confidered only the more common drefs of thefe ladies; the reader will conceive a ftill higher idea of their magnificence, when he is informed of the ornaments with which they are decorated in their vifits, and upon public occafions. We fhall begin with their manner of dreffing the hair, which being naturally black, and capable of reaching below their waifts, they difpofe in fuch a manner as to appear perfectly graceful. They tie it up behind in fix braided locks, through which a golden bodkin a little bent is inferted, and having a clufter of diamonds at each end. On this the locks are fufpended fo as to touch the fhoulder. On the front and upper part of the head they wear diamond egrets, and the hair is formed into little curls, hanging from the forehead to the middle of the ear, with a large black patch of velvet on each temple. Their ear-rings are of brilliants, intermixed with tuffs of black filk, covered with pearls, refembling thofe already

ready defcribed in the firft volume. Thefe are fo common an ornament, that befides their necklaces, they alfo wear about their neck rofaries, the beads of which are of pearls, either feparate or fet in clufters to the fize of a large filbert; and thofe which form the crofs are ftill larger.

BESIDES diamond rings, necklaces, girdles, and bracelets, all very curious both with regard to water and fize, many ladies wear other jewels fet in gold, or for fingularity fake, in tombago. Laftly, from their girdle before is fufpended a large round jewel enriched with diamonds; much more fuperb than their bracelets, or other ornaments. A lady covered with the moft expenfive lace inftead of linen, and glittering from head to foot with jewels, is fuppofed to be drefs'd at the expence of not lefs than thirty or forty thoufand crowns. A fplendor ftill the more aftonifhing, as it is fo very common.

A fondnefs for expence in thefe people, does not confine itfelf to rich apparel; it appears no lefs in the ftrange neglect, and the fmall value they feem to fet upon them, by wearing them in a manner the moft carelefs, and by that means bringing upon themfelves frefh expences in repairing the old or purchafing new jewels; efpecially pearls on account of their fragility.

THE moft common of the two kinds of dreffes worn when they go abroad, is the veil and long petticoat; the other is a round petticoat and mantelet. The former for church, the latter for taking the air, and diverfions; but both in the prevailing tafte for expence, being richly embroidered with filver or gold.

THE long petticoat is particularly worn on holy Thurfday; as on that day they vifit the churches, attended by two or three female negro or mulatto flaves, dreffed in an uniform like pages.

WITH regard to the perfons of the women of Lima, they are, in general, of a middling ftature,
handfome,

handsome, genteel, and of very fair complexions without the help of art; the beauty of their hair, has been already mentioned, but they have usually an enchanting lustre and dignity in their eyes.

These personal charms are heightened by those of the mind, clear and comprehensive intellects, an easiness of behaviour, so well tempered, that whilst it invites love, it commands respect; the charms of their conversation are beyond expression; their ideas just, their expressions pure, their manner inimitably graceful. These are the allurements by which great numbers of Europeans, forgetting the fair prospects they have at home, are induced to marry and settle here.

One material objection against them is, that being too well acquainted with their own excellencies, they are tainted with a haughtiness, which will scarce stoop to the will of their husbands. Yet by their address and insinuating compliance, they so far gain the ascendency over them, as to be left to their own discretion. There may indeed, a few exceptions be found; but these possibly are rather owing to a want of capacity. Another objection may be made to their being more expensive than other ladies: but this arises from the exorbitant price of stuffs, laces, and other commodities, in this country. And with regard to the independence they affect, it is no more than a custom long established in the country. To which may be added, that being natives, and their husbands generally foreigners, it is very natural, that the latter should not enjoy all that authority, founded on laws superior to custom; and hence this error remains uncorrected. The husbands conform to the manners of the country, as their character is not in the least affected thereby; and this complaisance is rewarded by the discretion and affection of their ladies, which are not to be paralleled in any other part of the world.

They

They are so excessively fond of perfumes, that they always carry ambergrise about them; putting it behind their ears, and other parts of the body; and also in several parts of their cloaths. Not content with the natural fragrancy of flowers, which are also a favourite ornament, they scatter perfumes even on their nosegays. The most beautiful flowers they place in their hair, and others, which are most valuable for their odour they stick in their sleeves; the effluvia therefore issuing from these ladies, the reader will conceive to reach to no inconsiderable distance. The flower most in use is the Chirimoya, of mean appearance, but of exquisite scent.

To this passion for flowers it is owing, that the grand square, every morning, on account of the vast quantity of beautiful vegetables brought thither, has the appearance of a spacious garden. The smell and the sight are there sufficiently gratified. The ladies resort thither in their calashes, and if their fancy happens to be pleased, they make but little difficulty with regard to the price. A stranger has the pleasure of seeing assembled here not only the ladies, but every body of rank whose health and avocations will admit of it.

The lower classes of women even to the very negroes, affect, according to their abilities, to imitate their betters, not only in the fashion of their dress, but also in the richness of it. None here are seen without shoes as at Quito, but they are made of so small a size, in order to diminish the natural bigness of the feet, that they must give infinite uneasiness in the wearing. A desire of being distinguished by an elegant dress is universal. Their linen is always starch'd to a great degree, in order to display the costly patterns of their laces. After this universal passion, their next care, and indeed a much more commendable one, is cleanliness; of which the uncommon

common neatnefs of their houfes are fufficient inftances.

They are naturally gay, fprightly, and jocofe, without levity; remarkably fond of mufick; fo that even among the loweft you are entertained with pleafing and agreeable fongs; for the gratification of this paffion, they have in general good voices, and fome of them are heard with admiration. They are very fond of balls, where they diftinguifh themfelves equally by the gracefulnefs and agility of their motions. In fine, the reigning paffions of the fair at Lima, are fhew, mirth, and feftivity.

The natural vivacity and penetration of the inhabitants of Lima, both men and women, are greatly improved by converfing with perfons of learning reforting thither from Spain. The cuftom of forming fmall affemblies, has alfo a great tendency to improve their minds, and give them a ready and happy manner of expreffion, from an emulation to diftinguifh themfelves in thefe engaging accomplifhments.

Tho' the natives have too great a fhare of pride, they are not wanting in docility when proper methods are taken. They inftantly fhew their reluctance to obey a command given with haughtinefs; but, when delivered with mildnefs and affability, equally obfequious and fubmiffive. They are charmed with gentlenefs of manners; and a few inftances of kindnefs make a lafting impreffion on their minds. They are remarkably brave, and of fuch unblemifhed honour, as never to diffemble an affront received, or give one to others; fo that they live together in a chearful and focial manner. The Mulattoes being lefs civilized, and having but flender notions of the turpitude of vice, and the importance of virtue, are haughty, turbulent and quarrelfome. Yet the mifchievous confequences of thefe vices are

lefs

less common, than might naturally be expected in such a populous city.

The manners and dispositions of the nobility, correspond with their rank and fortune. Courtesy shines in all their actions, and their complaisance to strangers is without limits. The reception they give them, is equally free from flattery and a haughty reserve; so that all the Europeans, whether they visit them out of curiosity or from commercial motives, are charmed with their probity, politeness, candour, and magnificence.

## CHAP. VI.

*Of the Climate of the City of* Lima *and the whole Country of* Valles: *And the divisions of the seasons.*

THE temperature of the air of Lima, and its alterations, would be greatly injured, by an inference drawn from what is felt in the same degree of north latitude; as Lima would from thence be concluded another Carthagena; the latitude of both cities, one in the northern and the other in the southern hemisphere, differing but very little; whereas in fact it is quite the reverse. For as that of Carthagena is hot to a degree of inconvenience, this of Lima is perfectly agreeable. And tho' the difference of the four seasons are sensible, all of them are moderate, and none of them troublesome.

Spring begins towards the close of the year, that is, towards the end of November, or beginning of December. But is to be understood only of the heavens, as then the vapours which filled the atmosphere during the winter subside; the sun to the

great

great joy of the inhabitants again appears, and the country now begins to revive, which during the abfence of his rays had continued in a ſtate of languor. This is ſucceeded by ſummer, which, tho' hot from the perpendicular direction of the ſun's rays, is far from being inſupportable; the heat, which would indeed otherwiſe be exceſſive, being moderated by the ſouth-winds, which at this ſeaſon always blow, tho' with no great force. At the latter end of June, or the beginning of July, the winter begins, and continues till November or December, the autumn intervening between both. About this time the ſouth winds begin to blow ſtronger, and bring the cold with them; not indeed equal to that in countries where ſnow and ice are known, but ſo keen that the light dreſſes are lain by, and cloth or other warm ſtuffs worn.

THERE are two cauſes of the cold felt in this country, and nature, wiſe in all her ways, provides others which produce the ſame effect at Quito. The firſt cauſe of cold at Lima is the winds, which paſſing over the frozen climes of the ſouth pole, bring hither part of the frigorific particles from thoſe gelid regions; but as a ſufficient quantity of theſe could not be brought over ſuch an immenſe ſpace as lies between the frozen and torrid zones of its hemiſphere, nature has provided another expedient: during the winter, the earth is covered with ſo thick a fog, as totally to intercept the rays of the ſun; and the winds, by being propagated under the ſhelter of this fog, retain the particles they contracted in the frozen zone. Nor is this fog confined to the country of Lima, it extends, with the ſame denſity, northward thro' all the country of Valles, at the ſame time filling the atmoſphere of the ſea; as will be ſhewn hereafter.

THIS fog ſeldom fails daily to cover the earth, with a denſity that obſcures objects at any diſtance:

About 10 or 11 it begins to rife, but without being totally difperfed, tho' it is then no impediment to the fight, intercepting only the rays of the fun by day, and by night thofe of the ftars; the fky being continually covered whatever height the vapours float at in the atmofphere. Sometimes, indeed, they are fo far difperfed as to admit of feeing the difk of the fun, but ftill precluding the heat of his rays.

It is not unworthy obfervation on this head, that at the diftance only of two or three leagues, the vapours are much more diffipated from noon to evening than in the city, the fun fully appearing fo as to moderate the coldnefs of the air. Alfo at Callao, which is only two leagues and a half from Lima, the winter is much more mild, and the air clearer, during that feafon, for the days at Lima, are very melancholy and difagreeable, not only on account of the darknefs, but frequently during the whole day the vapours continue in the fame degree of denfity and pofition, without breaking, or being elevated above the earth.

It is in this feafon only that the vapours diffolve into a very fmall mift or dew, which they call garua, and thus every where equally moiftens the earth; by which means all thofe hills, which during the other part of the year offer nothing to the fight but rocks and waftes, are cloathed with verdure, and enamelled with flowers of the moft beautiful colours, to the great joy of the inhabitants, who, as foon as the feverity of winter is abated, refort into the country, which exhibits fo elegant an appearance. Thefe garuas or dews never fall in quantities fufficient to damage the roads, or incommode the traveller; a very thin ftuff will not foon be wet thro'; but the continuance of the mifts during the whole winter without being exhaled by the fun, renders the moft arid and barren parts fertile. For the fame reafon they turn

the

the difagreeable duft in the ftreets of Lima into a mud, which is rather more offenfive.

THE winds which prevail during the winter, are nearly, though not exactly fouth; fometimes fhifting a little to the S. E. between which and the fouth they always blow. This we obferved to have conftantly happened during the two winters we fpent in this country, one at Lima, and the other at Callao; The former in the year 1742, and the latter in 1743. The firft was one of the moft fevere that had been felt, and the cold general in all that part of America to Cape Horn. In Chili, Baldivia, and Chiloe, the cold was proportionable to the latitudes; and at Lima it occafioned conftipations and fluxions, which fwept away fuch numbers, that it feemed to refemble a peftilence. And tho' diforders of this kind are very common in the winter feafon, they are rarely attended with the danger which then accompanied them.

THE extraordinary fingularity obferved in the kingdom of Peru, namely, that it never rains; or to fpeak more properly, that the clouds do not convert themfelves into formal fhowers, has induced many naturalifts to enquire into the caufe; but in their folutions of this difficulty they have varied, and invented feveral hypothefes to account for fo ftrange an effect. Some attribute it to the conftancy of the fouth winds, concluding, that as they are inceffant, they propel the vapours rifing from the fea, to the fame point; and thus by never refting in any part, as no oppofite winds blow during the whole year to check their courfe, there is not time fufficient for the mifts to collect themfelves, and, by an increafe of gravity to defcend in the manner of rain. Others have attributed it to the natural cold brought by the fouth wind, which continue the atmofphere in a certain degree of heat during the whole year, and thus increafe the magnitude of the particles of the air,

which

which with the nitrous effluvia acquired in its paſſage over the ſurface of the ſea, together with thoſe of the ſeveral minerals with which this country abounds, leſſen its velocity, and conſequently its power of uniting the vapours ſo as to form drops, whoſe gravity is greater than that of the air. To this we may add, that the rays of the ſun not exerting a force ſufficient for uniting and putting them in motion, the heat being greatly leſſened by the coldneſs of the wind, the fog cannot be converted into drops of rain. For while the weight of the cloud does not exceed that of the air, by which it is ſupported, it cannot precipitate.

I SHALL not cenſure this, or any other hypotheſis, formed for explaining the above phænomenon, not being certain that I have myſelf diſcovered the true cauſe; I ſhall however give the reader my thoughts, and leave them to the diſcuſſion of philoſophers. In order to this I ſhall lay down ſome preliminary principles, which may ſerve as a foundation to thoſe who ſhall apply themſelves to diſcover the true cauſe of this phænomenon, with ſome inſtructions for judging of the ſeveral hypotheſes that have been formed on this extraordinary ſubject.

1. IT is to be ſuppoſed, that throughout the whole country of Valles, no other winds are known during the whole year, than the ſoutherly, that is between the S. and S. E. and this not only on the land, but alſo to a certain diſtance at ſea; it evidently appearing that the winds are limited between the S. and S. E. It is therefore very ſtrange that ſome writers ſhould aſſert that they are confined between the S. and S. W. as this is abſolutely falſe. There are indeed intervals when theſe winds are ſcarce felt, and an air, tho' extreamly ſmall, ſeems to come from the north, and which forms the fog. 2. In winter the S. wind blows harder than in ſummer, eſpecially near the ſurface of the earth. 3. Tho' no formal rain is

is ever known in the country of Valles, there are wetting fogs called Garuas, which continue the greatest part of the winter; but are never seen in summer. 4. When the Garuas fall, it is observed that the clouds, mist, or vapours, which rise from the earth, remain almost contiguous to its surface; and the same fog which is converted into a Garua, begins by a moist air, till the humidity gradually increasing to its greatest condensation, the small drops which fall, are easily distinguishable. This is so natural, that it is known in all other countries subject to any degree of cold, and, consequently, not to be wondered at in this.

I give the name of cloud, mist, or vapours, to that which produces the Garua or small rain; for tho' there may be some accidental distinctions between these three kinds, they are not such as cause any material difference: The fog being only the vapour condensed more than when it first rose; and the cloud only a fog elevated to a greater height, and still more condensed than the former; so that in reality they may all be considered as one and the same thing, differing only in degrees of density, and therefore it is of little importance whatever name it is called by.

5. The rays of the sun during the summer, cause a prodigious heat all over Valles, and the more so as they are received upon a sandy soil, whence they are strongly reverberated, the winds being at the same time very weak. Hence it appears that the second hypothesis above related, is not founded on truth; for if the force or agitation of the south winds be the cause which hinders the vapours from rising to the height necessary for forming rain, this cause generally ceasing in the summer, the rain might be expected to descend; whereas quite the reverse happens, the Garuas being then much less common.

6. Particular times have been known when the nature

of the country departing as it were from its ufual courfe, formal fhowers have fallen, as we have already mentioned (chap. i.) in defcribing the towns of Chocope, Truxillo, Tumbez, and other places; but with this fingularity, that the winds continued at fouth, and blew much ftronger during the time of the rain, than is ufual either in winter or fummer.

THESE fix preliminary principles are fo common to this climate, that they may be applied to all the places mentioned in this chapter; and are the only guides that muft be followed in determining the true caufe why it does not rain in Peru as in Europe, or, more properly, as is common in the torrid zone.

IT will readily be granted, that the wind blows more ftrongly in fome regions of the atmofphere than in others; experience itfelf having fufficiently proved this to be fact: as on high mountains, along whofe fummits a ftrong wind is felt, when at the foot, hardly any can be perceived; at leaft we found this to be the cafe in all the mountains of the Cordilleras, one of the greateft inconveniences to us being the ftrength of the wind. And indeed this is every where fo common, that any perfon may be convinced of it by only afcending a high tower, when he will foon perceive the difference between the ftrength of the wind at the top and at the bottom. I am not ignorant that fome have endeavoured to prove, that on the land this proceeds from the inequalities of its furface, which hinder the winds from blowing in the plains or low countries with that force which is felt on eminences; but the fame thing happening at fea, as experience has abundantly proved, it appears beyond difpute, that the furface is not the place where the wind exerts its greateft force. This being granted, it may be confidently afferted, that the fouth winds blow with the greateft force in a portion of the atmofphere at fome diftance from the earth; but not generally higher than that in which the rain is formed;

or

## Ch. VI.   SOUTH AMERICA.   71.

or where the aqueous particles unite so as to form drops of any sensible gravity or magnitude. In this country therefore the clouds or vapours elevated above this space, that is, those which have the greatest degree of altitude, move with a much less velocity than the winds under them. Nor is it uncommon in other climates, besides that of Valles, for these clouds to move in a direction contrary to the more dense ones below it. Thus it appears to me, that without the danger of advancing irregular suppositions, the space of the atmosphere, where the winds generally blow with the greatest force, is that where the large drops commonly called rain, are formed.

Now in order to explain the singularity of this remarkable phænomenon, I conceive that in summer, when the atmosphere is most rarified, the sun, by the influence of his rays, proportionally elevates the vapours of the earth, and gives them a greater degree of rarifaction; for his beams being then in a more perpendicular direction to the earth, they have the power of raising them to a greater height. These vapours on their touching the lower part of the atmosphere, where the winds blow with the greatest force, are carried away before they can rise to the height required for uniting into drops, and consequently no rain can be formed. For as the vapours issue from the earth, they are wafted along the lower region of the atmosphere, without any stop; and the winds blowing always from the south, and the vapours being rarified proportionally to the heat of the sun, its too great activity hinders them from uniting: Hence in summer the atmosphere is clear, or free from vapours.

In winter the rays of the sun being less perpendicular to the surface of the earth, the atmosphere becomes considerably more condensed, but the winds from the south much more so, as being loaded with

F 4   the

the frigorific particles from the frozen zone, which particles it communicates to the vapours as they iffue from the earth; and confequently renders them much more condenfed than in fummer: Hence they are hindered from rifing with the fame celerity as before.

To thefe muft be added two other reafons, one, that the rays of the fun for want of fufficient activity diffipates the vapours lefs, fo that they rife much flower. The other that the region where the wind has its greateft velocity, being, in this feafon, near the earth, will not admit of their rifing to any height; and thus they continue contiguous to its furface, where they ftill follow the fame direction, and form the moift fog then felt; and having lefs fpace to dilate themfelves than at a greater height, they, confequently, fooner come into contact, and when fufficiently condenfed, defcend in a Garua.

In the middle of the day the garua ceafes, being then difperfed, which proceeds from the fun's rarifying the atmofphere, whence the vapours afcend and remain fufpended at a greater height, and thus they are rendered more tenuious, and being raifed to a region where they have more room to dilate, they are fo far difperfed as to become imperceptible.

After all, it muft be owned that both in fummer and winter, fome vapours muft furmount the difficulty of the wind in that region where its velocity is greateft, and getting above it afcend to a greater height; tho' not indeed in the very part where they firft reached this current of wind, but at fome diftance from it; fo that thefe vapours are to be confidered, on one hand, as yielding to the current of the air, and, on the other, as afcending in proportion to the rarefaction they have received from the rays of the fun. Hence it follows, that thefe vapours cannot be thofe which are moft condenfed, as the difficulty of rifing is always proportional

onal to the degree of condenfation; and at the fame time their magnitude would render them more fufceptible of the impulfe of the wind. So that thefe confequently being the moſt fubtile or tenuious, on having paffed that region, the celerity with which they were before carried upwards is decreafed, and great numbers of them being united from that lofty miſt which is feen after the cloud is totally diffipated. This miſt cannot be converted into rain; for having paffed above the region proper for its formation, all the parts become congealed, and their weight can never be increafed fufficiently to overcome the refiſtance of the air which fupports them; for the quantity of thofe which have overcome this obſtacle being inconfiderable, they cannot be united with a fufficient quantity of others to withſtand the continual diffipation occafioned by the action of the rays of the fun. Nor can they defcend in either fnow or hail, as might be expected from their prefent ſtate. Befides following always, tho' with lefs velocity, the current of the wind, any fuch concretion of them as to form a thick cloud is prevented; for as we have already obferved, thefe miſts are fo tenuious, as to afford in the day time a confufed view of the difk of the fun, and of the ſtars in the night.

In order to render the premifes agreeeable to obfervation, one difficulty ſtill remains, namely, that thofe lofty miſts are feen only in winter, and not in fummer. But this, in my opinion, muſt naturally be the confequence; for befides the general reafon that the ſtronger influence of the rays of the fun difperfes them, it proceeds from the increafe of the force of the winds during the winter, in a region nearer the earth than in fummer; and the nearer the lower part of this region is to the furface of the earth, the nearer alfo will be the upper part; while, on the contrary, in the fummer, the higher the lower part of this current of air is, the higher will be alfo

its

its upper part; and, as we muſt ſuppoſe, with all philoſophers, that the vapours of the earth can aſcend only to that height, where the gravity of the particles of the vapours are equal to thoſe of the air; and the rapidity of the wind extending in ſummer to theſe limits, they are conſequently involved in its violent impulſe; and thence there cannot be ſuch a multitude of conglomerations as to form the miſt ſo common in winter; for the winds in this ſeaſon ſtrongly blowing thro' a region nearer the earth, the agitation in the upper parts is proportionally leſs. And this current of air being below the region to which vapours can aſcend, the ſpace intercepted between the upper part of this current, and the part to which vapours riſe, becomes filled with them. All this ſeems natural, and is confirmed by experience; for in winter the ſouth winds are ſtronger on the land than in ſummer. But as a further proof may be thought neceſſary, I have added the following.

It has been ſaid that in the town of Chocope, two very hard and continual rains have happened; and that the ſame thing is more frequently ſeen at Tumbez, and other towns of thoſe parts, after ſome years of continual drought, which ſeems ſtrange; for that being in the country of Valles, and not at all different from Lima, no rain would naturally be expected there. Two cauſes for this, however, have occurred to me, one of them flowing from the other. I ſhall begin with the firſt as productive of the ſecond.

From what has been ſaid, it may be inferred, that in a country or climate, where one and the ſame wind perpetually prevails, there can be no formal rain; and in order to form it, either the wind muſt entirely ceaſe, or an oppoſite wind muſt ariſe, which by checking the courſe of the vapours, brings them into contact with thoſe lately exhaled from the earth,

and

and causes them to condense in proportion as they rise by the attraction of the sun, till being rendered heavier than the air by which they were supported, they descend in drops of water.

On reconsidering the circumstances of what happened at Chocope, it will appear, that during the whole day, the sky was clear, and that it was not before five in the evening that the rain began, and with it the violence of the wind. It should also be observed that in the time of the Brisas in those climates where they are periodical, they blow strongest between the setting and rising of the sun; and this happening in September and the following months, forms the summer in Valles, when they enjoy clear days and a lucid atmosphere. This was the case at Chocope at the time of that rain; for tho' the inhabitants did not precisely mention the season in which that event happened, yet the several particulars related, especially that the south winds then prevailed with an uncommon force, sufficiently indicate that it was in the summer; as this would not have been at all remarkable in winter, when they are very variable and sometimes stormy. It may therefore be safely concluded that these events happened during the summer; and, by way of corollary, that the Brisas being stronger than usual, and advancing so far on the continent as even to reach the south winds, they were overpowered by them, and shifted their point; but the succeeding south winds rendering it impossible to return in the same place, they left their former region and blew in a current nearer the earth. By which means the vapours which had been exhaling during the whole day, after being carried by the strongest current of wind to a certain distance, ascended to the region where the Brisas prevailed; and being there repelled by them, had time to condense; for being within that region where the rain is formed, or where many imperceptible drops compose one of a larger magnitude and gravity, and being more minutely divided by the influence of the fun they continued to afcend, till that power ceafing by the fetting of the fun, they again condenfed, and their weight becoming too heavy to be fupported in the air, they defcended in rain, which was the more violent as the vapours were ftrongly repulfed by the Brifas. At the dawn, thefe winds as ufual, began to decreafe, and the rain gradually leffened. The fouth winds blew all day as before; and there being then in the atmofphere, no other winds to oppofe them, they carried with them the vapours as they exhaled, and the atmofphere continued clear and ferene.

THIS happened at Chocope, fituated at a much greater diftance from the parts to which the Brifas extend than Tumbez, Piura, Sechura, and other towns where this is more frequent, as being nearer the equinoctial : notwithftanding, no Brifas or north-winds are felt in that part of the atmofphere near the furface of the earth. So that it is probable, or rather, indeed, evident from experience, that the north winds at the time they prevail, more eafily reach to the countries neareft the equinoctial, than to thofe at a greater diftance, tho' not fo as to be felt in the atmofphere near the earth, but in a more elevated region. Confequently, it is natural for rains to be more frequent in the former than in the latter, where thefe winds very feldom reach, whether in that part of the atmofphere contiguous to the earth, or another, which being more diftant from it they blow there more violently.

I AT firft declared againft any pofitive affertion that the opinion I have now laid before the reader, is founded on fuch undoubted phyfical principles, that no other can be advanced more conformable to phænomena; it being difficult immediately to fix on caufes which agreeing with all circumftances,

leaves

leaves the mind entirely satisfied: And as all within the reach of human perspicuity cannot be accommodated to every particular, as entire conviction requires, let it suffice that I have here delivered my thoughts; leaving the naturalists at full liberty to investigate the true cause, and when discovered, to reject my hypotheses.

As rain is seldom or never seen at Lima, so that place is also equally free from tempests; that those who have neither visited the mountains nor travelled into other parts, as Guayaquil or Chili, are absolute strangers to thunder and lightning; nothing of that kind being known here. Accordingly the inhabitants are extreamly terrified when they first hear the former or see the latter. But it is very remarkable, that what is here entirely unknown, should be so common at thirty leagues distant, or even less, to the east of Lima; it being no farther to the mountains, where violent rains and tempests are as frequent as at Quito. The winds, tho' settled in the abovementioned points, are subject to variations, but almost imperceptible, as we shall explain. They are also very gentle, and even in the severest winters, never known to do any damage by their violence; so that if this country was free from other inconveniences and evils, its inhabitants could have nothing to desire, in order to render their lives truly agreeable. But with these signal advantages, nature has blended inconveniences, which greatly diminish their value; and reduce this country even below those, on which nature has not bestowed such great riches and fertility.

It has been observed, that the winds generally prevailing in Valles, throughout the whole year, comes from the south; but this admits of some exceptions, which, without any essential alteration, implies that sometimes the winds come from the north, but so very faint, as scarcely to move the

vanes

vanes of the ſhips, and confiſt only of a very weak agitation of the air, juſt ſufficient to indicate that the wind is changed from the ſouth. This change is regularly in winter, and with it the fog immediately begins, which in ſome meaſure ſeems to coincide with what has been offered with regard to the reaſon why ſhowers are unknown at Lima. This breath of wind is ſo particular, that from the very inſtant it begins, and before the wind is condenſed, the inhabitants are unhappily ſenſible of it by violent head-aches, ſo as eaſily to know what ſort of weather is coming on before they ſtir out of their chambers.

## CHAP. VII.

*Inconveniences, Diſtempers, and Evils, to which the City of* LIMA *is ſubject; particularly Earthquakes.*

ONE of the inconveniences of Lima, during the ſummer, is that of being tormented with fleas and bugs, from which the utmoſt care is not ſufficient to free the inhabitants. Their prodigious increaſe is partly owing to the duſt of that dung, with which the ſtreets are continually covered; and partly to the flatneſs of the roofs, where the ſame duſt, wafted thither by the winds, produce theſe troubleſome inſects, which are continually dropping thro' the crevices of the boards into the apartments, and by that means render it impoſſible for the inhabitants, notwithſtanding all their pains, to keep their houſes free from them. The moſchitos are very troubleſome, but much leſs ſo than the former.

THE next, and indeed a moſt dreadful circumſtance, is that of earthquakes, to which this country

try is so subject, that the inhabitants are under continual apprehensions of being, from their suddenness and violence, buried in the ruins of their own houses. Several deplorable instances of this kind have happened in this unfortunate city; and lately proved the total destruction of all its buildings. These terrible concussions of nature are not regular, either with regard to their continuance or violence. But the interval between them is never of a length sufficient to obliterate the remembrance of them. In the year 1742 I had the curiosity to observe the distance of time between those which happened successively for a certain space. 1. On the 9th of May at three quarters after nine in the morning. 2. The 19th of the same month at midnight. 3. The 27th at 35 minutes after three in the evening. 4. The 12th of June at three quarters past five in the morning. 5. The 14th of October at nine at night; all which I carefully noted. And it must be observed that these concussions were the most considerable, and lasted near a minute; particularly that of the 27th of May, which continued near two minutes, beginning with one violent shock, and gradually terminating in tremulous motions. Between these above noted were several others, which I omitted, as being neither so lasting nor violent.

These earthquakes, tho' so sudden, have their presages, one of the principal of which is, a rumbling noise in the bowels of the earth, about a minute before the shocks are felt; and this noise does not continue in the place where it was first produced, but seems to pervade all the adjacent subterraneous parts. This is followed by dismal howlings of the dogs, which seem to have the first perception of the approaching danger. The beasts of burden passing the streets, stop, and, by a natural instinct spread open their legs, the better to secure themselves from falling. On these portents the terrified inhabitants fly

from

from their houses into the streets with such precipitation, that if it happens in the night, they appear quite naked; fear and the urgency of the danger, banishing at once all sense of decency. Thus the streets exhibit such odd and singular figures, that might even afford matter for diversion, were it possible, in so terrible a moment. This sudden concourse is accompanied with the cries of children waked out of their sleep, blended with the lamentations of the women, whose agonizing prayers to the saints, increase the common fear and confusion: The men also are too much affected to refrain from giving vent to their terror; so that the whole city exhibits one dreadful scene of consternation and horror. Nor does this end with the shock, none venturing to return to their houses thro' fear of a repetition, which frequently demolishes those buildings which had been weakened by the first.

My attention to set down the exact time of the abovementioned shocks, taught me, that they happen indifferently at half ebb, or half flood; but never at high or low water; which sufficiently confutes what some have confidently advanced, namely, that earthquakes always happen during the six hours of ebb, but never during the flood; because this favours the hypothesis they have advanced to account for their origin and causes; an hypothesis which, in my opinion, does not so sufficiently correspond with observations, as to recommend itself to the assent of intelligent persons.

The nature of this country is so adapted to earthquakes, that all ages have seen their terrible devastations; and that nothing may be wanting to satisfy the curiosity of the reader, I shall introduce the account of that which laid this large and splendid city totally in ruins, with a short narrative of the most remarkable that have been felt in latter ages.

1. The first concussion since the establishment of
the

## CH. VII. SOUTH AMERICA. 81

the Spaniards in these parts, happened in 1582, a few years after the foundation of Lima; but the damage was much less than in some of the succeeding, being chiefly confined to the city of Arequipa, which being situated near that spot, where the motion of the earth was most violent, the greatest part of it was destroyed.

2. On the 9th of July 1586, Lima was visited with another earthquake, and so violent, that even to this time it is solemnly commemorated on the day of the visitation of Elizabeth.

3. In 1609, another like the former happened.

4. On the 27th of November 1630, such prodigious damage was done in the city by an earthquake, and the entire ruin of it apprehended, that in acknowledgment of its deliverance, a festival, called Nuestra Senora del Milagro, is annually celebrated on that day.

5. In the year 1655, on the 3d of November, the most stately edifices, and a great number of houses, were thrown down by an earthquake; the inhabitants fled into the country, and remained there several days, to avoid the danger they were threatened with in the city.

6. On the 17th of June 1678, another earthquake happened, by which several houses were destroyed, and the churches considerably damaged.

7. One of the most dreadful of which we have any account, was that of the 20th of October, 1687. It began at four in the morning, with the destruction of several publick edifices and houses, whereby great numbers of persons perished; but this was little more than a presage of what was to follow, and preserved the greatest part of the inhabitants from being buried under the ruins of the city. The shock was repeated at six in the morning with such impetuous concussions, that whatever had withstood the first, was now laid in ruins; and the inhabitants

VOL. II. G thought

thought themselves very fortunate in being only spectators of the general devastation from the streets and squares, to which they had directed their flight on the first warning. During this second concussion the sea retired considerably from its bounds, and returning in mountainous waves, totally overwhelmed Callao, and the neighbouring parts, together with the miserable inhabitants.

8. On the 29th of September, 1697, this place was visited by another terrible earthquake.

9. On the 14th of July, 1699, a great number of houses were destroyed by another concussion.

10. The 6th of February, 1716, a like disaster.

11. On the 8th of January, 1725, another.

12. On the 2d of December, 1732, was another earthquake at one in the morning.

13, 14, 15. In the years 1690, 1734, and 1745, three others happened, but neither violent nor lasting. But all these were less terrible than the last, as will appear from the following account of it.

16. On the 28th of October, 1746, at half an hour after ten at night, five hours and three quarters before the full of the moon, the concussions began with such violence, that in little more than three minutes, the greatest part, if not all the buildings, great and small in the whole city, were destroyed, burying under their ruins those inhabitants who had not made sufficient haste into the streets and squares; the only places of safety in these terrible convulsions of nature. At length the horrible effects of this first shock ceased; but the tranquility was of short duration, concussions returning with such frequent repetitions, that the inhabitants, according to the account sent of it, computed two hundred in the first twenty four hours, and to the 24th of February of the following year, 1747, when the narrative was dated, no less than four hundred and

and fifty shocks were observed, some of which, if less lasting, were equal to the first in violence.

The fort of Callao, at the very same hour sunk into the like ruins; but what it suffered from the earthquake in its buildings, was inconsiderable, when compared to the terrible catastrophe which followed; for the sea, as is usual on such occasions, receding to a considerable distance, returned in mountainous waves foaming with the violence of the agitation, and suddenly turned Callao, and the neighbouring country into a sea. This was not, however, totally performed by the first swell of the waves; for the sea retiring further, returned with still more impetuosity; the stupendious water covering both the walls and other buildings of the place; so that whatever had escaped the first, was now totally overwhelmed by those terrible mountains of waves; and nothing remained except a piece of the wall of the fort of Santa Cruz, as a memorial of this terrible devastation. There were then twenty-three ships and vessels, great and small, in the harbour, of which nineteen were absolutely sunk, and the other four, among which was a frigate called St. Fermin, carried by the force of the waves to a great distance up the country.

This terrible inundation extended to other ports on the coast, as Cavallos and Guanape; and the towns of Chancay, Guaura, and the valleys della Baranca, Sape, and Pativilca, underwent the same fate as the city of Lima. The number of persons who perished in the ruin of that city, before the 31st of the same month of October, according to the bodies found, amounted to 1300; besides the maimed and wounded, many of which lived only a short time in torture. At Callao, where the number of inhabitants amounted to about 4000, two hundred only escaped; and twenty-two of these by means of the abovemention'd fragment of a wall.

According to an account sent to Lima after this accident,

accident, a volcano in Lucanas burſt forth the ſame night, and ejected ſuch quantities of water, that the whole country was overflowed; and in the mountain near Patas, called Converſiones de Caxamarquilla, three other volcanos burſt, diſcharging frightful torrents of water; like that of Carguayraſſo, mentioned in the firſt Vol. of this Work.

Some days before this deplorable event, ſubterraneous noiſes were heard at Lima, ſometimes reſembling the bellowing of oxen, and at others the diſcharges of artillery. And even after the earthquake they were ſtill heard during the ſilence of the night; a convincing proof that the inflammable matter was not totally exhauſted, nor the cauſe of the ſhocks abſolutely removed.

The frequent earthquakes to which ſouth America, particularly Lima, and all the country of Valles is ſubject, opens a field for enquiry not leſs ample than that juſt mentioned, concerning their cauſes. Many hypotheſes have been formed by philoſophers; but the generality, and with the greateſt appearance of truth, agree in deducing them principally from the violent force of the air contained in ſulphureous ſubſtances and other minerals, and alſo that confined in the pores of the earth; which being too much compreſſed by the incumbent load, make a very violent reſiſtance. This is ſo far from implying any contradiction, that beſides being countenanced by reaſon, it is alſo confirmed by experience. But the apparent difficulty conſiſts in explaining how the vents of the earth become again filled with air, after one concuſſion has happened; it being natural to think, that the quantity which ſtruggled for vent, was thereby diſcharged, and that a long interval of time was neceſſary before another could be produced. Alſo why ſome countries are more ſubject to theſe terrible convulſions than others. Though this ſubject has been treated of by

ſeveral

several authors, I think it my duty here to deliver the opinion which to me seems most probable.

Experience has sufficiently shewed, especially in this country by the many volcanoes in the Cordilleras which pass through it, that the bursting of a new burning mountain causes a violent earthquake, so as totally to destroy all the towns within its reach; as happened at the opening of the volcano in the desart of Carguagoazo as mentioned in Vol. I. This tremulous motion, which we may properly call an earthquake, does not so usually happen in case of a second eruption, when an aperture has been before made; or, at least, the motion it causes in the earth is comparatively but small. Whence it is inferred that an aperture being once made, however the substances in the bowels of the mountain may take fire, the convulsion of the earth is seldom or never felt a second time. The reason of which is, that the sudden reiteration of this accident greatly augments the volume of the air by rarefaction, and as it finds an easy passage without labouring in the bowels of the earth for a vent, no other concussion is produced than what must follow from the eruption of a great quantity of air through an aperture too narrow for its volume.

The formation of volcanoes is now well known; and that they owe their origin to sulphureous, nitrous, and other combustible substances in the bowels of the earth; for these being intermixed, and, as it were, turned into a kind of paste by the subterraneous waters, ferment to a certain degree, when they take fire, and by dilating the contiguous wind or air, and also that within their pores, so that its volume is prodigiously increased beyond what it was before the inflammation, it produces the same effect as gunpowder, when fired in the narrow space of a mine; but with this difference, that powder on being fired immediately disappears, whereas the volcano being once ignited continues so till all the oleaginous and sulphureous particles contained in the mountain are consumed.

Volcanoes are of two kinds, contracted and dilated. The former are found where a great quantity of inflammable matter is confined in small space; the latter where these combustibles are scattered at a considerable distance from one another. The first are chiefly contained in the bowels of mountains, which may be considered as the natural depositaries of these substances. The second may be considered as ramifications, which, tho' proceeding from the former, are, however, independent, extending themselves under the plains, and traversing them in several directions. This being admitted it will appear, that in whatever country volcanoes, or depositaries of these substances, are very common, the plains will be more diversified with these ramifications; for we are not to imagine that it is only within the bosoms of mountains that substances of this nature exist, and that they are not disseminated through all the parts of the adjacent region. Thus the country now under consideration, abounding in these igneous substances more than any other, must, by the continual inflammation which necessarily follows their natural preparation for it, be more exposed to earthquakes.

Besides the suggestions of natural reason, that a country containing many volcanoes must also be every where veined with ramifications of correspondent substances, it is confirmed by experiment in Peru; where we find almost universally, mines of nitre, sulphure, vitriol, salt, bitumen, and other inflammatory substances, which sufficiently confirm the truth of these inferences.

The soil both of Quito and Valles, particularly the latter, is hollow and spongy, so as to be fuller of cavities or pores, than is usually seen in that of

other

other countries; and consequently abounds with subterraneous waters. Besides which, as I shall presently shew more at large, the waters, from the ice continually melting on the mountains, being filtrated through these pores during their descent, penetrate deep into the cavities of the earth; and during their subterraneous course, moisten, and turn into a kind of paste, those sulphureous and nitrous substances; and though they are not here in such prodigious quantities as in volcanoes, yet they are sufficient, from their inflammatory quality, to rarify the air contained in them, which easily incorporating itself with that confined in the innumerable pores, cavities or veins of the earth, compresses it by its greater expansion, and at the same time rarifies it by its heat; but the cavities being too narrow to admit of its proper dilatation, it struggles for a vent, and these efforts shake all the contiguous parts; till at last, where it finds the least resistance, it forces itself a passage, which sometimes closes again by the tremulous motion it occasions, and at others continues open; as may be seen in different parts of all these countries. When on account of the resistance being equal, it finds a passage in several parts, the chasms or fissures are generally smaller, so that rarely any vestiges remain after the concussion. At other times when the subterranean cavities are so large as to form subterranean caverns, they not only rend the earth, and at every shock leave it full of disruptions; but also cause it to sink into spacious hollows; as I particularly observed near the town of Guaranda, a place in the jurisdiction of Chimbo, in the province of Quito; where in the year 1744 all the ground on one side of the chasm sunk near a yard, the other side rising in the same proportion, though with some inequalities on both sides.

THE loud subterraneous noises preceding earthquakes,

quakes, and which imitate thunder at a diſtance, ſeem to correſpond with the abovementioned cauſe and formation of earthquakes, as they can only proceed from the rarefaction of the air, on the ignition of the exploſive ſubſtances, which being impetuouſly propagated thro' all the caverns of the earth; propelling, and at the ſame time dilating what is contained in them, till all the cavities being pervaded, and no vent found, the efforts for a further dilatation, begin, and form the concuſſion with which it terminates.

It muſt be obſerved that at the time when the air, which had been confined within the earth, burſts through it, neither the light nor fire emitted from the chaſms are ſeen. The reaſon is, that this light and fire exiſt only at the inſtant when the matter becomes inflamed, and the air ſpreading itſelf through all the veins, the light is extinguiſhed by its dilatation, and becomes afterwards imperceptible. It is neceſſary to ſuppoſe that there muſt be ſome, tho' a ſhort interval, between the inflammation and effect. Neither is the flame permanent, the ſubſtances ignited not containing thoſe ſolid and oleaginous particles which ſupply the volcanoes. Beſides they are not in ſufficient quantity to aſcend from the ſubterraneous caverns where they took fire to the ſuperficies of the earth. Farther, this not being the place where the matter was originally contained, but that where it has forced a paſſage for the quantity of air which its rarefaction augmented, the firſt light is loſt among the meanders of its courſe, and therefore not to be ſeen when the wind violently forces a paſſage. There have, however, been inſtances when the light has been ſeen, though much oftner the ſmoke; but this is generally loſt in the clouds of duſt aſcending at the time of the concuſſion.

The ſhocks are repeated at intervals, of a few days, ſometimes of a few hours; proceeding from the matter being diſperſed in different places, and

each

each in a different degree of aptitude for inflammation, one part kindling after another succeffively, as each is more or lefs prepared. Hence proceed alfo the different violence of the fhocks and the different intervals of time. For the quantity firft inflamed increafes, by its heat, other inflammable portions of matter; whence a part which would not have been ignited till after fome days, by means of this adventitious fire, becomes fo within a few hours. The fecond fhocks are more violent, and caufe a greater deftruction than the firft; for the fire of the portion of matter which is firft inflamed, though in itfelf fmall, is fufficient to accelerate the fermentation of a much larger quantity, and confequently muft be attended with more powerful effects.

Though the fummer here, as we have already obferved, is confiderably warm, yet is it not productive of venomous creatures, which in this country are not known; and the fame may be faid of all Valles, though there are fome parts, as Tumbez and Piura, where the heat is nearly equal to that at Guayaquil. This fingularity can therefore proceed from no other caufe than the natural drought of the climate.

The diftempers moft common at Lima are malignant, intermittent and catarrhous fevers, pleurifies, and conftipations; and thefe rage continually in the city. The fmall-pox is alfo known here as at Quito, but is not annual; though when it prevails, great numbers are fwept away by it.

Convulsions are likewife very common and no lefs fatal. This diforder though unknown at Quito, is frequent all over Valles, but more dangerous in fome parts than in others. Something has already been faid of this diftemper in our account of Carthagena, but a more circumftantial defcription of it was referved for this place.

This

This diftemper is divided into two kinds, the common or partial, and the malignant or arched convulfions. They both come on when nature is ftruggling in the crifis of fome acute diftemper; but with this important difference, that thofe attacked with the former, often recover, though the greater part die on the third or fourth day, the term of its duration; while thofe who have the misfortune of being attacked by the latter, fink under it in two or three days, it being very extraordinary to recover, and is therefore termed malignant.

The fpafms or convulfions confift in a total inactivity of the mufcles, and a conftriction of the nerves of the whole body, beginning with thofe of the head; and thefe nerves being the channels which convey nourifhment to the body, and this nourifhment being precluded by the conftriction of its conduits, they all fucceffively fuffer; the mufcles, by having loft their activity, cannot affift in the motion of the nerves, and thefe being conftringed, can no longer perform their office. Add to this, a pungent humour difperfing itfelf through all the membranes of the body, and caufing infupportable pains; fo that the groaning patient labours under inconceiveable tortures, which are ftill increafed on his being moved, though with the greateft care and gentlenefs, from one fide to the other. The throat is fo contracted that nothing can be conveyed into the ftomach. The jaws are alfo fometimes fo clofely locked, as impoffible to be opened. Thus the miferable patient lies without motion, and tortured in every part of his body, till nature quite exhaufted falls a victim to this deleterious diftemper.

In the partial kind, the pulfe is no more affected than in the diftemper which preceded it, and commonly abates the violence of a fever. But in the malignant kind it augments, the circulations being quickened; and whether it be the effect of the humour

impe-

impetuously circulating through every part, or of the pain proceeding from the laceration of the membranes, and abrading the muscles, the patient falls into a lethargy, but which does not remove the torturing sensation of these punctures, often so insupportable, that the miserable patient violently turns himself, and thus augments his agonies, as evidently appears from his piercing cries and groans.

The malignant or arched spasm, even in the first stage is so violent, as to cause a contraction of the nerves of the vertebræ from the brain downwards; and as the distemper increases, and the malignant humour acquires great activity, the nerves become more and more constricted, that the body of the patient, contrary to nature, inclines backward into an arch, and all the bones become dislocated. However terrible the pains resulting from hence may seem, they are still increased by those of the other species of convulsions, when the violence is such that the patient usually loses all sensation, and falls into a total inaction, not having breath to utter his complaints.

It is common at the beginning of this distemper to be totally convulsed, so that every part of the patient is affected, and, during the continuance, is, as it were, deprived of all sensation. Their return is more frequent and lasting as the distemper increases, till nature becomes entirely spent; when the lethargic fits succeed, and it is generally in one of these that the patient breathes his last.

The usual method of treating this distemper is by keeping both the bed, and the chamber very close, even with a fire in it, that the pores being opened by the heat, the transpiration may be more copious. Laxative clysters are often injected to mollify the contractions of the intestines, and other internal parts. External applications are also applied to soften the parts, and open the ducts by
which

which nature may evacuate the morbid humour. For the fame intention and to check its progrefs, cordials and diuretic draughts are prefcribed; and alfo the bath; but the latter only at the beginning of the firft ftage of the diftemper; for if it is found to increafe on the fecond day, bathing is no longer ordered.

THE women of Lima are fubject to a diftemper, extreamly painful, very contagious, and almoft incurable: namely, a cancer in the matrix, which even at the beginning is attended with fuch excruciating pains, that their lives are one continued feries of groans and complaints. During its progrefs they difcharge great quantities of morbid humours, become attenuated, fall into a ftate of languor, which gradually puts a period to their lives. It ufually continues fome years, with intervals of eafe, during which if the evacuations do not entirely ceafe, they are confiderably intermitted; the pains feem over, and they are capable of dreffing themfelves and walking abroad; but the difeafe fuddenly returns with double violence, and the patient becomes totally difabled. This diftemper comes on fo imperceptibly, as not to be indicated either by the countenance or pulfe, till at its height; and fuch is the contagion of it, that it is contracted only by fitting in the fame chair commonly ufed by an infected perfon, or wearing her cloaths; but it has not been known to affect the men, hufbands ufually living with their wives till the laft ftage of the diftemper. Two caufes are affigned for this malady, their exceffive ufe of perfumes, which they always carry about them, and may doubtlefs contribute greatly to promote it; the other a continual riding in their calafhes, but this does not feem to be of fo much confequence as the former. For then the moft diftinguifhed of the fair fex in other countries, who ride in coaches, and

even

even ufe the more violent exercife of the horfe, would not be exempt from it.

Slow or hectic fevers alfo prevail greatly in thefe countries, and are likewife contagious, but more from a want of a proper care in the furniture and apparel of the perfons infected, than any malignancy of the climate.

The venereal difeafe is equally common in this country as in thofe we have already mentioned; it is indeed general in all that part of America; and as little attention is given to it till arrived to a great height, the general cuftom in all thofe parts, a repetition here would be needlefs.

---

## CHAP. VIII.

*Fertility of the Territories of* Lima, *and the manner of cultivating the foil.*

IT is natural to think that a country, where rain is feldom or ever known, muft, of neceffity, be totally barren; whereas the country of Lima enjoys a fertility to be envied, producing all kinds of grain, and a prodigious variety of fruits. Here induftry and art fupply that moifture which the clouds feem to withhold; and the foil is by this means rendered remarkably fruitful, amidft a continual drought.

It has already been obferved, that one of the principal cares of the Yncas was the cutting and difpofing in the moft advantageous manner, trenches or fmall canals, in order to conduct the waters of the rivers to nourifh every part, and render large fields capable of producing grain. The Spaniards finding thefe ufeful works ready executed to their hands, took care to keep them in the fame order; and by thefe are watered the fpacious fields of
wheat

wheat and barley, large meadows, plantations of sugar canes, and olive trees, vineyards and gardens of all kinds; all yielding uncommon plenty. Lima differs from Quito, where the fruits of the earth have no determined seasons; but here the harvests are gathered in, and the trees drop their leaves, according to their respective natures; for those which grow spontaneously in a hot climate, though the liveliness of their verdure fades, their leaves do not fall off till others supply their place. The blossoms also have their respective times, and are correspondently succeeded by fruits; so that this country resembles those of the temperate zones, no less in the product and seasons of corn, blossoms, fruits and flowers, than in the difference of winter and summer.

BEFORE the earthquake 1687, when this city suffered in so deplorable a manner, the harvests of wheat and barley were sufficient to supply the wants of the country without any importation, especially of wheat; but by this convulsion of nature, the soil was so viciated, that the wheat rotted soon after it was sown, occasioned, probably, by the vast clouds of sulphureous particles then exhaled, and the prodigious quantities of nitrous effluvia diffused thorough it. This obliged the owners of the lands to apply them to other uses, and accordingly many of them were turned into meadows of clover, plantations of sugar-canes, and other vegetables, which they found not subject to the same misfortune. After the land had continued forty years in this state of sterility, the husbandmen began to perceive such an alteration in the soil, as promised a speedy return to its former goodness. Accordingly some trials were successfully made with wheat, and by degrees that grain was found to thrive as before that dreadful event. But whether it be from the other plants, which have been cultivated in those parts, or from any mistrust of the

hus-

husbandmen, the same quantity has not been sown as before. It is natural to think that the late dreadful earthquake must have had the same pernicious effects on the soil. Tho' by means of the establishment of the corn trade with Chili since that time, the consequences will not be so sensibly felt. The fields in the neighbourhood of Lima are chiefly sown with clover, of which there is here a consumption not to be paralleled in any other place; it being the common fodder for all beasts, particularly the mules and horses, of which there is here an inconceivable number.

The other parts of the country are taken up with plantations already mentioned, among which those of canes are not the least, and yield an excellent kind of sugar. All these fields and plantations are cultivated by negro slaves, purchased for this service; and the same is seen in the other improved parts of Valles.

The olive plantations appear like thick forests; for besides the height, magnitude, and fulness of leaves of these trees, in all which they exceed those of Spain, they are never pruned, by which means their branches became so interwoven, that the light cannot penetrate through their foliage. The plough is not used here, the only cultivation they require, being to clear the holes made at the foot of each for receiving the water, to keep the trenches open which convey it, and every three or four years to cut down all shoots or cions, in order to form passages for gathering the fruit. With this small trouble the inhabitants have an uncommon plenty of the finest olives, which they either commit to the press for oil, or pickle, they being particularly adapted to the latter, both with regard to their beauty, largeness, and flavour. Their oil is much preferable to that of Spain.

The country contiguous to the city is covered

with gardens, producing all the herbs and fruits known in Spain, and of the fame goodnefs and beauty, befides thofe common to America; all which flourifh here in a very uncommon degree; fo that none of the parts of Peru, at leaft fuch as we vifited, are to be compared with thofe of the neighbourhood of Lima, where every place is covered with fruits and efculent vegetables.

It alfo enjoys another fingular advantage, the whole year being as it were fummer with regard to the plenty and frefhnefs of fruits; for the feafons of the year varying alternately in Valles and the mountains, when the time of fruits is over in Valles, it begins on the fkirts of the mountains; and the diftance from Lima being not above twenty five or thirty leagues, they are brought thither, and by this means the city is conftantly fupplied with fruits, except a few, as grapes, melons and water-melons, which requiring a hot climate, do not come to perfection in the mountains.

The grapes are of various kinds; and among them, one called the Italian, very larege and delicious. The vines extend themfelves on the furface of the ground, which is very well adapted to fupport them, being either ftony or full of fand. Thefe vines are pruned and watered at proper times, and thrive remarkably without any other care.

No other culture is beftowed on thofe defigned for wine, for both at Ica, Pifco, Nafca, and all other parts where they grow, they are form'd into efpaliers. None of the grapes near Lima are ufed in making wine, the demand for them in other refpects being too large.

The foil is ftony and fandy, that is, confifting of fmooth flints or pebbles, which are fo numerous that as other foils are entirely fand, rock, or earth, this is wholly of the above ftones; and in fome parts prove very inconvenient to travellers, whether in a

carriage

Ch. VIII.   SOUTH AMERICA.   97

carriage or on horfeback. The arable lands have a ftratum of about a foot or two of earth, but below that the whole confifts entirely of ftones. From this circumftance, the fimilarity of all the neighbouring coafts, and the bottom of the fea, this whole fpace may be concluded to have been formerly covered by the ocean, to the diftance of 3 or 4 leagues, or even farther, beyond its prefent limits. This is particularly obfervable in a bay about five leagues north of Callao, called Marques, where in all appearance, not many years fince, the fea covered above half a league of what is now Terra Firma, and the extent of a league and a half along the coaft.

The rocks in the moft inland part of this bay are perforated and fmoothed like thofe wafhed by the waves; a fufficient proof that the fea formed thefe large cavities, and undermined fuch prodigious maffes as lie on the ground, by its continual elifions; and it feems natural to think that the like muft have happened in the country contiguous to Lima, and that the parts, confifting of pebbles like thofe at the bottom of the adjacent fea, were formerly covered by the water.

Another fingularity in this arid country is, the abundance of fprings, water being found every where with little labour, by digging only four or five feet below the furface. This may arife from two caufes; the one, that the earth, being, from its compofition very fpungy, the water of the fea eafily infinuates itfelf to a great diftance, and is filtrated in paffing through its pores. The other, that the many torrents after defcending from the mountains, foon lofe themfelves in thefe plains, but continue their courfe along the fubterranean veins of the earth; for this ftony quality of the foil from the nature of the fprings cannot extend to any great depth, and underneath it the ftratum is hard and compact; confequently the water muft be conveyed to the

Vol. II.   H   moft

moſt porous parts, which being the ſtony, it there precipitates into a ſubterranean courſe, leaving the ſurface dry. We have already obſerved * that from many of the rivers in Valles, though apparently dry, the inhabitants procure a ſufficient quantity of water by digging wells in the beds over which their waters run in the winter: others might be paſſed without being known, but the bottom confiſting entirely of pebbles, wherever the beaſts ſet their feet, the water immediately oozes out. The reaſon of this is, that the water at that time runs a little below the ſurface, and I do not doubt but the ſame will be found in all Valles, though at different depths in different places.

This plenty of ſubterraneous ſtreams is doubtleſs of great advantage to the fertility of the country, particularly with regard to the larger plants, whoſe roots ſtrike deepeſt; and this ſeems a bountiful indulgence of the wiſe author of nature, who to provide againſt the ſterility which would certainly affect theſe countries from a want of water, has ſent a ſupply from the mountains, either in open rivers or ſubterraneous canals.

The lands in the juriſdiction of Chancay, like the other parts of the coaſts of Peru, are manured with the dung of certain ſea birds, which abound here in a very extraordinary manner. Theſe they call Guanoes, and the dung Guano, the Indian name for excrement in general. Theſe birds, after ſpending the whole day in catching their food in the ſea, repair at night to reſt on the iſlands near the coaſt, and their number being ſo great as entirely to cover the ground, they leave a proportionable quantity of excrement or dung. This is dried by the heat of the ſun into a cruſt, and is daily encreaſing, ſo that notwithſtanding great quantities are taken away, it is never exhauſted. Some will have this Guano to be,

* Chap. 1. of this Vol.

be only earth endowed with the quality of raifing a ferment in the foil with which it is mixed. This opinion is founded on the prodigious quantities carried off from thofe iflands, and on the experiment made by digging or boring, by which the appearance at a certain depth, was the fame as at the fuperficies; whence it is concluded, that the earth is naturally endowed with the heating quality of dung or Guano. This would feem lefs improbable, did not both its appearance and fmell prove it to be the excrement in queftion. I was in thefe iflands when feveral barks came to load with it; when the infupportable fmell left me no room to doubt of the nature of their cargo. I do not however pretend to deny, but that it may be mixed with earth, or that the moft fuperficial part of the earth does not contract the like virtue, fo as to produce the fame effect. But however it be, this is the manure ufed in the fields fowed with maize, and with proper waterings is found greatly to fertilize the foil, a little of it being put clofe to every ftem, and immediately watered. It is alfo of ufe in fields of other grain, except wheat and barley, and, confequently, prodigious quantities of it yearly ufed in agriculture.

BESIDES the orchards, fields, and gardens, with which this country is fo delightfully variegated, there are other parts where nature itfelf fpontaneoufly furnifhes beautiful profpects for the inhabitants, and plenty of excellent food for their cattle; particularly the hills of St. Chriftopher and Amancaes, whofe perpetual verdure diverfified in fpring with elegant flowers, feems to invite the neighbouring inhabitants to a nearer enjoyment of the beauties it prefents at a diftance to their view. The parts in the neighbourhood of the city to the diftance of fix or eight leagues, offer the like entertainment; and accordingly many families refort thither for the change of air, and the tranquility of rural amufements. The hills called Amancaes, already mentioned, have their name from a certain flower growing on them. It is yellow and of the campanula form, with four pointed leaves. Its colour is remarkably brilliant, and in that wholly confifts its value, being totally void of fragrancy.

BESIDES thefe delightful retreats, the city has a publick walk in the fuburb of St. Lazaro, called Alameda, confifting of rows of orange and lemon trees; along the banks of the river is another called the Acho, to which there is a daily refort of coaches and calafhes.

THE only monuments of antiquity remaining in the neighbourhood of Lima are the Guacas, or fepulchres of the Indians, and fome walls, which were built on both fides of the roads, and are frequently feen all over this country. But three leagues north eaft of the city, in a valley called Guachipa, are ftill ftanding the walls of a large town. Through ignorance I did not vifit them whilft I was at Lima; the account of them, however, which the ingenious marquis de Valde Lyrios was pleafed to give me, may be equally relied on, as if related from my own knowledge; efpecially as he took a very accurate furvey of the whole. He obferved that the ftreets were very narrow, that the walls of the houfes, which in common with all the buildings of that time were without roofs, were only of mud, and that each houfe confifted of three fmall fquare apartments. The doors towards the ftreet, were not fo high as the general ftature of a man, but the walls wanted little of three yards. Among all the houfes which compofed this large town, fituated at the foot of a mountain, is one, whofe walls overlook all the others, and thence it is concluded to have belonged to the Cafique or prince; though its ruinous condition render it impoffible to determine abfolutely. The inhabitants of this valley, where the fruitful fields are watered from the river Rimac, at no great dif-

ftance

## Ch. VIII. SOUTH AMERICA.

tance from thefe ruins, call them old Caxamarca, though it cannot now be difcovered whether that was the real name of the town in the times of Paganifm. For there neither remains any memorial of fuch tradition, nor any mention of it in the hiftories of that kingdom, written by Garcilazo, and Herrera; fo that all we know is, that the epithet old is now applied to it by way of diftinction from the prefent town of Caxamarca.

One aftonifhing particular in the walls of this town, and in all others in the neighbouring valleys, is, that though built on the furface of the earth, without any foundation, they have withftood thofe violent earthquakes which overthrew the more folid buildings of Lima and other large towns erected in the Spanifh manner; having received no other damage than what naturally refults from being forfaken, or what the drivers have done, who make it a refting place for their cattle in the road to Lima.

From the conftruction of thefe houfes it may be inferred, that long experience has inftructed the natives, that in parts fo fubject to earthquakes, it was improper to lay a foundation in order to ftrengthen the walls; and tradition informs us, that when the newly conquered Indians faw the Spaniards dig foundations for lofty buildings, they laughed at them, telling them they were digging their own fepulchres; intimating that the earthquakes would bury them under the ruins of their houfes. It is indeed a melancholy proof of pride and obftinacy, that after having the prudent example of the Indians before their eyes, the total ruin of the city at four different times in lefs than the fpace of two hundred years, has not been able entirely to eradicate the deftructive paffion for airy and elegant buildings, tho' thefe neceffarily require large and lofty walls, which muft have a foundation proportional to the

mag-

A VOYAGE TO Book I.
magnitude of the ſtructure, and the weight they are to ſupport.

## CHAP. IX.

### *Of the Plenty and different Kinds of Proviſions at* LIMA.

THE fertility of the ſoil, the goodneſs of the climate, and the convenient ſituation of Lima, concur to maintain in it a conſtant plenty. The fruits and herbs have been already mentioned; it remains that we conſider the meat and fiſh with which it is alſo equally provided.

THE bread at Lima is inconteſtibly the beſt in all this part of America, both with regard to its colour and taſte, the goodneſs of the corn being improved by the manner of working it; and at the ſame time ſo reaſonable, that the inhabitants uſe no other. It is of three kinds, one called Criollo, the crumb of which is very light and ſpongy; the ſecond French bread; and the laſt ſoft bread. It is kneaded by negroes employed by the bakers, many of whom are very rich, and their ſhops always well provided. Beſides their own ſlaves, the bakers are alſo obliged to receive any delivered up to them by their maſters to work as a puniſhment, and for theſe, beſides finding the ſlaves in proviſions, they pay the maſter the uſual wages in money or in bread. This puniſhment is the ſevereſt that can be inflicted on them, and, indeed, all the hardſhips and cruelties of the galleys are leſs than what theſe wretches are obliged to undergo. They are forced to work the whole day and part of the night, with little food and leſs ſleep; ſo that in a few days the moſt vigorous and ſtubborn

ſlave

slave becomes weak and submissive, and prostrates himself before his master, with tears, intreaties and promises of amendment on being removed from that place, the dread of which is doubtless of the greatest use in awing the vast number of slaves, both within and without the city.

THEIR mutton is the most common food, and is very palatable, from the nitrous pastures where the sheep are fattened. The beef also is good; but little eaten except by the Europeans, so that two or three beasts supply the city for a week. Here is also plenty of poultry, partridges, turtle-doves, &c. Pork is also in great abundance, though not equally delicate with that of Carthagena. The lard is used in dressing all kinds of dishes whether of flesh or fish, oil being only used in sallads and the like. This method of cookery is said to have had its rise when the country afforded no oil, and has been continued to the present time, notwithstanding it is now produced in great quantities. Antonia de Rivero, an inhabitant of Lima in the year 1660, planted the first olive-tree ever seen in Peru.

FROM the mountains, are often sent by way of present, frozen calves; being killed there, and left two or three days on the heaths to freeze; after which they are carried to Lima, where they may be kept any time required, without the least tendency to putrefaction.

OF fish there is still a greater variety daily brought from the neighbouring parts of Chorillos, Callao, and Ancon, the Indian inhabitants of which make fishing their whole business. The most palatable are the Corbinas, and the Pege Reyes, or king's fish; but those in the greatest plenty, and at the same time very palatable, are the anchovies. The Corbinas, and the king's fish, infinitely excel those of Spain; the latter is also remarkable for its size, being generally six or seven Paris inches in length;
yet

yet even thefe are thought to be furpaffed by thofe caught in Buenos Ayres river. It is a falt water fifh, but very little different from that caught in the rivers of Spain. The river of Lima affords a fort of prawns, two or three inches in length, but thofe fhould rather be called Cray-fifh.

THE whole coafts abound with fuch fhoals of anchovies, as exceed all comparifon; and befides the vaft quantities caught by fifhermen, they are the chief food of innumerable flights of birds, with which all thofe iflands abound, and commonly called Guanoes, poffibly from the Guano or dung mentioned in the preceding chapter; many of them are indeed alcatraces, a kind of gull, though all comprehended under the generical name of Guanoes. A little after the appearance of the fun, they rife from thofe iflands in fuch large and thick flights as totally to cover them, and fly towards the fea for an hour or two, without any vifible decreafe of their number. When at fome diftance from the land they divide themfelves, and begin their fifhing in a very entertaining manner. They fly in a circle at a confiderable height above the water, and on feeing a fifh, they dart down with their beak foremoft and their wings clofed, with fuch force that the agitation of the water is feen at a diftance; after which they rife again into the air and devour the fifh. Sometimes they remain a confiderable time under water, and rife at fome diftance from the place where they fell, doubtlefs becaufe the fifh has endeavoured to efcape, thus difputing celerity with them in their own element. They are continually feen in the place they frequent, fome watching in gyrations, fome darting down, others rifing with their prey; while their great numbers render this confufion diverting to the fpectator. When they are either tired or fatisfied they alight upon the waves,

and

## Ch. IX.   SOUTH AMERICA.   105

and at fun fet, forming themfelves into one body, withdraw to the iflands where they pafs the night.

At the port of Callao it is obferved that all the birds which reft on thofe iflands to the N. of it, in the morning univerfally fly towards the S. in queft of prey, returning in the evening to their place of reft; when the middle of the flight is over the harbour neither the beginning nor end can be feen, and the whole flock take up two or three hours in pafling over.

Though fhell fifh are very fcarce along this coaft, fome are found near Callao; particularly a kind, the fhell of which refembles that of a mufcle, though much larger. The fifh itfelf has more the appearance of an oyfter, and much the fame tafte.

The wines at Lima are of different forts, white, red, and dark-red: and of each fort fome are very generous and delicious. They are imported from the coafts of Nafca, Pifco, Lucumba, and Chili; but the latter produces the beft, and among them fome Mufcadel. The wine of Nafca is white, and has the leaft demand of any, being inferior to the others both in quality and tafte. That from Pifco has the greateft fale, and from the fame place come all the brandies either ufed at Lima or exported; no rum being either made or ufed here.

Most of the dried fruits are brought from Chili; and by means of the trade carried on between the two kingdoms, Lima is fupplied with all forts of fruits known in Spain, as almonds, walnuts, filberts, pears, apples, &c. fo that their tables cannot in this refpect fail of plenty and elegance, having at one time the fruits of the different feafons, both of America and Europe. But amidft this plenty, every thing is very dear, the price being four or five times as much as at Quito, bread only excepted. Wine, oil and dried fruits, are fome of the cheapeft. The poorer clafs however, as the negroes and other cafts, live tolerably well, fifh, which is little efteemed by

the

the opulent, felling at a low price; the fame may be faid of mutton and beef, with regard to the inhabitants of this country in general.

SWEETMEATS are alfo here in the fame plenty as in the other parts of South America, tho' feldom eaten, except as deferts, and even then very moderately. Inftead of chocolate, Mate, or Paraguay tea is generally ufed, and prepared twice a day. Though this has here the defect already obferved, it is better prepared than in any other part.

## CHAP. X.
### Trade and Commerce of LIMA.

THE city of Lima could not have attained to fuch fplendor, if, befides being the capital of Peru, it had not been alfo the general ftaple of the kingdom. But as it is the refidence of the government and chief tribunals, fo it is alfo the common factory for commerce of every kind, and the center of the products and manufactures of the other provinces, together with thofe of Europe, brought over in the galleons or regifter fhips; and from hence they are diftributed through the vaft extent of thefe kingdoms, whofe wants are fupplied from Lima, as their common mother. At the head of this commerce is the tribunal del Confulado, which appoints commiffaries to refide in the other cities of its dependencies, extending through all Peru.

ALL the wealth of the fouthern provinces, is brought to Lima, where it is embarqued on board the fleet, which, at the time of the galleons fails from Callao, to Panama. The proprietors of the treafure, commit it to the merchants of Lima, who traffic at the fair with this and their own ftock. The fame fleet returns to the harbour of Paita, where

where the European merchandizes of value purchased at Porto Bello fair are landed, in order to avoid the delay of sailing to Callao, and sent by land to Lima, on droves of mules; but those of less value are carried thither by the same ships.

On the arrival of these commodities at Lima, the merchants remit to their correspondents such parts as they had a commission to purchase, reserving the rest in ware-houses to dispose of on their own account to traders, who at this time resort to Lima; or send them to their factors in the inland provinces, who remit the returns in money or bills of exchange to their principals at Lima. These consignments are repeated till they have disposed of their whole stock. Thus the cargo of a flotilla lasts a considerable time, there being no immediate vent for the whole.

The produce of the sales in the inland parts of the kingdom, is sent to Lima in bars of silver, and Pignas†; and is coined at the mint in this city. Thus the traders have not only a great profit in the sale of their goods, but also in the returns of their silver, which they take at a lower rate than is allowed them for it. All these sales may therefore be considered as an exchange of one commodity for another; for he who sells the goods agrees both with regard to their price, and the rate in which he is to take the silver bars, or pignas; and thus two species of trade are transacted at the same time, one a sale of goods, and the other of silver.

The remittances sent to Lima during the interval between the Flotillas, are laid out in manufactures of the country, great quantities of which come from the province of Quito; and this trade is carried on in all respects like the former; for the consumption of them being equal or rather larger;

† Pignas are porous and light masses of silver, being an amalgama of mercury and dust taken out of the mines.

they

they are not lefs neceffary here than in Europe, being worn by all the lower clafs of people, who cannot afford the price of European ftuffs; and the generality of traders who come to Lima purchafe ftuffs of both kinds, that they may be provided with affortments for cuftomers of all ranks.

BESIDES this commerce, which is the moft confiderable, and tranfacted wholly by means of this city, Lima has alfo its particular trade with the kingdoms both of north and fouth America. The moft confiderable commodity received from the former is fnuff, which is brought from the Havannah to Mexico, and after being there improved is forwarded to Lima, and from thence fent into the other provinces. This trade is carried on nearly in the fame manner as that of Panama; but thofe who deal in this commodity, never trouble themfelves with any other except perfumes, as ambergrife, mufk, &c. and porcelain ware. Some of thefe traders are fettled at Lima, others refide there occafionally, but are in general factors to the merchants at Mexico. Lima alfo receives from the ports of new Spain, Naphtha, tar, iron, and fome indigo for dying.

THE kingdom of Terra Firma fends to Lima leaf-tobacco, and pearls, which here meet with a good market; for befides the great numbers worn by the ladies, no mulatto woman is without fome ornament or other made of them. During a free affiento of negroes, this commerce is always carried on by way of Panama, and to a confiderable amount.

THE ladies, and indeed women of all ranks, have a very antient cuftom, namely, the carrying in their mouths a Limpion, or cleanfer, of tobacco. The firft intention of this was to keep the teeth clean, as the name itfelf intimates. Thefe Limpions are fmall rolls of tobacco, four inches in length, and nine lines in diameter, and tied with a thread, which they untwift as the Limpion waftes. One end of they this put

into

their mouth, and after chewing it for some time, rub the teeth with it, and thus keep them always clean and white. The lower class of people, who generally pervert the best things, carry this custom to such excess, as to keep continually in their mouths a roll of tobacco, an inch and a half in diameter; affecting to distinguish themselves by the largeness of their Limpions, tho' it absolutely disfigures them. This custom, together with that of smoaking, which is equally common among the men, occasions a great demand for leaf tobacco. The Limpions are made of Guayaquil tobacco mixed with some of that brought from the Havannah to Panama; but that used in smoaking comes from Santa Mayobamba, Jaen de Bracamaros, Llulla, and Chillaos, where it grows in the greatest plenty, and is best adapted to that purpose.

All the timber used in building houses, refitting ships, or building small barks at Callao, is brought from Guayaquil, together with the Cacao; but the consumption of the latter is here very small, the Paraguay tea being more generally used. The timber trade is carried on by the masters of ships, who bring it hither on their own account, as we have already observed, in describing Guayaquil, and depositing it in store-houses at Callao, sell it as opportunity offers.

The coasts of Nasca and Pisco, send to Lima, wine, brandy, raisins, olives and oil: and the kingdom of Chili, wheat, flour, lard, leather, cordage, wines, dried fruits, and some gold. Besides these all sorts of goods are also laid up at Callao, in storehouses built for that purpose; some on account of the owners who remit them, others for masters of ships who purchase them on the spot where they grow, or are made. Every Monday during the whole year there is a fair at Callao, whither the proprietors and dealers resort from all parts; and the

the goods are carried according to the buyers direction on droves of mules kept there for that purpofe by the mafters of the warehoufes, and whofe profit wholly confifts in the hire of thefe beafts.

THE provifions brought to Lima are not only fufficient to fupply its numerous inhabitants, but great quantities of all kinds are fent to Quito, and its jurifdiction, to Valles and Panama. Copper and tin in bars are brought from Coquimbo; from the mountains de Caxamarca, and Chacapoyas, canvas made of cotton for fails and other ftuffs of that kind, and alfo of Pita: Cordovan leather, and foap are made all over Valles. From the fouthern provinces, as Plata, Oruro, Potofi, and Cufco, is fent Vicuna wool for making hats, and fome ftuffs of a peculiar finenefs. Laftly, from Paraguay the herd called by that name is fent, of which there is an amazing confumption, it being fent from Lima among the other provinces, as far as Quito. There is no province in Peru, which does not remit to Lima, its products and manufactures; and fupplies itfelf from hencewith the neceffary commodities. Thus Lima is the emporium to which people refort from all parts; and trade being always in a conftant circulation, befides the continual refort of ftrangers, the families of rank are enabled to fupport the expences of that fplendor I have already mentioned; for without fuch continual affiftance they muft either contract their expences, or fall victims to their oftentation.

IT would naturally be imagined that by a commerce fo extenfive and important, many vaft fortunes muft be acquired, efpecially as every branch of it is attended with great profits; but if there are fome who actually do acquire great riches, neither their number nor opulence are equal to what might be expected; for by a narrow infpection there will hardly be found above ten or fifteen houfes-of-trade, exclufive

## Ch. X.  SOUTH AMERICA.  111

five of immoveables as lands and offices, whofe ftock in money and goods amounts to five or fix hundred thoufand crowns; and to one that exceeds this fum, there are more that fall fhort of it. Many poffefs from one to three hundred thoufand crowns, and thefe are indeed the perfons who compofe the main body of trade. Befides thefe there are great numbers of inferior traders, whofe capitals do not exceed fifty or a hundred thoufand crowns. The paucity of immenfe fortunes amidft fuch advantages is doubtlefs owing to the enormous expences; whence, though their gains are great, they can hardly fupport their credit; fo that after paying the fortunes of their daughters, and the eftablifhing their fons, the wealth of moft families terminates with the life of him who raifed it, being divided into as many fmall ftocks as he had dependents; unlefs fome either by induftry or good fortune, improve the portion they obtained by inheritance.

THE inhabitants of Lima have a natural difpofition and aptitude for commerce, and the city may be confidered as an academy to which great numbers repair to perfect themfelves in the various arts of trade. They both penetrate into the fineffes of the feller; and artfully draw the purchafer into their views. They are bleffed with a remarkable talent of perfuafion, at the fame time that they are incapable of being perfuaded, as well as of artfully eluding objections. They affect to flight what they are moft defirous of purchafing, and by that means often make very advantageous bargains, which none can obtain from them. But after all thefe precautions and fineffes in buying and felling, for which they are fo diftinguifhed, none are more punctual and honourable in performing their contracts.

BESIDES the fhops where ftuffs and goods of that kind are fold; there are others for fnuff, and in thefe may be purchafed the wrought plate, which is bought in the cities near the mines, where it is made.

THE wholefale traders, who have large warehoufes, are not above keeping fhops where they fell by retail, which is reckoned no difgrace; and thus they gain that profit which they muſt otherwife allow to others. And from this indulgence granted to every branch of commerce, it flourifhes very greatly. There are, however, many families, who, as I have already obferved, fupport a proper fplendor entirely by the revenue of their eftates, without joining in the cares and hurry of commerce. But a greater number with eftates, add the advantages of commerce, in order to preferve them. Thefe, however, deal only at the fairs of the galleons, and in other large branches of commerce; and find the benefit of having abandoned thofe fcruples brought by their anceftors from Spain, namely, that trade would tarnifh the luftre of their nobility.

## CHAP. XI.

*Extent of the jurifdiction of the Vice-roy of* PERU: *together with the audiences and diocefſes of that kingdom.*

THE foregoing accounts naturally lead to the extent of the audience of Lima, and the juriſdiction of the vice roy of Peru. But fuch a particular defcription as I have already given † of Quito, requiring a perfonal knowledge of all its provinces and jurifdictions, and alfo a particular work, from the extenfivenefs of the fubject, I fhall confine myfelf to fome principal accounts, but which will convey an adequate idea of the vaft dominions of this country. In order to this I have confulted feveral perfons, fome

of

† Vol. I.

Ch. XI.   SOUTH AMERICA.   113

of which have been vested with high employments here, and others, whose commendable curiosity, as natives of this country, had prompted them to acquire an exact knowledge of it. This was a resource of absolute necessity; no opportunity having offered of visiting the inland parts of these countries; and the accounts we received of them at Lima, were not to be depended upon, with that confidence necessary to their being inserted here; for considering the vast distance between the capital and some provinces, it is no wonder they are but little known at Lima. The reader will therefore indulge me in giving a superficial account of some; for according to the method in which I began to write the history, we shall insert such particulars only as are authentic; it being undoubtedly more advantageous to say a little with truth, than to engage in prolix and uncertain particulars.

In order the better to describe the countries governed by the vice-roy of Peru, without departing from the plan hitherto observed, I shall divide the whole jurisdiction of its government, into those audiences of which it consists; these into the dioceses they contain; and the dioceses into jurisdictions under a Corregidor.

The vice royalty of Peru in south America, extends over those vast countries, included in the jurisdictions of the audiences of Lima, Los Charcas, and Chili; and in these are comprehended the governments of Santa Cruz de la Sierra; Paraguay, Tucuman, and Buenos Ayres. Though these three provinces and the kingdom of Chili have particular governors invested with all the authority agreeable to such a character; and as such are absolute in political, civil, and military affairs, yet, in some cases, are subordinate to the vice-roy; for instance, on the death of any inferior governor, the vacancy is supplied by him. Before the erection of the vice-

Vol. II.        I        royalty

royalty of the new kingdom of Granada in 1739, that of Peru, as we have already obferved, extended to the countries of the two audiences of Terra Firma and Quito; but thofe being then feparated from it, the bounds of it on the north were the jurifdiction of Piura, which extends to thofe of Guayaquil and Loxa, and that of Chacapayas, which joins to the government of Jaen de Bracamoros. Thus the vice-royalty of Peru begins at the bay of Guayaquil, at the coaft of Tumbez, in 3° 25' fouth latitude, and reaches to the land of Magellan in 50° confequently it extends 1012 fea leagues. Eaftward it partly terminates on Brazil, being bounded by the celebrated line, or meridian of demarkation, or that which feparates the dominions of Spain and Portugal, and on the coaft of the north fea: and on the W. is terminated by the fouth-fea.

THE audience of Lima erected in the year 1542, though it was the year 1544 before any feffion was held in that city, contains within its jurifdiction one arch-bifhoprick, and four bifhopricks, viz.

The archbifhoprick of Lima, and the bifhopricks of Truxillo, Guamanga, Cufco, and Arequipa.

The arch-bifhoprick of Lima, to which the precedence in every refpect belongs, fhall be the fubject of this chapter. It contains fourteen jurifdictions, which I fhall treat of in the order of their fituation, beginning with thofe neareft the capital, and concluding with thofe which are moft remote: the fame method fhall alfo be obferved in the other dioceffes.

I. The Curcado or circuit of Lima.
II. Chancay.  
III. Santa.  
IV. Canta.  
V. Canete.  
VI. Ica, Pifco, and Nafca.  
VII. Guarachia.  
VIII. Guanuco.  
IX. Yauyos.  
X. Caxatambo.  
XI. Sarma.  
XII. Jouxa.  
XIII. Conchucos.  
XIV. Guyalas.  
XV. Guamalies.

I. II.

I. II III. The jurifdiction of Lima, Chancay, and Santa have been already defcribed in Chap. III.

IV. The jurifdiction of Canta begins at the diftance of five leagues N. N. E. of Lima, where it terminates on the Circado of that city. It extends above thirty leagues, and the greater part of them taken up by the firft branch of the Cordillera of the Andes; fo that the temperature of the air is different in different parts of the country; that part which lies low, or among the valleys being hot, thofe on the fkirts of the mountains, which are alfo intermixed with fome plains, temperate; and thofe in the upper parts of the mountains cold. This difference of air is of great advantage both to the fruits of the earth and paftures; for by appropriating every fpecies to its proper degree of heat, the produce is large, and exceeding good. Among all the fruits the Papa is particularly diftinguifhed, and the roots carried to Lima where they meet with a good market. The vaft fields of Bombon, part of which belongs to this jurifdiction, are by their high fituation, always cold; yet they afford pafture for innumerable flocks of fheep. Thefe extenfive tracts of land are divided into Haciendas, or eftates belonging to noble families of Lima. At Guamantanga, one of the towns in this jurifdiction is a miraculous crucifix, devoutly worfhipped; the inhabitants of Lima, and the neighbouring country, go thither in pilgrimage at Whitfuntide to affift at a feftival, inftituted particularly in honour of it.

V. The town of Canete is the capital of the jurifdiction of its name. Its jurifdiction begins at the diftance of fix leagues fouth from Lima, and extends along the coaft in the fame rhumb above thirty leagues. The temperature of the air in this jurifdiction is the fame with that in the valleys of Lima; and the country being watered by a large river, and other leffer ftreams, produced vaft quantities

tities of wheat and maize. Great part of the lands are planted with canes, from whence they extract an excellent sugar. These profitable tracts of land belong also to noble families. In the neighbourhood of Chilca, situated about ten leagues from Lima, is found salt petre of which gunpowder is made at that city. Besides these advantages it has a good fishery, which affords a comfortable subsistence to the Indian inhabitants of the towns, particularly those situated near the sea coast; together with plenty of fruits, pulse, and poultry, the breeding of which is another occupation of the Indians. Whence a large trade is carried on between this jurisdiction and Lima.

VI. Ica, Pisco, and Nasca are three towns which denominate this jurisdiction; one part of it runs along the coast southward, and its territories extend above 60 leagues; but are intermixed with some deserts, and the country being sandy, those parts which are beyond the reach of the trenches cut from the rivers are generally barren. I say generally, because there are some tracts, which, without the benefit of an artificial watering, are planted with vines, and produce excellent grapes, the roots being supplied with moisture from the internal humidity of the earth. Great quantities of wines are made from them, and chiefly exported to Callao, and from thence to Guayaquil and Panama; also to Guamanga, and other inland provinces: they also extract from these wines great quantities of brandy. Some parts of this jurisdiction are planted with olive-trees, which produce excellent fruit either for eating, or oil. The fields, which are watered by the trenches, yield an uncommon plenty of wheat, maize, and fruits. The jurisdiction of Ica is remarkable for spacious woods of Algarrobales or carob-trees, with the fruit of which the inhabitants feed vast numbers of asses, for the uses of agriculture. The Indians who live near the sea apply themselves

selves to fishing, and after salting carry it to the towns among the mountains, where they never fail of a good market.

VII. The jurisdiction of Guarachiri contains the first chain and part of the second of the mountains, extending itself along these chains above forty leagues. This province begins about six leagues east of Lima. From the disposition of its parts, those places only which lie in the valleys and in the breaches of the mountains are inhabited; and these are very fertile, producing great quantities of fruit, wheat, barley, maize, and other grain. In its mountains are several silver mines, though but few of them are wrought, being none of the richest.

VIII. Guanuco is a city and the capital of its jurisdiction, which begins forty leagues north-east of Lima. This city was formerly one of the principal in these kingdoms, and the settlement of some of the first conquerors; but at present in so ruinous a condition, that the principal houses where these great men lived remain as it were only monuments of its former opulence. The other parts of it can hardly be compared to an Indian town. The temperature of the air in the greatest part of its territories is very pure and mild; and the soil fruitful. Several kinds of sweetmeats and jellies are made here, and sold to other provinces.

IX. The jurisdiction of Yauyos, begins twenty leagues south-east from Lima, and takes up part of the first and second chain of the Cordilleras; consequently the temperature of the air is different in different parts. The greatest length of this jurisdiction is about thirty leagues, and abounds in fruits, wheat, barley, maize, &c. whilst other parts are continually cloathed with verdure, and feed numerous herds and flocks for the markets of Lima; and these are the most considerable articles of its commerce.

X. The jurisdiction of Caxatambo, which begins

35 leagues north of Lima, extends about 20 leagues and partly among the mountains, whence the temperature of the air is various; but the whole territory is very fertile in grain. It has also some silver mines, which are worked, and the Indians have manufactures of bays, which make part of the trade of this jurisdiction.

XI. The jurisdiction of Tarma is one of the largest in this archbishoprick. It begins forty leagues north-east from Lima, and terminates eastward on a tract of land inhabited by wild Indians, called Maran-cochas, who often make inroads into the territories of this jurisdiction. The difference of the air in its several parts, render it capable of producing all kinds of grain and fruits, which the inhabitants are not wanting to improve. The temperate parts are sown with wheat, barley, maize, and other grain; while the colder parts afford pasture to infinite numbers of cattle of all kinds. This province is also rich in silver mines; and as many of them are worked, they spread affluence all over the country. Besides these important sources of commerce, and that of the cattle, the making of bays and other coarse stuffs, profitably employ great numbers of Indians in most of its towns.

XII. The jurisdiction of Jauxa borders on the southern extremity of the former, and begins about forty leagues east of Lima, and extends forty more along the spacious valleys and plains between the two Cordilleras of the Andes. In the middle of it runs a large river, called also Jauxa, the source of which is in the lake of Chincay-Cocha, in the province of Tarma. It is also one of the branches of the river of the Amazons. The whole jurisdiction of this province is divided into two parts by the river, and in both are several handsome towns, well inhabited by Spaniards, Mestizos, and Indians. The soil produces plenty of wheat and other grain, together with a great variety of fruits. It has also a considerable share of trade, being the great road to the provinces of Cusco, Paz, Plata,

Plata, and others to the southward, here called Tiera de Ariba, or the upper country. Like the former it borders eastward on the wild Indians of the mountains; but among which the order of St. Francis has established several missions, the first being in the town of Ocopa. Within its dependances are several silver mines, some of which being worked, greatly increase the riches of this province.

XIII. The jurisdiction of Conchucos begins forty leagues N. N. E. of Lima, and extends along the center of the Cordillera; so that its air is different according to the height of the situation of its several parts, the mildest of which produce all kinds of grain and fruits, and the others, where the effects of the cold checks this fertility, afford pasture for cattle of all kinds. In this jurisdiction are great number of looms; the principal occupation of the Indians being several kinds of woollen manufactures, and these constitute the greatest part of its commerce with other provinces.

XIV. The province of Guaylas, like the former, extends along the center of the Cordillera, beginning fifty leagues from Lima, and in the same direction as the other; this jurisdiction is large, and has different temperatures of air. The low parts produce grain and fruits, the upper abound in cattle and sheep, which form the greatest branch of their trade.

XV. The last is that of Guamalies, which, like the former, is situated in the center of the Cordillera, consequently its air very different. This jurisdiction begins eighty leagues N. E. of Lima, and its situation being rather cold than temperate, few places are fertile in its whole extent, which is above forty leagues. The Indian inhabitants of the towns apply themselves to weaving, and make a great variety of bays, serges, and other stuffs, with which they carry on a very considerable trade with the other provinces, destitute of such manufactures.

The preceding provinces, together with the following in the audience of Lima, as in those belonging to that of Charcas, are full of towns, villages and hamlets, inhabited by Spaniards, Mestizos, and Indians; but with some difference, the number of Spaniards being greater in some, and in others that of the Indians. Many of them are indeed solely inhabited by the latter. The distance from the capital of the province, especially to the towns situated on its frontiers, being so great, as to render it impossible for the corregidor to discharge his office every where with the necessary punctuality and attention, the province is divided into several districts, consisting of three or four towns, more or less, according to their largeness and distance; and over these is placed a delegate.

EVERY settlement of any consequence maintains a priest; and so commendable is their provision in this respect, that sometimes two, three, or more small places join to support one, either alone or with a curate; so that some ecclesiastics have distant settlements under their care. These incumbents are either seculars or regulars, according to the right acquired by each of these classes, as having been employed in the conversion of the Indians immediately after the Conquest.

## CHAP. XII.

*Of the Provinces in the Dioceses of* TRUXILLO, GUAMANGA, CUSCO, *and* AREQUIPA.

NORTH of the archiepiscopal diocess of Lima lies the bishopric of Truxillo, and with it terminates on that side both the jurisdiction of that audience, and the vice-royalty of Peru; but the whole extent of this diocess is not under the jurisdictions of this audience, nor of that of the vice-roy; for it also includes

## Ch. XII. SOUTH AMERICA.

includes the government of Jaen de Bracamoros, which, as we have already obferved (Vol. I.) belongs to the province and audience of Quito. We fhall therefore exclude it, and only give an account of the feven jurifdictons in the diocefe of Truxillo belonging to the vice-royalty of Peru, and the audience of Lima.

Jurifdictions in the diocefs of Truxillo.

      I. Truxillo.
II. Sana.     V. Chachapayas.
III. Piura.     VI. Llulia, and Chilloas.
IV. Caxamarca.   VII. Pataz, or Coxamarquilla.

 I. II. III. A fufficient account having already been given (Chap. I. II.) of the jurifdictions of Truxillo, Sana, and Piura, it only remains to fpeak of the other four.

 IV. Caxamarca lies to the eaftward of Truxillo, and its jurifdiction extends along a vaft interval betwixt the two Cordilleras of the Andes. It enjoys a fertility of all kinds of corn, fruits, and efculent vegetables; alfo cattle, fheep, and efpecially hogs, of which they fell vaft numbers to the farmers in the valleys, who after fattening them with maize, fend them to the markets in the great towns; particularly the farmers of the valley of Chincay and others, who drive a confiderable trade in thefe creatures at Lima, Truxillo, and other flourifhing places. The Indians throughout this jurifdiction weave cotton for fhip's fails, bed-curtains, quilts, and other ufes, which are fent into the other provinces. Here are alfo fome filver mines, but of little confequence.

 V. On the fame fide, but more towards the eaft, lies the jurifdiction of Chachapoyas. Its temperature is hot, being without the Cordilleras, and to the eaftward its territories have a low fituation. It is of great extent, but very thinly inhabited; and the products of the earth only fuch as naturally flourifh in fuch a climate. The Indians here are very ingenious in making cottons, particularly tapeftry, which for the livelinefs of
                  the

the colours, and delicacy of the work, make an elegant appearance: thefe, together with the fail-cloth, bring great profits to this country, being highly valued in the other provinces.

VI. SOUTH of Chachapayas, and alfo on the eaftfide of the cordillera of the Andes, lies the jurifdiction of Llulla and Chiloas, which is low, warm and moift, and covered with woods, fo that great parts of it are uninhabited. It borders on the river of Moyabamba, which beginning its courfe from thefe fouthern provinces of Peru, forms the river of the Amazones, as we have already obferved.* The principal commodity of this country is tobacco, which, with a particular kind of almonds called andes, and a few other fruits natural to its climate, form the commerce carried on by this province with the others.

VII. THE laft jurifdiction of this diocefs is that of Pataz, or Caxamarquilla. From its different fituations it has a variety of products: but is particularly remarkable for gold mines; its chief commerce confifting in exchanging that metal for current money, efpecially filver coin, which is the more efteemed here for its fcarcity.

GUAMANGA the fecond diocefs.

THE city of Guamanga, the capital of this diocefs, was founded in the year 1539, by Don Francifco Pizarro, on the fite of an Indian village of the fame name. The Spaniards added the name of San Juan del la Victoria, in memory of the precipitate retreat of Manco the Ynca, from Pizarro, who offered him battle. This city was founded for the conveniency of the trade carried on between Lima and Cufco; for during this long diftance, there was at that time no town, whence the travellers frequently fuffered by the incurfions of Manco's army. This gave occafion to building the city on the fpot where the Indian village ftood, tho' extreamly inconvenient with regard to

pro-

* Vol. I.

provisions, as lying contiguous to the great chain of the Andes; but the war being happily terminated by the entire defeat of Manco's party, the city was removed to its present situation. Its jurisdiction, regulated at the time of its foundation, began at the frontiers of Joxa, and reached to the bridge of Valcas; but at present it is bounded by the provinces which surround it, and contains the town of Anco, about three leagues from it: The city is situated on the declivities of some mountains not remarkable for their height, which extending southward inclose a spacious plain to the eastward of the town, watered by a small stream descending from the neighbouring mountains; but the ground on which the city is built, being higher than the breach thro' which the river flows, the inhabitants were obliged to provide themselves with small fountains. Among the number of inhabitants, Guamanga boasts at least of twenty noble families, who live in the center of the town, in spacious houses of a considerable height, built partly of stone, and covered with tiles. Besides the largeness of the apartment, they have extensive gardens and orchards, tho' it is no small difficulty to keep these in order, on account of the scarcity of water. The large Indian suburbs round the city, add greatly to its extent, and the houses tho' low, are chiefly of stone, and roofed, which considerably augments the appearance of the city. This is indeed the general manner of building in the towns of this kingdom, remote from the coast.

THE cathedral is very splendid, and its chapter, besides the bishop, consists of a dean, archdeacon, chanter, two canons by composition, a penitentiary, and two prebendaries. It has a seminary for the service of the church, under the title of St. Christopher. The church of this seminary is that belonging to the parish of the Spaniards, and another dedicated to St. Ann, the parish church of the Indians. Besides these are the chapels of Carmenca, Belen, St. Sebastian,

and

and St. John the Baptift depending on it. The parifh of Magdalena inhabited by Indians, is under the care of the Dominicans, and the incumbent has the title of prieft. The city has alfo an univerfity, with profeffors of philofophy, divinity and law, and equal privileges with that of Lima, they being both royal foundations. The corporation is compofed of the principal nobility of the city, at the head of which is the corregidor, and out of this body the Alcaldes are chofen, to fuperintend the civil and political government.

WITHIN the walls of this city are the convents of St. Dominic, St. Francis, the fathers of Mercy, St. Auguftine, St. Juan de Dios, a college of Jefuits, a hofpital of St. Francis de Paula. The nunneries are of the orders of St. Clare, and the Carmelites; and a religious fifterhood.

The jurifdictions in the diocefs of Guamanga, are
I. Guamanga.
II. Guanta.
III. Vilcas Guaman.
IV. Andoguaylas.
V. Guanca Belcia.
VI. Angaraes.
VII. Caftio Vineyna.
VIII. Parina-Cocha.
IX. Lucanas.

I. THE jurifdiction of Guamanga, enjoys in every part, fo good a temperature, that it abounds in variety of grain, fruit and cattle, and is very populous. One part of its commerce confift in Bend leather for foles of fhoes, which are cut out here. Conferves and fweatmeats are here made in great quantity.

II. THE jurifdiction of Guanta which lies N. N. W. of Guamanga, begins a little above four leagues from that city; and is in length about thirty leagues. It is very happy in the temperature of the climate, and fertility of the earth; but its filver mines, which were formerly very rich, are now greatly exhaufted. In an ifland formed by the river Jauxa, called in that country Tayacaxa, grows in remakable plenty the Caca already mentioned in Vol. I. This herb, and the lead produced from the mines of that metal in this country,

try, are the branches of its commerce. It supplies the city of Guamanga with great part of its corn and fruits.

III. S. E. of Guamanga, and between six and seven leagues from that city is Vilcas Guaman, which extends above 30 leagues. The greatest part of this country, lying in a temperate air, besides a sufficiency of corn, and fruits, and esculent vegetables, has very fine pastures, in which are bred vast quantities of cattle of all kinds. The Indians in the towns of this jurisdiction apply themselves to weaving bays, corded stuffs, and other branches of the woollen manufactory, which are carried to Cusco, and other provinces; but this trade is rendered very laborious by the great distance of the several places. Here is still remaining a fort built by the old Indians, and resembles that already described, Vol. I. near the town of Cannar; at the town of Vilcas Guaman was another, very famous, but taken down in order to erect a church with the stones.

IV. East a little inclining to the S. of Guamanga is Andaguaylas, extending eastward along an intermediate space between two branches of the Cordillera, above twenty miles, having the advantage of being watered by several small rivers. Its climate is partly hot, and partly temperate, so that the soil being watered by these streams, produces all kinds of fruits and grain in great plenty, especially maize, wheat and sugar canes. This province is one of the most populous in all those parts; in it the gentry of Guamanga have large sugar plantations.

V. The government of Guanca Belica begins thirty leagues north of Guamanga. The town which gives name to this government, was founded on account of the famous rich quicksilver mine, and to the working of it, the inhabitants owe their whole subsistance; the coldness of the air checking the growth of all kinds of grains and fruits, so
that

that they are obliged to purchafe them from their neighbours. This town is noted for a water where fuch large petrefications are formed, that the inhabitants ufe them in building houfes, and other works. The quickfilver mines wrought here, fupply with that neceffary mineral, all the filver mines of Peru.; and notwithftanding the prodigious quantities already extracted, no diminution is perceived. Some attribute the difcovery of thefe mines to a Portuguefe, called Enrique Garces in the year 1566, who accidentally met an Indian with fome pieces of cinnaber, called by the Indians Llimpi, and ufed in painting their faces. But others, among whom are Acofta, Laett, and Efcalona, fay that the mines of Guanca Belica, were difcovered by a Navincopa, or Indian, and fervant to Amador Cabrera; and that before the year 1564, Pedro Contreras and Henrique Garces had difcovered another mine of the fame kind at Patas. But however it be, the mines of Guanca Belica are the only ones now worked; and the ufe of quickfilver for aggregating the particles of filver began in the year 1571, under the direction of Petro Fernandes Velafco. The mines of Guanca Belica immediately on the difcovery were claimed in the king's name, and alternately governed by one of the members of the audienza of Lima, with the title of fuperintendant, whofe office expired at the end of five years, till in the year 1735, when Philip V. appointed a particular governor of thefe mines, with the fame title of fuperintendant, but thoroughly acquainted with the nature of extracting this mineral, having been employed in thofe of the fame nature in Spain; and by his œconomy the mines are worked with lefs charge, and will not be fo foon exhaufted. Part of the quickfilver found here, is fold on the fpot to miners, and the remainder fent to all the royal offices of the kingdom of Peru, for

the

the more commodious supply of those whose mines are at a great distance.

VI. The jurisdiction of Angaraes, depends on the government of Guanca Belica, and begins about twenty leagues W. N. W. of the city of Guamanga. Its territories reach above twenty leagues; its air is temperate, and it abounds in wheat, maize, and other grains and fruits, and also breeds vast droves of cattle of all kinds.

VII. West of the city of Guamanga, is the jurisdiction of Castro Virreyna. In some parts this province extends above thirty leagues, and has such a variety of temperatures, that it produces every kind of grain and fruits. The heaths which are the coldest parts, are frequented by a kind of sheep called Vicunna, whose wool is the most considerable article of its commerce. This animal was also common in the provinces of Jauxa, Guanuco, and Chuquiabo, till the conquest of those countries, when every one hunted them at pleasure for the sake of their wool, without restraint from the government, they became, as it were, exterminated in those parts; now they are only to be found in the summits of mountains or the coldest heaths, where they are not caught without great difficulty.

VIII. About twenty leagues south of the city of Guamanga, is the jurisdiction of Parina-Cocha, which reaches about twenty five leagues; and lies principally in so temperate an air, that the soil, besides excellent pastures, abounds in grain and fruits. It has also several mines both of silver and gold, which now produce more considerably than heretofore. These valuable metals make the chief branch of its active commerce; its passive being the same as in the following jurisdiction.

IX. The jurisdiction of Lucanas begins about twenty-five or thirty leagues south-west of Guamanga. Its temperature is cold and moderate. The parts
of

of the former breed large droves of all forts of cattle; and thofe of the latter are fertile in grain, herbs and fruits. It alfo abounds in valuable filver mines, in which chiefly the riches of Peru confift, and by that means made the center of a very large commerce; great numbers of merchants reforting hither with their goods, and others for purchafing fuch provifions as their own countries do not afford, for which they give in exchange ingots and pinnas of filver.

III. *Diocefs of the audience of* LIMA.
CUSCO.

OF all the cities in Peru, Cufco is the moft ancient, being of the fame date with the eaft empire of the Yncas. It was founded by the firft Ynca Mango Capac, as the feat and capital of his empire. Having peopled it with the firft Indians who voluntarily fubmitted to him, he divided it into two parts, which he called high and low Cufco, the former having been peopled by Indians which the emperor himfelf had affembled, and the latter by thofe whom his confort Mama-Oello had prevailed upon to leave their wandring manner of life. The firft forms the N. and the latter the S. part of the city. The houfes originally were low and fmall like cottages; but as the empire encreafed they affumed a new appearance; fo that when the Spaniards landed in thefe parts, they were aftonifhed at the largenefs and fplendor of the city, efpecially the magnificence of the temple of the fun, the grandeur of the palaces of the Ynca, and the pomp and richnefs becoming the feat of fo vaft an empire. It was in the month of October 1534, when Don Francifco Pizarro entered and took poffeffion of it in the name of Charles V. emperor, and king of Spain. This was followed by a fiege of the Ynca Mango, who laid great part of it in afhes, but without diflodging the Spaniards.

THIS city ftands in a very uneven fituation on the fides of the mountains, there being no other more
con-

convenient near it. On a mountain contiguous to the north part of the city are the ruins of that famous fort built by the Yncas for their defence; and it appears from thence, that the design was to inclose the whole mountain with a prodigious wall, of such construction as to render the ascent of it absolutely impracticable to an enemy, and at the same time easily to be defended by those within; in order to prevent all approach to the city. This wall was entirely of free stone, and strongly built, like all the other works of the Yncas, described Vol. I. but still more remarkable for its dimensions and the largeness of the stones, which are of different magnitudes and figures. Those composing the principal part of the work are of such prodigious dimensions, that it is difficult to imagine how it was possible for the strength of man, unassisted by machines, to have brought them hither from the quarries. The interstices formed by the irregularities of these enormous masses are fill'd with smaller, and so closely joined as not to be perceived without a very narrow inspection. One of these large stones is still lying on the ground, and seems not to have been applied to the use intended, and is such an enormous mass, that it is astonishing to human reason to think by what means it could be brought thither. It is called la Cansada, or the troublesome, alluding probably to the labour of bringing it from the quarry. The internal works of this fortress consisting of apartments, and two other walls, are chiefly in ruins, but the outward wall is standing.

The city of Cusco is nearly equal to that of Lima. The north and west sides, are surrounded by the mountain of the fortress, and others called Sanca: on the south it borders on a plain, on which are several very beautiful walks. Most of the houses are of stone, well contrived, and covered with tiles, whose lively red, gives them an elegant appearance.

The apartments are very spacious, and finely decorated, the inhabitants being noted for their elegant taste. The moldings of all the doors are gilt, and the other ornaments and furniture answerable.

THE cathedral of Cusco, both with regard to materials, architecture, and disposition, greatly resembles that of Lima, but is a much smaller structure. It is built entirely of stone, and the architecture is even thought to exceed it. The Sacristy is called Nueftra Senora del Triumpho, being the place where the Spaniards defended themselves from the fury of the Indians, when surrounded by the army of the Ynca Manco; and though the whole city was several times set on fire, the flames had no effect on this part; which was attributed to the special protection of the holy virgin. It is served by three priests, one in particular for the Indians of the parish, and the other two for the Spaniards. Besides this, Cusco also contains eight other parishes; namely,

I. Belin. II. The church of the general hospital, which has also its priest and its parish. III. Santa Ana. IV. Santiago. V. San Blas. VI. San Chriftoval. VII. San Sebastian. VIII. San Geronymo. And though the first of the two last be a league, and the second two leagues from the city, they are reckoned among the number of its parishes.

HERE is also a convent of Dominicans, the principal walls of which were formerly those of the temple of the sun, and at present the high altar stands in the very place, where once was a golden image of that planet. There is likewise at Cusco a convent of Francifcans, which is the head of that order in this province. The convents of the Auguftines and the fathers of mercy in this city, are also the principal of their respective orders. The Jesuits have likewise a college here. The convent of St. Juan de Dios and that of the Bethlemites, which are both very large, are hospitals for the sick; the latter is

par-

Ch. XII.  SOUTH AMERICA.  131

particularly appropriated to the Indians, who are there used with the greatest care and tenderness. The nunneries are those of St. Clare, St. Catherine, the barefooted Carmelites, and a Nazarine sisterhood.

The government of this city consists of a corregidor, placed at the head of the magistrates, who are the chief nobility, and out of these are annually chosen two ordinary Alcaldes, according to the custom of all the cities in south America. The members of the cathedral chapter besides the bishop, are five dignitaries, namely, the dean, archdeacon, chanter, rector and treasurer; two canons by competition, a magistral, and penetentiary; three canons by presentation, and two prebendaries. Here are three colleges, in the first, called St. Anthony, a seminary for the service of the cathedral, are taught latin, the sciences and divinity. The second is under the direction of the Jesuits, where these fathers instruct youths of fortune. The third, called St. Francis de Borja, belongs also to the Jesuits, and is appointed for the education of the sons of Caziques, or Indian princes. The two former confer all degrees below that of doctor, and have been erected into universities.

Among the courts of justice, is one for the revenue, consisting of two judges. Here is also a court of inquisition, and of the croisade; together with the same offices as in the other large cities already described. Formerly this city was very full of Spaniards, and among them many noble families; but at present its inhabitants are very much declined.

*Jurisdictions in the Diocess of* Cusco.
I. Cusco.
II. Quispicanchi.
III. Avancay.
IV. Paucartambo.
V. Colcaylares.
VI. Chilques, and Masques.
VII. Cotabamba.
VIII. Canas,

VIII. Canas, and
Cances, or Tinta.
IX. Aymaraes.
X. Chumbi-Vilcas.
XI. Lampa.

XII. Carabaya.
XIII. Afangaro, and
Afilo.
XIV. Apolo-Bamba.

I. THE jurifdiction of Cufco extends two leagues; the temperature of air is various, but both the heat and cold very fupportable, except in fome parts where the cold is intenfe: thefe, however, afford good pafture for all kinds of cattle, whilft the valleys produce plenty of grain and fruits.

II. THE jurifdiction of Quifpicanchi, begins as it were at the fouth gates of Cufco, ftretching from E. to W. above twenty leagues. The lands belong in general to the gentry of Cufco, and produce plenty of wheat, maize, and fruits. Here are alfo manufactories of bays, and coarfe woollen ftuffs. Part of this province borders on the forefts inhabited by wild Indians, and produces great quantities of Coca, which forms one of the principal branches of its commerce.

III. FOUR leagues north-eaft from the city of Cufco, begins the jurifdiction of Avancay, and extends above thirty leagues; the air differing in temperature according to the fituation of its parts; but is in general rather hot than temperate, and, accordingly, many parts of it are taken up with large plantations of canes, which yield a very rich fugar. The lands where the air is more temperate, abound in wheat, maize and fruits, part of which are fent to the city of Cufco. In this province is the valley Xaquijaguana, corruptly called Xajaguana, where Gonzalo Pizarro was defeated and taken prifoner by Pedro de la Gafco.

IV. PAUCARTAMBO begins eight leagues eaft of Cufco, and is of a confiderable extent. This province produced in the time of the Yncas the greateft quantity of Coca, with which it carried on a very profitable commerce; but is greatly declined fince this

fhrub

shrub has been planted in other provinces. The soil is equally fertile in other products.

V. The jurisdiction of Calcaylares begins four leagues W. of the city of Cusco. The air every where excels that of all the other provinces, and, accordingly produces an exuberance of all kinds of grain and fruits. In the hottest parts called Lares, were formerly very large plantations of sugar canes, but for want of hands to cultivate them, they are at present so diminished, that instead of sixty or eighty thousand arobas, which they annually produced in the time of their prosperity, they are now reduced to something less than thirty; but the sugar is of such an excellent kind, that without any other preparation than that of the country, it is equal both in colour and hardness to the refined sugar of Europe. This diminution of its sugar, has greatly lessened the principal branch of its commerce.

VI. S. E. of Cusco, and at the distance of about seven or eight leagues, begins the jurisdiction of Chilques and Masques, extending above thirty leagues in length. The temperature of the air is proportioned to the situation of its several parts, some of which are very fertile in grain, and others feed vast numbers of cows and sheep. But besides these its commerce is greatly augmented by the woollen manufactures of the Indians.

VII. S. W. of Cusco, and about twenty leagues distance, begins the jurisdiction of Cotabamba, which afterwards extends above thirty leagues between the rivers Avancay and Apurimac: In which extent are different temperatures of air. It abounds in all kinds of cattle, and the temperate parts produce plenty of wheat, maize, and fruits. Here are also mines of silver and gold, the richness of which formerly rendered this province very flourishing; but at present their produce is greatly declined.

VIII. The jurisdiction of Canas and Carches or Tinta,

Tinta, begins about fifteen or twenty leagues S. of Cufco, and extends about twenty leagues in every direction. The Cordillera divides it into two parts; the highest called Canas and the lowest Canches. The latter by reason of its temperate air yields all kinds of grains and fruits; whilst the former affords pasture for very numerous flocks and herds; and in the meadows between the eminences are fed no less than twenty five or thirty thousand mules, brought thither from Tucuma to pasture. Here is a very great fair for these creatures, to which dealers resort from all parts of the diocefs. In the part called Canas is the famous silver mine Condonoma.

ABOUT forty leagues S. W. from Cufco is the jurisdiction of Aymaraes, which extends thirty farther, and like the former has different temperatures of air. The lands abound in sugar, cattle, and grain; and also in mines of gold and silver, which formerly produced large quantities of those valuable metals; but at present few of them are wrought, the country being too thinly inhabited.

X. SOMETHING more than forty leagues from Cufco, begins the jurifdiction of Chumbi Vilcas, which in some parts extends above thirty leagues, has different temperatures of air, great quantities of corn and fruits, and large herds of cattle; together with some mines of silver and gold.

XI. THE jurifdiction of Lampa begins thirty leagues S. of Cufco, and is the principal of all the provinces included under the name of Callao. Its plains are interrupted with small hills, but both abound in good pasture; and accordingly this province is particularly remarkable for its quantity of cattle, with which it carries on a very profitable trade; but the air being every where cold, the only fruits of the earth are Papas and Quincas. Another very confiderable advantage are its filver mines, being very rich, and constantly worked.

XII THE

XII. The jurisdiction of Carabaya begins sixty leagues S. E. of Cusco, and extends above fifty leagues. The greatest part of it is cold; but the valleys so warm as to produce Coca, and abounds in all kinds of fruits, grain, and pulse, together with sufficient pastures for cattle of all kinds. Here are several gold mines, and the two famous lavatories, called Lavaderos de San Juan del Oro, and Pablo Coya; also that of Monte de Ananea, two leagues from the town of Poto, where there is an office for collecting the Quintos or fifth, belonging to the king. In this province also is a river, which separates it from the mountains of the wild Indians, and is known to abound so greatly in gold, that at certain times the Caziques send out a certain number of Indians in companies from the towns in their respective districts to the banks of this river, where by washing the sands in small wells they dig for that purpose, they soon find a sufficient quantity of gold to pay the royal tribute. This kind of service they call Chichina. This province has also mines of silver, which produce vast quantities of that metal In 1713 was discovered in the mountain of Ucuntaya a vein or stratum nearly of solid silver, which though soon exhausted, yielded some millions, and hopes have been conceived from it of meeting with others, whose riches will be of a longer continuance. This jurisdiction is also famous for the gold mine called Aporama, which is very rich, and the metal twenty three carats fine.

XIII. The jurisdiction of Asangaro and Asilo, which lies about fifty leagues S. of Cusco, is every where cold, and consequently proper only for breeding cattle, in which, however, it carries on a very profitable trade. In the N. E. parts which border on those of Caravaya, are some silver mines, but a few of them only are worked. Some of its lands produce plenty of those roots and grains which naturally flourish in a cold air, as Papas, Quinoas, and Canaguas;

naguas; of the two laſt the natives makes Chica in the fame manner as it is made with maize. This juriſdiction belongs to the audience of Charcas.

XIV. ABOUT ſixty leagues from Cuſco, on the borders of the Moxos, which are miſſions of the Jeſuits, are others called Apolo-bamba, belonging to the Franciſcans. Theſe confiſt of ſeven towns of Indians newly converted, and who having received the doctrine of the goſpel, have abandoned the ſavage manner in which they formerly lived. In order to render the miſſionaries more reſpected by the Indians, and at the ſame time to defend the latter from the inſults of their idolatrous brethren, a major general is poſted here, who is both a civil and military officer, adminiſtring juſtice, and commanding in chief the ſeveral bodies of militia formed by he inhabitants of theſe towns and villages.

IV. Dioceſs of the Audience of LIMA.

AREQUIPA.

THE city of Arequipa was founded in 1539 by order of Don Franciſco Pizarro, in a place known by the ſame name; but this ſituation being found very diſadvantageous, the inhabitants obtain'd permiſſion to remove it to the valley of Quilca, where it at preſent ſtands about twenty leagues diſtant from the ſea. The lands in its dependency having been united to the empire of the Yncas by Maita Capac, the goodneſs of the ſoil and the purity of the air induced that monarch, for the farther improvement of the country, to draw 3000 families from ſuch adjacent provinces as were leſs fertile, and with theſe to people four or five towns.

THIS city is one of the largeſt in all Peru, delightfully ſituated in a plain, and the houſes well built of ſtone, and vaulted. They are not all of an equal height, though generally lofty, but commodious, finely decorated on the outſide, and neatly furniſhed within. The temperature of the air is remarkably good:

and

## Ch. XII. SOUTH AMERICA. 137

and though sometimes a small frost is seen, the cold is never excessive, nor is the heat troublesome; so that the fields are always cloathed with verdure and enameled with flowers, as in a perpetual spring. The inhabitants enjoy an exemption from many diseases common in other countries, partly owing to their care in keeping the streets clean by means of canals which extend to a river running near the city; and by these all the filth of the city is swept away.

But these pleasures and advantages are allayed by the dreadful shocks of earthquakes, to which, in common with all those parts of America, it is so subject, that it has been four times by these convulsions of nature laid in ruins; besides other small shocks not attended with such terrible consequences. The first of those was felt in 1582; the second on the 24th of February 1600, which was accompanied with an eruption of a volcano called Guayna-Patina, in the neighbourhood of the city; the third happen'd in 1604, and the last in 1725. And tho' the desolation attending the three last was not so universal, yet the publick buildings, and the most stately houses were laid in ruins.

The city is very populous, and among its inhabitants many noble families, this being the place where most of the Spaniards settled, on account of the goodness of the air, and the fertility of the soil; as also for the conveniency of commerce at the port of Aranta, which is only twenty leagues distant. The civil, political and military government of the city is executed by a corregidor, who is placed at the head of the regidores, from which are annually chosen two ordinary Alcaldes.

The city of Arequipa did belong to the diocefs of Cusco, till the year 1609, when it was erected into a particular bishoprick on the 20th of July. The chapter besides the bishop consist of the five usual dignitaries, namely, the dean, archdeacon, chantor,

tor, rector, and treafurer; three canons and two prebends. Befides the facrifty, which is ferved by two priefts for the Spaniards, the parifh of Santa Martha is appropriated to all the Indian inhabitants. Here are two Francifcan convents, one of obfervants, and the other of recollets, both belonging to the province of Cufco; alfo one of Dominicans, and another of Auguftines, depending on Lima; and a monaftery of the fathers of mercy, fubordinate to that of Cufco. Under their refpective fraternities of Lima here is alfo a college of Jefuits, and a convent and hofpital of St. Juan de Dios. Here is a feminary for the fervice of the cathedral; and two nunneries; namely, one of the Carmelites, and the other of St. Catharine. A third is now building for the order of Santa Rofa. There is alfo at Arequipa an office of revenue, under the direction of an accomptant and treafurer; together with commiffaries of the inquifition and croifades, with their fubalterns, as in all the other cities.

Jurifdictions in the Diocefs of AREQUIPA.
I. Arequipa.            IV. Caylloma.
II. Camana.             V. Monquegua.
III. Condefuyos de Arequipa.  VI. Arica.

I. AREQUIPA, comprehends the fuburbs and towns in its neighbourhood, where the climate being the fame as in the city, the country is perpetually covered with flowers, corn, and fruits; while the excellence of the paftures is fufficiently evident from the numbers of fine cattle fed in them.

II. ALONG the coaft of the fouth-fea, but at fome diftance from the fhore is the jurifdiction of Camana, which is very large, but contains many defarts, efpecially along the coaft. Eaftward it extends to the borders of the Cordillera; fo that the temperature of fome parts of its jurifdiction is nearly the fame with that of the former, while others are cold; both producing the grain and fruits of a correfpondent nature.

Its

Its principal trade confifts in affes. It has filver mines near the mountains, but of little advantage, as they are not worked.

III. N. of Arequipa and thirty leagues diftant from that city, is the jurifdiction of Condefuyos de Arequipa, extending about thirty leagues, with different temperatures of the air, and confequently produces grains and fruits. Here is bred the wild Cochineal, with which the Indians carry on a kind of trade with thofe provinces where the woollen manufactures flourifh. They firft pulverize the Cochineal by grinding, and after mixing four ounces of it, with twelve of violet maize, they form it into fquare cakes called Mango, each weighing four ounces, and fell it for a dollar per pound. This country abounds in gold and filver mines; but they are not worked with the care and diligence of former times.

IV. At about thirty leagues eaft from the city of Arequipa, begins Caylloma, famous for a mountain of the fame name, and the filver mines it contains. Though thefe mines have been long difcovered and conftantly and induftrioufly worked, their produce is ftill fo confiderable, that in the principal village, called by the fame name, there is a governor and office appointed for receiving the king's fifths, and vending the quickfilver ufed in feparating the metal from the ore. The cold in the greateft part of the country is fo intenfe, that the inhabitants are obliged to have recourfe to the neighbouring provinces, for the fruits of the earth. Even the declivities of mountains and valleys produce but little. In fome parts of this province are wild affes, like thofe already mentioned in Vol. I.

V. The jurifdiction of Monquegua lies about forty leagues S. of the city of Arequipa, and fixteen from the coaft of the fouth-fea. The principal town, which bears the fame name, is inhabited by Spaniards, and among them feveral noble and opulent families.

This

This jurifdiction extends at leaft forty leagues in length, and in a happy climate, adorned with large vineyards, from the produce of which great quantities of wine and brandy are made; thefe conftitute its whole commerce, fupplying all the provinces bordering on the Cordilleras as far as Potofi, by land carriage; while they are exported by fea to Callao, where they are greatly valued. Here are alfo Papas and Olives;

VI. THE laft jurifdiction of this diocefs is Arica, which extends along the coaft of the fouth-fea. Befides the heat, and inclemency of the air, the greateft part of the country is barren, producing only Aji, or Guinea pepper, from which alone it drives a very advantageous trade, as may eafily be imagined from the vaft confumption of it in all thefe parts of America. Accordingly the dealers in this commodity refort hither from the provinces on the other fide of the mountains, and by computation, the annual produce of thefe plantations amount to no lefs than 60000 dollars per annum. The pods of this pepper are about a quarter of a yard in length, and when gathered are dried in the fun, and packed up in bags or rufhes, each bag containing an aroba, or quarter of a hundred weight; and thus they are exported to all parts of the kingdom, and ufed as an ingredient in moft of their difhes. Other parts of this jurifdiction are famous for vaft quantities of large and excellent olives, far exceeding the fineft produced in Europe, being nearly as large as a hen's egg. They extract fome oil from their olives, and find a good market for it in the provinces of the Cordillera; others are pickled, and fome, together with a fmall quantity of oil, exported to Callao.

CHAP.

## CHAP. XIII.
*Of the Audience of* CHARCAS.

THE province of Charcas, in the extent of its jurifdiction, is equal to that of Lima; but with this difadvantage, that many of its parts are not fo well inhabited, fome being full of the vaft defarts and impenetrable forefts; while others are full of vaft plains intercepted by the ftupendous heights of the Cordilleras, fo that it is inhabited in thofe parts only which are free from thefe inconveniences. The name of Charcas formerly included many populous provinces of Indians, whom the Ynca Capac Yupanqui fubjected to his empire; but he carried his arms no farther than the provinces of Tutyras and Chaqui, where he terminated his conquefts towards Callafuyo. On the death of this monarch his fon Ynca Roca, the fixth in the fucceffion of thofe emperors, pufhed his conquefts farther in the fame part, till he became fovereign of all the intermediate nations to the province of Chaquifaca, where was afterwards founded the city of Plata, at prefent the capital of the whole province of Charcas. Its jurifdiction begins on the north fide, at Vilcanota, belonging to the province of Lampa in the diocefs of Cufco, and reaches fouthward to Buenos Ayres. Eaftward it extends to Brafil, being terminated by the meridian of demarcation; and weftward part of it reaches to the fouth-fea, particularly at Atacama, the moft northern part of it on this fide. The remainder of Charcas borders on the kingdom of Chili. Thefe vaft tracts of land give one archbifhop and five bifhops his fuffragans, namely,

The archbifhop of PLATA.
Bifhopricks.

I. La Pas.  II. Santa Cruz de la Sierra.
III. Tu-

dicated to St. Francis Xavier, the chairs of which are filled indifferently either by fecular clergy or lay men; but the rector is always a Jefuit. Here are alfo two other colleges in which lectures of all kinds are read. That of St. John is under the direction of the Jefuits; while the archbifhop nominates to that of St. Chriftopher, which is a feminary.

Two leagues from Plata runs the river Cachimayo along the plains, having on its banks feveral pleafant feats of the inhabitants; and about fix in the road leading to Potofi, is the river of Philco-mayo, which is paffed over by a large ftone bridge. During fome months of the year this river furnifhes the city of Plata with great plenty of delicious fifh; among which is one called the Dorado, which generally weighs between twenty and twenty five pounds. The other provifions, as bread, flefh and fruits, are brought from the adjacent provinces.

THE chief tribunal in Plata is that of the Audience, erected in the year 1559, and whofe prefident has the titles of governor and captain-general of the province, exclufive of the governments of Santa Cruz de la Sierra, Tucuman, Paraguay and Buenos Ayres, which are independent, and in military cafes abfolute. It has alfo a Fifcal, a protector-fifcal of the Indians, and two fupernumerary auditors.

THE magiftracy or corporation, as in all other cities of this country, confifts of regidores, who are perfons of the firft diftinction, with the Corregidor at their head, and from them are annually chofen two ordinary Alcaldes, for maintaining order and the police. Plata was erected into a bifhopric in 1551, the place having then the title of city; and in the year 1608 was raifed to a metropolis. Its chapter confifts of a dean, archdeacon, chantor, treafurer and rector; five canons, four prebendaries and four minor prebendaries. The archbifhop and his chancellor conftitute the ecclefiaftical tribunal.

HERE

Ch. XIII.   SOUTH AMERICA;   145

Here is also a tribunal of Croisade, with a commissary, subdelegate, and other officers: likewise a court of inquisition subordinate to that of Lima, and an office for taking care of the effects of persons dying intestate; all established on the same foundation with those in other cities already mentioned.

The jurisdictions belonging to the archbishopric of Plata, are the fourteen following:

I. The city of Plata, and Imperial Town of Potosi.
II. Tomina.
III. Porco.
IV. Tarija.
V. Lipes.
VI. Amparaes;
VII. Oruro.
VIII. Pilya, and Paspaya.
IX. Cochabamba.
X. Chayantas.
XI. Paria.
XII. Carangas.
XIII. Cuacica.
XIV. Atacama.

I. The jurisdiction of the city of Plata is of such prodigious extent, as to include the imperial town of Potosi, which is the continual residence of the Corregidor. There also is established the office of revenue, which consists of an accountant and treasurer, with clerks; as most convenient on account of its vicinity to the mines, for taking account of the silver produced by them.

The famous mountain of Potosi, at the foot of which on the south side stands the town of the same name, is known all over the commercial world, as having been greatly enriched by the silver it produces. The discovery of these immense mines happened in the year 1545, by an accident seemingly fortuitous. An Indian, by some called Gualca, and by others Hualpa, pursuing some wild goats up this mountain, and coming to a part very steep, he laid hold of a small shrub in order to climb it with the greater celerity; but the shrub being unable to support his weight came up by the roots, and discovered a mass of fine silver; and at the same time

Vol. II.            L                        he

dicated to St. Francis Xavier, the chairs of which are filled indifferently either by fecular clergy or lay men; but the rector is always a Jefuit. Here are alfo two other colleges in which lectures of all kinds are read. That of St. John is under the direction of the Jefuits; while the archbifhop nominates to that of St. Chriftopher, which is a feminary.

Two leagues from Plata runs the river Cachimayo along the plains, having on its banks feveral pleafant feats of the inhabitants; and about fix in the road leading to Potofi, is the river of Philco-mayo, which is paffed over by a large ftone bridge. During fome months of the year this river furnifhes the city of Plata with great plenty of delicious fifh; among which is one called the Dorado, which generally weighs between twenty and twenty five pounds. The other provifions, as bread, flefh and fruits, are brought from the adjacent provinces.

The chief tribunal in Plata is that of the Audience, erected in the year 1559, and whofe prefident has the titles of governor and captain-general of the province, exclufive of the governments of Santa Cruz de la Sierra, Tucuman, Paraguay and Buenos Ayres, which are independent, and in military cafes abfolute. It has alfo a Fifcal, a protector-fifcal of the Indians, and two fupernumerary auditors.

The magiftracy or corporation, as in all other cities of this country, confifts of regidores, who are perfons of the firft diftinction, with the Corregidor at their head, and from them are annually chofen two ordinary Alcaldes, for maintaining order and the police. Plata was erected into a bifhopric in 1551, the place having then the title of city; and in the year 1608 was raifed to a metropolis. Its chapter confifts of a dean, archdeacon, chantor, treafurer and rector; five canons, four prebendaries and four minor prebendaries. The archbifhop and his chancellor conftitute the ecclefiaftical tribunal.

Here

Ch. XIII.   SOUTH AMERICA.   145

HERE is also a tribunal of Croisade, with a commissary, subdelegate, and other officers: likewise a court of inquisition subordinate to that of Lima, and an office for taking care of the effects of persons dying intestate; all established on the same foundation with those in other cities already mentioned.

THE jurisdictions belonging to the archbishopric of Plata, are the fourteen following:

I. THE city of Plata, and Imperial Town of Potosi.
II. Tomina.
III. Porco.
IV. Tarija.
V. Lipes.
VI. Amparaes.
VII. Oruro.
VIII. Pilya, and Paspaya.
IX. Cochabamba.
X. Chayantas.
XI. Paria.
XII. Carangas.
XIII. Cuacica.
XIV. Atacama.

I. THE jurisdiction of the city of Plata is of such prodigious extent, as to include the imperial town of Potosi, which is the continual residence of the Corregidor. There also is established the office of revenue, which consists of an accountant and treasurer, with clerks; as most convenient on account of its vicinity to the mines, for taking account of the silver produced by them.

THE famous mountain of Potosi, at the foot of which on the south side stands the town of the same name, is known all over the commercial world, as having been greatly enriched by the silver it produces. The discovery of these immense mines happened in the year 1545, by an accident seemingly fortuitous. An Indian, by some called Gualca, and by others Hualpa, pursuing some wild goats up this mountain, and coming to a part very steep, he laid hold of a small shrub in order to climb it with the greater celerity; but the shrub being unable to support his weight came up by the roots, and discovered a mass of fine silver; and at the same time

VOL. II.   L   he

he found some lumps of the same metal among the clods which adhered to the roots. This Indian, who lived at Porco, hastened home with these first fruits of his discovery, washed the silver and made use of it, repairing when his stock was near exhausted, to his perpetual fund. At length an intimate friend of his called Guanca, observing such a happy change in his circumstances, was desirous of knowing the cause, and urged his questions with a warmth, that Gualca was unable to deny. For some time they retired in concert to the mountain for fresh supplies of silver, till Gualca refusing to discover his method of purifying the metal, Guanca revealed the whole secret to his master Villarroel, a Spaniard who lived at Porco. Immediately on this information he went on the 21st of April 1545, to view this fortunate breach in the mountain, and the mine was without delay worked, with immense advantage.

THIS first mine was called the discoverer, as having been the occasion of discovering other sources of riches inclosed in the bowels of this mountain; for in a few days another was found equally rich, and called the Tin mine: since that another has been discovered, and distinguished by the name of Rica, as surpassing all the rest: and was succeeded by the Mendieta. These are the principal mines of Potosi, but there are several smaller crossing the mountain on all sides. The situation of the former of these mines is on the N. side of the mountain, their direction being to the S. a little inclining to the W. and it is the opinion of the most intelligent miners in this country, that those which run in these directions are the richest.

ON a report of these important discoveries people from all parts retired to Potosi, particularly from the city of Plata, which is situated about twenty five leagues from the mountain; so that at present, be-

sides

sides its extraordinary riches, having among its inhabitants many noble families, particularly those concerned in the mines, the circuit of the town is near two leagues. The air of the mountain being extreamly cold and dry, renders the adjacent country remarkably barren, producing neither grain, fruits, herbs, or other esculents. The town, however, is so plentifully provided as to enjoy an abundance of every kind; and the trade for provisions is greater here than in any other place, that of Lima alone excepted. Nor will this appear at all strange if the great number of people employed in the mines be considered. Some provinces send the best of their grain and fruits; others their cattle; others their manufactures; and those who trade in European goods resort to Potosi, as to a market where there is a great demand, and no want of silver to give in exchange.

BESIDES this commerce, here are a set of persons called Aviadores, who find their account in advancing to the masters of the mines coined silver to pay their necessary expences, receiving in exchange silver in ingots and pinnas. Another article of great consequence is the trade of quickfilver for the use of these mines: but this branch the crown has reserved to itself. The vast consumption of this mineral may in some measure be conceived by the great quantity of silver produced by these mines; for before the invention of extracting the silver with less mercury, a mark of that mineral was consumed in obtaining a mark of fine silver; and often by the ignorance of the workmen, a still greater quantity; but the immense consumption of quickfilver in the mines of this mountain, and the riches extracted from it, will best appear from the following accounts, of two authors, who were perfectly masters of the subject, The first is that of the Rev. Alonzo Barba, parish priest in the imperial town of

Potofi, who, in a piece on metals publifhed in the year 1637, fays, that from the year 1574, when mercury was firft ufed here in extracting the filver, the royal office of Potofi has received, above 204700 quaintails of mercury, exclufive of what had been clandeftinely bought by private perfons, and which amounted to no fmall quantity. And as this was confumed in the fpace of fixty three years, the annual amount is about 3249 quintails. The fecond account is given us by don Gafper de Efcalona, who in his Gazophilacio Perubico (fol. 193.) declares, from very good authority, that before 1638, it appeared by the public accounts, that the produce of the filver amounted to 395619000 dollars, which in ninety three years, the time it had then been difcovered, amounted to 41255043 dollars per annum. Hence an idea may be formed of the vaft commerce, which has for many years been carried on in this town, and which is ftill like to continue for a long time: fuch enormous fums being annually bartered for goods fent hither, its whole trade confifting in filver extracted from this mountain; and if fome diminution has been perceived in its produce, it is ftill very confiderable

At a fmall diftance from Potofi are the hot medicinal baths called Don Diego, whither fome refort for health, and others for diverfion.

The jurifdiction of Tomina, begins about eighteen leagues S. E. from the city of Plata, borders eaftward on a nation of wild Indians called Chiriguanos. The climate is hot, and confequently its products are fuch as are common to hot countries. Some parts have vine-yards; and in others are made confiderable quantities of fugar. It abounds alfo in cattle and fheep. The extent in fome parts is near forty leagues. The vicinity of the Chiriguanos is a continual uneanefs to the towns in this jurifdiction, and even to the city of Plata itfelf, they having more than once attempted to furprize it.

III. The

III. The jurifdiction of Porco begins at the W. fide of the town of Potofi, and about 25 leagues diſtance from the city of Plata; extending about 20 farther. The coldneſs of its fituation occafions a fcarcity of grain and fruits; but, on the other hand, it abounds in fine cattle of all forts. In this jurifdiction is the mountain of Porco, whence it has its name, and from whofe mines the Yncas, as I have already obferved, extracted all the filver for their expences and ornaments; and accordingly was the firſt mine worked by the Spaniards after the conqueſt.

IV. About 30 leagues S. of Plata lies the jurifdiction of Tarija, or Chichas, the greateſt extent of which is about 35 leagues. The temperature of the air is various, being in fome parts hot, and in others cold; whence it has the advantage of corn, fruits, and cattle. This country every where abounds in mines of gold and filver, and efpecially that part called Chocayas. Between this province and the country inhabited by the wild Indians, runs the large river Tipuanys, the fands of which being mixed with gold, are wafhed like thofe of the river Caravaga, already mentioned.

V. In the fame part as the former, but with a fmall inclination towards the S. W. is the jurifdiction of Lipes, and extends alfo thirty-five leagues. The air is extreamly cold, fo that grain and fruit thrive very little here; but it abounds in cattle, particularly thofe natural to the country, as the Vicuna, Alpaca, or Taruga, and the Llama. It muſt, however, be obferved, that thefe creatures are common to all the other provinces of Punas, that is, to thofe where the heaths and mountains are of fuch a height, as to render the air continually cold. Here are alfo mines of gold, but at prefent forfaken, tho' the remains of the old works are ſtill vifible, particularly in one of the mountains near Colcha, known by the name of Abetanis, which in the Indian language fignifies a

golden

golden mine. That of St. Chriftopher de Acochala was formerly one of the moft famous in all Peru, for the richnefs of its filver mines, the meal being in fome parts cut out with a chifel; but now very greatly declined; which may in a great meafure be imputed to a want of people for working them; it being highly probable that the fame work would ftill produce nearly an equal quantity of that valuable metal.

VI. The jurifdiction of Amparaes begins at a little diftance to the eaftward of the city of Plata, and is terminated on the E. by the jurifdictions belonging to the d ocefs of Santa Cruz de la Sierra, particularly on that of Mifquepocona; and the corregidor of the province of Amparaes has the cognizance of the Indian inhabitants of Plata. Its warm parts abound in gra n, particularly barley, which together with the numerous droves of cattle in the colder parts, conftitute the chief branch of its trade.

VIII. N. W. of Plata is the province of Oruro, whofe capital San Phelipe de Auftria de Oruro is 30 leagues diftant from it. The greateft part of this jurifdiction is fo cold as to deny it any efculent vegetables; but on the other hand it feeds numerous flocks and herds, befides great numbers of cattle peculiar to the country, as Vicunas, Guanacos, and Llamas. Here are alfo many gold and filver mines; the former, tho' known even in the time of the Yncas, have been feldom worked; but thofe of filver have yielded great riches to the inhabitants of the province. They are now however, according to all appearance, under an irremediable decay, being overflowed, and all the endeavours hitherto ufed, in order to drain them, have proved ineffectual; fo that thofe of any confideration at prefent are in the mountains of Popo, about twelve leagues from the town, which is large and very populous, from the trade carried on there with the mines. It has a revenue office for collecting the fifths belonging to the crown.

VIII. The

CH. XIII.   SOUTH AMERICA.   151

VIII. The province of Pilaya and Pafpaya, or Cinti, lies S. of Plata, diftance about 40 leagues. The greateft part of its jurifdiction being among the breaches of the mountains, is the better adapted for producing all kinds of grain, pulfe, and fruits; which, with the great quantity of wine made here, enable it to carry on a very lucrative commerce with the other provinces, which are not fo happily fituated.

IX. The province of Cochabamba, lies fifty leagues S. E. of Plata, and fifty fix from Potofi. Its capital is one of the moft confiderable cities in Peru, with regard to largenefs, and the number and wealth of its inhabitants. The province in fome directions extends above forty leagues. Befides the fituation of the city in a moft fertile plain, the whole country is fo fertilized by the many rivers and ftreams, which every where traverfe it, that this province is efteemed the granary of the whole archbifhopric, and even of the diocefs de la Paz. The air alfo is in moft parts very mild and pure; and in fome fpots filver mines have been difcovered.

X. About fifty leagues N. W. from the city de la Plata, lies the province of Chayanta extending in fome parts about forty leagues. This country is very famous for its gold and filver mines. The former are indeed at prefent difcontinued, tho' the antient fubterraneous paffages are ftill open. This province is watered by the river Grande, in whofe fand confiderable quantities of gold duft, and grains of that metal are found. The filver mines are ftill worked to great advantage; but with regard to cattle, this province feeds no more than are barely fufficient for its inhabitants.

XI. The contiguous province to that of Chayanta, on the N. W. fide of Plata, and feventy leagues diftant from that city, is that of Paria, the extent of which is about forty leagues. The air here is cold, fo that it produces little grain, which is in fome

L 4                                     mea-

meafure compenfated by the great plenty of cattle of all kinds; and the cheefes made here, both from the milk of fheep and cows, are fo highly efteem'd, that they are fent into every part of Peru: It has alfo fome filver mines. The name of this province is derived from a very large lake, being an arm of that prodigious collection of waters called Titi-caca, or Chucuito.

XII. The province of Carangas, begins feventy leagues W. from the city of Plata, and extends above fifty leagues. The climate of this jurifdiction is fo cold, that the only efculent vegetables here are the Papa, Quinoa, and Canagua; but it abounds in cattle. Here are a great number of filver mines conftantly worked; among which that called Turco is very remarkable for a fort of ore termed by miners Machacado; the fibres of the filver forming an admirable intertexture with the ftone in which they are contained. Mines of this kind are generally the richeft. Befides this there are others in this jurifdiction, which if not richer, are equally remarkable; and thefe are found in the barren fandy defarts extending towards the coaft of the South Sea. And here, only by digging in the fands, are found detached lumps of filver, not mixed with any ore or ftone, fave what adheres in fome parts to the metal. Thefe lumps are called Papas, being taken out of the ground, in the fame manner as that root. It is doubtlefs very difficult to account for the formation of thefe maffes of filver, in a barren and moveable fand, remote from any ore or mine. Two conjectures may, however, be offered. The firft by admitting the continual reproduction of metals, of which there are indeed here fo many evident proofs; as the matrices of gold and filver, met with in many parts of this kingdom. Nay the very mines themfelves, after being long forfaken, have again been worked with great advantage; but the fkeletons of Indians found in old mines, and

covered

covered with fibres of silver, and the inward parts also full of the same metal, seem to put the matter beyond dispute. If this be admitted, it is natural to conclude, that the primordial matter of silver is first fluid, and when it has acquired a certain degree of perfection, some parts of it are filtrated through the pores of the sand, till stopping in a place proper for compleating the fixation, they there form a solid congeries of silver.

Tho' this conjecture be not destitute of probability, yet I am more inclined to embrace the second, as it is, in my opinion, more simple and natural. Subterraneous fires being very common in these parts of America, as I have already observed in speaking of the earthquake, their activity is doubtless so strong as to melt any metals deposited near the places where they begin; and to communicate to them a heat sufficient for keeping them a long time in a state of fusion, and hence a portion of silver thus melted necessarily spreads, and introduces itself through the larger pores of the earth, and continues to expand itself, till being beyond the reach of the heat, it fixes, and reassumes its former consistency, together with other heterogeneous substances collected in its passage. To this hypothesis, two objections may be offered ; one that the metal in fusion by changing its situation, must be exposed to the cold air, and, consequently, soon condense. The second that the pores of the earth being extreamly minute, particularly in a sandy soil, the silver should rather be found in filaments, or fine ramifications, than in large lumps or pieces, as is really the case. To both these objections I shall endeavour to give a brief but satisfactory answer.

Before the silver begins to run from the place where it was melted, the subterraneous fire had pervaded the pores of the earth, which by the dilatation of the body of air inclosed in them, became distended; the metal immediately follows, and finding a channel sufficiently capacious for introducing itself, farther compresses the particles of the earth contiguous to those it abrades, and, consequently, continues its course without obstruction. The subterraneous fire which preceded the fusion, communicates to the earth a degree of heat sufficient to expel the cold air, so that the metal runs through it, till by degrees, the heat is abated, and the metal becomes fixed. Another circumstance which contributes to prolong the heat, is, there being often no spiracle to these passages, whence the earth through which the metal flows, does not soon emit the first heat it contracted from the subterraneous fire; consequently the metal will not be fixed till at a considerable distance from the place of liquidation; but the first particles of the metal being checked by the cold they have gradually contracted, those which follow flow to the same place, and there forms a concreted mass, or mixed body of silver and scoria, brought with it from the original mine. It now remains that we examine whether what is actually observed in these lumps of silver, agrees with what has been advanced, in order to determine whether this opinion has a probable foundation.

These papas, or lumps of silver, are of a different composition from those found in the mine, having all the appearances of melted silver, as any person, a stranger to the manner of finding them, would immediately conclude. In them the silver forms a mass, and the surface is covered over with terrene particles, few or none of which are mixed with the silver; conformable to what is seen in metals melted, and suffered to cool without separating the dross. The terrene particles adhering to the silver are black, and exhibit all the marks of calcination, except that in some it is stronger than in others; and as this must happen if the lumps are formed by the fusion of the metal, it seems natural to conclude that they were really formed in this manner.

THE

The size and figure of these lumps are very different; some weighing about two marks, and others much more; for among several which I saw at Lima were two, one weighing 60, and the other above 150 marks, being a Paris foot in length; these indeed were the largest ever seen here. These lumps of silver are found in different parts of the same ground, tho' not often near one another. The metal in its course takes various directions, introducing itself into those places where it finds the least resistance; and as these parts are more or less capacious, the magnitude of the papa is greater or smaller.

XIII. About ninety leagues N. of the city of Plata, but only forty from Paz, lies the province of Ciacica. Its capital, which has the same name, and all the places situated to the southward of it, belong to the archbishopric of Plata; but many of those to the northward of it are in the diocess of Paz. The countries in this jurisdiction extend in some parts above a hundred leagues, and consequently the temperature is various. Some spots are very hot, and produce an exuberance of coca, which shrub alone is the source of a very considerable commerce, supplying all the mine towns from Charcas to Potosi. The leaves of this plant are packed in frails, each of which must, according to the ordinance, contain eight pounds; and its current price at Oruro, Potosi, and the other mine towns, is from nine to ten pieces of eight, and sometimes more. The colder parts feed large herds of cattle; together with Vicunas, Guanacos, and other wild creatures. This province has also some silver mines, but not so many, nor so rich, as the preceding province.

XIV. Attacama is the western boundary of the audience of Charcas, extending to the south sea; and the principal town, called also Attacama, is no less than 120 leagues from Plata. Its jurisdiction is of a considerable extent, and a great part of it very fruitful;
but

but intermixed with some deserts particularly towards the S. where it divides the kingdoms of Peru and Chili. On the coast in this province there is every year a large fishery of Tolo, a sort of fish common in the S. sea, with which a very great trade is carried on with the inland provinces, it being there the chief food during Lent, and the other days of abstinence.

## CHAP. XIV.

*Account of the three Diocesses of* LA PAZ, SANTA CRUZ DE LA SIERRA, *and* TUCUMAN; *and of their respective Provinces.*

THE province in which the present city of la Paz, is situated, was formerly known by the name of Chuquiyapu, which in the idiom of that country is commonly thought to signify Chacra, or an inheritance of gold, and is there corruptly called Chuquiabo. Accordingly Garcelaso pretends that Chuquiapu signifies Lanza Capitana, or principal lance; but this is deriving it from the general language of the Yncas, and with a difference in the penultima, it not being uncommon for a word nearly alike in sound to have a very different signification in each idiom. This province was first conquered by Mayta-Capac, the fourth Ynca; and the Spaniards having afterwards taken possession of it, and quelled all disturbances, this city was founded by Pedro de la Gasca, that in the vast distance of an hundred and seventy leagues between Arequipa and Plata, there might be a settlement of Spaniards, for the improvement of commerce, and the safety and conveniency of the traders. The president Gasca, committed the care of building it to Alonso de Mendoza, with orders that it should be erected on a spot, midway between Cusco and

Charcas,

## CH. XIV.  SOUTH AMERICA.  157

Charcas, which are one hundred and sixty leagues from each other; and that it should be called Nueftra Senora de la Paz, in memory of the publick tranquility recently fettled by the defeat and execution of Gonzalo Pizarro, and his adherents. With regard to its fituation, a valley in the country called las Pacafas, was pitched upon, on the 8th of October 1548, as a place abounding in grain, and cattle, and full of Indians.

ALONG the valley de la Paz, flows a large river, but fometimes greatly increafed by torrents for the cordillera, about twelve leagues diftant from the city; but from its vicinity, great part of the country is expofed to fo cold an air, as hard frofts, fnow, and hail are not uncommon; but the city itfelf is fecured from them by its happy fituation. Other parts are alfo fo well fheltered, that they produce all the vegetables of a hot climate, as fugar canes, coca, maize, and the like. In the mountainous part are large woods of valuable timber, but infefted with bears, tigers, and leopards; they have alfo a few deer: While on the heaths are found Guanacos, Vicunas, and Llamas, with great numbers of cattle of the European fpecies, as will be feen in the account of each refpective province.

THE city is of a middling fize, is furrounded with mountains, and commands the profpect of the river. When the river is increafed either by rains, or the melting of the fnow on the mountains, its current forces along huge maffes of rocks, with fome grains of gold, which are found after the flood has fubfided. Hence fome idea may be form'd of the riches inclofed in the bowels of thefe mountains; but a more remarkable demonftration appeared in the year 1730, when an Indian happening to wafh his feet in the river, difcovered a lump of gold, of fo large a fize that the marquis de Caftel-Fuerte, gave twelve thoufand pieces of eight for it, and fent it to Spain, as a prefent worthy the curiofity of his fovereign.

THIS

This city is governed by a corregidor, under whom are regidores, and ordinary alcaldes, as in all other towns. Besides the cathedral, and the parish church del Sagrario, where two priests officiate, here are also those of St. Barbara, St. Sebastian, and St. Peter: The religious fraternities of Francifcans, Dominicans, Auguftines, the fathers of mercy, a college of Jefuits, and a convent and hofpital of St. Juan de Dios; together with a nunnery of the order of the Conception, and another of Santa Terefa. Alfo a college of St. Jerom, for the education of youth, designed for ecclefiaftic or civil employment.

In 1608 the church de la Paz was feparated from the diocefs of Chuquifaca, to which it before belonged, and erected into a cathedral. Its chapter confifts of the bifhop, dean, archdeacon, chantor, four canons and prebendaries; but with regard to other circumftances, being the fame with feveral cities already defcribed, I fhall proceed to the provinces in its diocefs.

I. Bifhopric of the audience of charcas.

La Paz.

The provinces or jurifdictions in the diocefs of Paz, are the fix following.

I. La Paz.       IV. Laricaxas.
II. Omafuyos.    V. Chucuito.
III. Pacages.    VI. Paucar-Colla.

I. The jurifdiction of la Paz, is of no great extent, and the city almoft the only place worth notice in it. In the adjacent cordillera is a mountain of remarkable height called Illimani, which doubtlefs contains immenfe riches. A crag of it being fome years fince ftruck from it by a flafh of lightning, and falling on a neighbouring mountain, fuch a quantity of gold was found in the fragments, that for fome time that metal was fold at Paz, at eight pieces of eight per ounce. But its fummit being perpetually covered with ice and fnow, no mine has been opened in this mountain. The fame we have already obferved of thofe high

moun-

mountains in the province of Quito, Vol. I. all attempts having been rendered abortive.

II. N. W. and almoſt at the gates of Paz, the juriſdiction of Omaſuyos begins and extends about 20 leagues, being bounded on the W. by the famous lake of Titi-caca, or Chucuito, of which a farther account will be given in the ſequel. The air here is ſomewhat cold, ſo that it produces little grain; but that deficiency is abundantly compenſated by the great numbers of cattle; beſides an advantageous trade for fiſh, carried on in other provinces by the Indians living on the borders of the lake, who are very induſtrious in improving that advantage.

III. Almost S. W. of Paz, is the juriſdiction of Pacajes, the greateſt part of which being in a cold climate produces little grain or fruits; ſo that the inhabitants apply themſelves to the breeding of cattle. This province is however very rich in ſilver mines, tho' but a ſmall part of them are worked; and it is known from undoubted ſigns that theſe mines were worked in the time of the Yncas. Here are alſo mines of talc, called jaſpas blancos de Verenguela. It is of a beautiful white, and on account of its tranſparency is tranſported to different parts of Peru, for making panes of windows, both in churches and houſes; as the ſtone called Tecali ſerves for the ſame uſes in New Spain. In theſe mountains are alſo a great number of mines of gems, particularly one of emeralds, well known in Europe, but for ſome latent reaſons not worked; together with quarries of different ſpecies of marble. In this province is the famous ſilver mine Verenguela; and the mountains of Santa Juana, Tampaya, and others, well known for the immenſe treaſures extracted from them.

IV. Adjacent to the territories of the juriſdiction of la Paz, and to the N. of that city is the province of Laricaxas, which extends 118 leagues from E. to W. and about thirty from N. to S. The temperature of the air is different in different parts, and some of its product are the same with those of Carabaya, by which it is terminated to the northward. This whole province abounds in gold mines, whose metal is of so fine a quality, that its standard is twenty-three caracts, and three grains. In this province is the celebrated mountain of Sunchuli, in which, about fifty years since was discovered, a gold mine remarkably rich, and of the standard above-mention'd; but when in its highest prosperity, it was unfortunately overflowed; and notwithstanding prodigious sums were expended in endeavours to drain it, all the labour and expence, from the works being injudiciously conducted, were thrown away.

V. THE jurisdiction of Chucuito begins about twenty leagues W. of Paz, and some part of it bordering on the lake of Titi-caca, that collection of waters is also called the lake of Cucuito. The extent of this province from N. to S. is betwixt twenty-six and twenty eight leagues. Its temperature is in general, cold and very disagreeable, the frosts continuing one half of the year, and the other either snow or hail is continually falling. Accordingly the only esculent productions of the vegetable kingdom are the Papas and Quinoas. The inhabitants have however a very beneficial trade with their cattle, which abound in this jurisdiction, by salting and drying the flesh. The traders who carry it to the coast exchange it for brandy and wine; and those who go to Cochabamba, carry also Papas, and Quinoas, which they barter for meal.

ALL the mountains in this province have their silver mines, and formerly produced largely, but at present are totally abandoned.

THE territories of the province of Chucuito, are on one side bounded by the lake of Titi-caca, the magnitude of which merits some account to be given of it. This lake lies between these provinces, comprehended under the general name of Calloa, and is

of

CH. XIV. SOUTH AMERICA. 161

of all the known lakes of America, much the largeſt. Its figure is ſomewhat oval, inclining nearly from N. W. to S. E. its circumference is about 80 leagues, and the water in ſome parts 70 or 80 fathoms deep. Ten or twelve large rivers, beſides a great number of ſmaller ſtreams empty themſelves into it. The water of this lake, tho' neither bitter or brackiſh, is turbid, and has in its taſte ſomething ſo nauſeous that it cannot be drank. It abounds with fiſh, of two oppoſite kinds; one large and palatable, which the Indians call Suchis; the other ſmall, inſipid and bony, termed long ſince by the Spaniards Boyas. It has alſo great number of geeſe and other wild fowl, and the ſhores covered with flags and ruſhes, the materials of which the bridges are made, and of which an account will be given in the ſequel.

As the weſtern borders of this lake are called Chucuito, ſo thoſe on the E. ſide are diſtinguiſhed by the name of Omaſcuyo. It contains ſeveral iſlands, among which is one very large, and was anciently one mountain, but ſince levelled by order of the Yncas; it, however, gave to the lake its own name of Titicaca, which, in the Indian language, ſignifies a mountain of lead. In this iſland the firſt Ynca Mancho-Capac, the illuſtrious founder of the empire of Peru, invented his political fable, that the ſun, his father, had placed him, together with his ſiſter and conſort Mama Oello Huaco, there, enjoining them to draw the neighbouring people from the ignorance, rudeneſs, and barbarity in which they lived, and humanize them by cuſtoms, laws, and religious rights dictated by himſelf; and in return for the benefits reſulting from this artful ſtratagem, the iſland has, by all the Indians, been conſidered as ſacred; and the Yncas determining to erect on it a temple to the ſun, cauſed it to be levelled, that the ſituation might be more delightful and commodious.

THIS was one of the moſt ſplendid temples in the whole

whole empire. Befides the plates of gold and filver with which its walls was magnificently adorned, it contained an immenfe collection of riches, all the inhabitants of provinces which depended on the empire, being under an indifpenfible obligation of vifiting it once a year, and offering fome gift. Accordingly they always brought in proportion to their zeal or ability, gold, filver, or jewels. This immenfe mafs of riches, the Indians, on feeing the rapacious violence of the Spaniards, are thought to have thrown into the lake; as it is certainly known, they did with regard to a great part of thofe at Cufco, among which was the famous golden chain made by order of the Ynca Huayna Capac, to celebrate the feftival of giving name to his eldeft fon. But thefe valuable effects were thrown into another lake, fix leagues S. of Cufco, in the valley of Orcos: and tho' numbers of Spaniards animated with the flattering hopes of fuch immenfe treafures made frequent attempts to recover them, the great depth of the water, and the bottom being covered with flime and mud, rendered all their endeavours abortive. For notwithftanding the circuit is not above half a league, yet the depth of water is in moft places not lefs than twenty-three or twenty-four fathoms.

TOWARDS the S. part of the lake Titi-caca, the banks approach each other, fo as to form a kind of bay, which terminates in a river called el Defaguadero, or the drain, and afterwards forms the lake of Paria, which has no vifible outlet; but the many whirlpools fufficiently indicate that the water iffues by a fubterraneous paffage. Over the river Defaguadero is ftill remaining the bridge of rufhes, invented by Capac Yupanqui, the fifth Ynca, for tranfporting his army to the other fide, in order to conquer the provinces of Collafuyo. The Defaguadero is here between eighty and a hundred yards in breadth, flowing with a very impetuous current under a fmooth, and, as it were, a fleeping furface. The Ynca to

over-

overcome this difficulty, ordered four very large cables to be made of a kind of grafs which covers the lofty heaths and mountains of that country, and called by the Indians Ichu; and thefe cables were the foundation of the whole ftructure. Two of thefe being laid a-crofs the water; fafcines of dry juncia and totora, fpecies of rufhes, were faftened together, and laid a-crofs them. On thefe the two other cables were laid, and again covered with other fafcines fecurely faftened, but fmaller than the firft, and arranged in fuch a manner as to form a level furface; and by this means he procured a fafe paffage to his army. This bridge, which is about five yards in breadth, and one and a half above the furface of the water, is carefully repaired, or rebuilt every fix months, by the neighbouring provinces, in purfuance of a law made by that Ynca, and fince often confirmed by the kings of Spain, on account of its prodigious ufe; it being the channel of intercourfe between thofe provinces feparated by the Defaguadero.

VI. The laft jurifdiction of this bifhopric is that of Paucar-Colla, whofe capital is the town of Puno. Its jurifdiction fouthward borders on that of Chuquito, and has the fame temperature: confequently is obliged to have recourfe to other provinces for the greateft part of its grain, and efculent vegetables; but abounds in all kinds of cattle, both of the European and American kinds. The Indians of the town weave bags with their wool, and fell them to great advantage. The mountains in this province contain feveral filver mines, and among the reft the famous Laycacota, which formerly belonged to Jofeph Salcedo, and where the metal was often cut out of the mine with a chiffel; but its prodigious richnefs accelerated the death of its owner, foon after which the waters broke in to it; nor has any labour and expence been able to drain it, fo that it is at prefent abandoned. Few of the reft are worked, the general cafe with almoft all the filver mines in this audience, especially of those in the archbishopric of Charcas, and this diocess of La Paz.

II. Bishopric in the audience of Charcas. Santa Cruz de la Sierra.

The province of Santa Cruz de la Sierra, is a government and captain generalship: and tho' its jurisdiction is of a large extent, not many Spaniards are found in it, and the few towns are in general missions, comprehended under the common name of Paraguay missions. The capital of the same name was erected into a bishopric in the year 1605. Its chapter consists only of a bishop, dean, and archdeacon, having neither canons, prebendaries, or other dignitaries. The usual residence of the bishop is the city of Misque Pocona, eighty leagues from Santa Cruz de la Sierra.

The jurisdiction of Masque-Pocona, reaches above thirty leagues; and tho' the city itself is very thinly inhabited, there are, in other parts of it, several populous towns. The temperature is hot, but not in a degree too great for vineyards. The valley in which the city stands is above eight-leagues in circumference, and produces all kinds of grain and fruits; and the woods and uncultivated mountains afford great quantities of honey and wax, which constitute a principal branch of its commerce.

The missions belonging to the Jesuits in the parts dependent on this bishopric, are those called Indios Chiquitos, or little Indians, a name given them by the Spaniards, on account of the extreme smallness of the doors of their houses. Their country lies between Santa Cruz de la Sierra, and the lake Xarayes, from whence the river Paraguay has its rise, and being increased by the conflux of others, forms the famous river de la Plata. It was about the close of the last century, when the fathers first began their preaching in this nation, and so great has been their success, that in the year 1732, they had form'd seven towns, each consisting of above 600 families; and were then

build-

## Ch. XIV.  SOUTH AMERICA.

building others for affembling under the fame laws, the great number of Indians, daily converted. Thefe Indios Chiquitos are well made and active; and their courage has been often experienced by the Portuguefe, who ufed to make incurfions, in order to carry off the inhabitants for flaves: But the valour of thefe people has taught them to defift from fuch inhuman attempts, and, for their own fafety, to keep within their limits. The arms of thefe Indians are mufquets, fabres, and poifoned arrows. Though their language is different from that of the other nations of Paraguay, the fame cuftoms nearly obtain here, as among all the other Indians.

BORDERING on this nation of Chiquitos is another of Pagan Indians called Chiriguanos, or Chiriguanaes, who have always refufed to liften to the miffionaries; though the fathers ftill continue to vifit them at certain times, and preach to them, but prudently take care to be accompanied with fome Chiquitos for their fecurity; and thus they make now and then a few converts, who are fent to their towns, and there lead a focial life. This generally happens after fome misfortune in the wars continually carried on between them and the Chiquitos; when in order the more eafily to obtain a peace, and that the Chiquitos may not abfolutely exterminate them, they fend for miffionaries; but foon difmifs them again, pretending that they cannot bear to fee punifhments inflicted on perfons merely for deviating from the rules of reafon. This plainly demonftrates, that all they defire or aim at, is an unbounded licentioufnefs of manners.

SANTA Cruz de la Sierra, the capital of this government, lies eighty or ninety leagues E. of Plata. It was originally built fomething farther toward the S. E. near the Cordillera of the Chiriguanos. It was founded in the year 1548, by captain Nuflo de Chaves, who called it Santa Cruz, from a town of that name near

Truxillo in Spain, where he was born. But the city having been deſtroyed, it was rebuilt in the place where it now ſtands. It is neither large nor well built, nor has it any thing anſwerable to the promiſing title of city.

III. Biſhopric of the Audience of CHARCAS.

El Tucuman.

TUCMA, by the Spaniards called Tucuman, lies in the center of this part of America, beginning S. of the Plata, beyond the towns of Chicas, which furniſh Indians for the mines in Potoſi. On the E. it borders on Paraguay and Buenos Ayres; reaches weſtward to the kingdom of Chili, and ſouthward to the Pampas or plains belonging to the land of Magellan. This country, though united to the empire of the Yncas, was never conquered by them; having, when Vira Cocha the eighth Ynca had made himſelf ſovereign in Charcas, ſent a deputation of their chiefs, with a requeſt of being admitted among the number of his ſubjects, and that he would be pleaſed to ſend them governors, that their country might partake of the benefits of thoſe wiſe laws, and uſeful improvements he had introduced into all the parts of his empire.

THE Spaniards having penetrated into Peru, and finiſhed the conqueſt of far the greateſt part of that empire, proceeded to that of Tucuman in 1549, under the conduct of Juan Nunez de Prado, whom the preſident Pedro de la Gaſca intruſted with the conduct of this expedition. He had, indeed, no opportunity of diſplaying his military talents; for the inhabitants being of a mild and eaſy diſpoſition, readily ſubmitted; on which the following four cities were built in that country; namely Santiago del Eſtero, ſo called from a river of the ſame name on which it is built, and whoſe inundations greatly contribute to increaſe the fertility of the ſoil; it ſtands above a hundred and ſixty leagues S. of Plata: San Miguel del Tucuman,

twenty-

twenty five or thirty leagues W. of the former: Nueſtra Sennora de Talavera, ſomething more than forty leagues N. W. of Santiago. The fourth was called Cordova de la Nueva Andalucia, and is above eighty leagues S. of Santiago.

THE territories of this government being of ſuch extent that they reach from N. to S. above two hundred leagues, and little ſhort of a hundred in ſome parts from E. to W. it was judged proper to increaſe the number of Spaniſh ſettlements; and accordingly orders were given for building two other cities, which are Rioja, about eighty leagues S. W. of Santiago, and Santa, between ſixty and ſeventy leagues N. W. of the ſame city; together with a village called San Salvador, or Xuxui, about twenty leagues N of Salta. But all theſe places are ſmall, and built without either order or ſymmetry. The governor, notwithſtanding Santiago was the firſt, reſides at Salta; and even the biſhop with his chapter at Cordova, which is the largeſt. The others have their reſpective Corregidors, under whom alſo are the Indian villages within the dependencies of their proper cities. But of theſe there is no great number, the principal part of the country not being inhabitable, either from a want of water, or from their being covered with impenetrable foreſts. This want of inhabitants is alſo greatly owing to the cruelties and ravages of the ſavage Indians, in their frequent incurſions.

THE epiſcopal church of Tucuman, which, as we have already obſerved, is in Cordova, was in the year 1570 erected into a cathedral, and its chapter now conſiſts of the biſhop, dean, archdeacon, chantor, rector and treaſurer, who is elected; but has neither canons nor prebendaries.

THOSE parts of the country which are watered by the rivers, are ſo remarkably fertile in grain and fruits, that they produce ſufficient for the common conſumption of the inhabitants. The woods abound in wild honey and wax, whilst the hot parts produce sugar and cotton; the last is manufactured here, and with the woollen stuffs also wove by the inhabitants, form an advantageous branch of trade. But its great article consists in the mules bred in the luxuriant pastures of its valleys. Inconceivable droves of these creatures are sent to all parts of Peru, the Tucuman mules being famous over these countries, far exceeding all others in strength, and docility.

## CHAP. XV.

*Account of* PARAGUAY *and* BUENOS AYRES; *the two last Governments of the Audience of* CHARCAS.

IV. Bishopric of the Audience of CHARCAS.

### PARAGUAY.

THE government of Paraguay lies S. of Santa Cruz de la Sierra, and E. of Tucuman. Southward it joins to that of Buenos Ayres; and is terminated eastward by the captainship of St. Vicente in Brazil, whose capital is the city of St. Pablo. These countries were first discovered by Sebastian Gaboto, who, coming to the river of Plata in the year 1526, sail'd up the river Parana in some small barks, and thence entered that of Paraguay. He was succeeded in 1536 by Juan de Ayolas, to whom Don Pedro de Mendoza, the first governor of Buenos Ayres, had given a commission, together with a body of troops, military stores and other necessaries; and afterwards, by his orders, Juan de Salinas, founded the city of Nuestra Senora de la Assumption, the capital of the province; but the discovery of the whole, and consequently the conquest of people who inhabited it, it, being still imperfect, it was prosecuted by Alvar Nunez, surnamed Cabeza de Baca, or Cowhead, whose eminent services, on the death of Don Pedro de Mendozo, procur'd him the government of Buenos Ayres.

The only settlements in the whole extent of this government, are the city of Assumption, Villa Rica, and some other towns, whose inhabitants are a mixture of Spaniards, Mestizos, and some Indians, but the greatest part of the several casts. As the city itself is but small and irregular, nothing better can be expected in Villa Rica, and other towns and villages. Its houses are indeed intermixed with gardens and plantations, but without any symmetry. It is the residence of the governor of the province, who had formerly under his jurisdiction, part of the towns composing the missions of Paraguay; but a few years since they were separated from it, and are now annexed to the government of Buenos Ayres; but without any change in the ecclesiastical government. In the city of Assumption is a cathedral, whose chapter consists of the bishop, dean, archdeacon, treasurer, and two canons. The parishes of the city of Villa Rica, and of the other towns depending on this government are served by the Franciscans: but in the missionary towns they are solely under the care of the Jesuits; and these composing the greater number of towns in this province, I shall speak particularly of them, still keeping to that concisenefs I have observed in the other jurisdictions.

The missions of Paraguay, besides those in the province of that name, include also a great many of Santa Cruz de la Sierra, Tucuman and Buenos Ayres. Within a century and a half, the epocha of their first establishment, they have been the means of bringing into the bosom of the church, many Indian nations, who lived in the blindness of idolatry, and the turpitude of the savage customs

trans-

transmitted to them by their anceſtors. The firſt inſtance of this apoſtolic zeal was the ſpiritual conqueſt of the Guacanies Indians, ſome of whom inhabited the banks of the rivers Uruguay and Parana; and others near an hundred leagues up the countries N. W. of the Guayra. The Portugueſe, then only intent on the improvements of their colonies, in violation of the moſt ſacred laws, did not even after the converſion of theſe people, ceaſe from making incurſions, in order to carry off the young inhabitants as ſlaves for their plantations; ſo that it became abſolutely neceſſary, in order to preſerve theſe converts, to remove into Paraguay, about 12000 of all ages, and both ſexes; a like number of emigrants was alſo brought from Tappe, and formed into communities, living here in peace and ſafety; and at the ſame time in a decency becoming their new profeſſion.

But the number of ſucceeding converts was ſo great, that continual additions were neceſſary to theſe towns, ſo that I was at Quito informed by a perſon of undoubted veracity, and thoroughly acquainted with ſuch matters, that the number of towns of the Guaranies Indians in the year 1734, amounted to thirty-two, and ſuppoſed to contain between thirty and forty thouſand families: That from the increaſing proſperity of the Chriſtian religion, they were then deliberating on the manner of building three other towns, theſe thirty-two being in the dioceſſes of Buenos Ayres, and Paraguay. Beſides the Indios Chiquitos belonging to the dioceſs of Santa Cruz de la Sierra, there were at that time ſeven very populous towns; and by reaſon of the great reſort of converted Indians, preparations were making for building others.

The Paraguay miſſions are on all ſides terminated by nations of idolatrous Indians; ſome of which however live in perfect harmony with them, but others do

all

all in their power to exterminate them by frequent incurfions; and it is with the latter that the fathers chiefly employ their zeal, in order to reclaim them from their inhumanity, by preaching to them the glad tidings of the gofpel. Nor is this fortitude deftitute of fruit, the moft rational receiving with joy the knowledge of the true God, and quitting their country, are conducted to the Chriftian towns, where, after proper inftructions, they are admitted to baptifm.

About a hundred leagues from the miffions is a nation of idolaters called Guanoas. It is with great difficulty any of thefe are brought to embrace the light of the gofpel, as they are extreamly addicted to a licentious life; and a great number of Meftizos, and even fome Spaniards, whofe crimes have obliged to take fhelter among them, by their ill example harden the Indians in their contempt of inftruction. Befides they are fo indolent and flothful, that they will not take the pains to cultivate the lands, chufing to live by the more expeditious way of hunting; and being convinced, that if they embrace the Chriftian religion, and fubmit to the miffionaries, they muft labour, they cannot bear to think of a change which will inevitably deprive them of their favourite indolence. Many, however, of thofe who come to the Chriftian towns to vifit their relations, cannot withftand the order and decency in which they fee them live, and accordingly embrace the Chriftian religion.

It is nearly the fame with the Charuas, a people inhabiting the country between the rivers Parana and Uruguay. Thofe dwelling on the banks of the river Parana, from the town of Corpus upwards, and called Guananas, are more tractable, and their induftry in agriculture and other rural arts, render them more fufceptible of liftening to the preaching of the miffionaries: befides no fuch thing as a fugitive is to be found among them. Near Cordova is another nation of idolaters, called Pampas, who, notwithftanding they
fre-

frequently come to the city, to fell different productions of the earth, are very obstinate in their opinions, and, consequently, are not reclaimed without the greatest difficulty. These four nations of idolatrous Indians live, however, in peace with the Christians.

IN the neighbourhood of the city of Santa Fé, situated in the province of Buenos Ayres, are others who absolutely reject all terms of peace; so that even the villages and estates near Santiago and Salta in the government of Tucuman have felt the effects of their daring incursions. The other nations between these and the Chiquitos, and the lake of Xarayes, are little known. Not many years since some Jesuit missionaries ventured to visit their country up the river Pilcomayo, which runs from Potosi to Assumption; but their territories being very large, and living a vagrant sort of lives, without fixed habitations, the zeal of the good fathers was frustrated; as it has indeed on many other occasions, even after repeated trials.

THE idolatrous Indians, who inhabit the country from the city of Assumption northward, are but very few. The missionaries have been so fortunate to meet with some of these in their journies after them, and prevailed on them to accompany them to the Christian towns, where, without much reluctancy, they have embraced Christianity. The Chiriguanos, already mentioned, also reside in these parts; but are so infatuated with the pleasures of a savage life, that they will not hear of living under laws.

FROM what has been said, it will easily be conceived that the country occupied by the Paraguay missions, must be of a very great extent. The air in general is moist and temperate; tho' in some parts, it is rather cold. The temperate parts abound with all kinds of provisions. Cotton contributes considerably to their riches, growing here in such quantities, that every little village gathers of it annually above two thousand arobas; and the industrious are very ingenious

nious in weaving it into stuffs for exportation. A great deal of tobacco is also planted here. But these articles are far less advantageous to the inhabitants than the herb called Paraguay, which alone would be sufficient to form a flourishing commerce in this province, it being the only one which produces it; and from hence it is sent all over Peru, and Chili, where its use is universal; especially that kind of it called Camini, which is the pure leaf; the other, distinguished by the name of Palos, being less fine, and not so proper for making mate, is not so valuable.

These goods are carried, for sale, to the cities of Santa Fe, and Buenos Ayres, where the fathers have factors; the Indians, particularly the Guaranies, wanting the sagacity and address, so absolutely necessary to procure success in commercial affairs. These factors dispose of what is consigned to them from Paraguay, and lay out the money in such European goods as the towns are then in want of, in ornaments for the churches, and the decent support of the priests officiating in them. But the greatest care is taken in deducting from what each town sends, the amount of the tribute of its Indian inhabitants, which is remitted immediately to the revenue office, without the least deduction, except the stipends for the priests, and the pensions allowed the Caciques.

The other products of their lands, together with their cattle, are made use of for the subsistance of the inhabitants, among whom they are distributed with such regularity and œconomy, that the excellent police under which those people live so happily cannot be passed over in silence, without great injustice to these wise legislators.

Every town of the missions of Paraguay, like the cities, and great towns of the Spaniards, are under a governor, regidores and alcaldes. That the important office of governor may be always filled by a person duly qualified, he is chosen by the Indians, with the approbaton tion of the priefts. The alcaldes are annually appointed by the regidores, and jointly with them, the governor attends to the maintainance of good order and tranquility among the inhabitants; and that thefe officers, who are feldom perfons of the moft fhining parts, may not abufe their authority, and either thro' intereft, or paffion, carry their revenge too far againft other Indians, they are not to proceed to punifhment without previoufly acquainting the prieft with the affair, that he may compare the offence with the fentence. The prieft, on finding the perfon really guilty, delivers him up to be punifhed, which generally confifts in imprifonment for a certain number of days, and fometimes fafting is added to it; but if the fault be very great, the delinquent is whipt, which is the moft fevere punifhment ufed among them; thefe people being never known to commit any crime that merits a greater degree of chaftifement; for immediately on being regiftered as converts, the greateft care has been taken in thefe miffions, to imprint on the minds of thefe new Chriftians, a deteftation of murther, robbery, and fuch atrocious crimes. The execution of the fentence is preceded by a difcourfe made by the prieft before the delinquent, in which he reprefents to the offender, with the greateft foftnefs, and fympathy, the nature of his crime, and its turpitude; fo that he is brought to acknowledge the juftnefs of the fentence, and to receive it rather as a brotherly correction, than a punifhment; fo that tho' nature muft feel, yet he receives the correction with the greateft humility and refignation, being confcious that he has brought it upon himfelf. Thus the priefts are in no danger of any malice being harboured againft them; indeed the love and veneration the Indians pay them is fo great, that could they be guilty of enjoyning an unjuft punifhment, the fuffering party would impute it to his own demerits, being firmly

per-

persuaded that the priests never do any thing without a sufficient reason.

Every town has a particular armory, in which are kept all the fire-arms, swords, and weapons used by the militia, when they take the field, whether to repel the insults of the Portuguese, or any heathen Indians inhabiting on their frontiers. And that they may be dextrous in the management of them, they are exercised on the evening of every holiday in the market-places of the towns. All persons capable of bearing arms in every town, are divided into companies, and have their proper officers, who owe this distinction to their military qualifications: their uniform is richly laced with gold or silver, according to their rank, and embroidered with the device of their towns. In these they always appear on holidays, and at the times of exercise. The governor, alcaldes, and regidores, have also very magnificent habits of ceremony, which they wear on solemn occasions.

No town is without a school for teaching reading, writing, dancing, and music: and in whatever they undertake they generally excel, the inclination and genius of every one being carefully consulted before they are forwarded in any branch of science. Thus many attain a very good knowledge of the Latin tongue. In one of the courts of the house belonging to the priest of every town, are shops or workhouses for painters, sculptors, gilders, silversmiths, locksmiths, carpenters, weavers, watchmakers, and all other mechanic arts and trades. Here every one works for the benefit of the whole town, under the inspection of the priests coadjutors; and boys are there also instructed in those trades or arts, to which they have the greatest inclination.

The churches are large, and well built: and, with regard to decorations, not inferior to the richest in Peru. Even the houses of the Indians are built with that symmetry and convenience, and so compleatly and

elegantly

elegantly furnished, as to excel those of the Spaniards in many towns in this part of America. Most of them however are only of mud walls, some of unburnt bricks, and others of stone; but all, in general, covered with tiles. Every thing in these towns is on such good footing, that all private houses make gun-powder, that a sufficient quantity of it may not be wanting, either on any exigency, or for fireworks on holidays, and other anniversary rejoicings which are punctually kept. But the most splendid ceremony is on the accession of the new monarch to the Spanish throne, when the governor, alcaldes, regidores, together with all the civil and military officers, appear in new uniforms, and other ornaments, to express the ardent affection they bear their new sovereign.

Every church has its band of musick, consisting of a great number both of vocal and instrumental performers. Divine service is celebrated in them with all the pomp and solemnity of cathedrals. The like is observed in publick processions, especially that on Corpus Christi day, at which the governor, alcaldes, and regidores, in their habits of ceremony, and the militia in their uniforms, assist: the rest of the people carry flambeaux; so that the whole is conducted with an order and reverence suitable to the occasion. These processions are accompanied with fine dancing, but very different from that in the province of Quito, described in the first volume; and the performers wear particular dresses, extreamly rich, and well adapted to the characters represented. In short, a missionary town omits no circumstance either of festivity or devotion, practised in opulent cities.

Every town has a kind of Beaterio, where women of ill fame are placed: it also serves for the retreat of married women who have no families, during the absence of their husbands. For the support of this house, and also of orphans and others, who by age or any other circumstance are disabled from earning a livelihood, two days in the week are set apart; when the inhabitants of every village are obliged to sow and cultivate a certain piece of ground, called Labor de la Comunidad, the labour of the community; and the surplus of the produce is applied to procure furniture and decorations for the church, and to clothe the orphans, the aged, and the disabled persons. By this benevolent plan all distress is precluded, and the inhabitants provided with every necessary of life. The royal revenues are punctually paid; and by the union of the inhabitants, the uninterrupted peace they enjoy, and the wisdom of their polity, which is preserved inviolable, these places, if there are any such on earth, are the habitations of true religion and felicity.

The Jesuits, who are the priests of these missions, take upon them the sole care of disposing of the manufactures and products of the Guaranies Indians, designed for commerce; these people being naturally careless and indolent, and doubtless without the diligent inspection and pathetic exhortations of the fathers, would be buried in sloth and indigence. The case is very different in the missions of the Chiquitos, who are industrious, careful, and frugal; and their genius so happily adapted to commerce, as not to stand in need of any factors. The priests in the villages of this nation are of no expence to the crown, the Indians themselves rejoicing in maintaining them; and join in cultivating a plantation filled with all kinds of grain and fruits for the priest; the remainder, after this decent support, being applied to purchase ornaments for the churches.

That the Indians may never be in any want of necessaries, it is one part of the minister's care to have always in readiness a stock of different kinds of tools, stuffs, and other goods; so that all who are in want repair to him, bringing by way of exchange wax, of which there are here great quantities;

cities; and other products. And this barter is made with the strictest integrity, that the Indians may have no reason to complain of oppression; and that the high character of the priests for justice and sanctity may be studiously preserved. The goods received in exchange are by the priests sent to the superior of the missions, who is a different person from the superior of the Guaranies: and with the produce, a fresh stock of goods is laid in. The principal intention of this is, that the Indians may have no occasion to leave their own country, in order to be furnished with necessaries; and by this means are kept from the contagion of those vices, which they would naturally contract in their intercourse with the inhabitants of other countries, where the depravity of human nature is not corrected by such good examples and laws.

If the civil government of these towns be so admirably calculated for happiness, the ecclesiastical government is still more so. Every town and village has its particular priest, who in proportion to its largeness, has an assistant or two of the same order. These priests, together with six boys who wait on them, and also sing in the churches, form in every village a kind of small college, where the hours are under the same regulation, and the exercises succeed each other with the same formalities as in the great colleges of cities. The most laborious part of the duty belonging to the priest, is to visit personally the chacaras or plantations of the Indians; and in this they are remarkably sedulous, in order to prevent the ill consequences of that slothful disposition so natural to the Guaranies; who, were they not frequently roused and stimulated by the presence of the priest, would abandon their work, or, at least, perform it in a very superficial manner. He also attends at the public slaughter-house, where every day are killed some of the cattle; large herds of which are

## Ch. XV. SOUTH AMERICA.

are kept for the public use by the Indians. The flesh of these beasts are dealt out by the priest, in lots proportionable to the number of persons each family consists of; so that every one has a sufficiency to supply the calls of nature, but nothing for waste. He also visits the sick, to see that they want for nothing, and are attended with that care and tenderness their state requires. These charitable employments take up so great a part of the day, as often to leave him no time for assisting the father coadjutor in the services of the church. One useful part of the duty of the latter is to catechize, and explain some portion of scripture in the church every day in the week, thursdays and saturdays excepted, for the instruction of the young of both sexes; and these in every town are not less than two thousand. On sundays all the inhabitants never fail to attend divine service. The priest also visits the sick to confess them; and, if the case requires it, to give them the Viaticum; and to all these must be added the other indispensible duties of a priest.

By the strictness of the law these priests should be nominated by the governor, as vice-patron, and be qualified for their function by the consecration of the bishop; but as among the three persons recommended on such occasions to the governor, there will of consequence be one, whose virtues and talents render him most fit for the office; and as no better judges of this can be supposed than the provincials of the order, the governor and bishop have receded from their undoubted rights, and the provincials always collate and prefer those whose merits are most conspicuous.

The missions of the Guaranies are all under one superior, who nominates the assistant priests of the other towns. His residence is at Candelaria, which lies in the center of all the missions; but he frequently visits the other towns in order to superintend their governments; and, at the fame time, concerts meafures that fome of the fathers may be fent among the heathen Indians, to conciliate their affections, and by degrees work their converfion. In this important office he is affifted by two vice-fuperiors, one of whom refides at Parana, and the other on the river Uruguay. All thefe miffions, tho' fo numerous and difperfed, are formed as it were into one college, of which the fuperior may be confidered as the mafter or head; and every town is like a family governed by a wife and affectionate parent, in the perfon of the prieft.

In the miffions of the Guaranies the king pays the ftipends of the priefts, which, including that of the affiftant, is three hundred dollars per annum. This fum is lodged in the hands of the fuperior, who every month fupplies them with neceffary food and apparel, and on any extraordinary demand, they apply to him, from whom they are fure of meeting with a gracious reception.

The miffions of the Chiquito Indians have a diftinct fuperior; but with the fame functions as he who prefides over the Guaranies; and the priefts alfo are on the fame footing, but have lefs anxiety and labour; the induftry and activity of thefe Indians, faving them the trouble of coming among them to exhort them to follow their employments, or of being the ftorekeepers and agents in difpofing of the fruits of their labours; they themfelves vending them for their own advantage.

All thefe Indians are very fubject to feveral contagious diftempers; as the fmall-pox, malignant fevers, and others, to which, on account of the dreadful havock attending them, they give the name of peftilence. And to fuch difeafes it is owing, that thefe fettlements have not increafed in a manner proportional to their numbers, the time fince their eftablifhment, and the quietnefs and plenty in which thefe people live.

THE

The missionary fathers will not allow any of the inhabitants of Peru, whether Spaniards or others, meftizos, or even Indians, to come within their miffions in Paraguay. Not with a view of concealing their tranfactions from the world; or that they are afraid left others fhould fupplant them of part of the products and manufactures; nor for any of thofe caufes, which even with lefs foundation, envy has dared to fuggeft; but for this reafon, and a very prudent one it is, that their Indians, who being as it were new born from favagenefs and brutality, and initiated into morality and religion, may be kept fteady in this ftate of innocence and fimplicity. Thefe Indians are ftrangers to fedition, pride, malice, envy, and other paffions which are fo fatal to fociety. But were ftrangers admitted to come among them, their bad examples would teach them what at prefent they are happily ignorant of; but fhould modefty, and the attention they pay to the inftructions of their teachers, be once laid afide, the fhining advantages of thefe fettlements would foon come to nothing; and fuch a number of fouls, who now worfhip the true God in the beauty of holinefs, and live in tranquility and love (of which fuch flender traces are feen among civilized nations) would be again feduced into the paths of diforder and perdition.

These Indians live at prefent in an entire affurance, that whatever their priefts advife them to is good, and whatever they reprehend is bad. But their minds would foon take a different turn, by feeing other people, on whom the doctrine of the gofpel is fo far from having any effect, that their actions are abfolutely repugnant to its precepts. At prefent they are firmly perfuaded, that in all bargains and other tranfactions, the greateft candor and probity muft be ufed, without any prevarication or deceit. But it is too evident, that were others admitted among them, whofe leading maxim is to fell as dear, and buy as cheap as they are able, thefe innocent people would foon imbibe the fame practice, together with a variety of others which feem naturally to flow from it. The contamination would foon fpread thro' every part of their behaviour, fo as never more to be reclaimed. I do not here mean to leffen the characters of thofe Spaniards or inhabitants of other nations, whofe countries are fituated conveniently for trading with Paraguay, by infinuating that they are univerfally fraudulent and diffolute: but, on the other hand, among fuch numbers, it would be very ftrange if there were not fome; and one fingle perfon of fuch a character would be fufficient to infect a whole country. And who could pretend to fay, that, if free admiffion were allowed to foreigners, there might not come in, among a multitude of virtuous, one of fuch peftilent difpofitions? Who can fay that he might not be even the very firft? Hence it is that the jefuits have inflexibly adhered to their maxim of not admitting any foreigners among them: and in this they are certainly juftified by the melancholy example of the other miffions of Peru, whofe decline from their former happinefs and piety is the effect of an open intercourfe.

Though in the feveral parts of Paraguay, where the miffions have been always fettled, there are no mines of gold and filver; feveral are to be found in fome adjacent countries under the dominion of the king of Spain; but the Portuguefe reap the whole benefit of them: for having encroached as far as the lake Xarayes, near which, about twenty years ago, a rich mine of gold was difcovered; they, without any other right than poffeffion, turned it to their own ufe: the miniftry in Spain, in confideration of the harmony fubfifting between the two nations, and their joint intereft, forbearing to make ufe of any forcible methods.

V. Bifhop-

## V. Bishopric of the audience of Charcas.
### Buenos Ayres.

THE ecclesiastical jurisdiction of the bishop of Buenos Ayres extends to all the countries under the temporal government of the same name; and this begins on the oriental and southern coast of that part of America, and extends westward as far as Tucuman; on the N. it terminates on Paraguay, and is bounded towards the S. by the land of Magellan. Its countries are watered by the great river de la Plata, the discovery of which was owing to Juan Dias de Solis, who, in 1515 having sailed from Spain with two vessels to make discoveries, arrived at the mouth of this river, and took possession of it in the name of the king of Spain. But being unhappily deluded by the signs of joy and friendship made by the Indians, he landed, and was immediately killed, together with his few attendants. The same voyage was repeated in 1526 under Sebastian Gabot, who entering the river, discovered an island, which he called St. Gabriel; and advancing further, came to another river, which emptied itself into that of La Plata; to this he gave the name of St. Salvador, causing his fleet to enter the river, and there disembark their troops. Here he built a fort, and leaving in it part of his men, he sailed above two hundred leagues up the river Parana, discovering also that of Paraguay. Gaboto, having purchased some ingots of silver from the Indians he met with, and particularly from the Guaranies, who brought the metal from the other parts of Peru, imagined that they had found it in the neighbourhood of the river, and thence called the river Rio de la Plata, or Silver River, which has superseded that of Solis, as it was before called from its first discoverer, whose memory is still preserved by the little river Solis, about seven or eight leagues W. of Maldonado bay.

The capital of this government is called Neuestra Senora

Senora de Buenos-Ayres. It was founded in the year 1535 by Don Pedro de Mendoza, purfuant to his orders, which alfo appointed him governor. He chofe for it a Place called Cape Blanco, on the S. fide of Rio de la Plata, clofe by a fmall river. Its latitude, according to father Feville, is 34°, 34′, 38″, S. He gave it the name of Buenos Ayres, on account of the extreme falubrity of the air. The city is built on a large plain, gently rifing from the little river. It is far from being fmall, having at leaft three thoufand houfes, inhabited by Spaniards and different cafts. Like moft towns fituated on rivers, its breadth is not proportional to its length. The ftreets are however ftrait, and of a proper breadth. The principal fquare is very large, and built near the little river; the front anfwering to it, being a caftle where the governor conftantly refides; and, with the other forts, has a garrifon of a thoufand regular troops. The houfes, formerly of mud walls, thatched with ftraw and very low, are now much improved, fome being of chalk, and others of brick, and having one ftory befides the ground floor, and moft of them tiled. The cathedral is a fpacious and very elegant ftructure, and is the parifh church for the greateft part of the inhabitants; the other at the farther end of the city being only for the Indians. The chapter is compofed of the bifhop, dean, arch-deacon, and two canons, one by compofition, the other by prefentation. Here are alfo feveral convents, and a royal chapel in the caftle where the governor refides. With regard to the civil and œconomical government, and the magiftracy, it will be unneceffary to enter into particulars, they being on the fame footing as thofe of the places already mentioned.

The climate here is very little different from that of Spain; and the diftinctions between the feafons are the fame. In winter indeed violent tempefts of

winds

## Ch. XV.   SOUTH AMERICA.   185

winds and rain, are here very frequent, accompanied with such dreadful thunders and lightnings, as fill the inhabitants, though used to them, with terror and consternation. In summer the excessive heats are mitigated by gentle breezes, which constantly begin at eight or nine in the morning.

The city is surrounded by a spacious and pleasant country, free from any obstruction to the sight; and from these delightful fields, the inhabitants are furnished with such a plenty of cattle, that there is no place in America or Europe where meat is better or cheaper. It is the usual custom to buy the hides of the beast, the carcase being in some measure a gratuitous addition; and the meat is always fat and very palatable. The country to the W. S. and N. of Buenos Ayres, lately abounded so greatly in cattle and horses, that the whole cost consisted in taking them; and even then a horse was sold for a dollar of that money, and the usual price of a beast, chosen out of a herd of two or three hundred, only four rials. At present there is no scarcity, but they keep at a greater distance, and are more difficult to be catched, by reason of the prodigious havock made of them by Spaniards and Portuguese, merely for the sake of their hides; the grand commerce of Buenos Ayres.

All kinds of game and fish are also here in the same plenty; several sorts of the latter being caught in the river running by it; but the Pexereyes are very remarkable, some of them being half a yard or more in length. Both the American and European fruits come to full perfection, and are in great plenty. In a word, for the enjoyments of life, especially with regard to the salubrity of the air, a finer country cannot be imagined.

This city is situated about seventy-seven leagues from Cape Santa Maria, which lies on the N. coast near the entrance of the river de la Plata; and its little river not having water sufficient for ships of

burden

burden to come up to Buenos Ayres, they anchor in one of the two bays on the fame coaft. That fartheft to the eaftward is called Maldonado, and is nine leagues from the above cape: the other bay, is, from a mountain near it, named Monte-video, and is about twenty leagues from it.

WITHIN the government of Buenos Ayres, are three other cities, namely, Santa Fè, las Corientes, and Monte-video. The laft which was lately built, ftands on the border of the bay, from whence it derives its name. Santa Fè, lies about ninety leagues N. W. of Buenos Ayres, between the Rio de la Plata, and the Rio Salado, which after running thro' the country of Tucuman, joins the former. The city is but fmall, and meanly built; owing in a great meafure, to the infults it has frequently fuffered from the heathen Indians, who not long fince pillaged it, maffacring the inhabitants of the city, and thofe of the neighbouring villages; and they ftill keep the country under continual apprehenfions of another vifit. It is however the channel of the commerce between Paraguay and Buenos Ayres, for the herb Camini and Palos. The city de las Corientes, fituated on the eaftern banks of the river de la Plata, betwixt it and the river Paranaʃ is about a hundred leagues N. of the city of Santa Fè. Its magnitude and difpofition are both inferior to Santa Fè, and indeed has no marks of a city except the name. Each of thefe cities has its particular corregidor, as lieutenant of the governor; and its inhabitants, together with thofe of the neighbouring country are formed into a militia, which on any appearance of an invafion from the Indians, affemble, and have often fhewn a great deal of refolution in repelling the attacks of their Pagan enemies. It has already been obferved, that part of the towns of the miffions of Paraguay belong to this diocefs, and with regard to the royal jurifdiction, thefe miffions univerfally depend on Buenos Ayres;

thofe

those which formerly belonged to the government of Paraguay having been separated from it.

Having thus with the government of Buenos Ayres, finished my account of every thing worthy of notice in the audiences of Lima and Charcas; together with the jurisdictions included in their dioceses, it now remains only to conclude my description of the kingdom of Peru, with an account of the kingdom and audience of Chili; but the many objects of importance in it so well deserves to be fully treated of, that I thought proper to reserve them for the following book; those included in this, as I have mentioned in its place, merited a much greater prolixity; for from what has been said in the first volume of the province of Quito, some idea of the difference between the two with regard to the number of people, towns and villages, trade and commerce, may be conceived; the province of Quito having only one diocess and part of another; whereas Lima contains one archbishopric, and four bishoprics; and that of Charcas one bishopric more than that of Lima. In the province of Quito only a few mines are worked, and those to little advantage; whereas the mines of Lima and Charcas, by their immense riches, draw thither great numbers of traders and industrious people, and thus spread wealth and affluence through the whole country, by the brisk circulation of trade. It must however be owned, that the number of people in these provinces bear no proportion to their extent; and it is with too much truth said, that they are in many places almost destitute of people; for supposing a corregidor to have twenty villages under his jurisdiction; yet if the least extent of it be thirty leagues one way, and fifteen another, they must be very thin. For draw a parallelogram of that dimensions, it will contain 450 square leagues of ground, and consequently the share to each village will be

twenty

twenty two square leagues and a half. This calculation is made from the smallest distances, there being jurisdictions of a far greater extent; and others, which, tho' equal in dimensions, have not twenty villages. What has been said of the products and manufactures in each jurisdiction must be understood in a general sense, not having entered into many particulars made or produced in some towns, and not common to others; as may be observed in the description of Quito. But these accounts drawn from our own experience, and the relations of persons of undoubted veracity, we hope will not prove unacceptable to the reader, who is desirous of forming a true idea of these parts, which for their riches, fertility, prodigious extent, and many other particulars, merit the greatest attention; especially for the amazing success which has attended the propagation of the christian religion, in countries formerly involved in ignorance and inhumanity.

B O O K.

# BOOK II.

*Return from* LIMA *to* QUITO: *Voyage from* CALLAO *to* GUAYAQUIL, *for putting that City in a Posture of Defence against the Attack apprehended from the* ENGLISH *Squadron, under Commodore* ANSON. *Second Voyage to* LIMA, *and from thence to the Island of* JUAN FERNANDES, *and the Coast of* CHILI; *with an Account of that Kingdom, and the adjacent Sea, and return to the Port of* CALLAO.

## CHAP. I.

*Voyage from* CALLAO *to* PAITA, *with nautical Remarks.*

THE time of our stay at Lima and Callao was taken up in the diligent execution of several commissions with which the Vice-roy had been pleased to honour us, for putting the coasts, and other parts of that kingdom in the best posture of defence; that in case an English squadron should make any attack\*, so a vigorous resistance might discourage any farther attempt of that nature. Having made the necessary dispositions to the Vice-roy's satisfaction, and four men of war which had been sent at the beginning of the summer to cruize off the coast of Chili, in order to attack the English squadron at their first appearance, being returned without the least information of any foreign ships having been seen in those seas; and the season of

\* At this time Spain and England were at war.

the

the year now inclining to winter, when every one was of opinion that it was utterly impracticable for Mr. Anson and his ships to get round Cape Horn that year, if (as indeed we concluded) he had not already perform'd it; we defired leave, as our longer stay could be of no service, to return to Quito, in order to profecute the original defign of our voyage. This leave, we, with some difficulty, obtained; by reason of the great want of officers in Peru, and the certain advice the Vice-roy received, that the Spanish squadron, under the command of Don Joseph Pizarro, had not been able to get round Cape Horn. But at length, convinced that our stay would greatly retard the execution of his majefty's particular commands, and confident that on any sudden exigency he would find the same alacrity in us to obey his orders, he was pleased to grant our request, and difmiffed us in the most polite manner.

THERE happened at this time to be one of the largest merchant ships trading in the south feas, at Callao, just ready to fail for Guayaquil, called the Chaldas. On board this ship we embarked on the 8th of August 1741, and on the 15th of the same month anchored at Paita: continued our voyage from thence on the 18th, and on the 21st entered the harbour of Puna. We immediately set out for Guayaquil, and from thence continued our journey for Quito, which we reached on the 5th of September.

THE course generally steered from Callao to Paita, is first W. N. W. till the ships are past the Feralones* of the island of Guara. From thence N. W. and N. W. one quarter northerly, to a latitude a little beyond the outermost island of Lobos, or Wolves. Afterwards they steer N. and N. E. till they make the continent within them, and which is continued in sight

* The Feralones are two old walls on the island of Guara, and serve as light-houses.

till

till they arrive at the Port of Paita; being very careful to keep at a proper diftance from Ogujia, which is very low, and projecting a great diftance into the fea. Accordingly cautious navigators, after paffing the iflands of Lobos, fteer a north courfe till they get fight of that of Nonura.

The land of this whole coaft is low; but there are two figns which evidently indicate its being near. Firft the fea-wolves, which are feen near thefe iflands, and at three or four leagues diftant from them. The fecond is the great flocks of birds all along this coaft, flying two or three leagues from the fhore, in queft of food. And tho' fogs are very frequent here, and fo thick as to hide the land, yet its diftance may be nearly known from thefe figns in the day time; but at night more circumfpection is neceffary on account of the extream lownefs of the fhore. And tho' the iflands of Lobos are fomething higher than the coaft, too much caution cannot be ufed in approaching them.

It is common in this voyage if the fhip is intended to touch at Paita, and has not had fight of the iflands of Lobos in the day-time, when in their latitude, to lie to all night. But if they do not propofe to ftop at Paita, proper attention muft be given to the courfe, and the voyage continued. If the fhip be bound to Paita, there is a neceffity for making thefe iflands, or the continent near them to the N. in order to avoid being carried beyond the port by the currents; as in fuch a cafe a great deal of time would be loft in getting back, both the wind and currents being contrary.

From Paita, the coaft is always kept in fight; but a careful look out is neceffary in order to difcover the Negrilos, rocky fhoals, projecting four or five leagues diftant from the fhore, and lying betwixt Paita and cape Blanco, one of the points of Guayaquil bay. The winds during this whole paffage are ufually S. but

in

in the summer, that is, from November to May, sometimes veer as far as S. E. Near the coast is a periodical morning breeze, or faint easterly wind, which shifts round to the S. E. or S. S. E. and in this season, at any distance from the coast, the S. winds are also faint; nor are calms uncommon, tho' they are of short continuance; but the Brisas never reach so far: and this renders the voyage from Paita to Callao so very long in all seasons. For if a ship stretches out to a great distance from the coast, the winds, even within ten or twelve leagues, shift from S. to S. W. but if she keeps along the shore, and endeavours to perform her voyage by tacking, she loses on one, what she gained on another. Besides, during the winter the currents set strongly towards the N. or N. W. and consequently render the voyage still more tedious. In summer there is here generally no current, or if any do set to the northward, it is scarcely perceived; the direction of the current in that season being generally W. This proceeds from the Brisas blowing from the N. of the equator, tho' they are unable to change the set of the current to the S. as would be the natural consequence, were it not for the resistance it meets with from the waters agitated by the S. winds to the southward of the equinoctial; but by meeting each other they run towards the W. There are, however, some short intervals during the summer, when the currents suddenly change their direction, and run to the southward, but at no great distance from the shore; and in the same instantaneous manner shift about to an opposite point; and this is the reason why most ships coming from Paita to Callao in this season keep near the shore, and work up to windward, hoping, by the favourable change of the currents, to acquire that assistance which the winds deny.

At all times this voyage is of a most disagreeable and fatiguing length; for tho' the distance according to the latitude of these ports, be only 140 leagues, a

ship

Ch. I.    SOUTH AMERICA.    193

ship is very fortunate to perform it in forty or fifty days; and even if after spending that time in continual labour, she be not obliged to return again to Paita; such accidents being very common; and it is nothing extraordinary to meet with two or three misfortunes of the same kind succeffively, especially if the ships make a great deal of lee-way, when it is often a twelve month's task. They relate here a story to this purpose, that the master of a merchant ship, who had been lately married at Paita, took his wife on board with him, in order to carry her to Callao. In the vessel she was delivered of a son, and before the ship reached Callao, the boy could read distinctly. For after turning to windward, two or three months, provisions growing short, the master put into some port, where several months were spent in procuring a fresh supply; and after another course of tacking, the same ill fortune still pursued him; and thus four or five years were spent in tacking and victualling to the ruin of the owner, before the ship reached Callao. This misfortune was, in a great measure, owing to the ill construction of the ship; and every other circumstance tending to obstruct her passage, the transaction has nothing very wonderful in it.

According to observations made by Don George Juan at Paita, in the year 1737, its latitude is 5° 5' S. It is a small place, having only one street, and about 172 houses; and these only of Quinchas and canes covered with leaves; the only house built of stone being that of the governor. It has a parish church and a chapel dedicated to our lady of mercy, and served by a religious of that order. A little to the southward of the town is a mountain, called from its figure Silla de Paita, or the saddle of Paita. The soil round Paita is wholly of sand, and extreamly barren; for besides the total want of rain, it has not a single river for the conveyance of water; so that it is entirely destitute of that necessary fluid, unless what

Vol. II.          O             is

is daily brought with great fatigue, from Colan, a town on the fame bay, four leagues N. of Paita, and near which runs the river Chera, the fame ftream which waters Amotape. The Indians of the town of Colan are under an obligation of daily fending to Paita, one or two balzas loaded with water, which is diftributed among the inhabitants by ftated proportions. From the fame town Paita has alfo the greateft part of its provifions. The nature of the foil, and the fituation of the place render it extreamly hot. Its inhabitants, who are about thirty-five or forty families, and confift of Spaniards, Mulattoes, and Meftizos, live chiefly by paffengers going or returning from Panama to Lima. So that the town owes its whole fupport to the harbour, which, as I have before obferved, is the place where the cargoes of goods fent from Panama are landed, together with thofe coming from Callao to the jurifdictions of Piura and Loja.

IN the bay of Paita, and that of Sechura, which lies a little farther to the fouthern, fuch large quantities of tollo are taken as to anfwer the demands of the provinces of the mountains, and part of thofe of Quito and Lima. The feafon for this fifhery begins in October, when great numbers of barks go from Callao, returning when the feafon is over. Fifhing is alfo the conftant employment of the Indians of Colan, Sechura, and the fmall hamlets near the coaft; thefe feas abounding in feveral kinds of fifh, befides the tollo, all palatable, and fome delicious.

CHAP.

## CHAP. II.

*Account of the Transactions at* QUITO: *unhappy occasion of our sudden return to* GUAYAQUIL.

ON our arrival at Quito, we made it our first business to join the French company, who were pleased to express a great deal of joy at our return. Mr. Godin, during our absence, had finished the astronomical observation to the northward, and tho' Mess. Bouguer and de la Condamine, had also gone thro' them, yet they still purposed to repeat them; for these able academicians, who had always shewn an indefatigable zeal for the perfection of the work, were particularly attentive in observing the greatest obliquity of the ecliptic; at which observations we also assisted; but several accidents hindered them from being carried on without interruption. They therefore thought it most agreeable to their character, and the commission with which they had been honoured, to spend some more time in ascertaining this important point, than to leave the country before their observations were compleated. Notwithstanding their stay was attended with so much inconvenience and fatigue, they could not think of leaving undetermined a difficulty, occasioned by a certain motion which they observed in the stars. In order to ascertain with the greater accuracy the quantity of the arch, they divided themselves into two companies, Bouguer being at the head of one, and M de la Condamine accompanied by M. Berguin, at that of the other; the latter, while the geometrical mensuration was carrying on, applied himself with indefatigable labour, and admirable skill in drawing maps of the country, in order to erect the signals in the most advantageous places. He also assisted both companies in their menfurations of the two bafes, which ferved to prove the accuracy of the operations. And, laftly, he was prefent at making the aftronomical obfervations. But before the repetition was undertaken, M. de la Condamine employed himfelf in erecting two obelifques at the extremities of the bafe of Yaruqui, as monuments of this tranfaction: This fpot having been the foundation of the whole work. Various were the fentiments with regard to the infcription proper to be engraved on them; and indeed the difficulties attending this particular, feemingly of no great importance, were fuch, as could not be removed till the affair was intirely dropt on account of other things of real concern, and which would admit of no delay. It was however unanimoufly concluded, that the whole affair fhould be referred to his Majefty's pleafure after our arrival in Spain. Accordingly in the year 1746, the marquis de la Enfenada, equally diftinguifhed as a ftatefman, and a patron of real knowledge, being at that time fecretary of ftate for the Indies, fent over, in his majefty's name, the following infcription.

PHILIPPO V.
Hifpaniarum, & Indiarum Rege Catholico.
LUDOVICI XV.
Regis Chriftianiffimi Poftulatis, Regiæ Scientiarum
Academiæ Parifienfis.
Votis Annuente, ac Favente.
LUDOV. GODIN, PETRUS BOUGUER,
CAR. MARIA DE LA CONDAMINE,
Ejufdem Academiæ Socii,
Ipfius Chriftianiffimi Regis Juffu, & Munificentia.
Ad Metiendos in Æquinoctiali Plaga
Terreftres Gradus,
Quo vera Terræ Figura, Certius Innotefceret,
In Peruviam Miffi;
Simulque

GEORGIUS

GEORGIUS JUAN S. JOHANNIS Hierofolymitani Ord.
Eques, &
ANTONIUS DE ULLOA,
Uterque Navium Bellicarum Vice-præfecti, et Mathematicis Disciplinis Eruditi.
Catholici Regis Nutu, Auctoritate Impensa ad ejusdem mensionis Negotium eodem allegati Communi Labore, Industria, Consensu in hac Yaruquensi Planitie distantiam Horizontalem 6272 $\frac{511}{726}$ Paris.
Hexapedarum.
In Linea a Borea Occidentem versus grad. 19 min.
$25\frac{1}{2}$ intra hujus & alterius
Obelisci Axes Excurrentem,
Quœque ad Basim primi Trianguli Latus Eliciendam & Fundamenti Toti Operi jaciendum inserviret, statuere.
Anno CHRISTI MDCCXXXXVI. Mense NOVEMBRI.
Cujus Rei Memoriam duabus hinc inde Obeliscorum molibus extructis Alternum consecrari placuit.

" In the reign of his catholic majesty Philip V.
" king of Spain and the Indies; agreeable to the
" request of his most christian majesty Lewis XV.
" king of France, and in condescension to the de-
" sire of the royal academy of sciences at Paris,
" Lewis Godin, Peter Bouguer, Charles Maria de
" la Condamine, members of that academy, were,
" by the command and munificence of the most
" Christian king, sent into Peru, to measure the
" terrestrial degrees under the equinoctial, in order
" to obtain a more accurate knowledge of the true
" figure of the earth. At the same time, by the
" command, and at the expence of his Catholic ma-
" jesty, were sent, George Juan, knight of the
" order of St. John of Jerusalem, and Antonio de
" Ulloa, both lieutenants in the royal navy, and
" well acquainted with all the branches of the ma-
" thematics: During the whole process of this men-
" suration they all equally shared in the fatigues,
" hardships,

"hardships, and operations; and with an unani-
"mous consent determined in this plain of Yaruqui
"a horizontal distance of 6272 $\frac{55}{216}$ Paris toises in
"a line whose direction was N. 19° 25′ 30″ wester-
"ly, and intercepted between the axes of this and
"the other obelisque, as the base or side of the first
"triangle, and a foundation for the whole work.
"In the month of November 1736. In memory
"of which transaction an obelisque has been erected
"at each extremity of the said base."

WE had now been three months at Quito, waiting till Mr. Hugot, instrument maker to the company, had finished some indispensible works in which he was then employed, that he might accompany us to the place where M. Godin, after finishing the observations, had left the instrument, which required some repairs in order for our making use of it in finishing our part of the work. But on the 5th of December 1741, when we were animated with the hopes of concluding our task in two or three days, the melancholy news arrived at Quito, that Paita had been pillaged and burnt by a squadron of men of war commanded by commodore Anson; and was too soon confirmed in all its circumstances, by letters from the Corregidor and other officers of Piura, giving an account that on the 24th of November, at two in the morning, the Centurion man of war, being the commodore's ship, had entered that harbour, and sent her long-boat a shore with forty armed men, under the advantage of the night, whereby the inhabitants and strangers who happened to be in the place, were waked from their sleep by the shocking surprize of an invasion, the first notice of which were given by the cries of a negro; so that filled with confusion and terror, like persons unable to recollect themselves, most of them had leaped from their beds, and fled naked from their houses, without knowing whether their enemies were in possession

of

of the town; or whether by a vigorous refiftance they might not be repelled: The mind, on fo great and fudden a perturbation, being but little capable of fuch reflections.

Not fo Don Nicholas de Salaza, the accomptant of Piura, who happened to be then at Paita, on fome affairs of his office. This gentleman attended only by a negro flave, with an equal prefence of mind and refolution, threw himfelf into the little fort, built for the defence of that fmall town, and fired two or three fhot towards the place where he heard the noife of the oars. Upon this the long boat ftopped; but the fort was obliged to give over firing for want of hands to affift an officer who had fhewn fo generous an example of refolution. The Englifh, concluding very naturally, that the fort was alfo abandoned, landed about half a league N. of the town, to which they immediately marched, and finding it forfaken, entered the fort, where, for fear of any furprize, they kept themfelves all night. But the inhabitants thought of nothing but faving their lives, and accordingly fled to a mountain, betwixt the Silla and the town, where they concealed themfelves, except a few flaves, who finding that the enemy were all retired into the fort, took the advantage of the night, and boldly returned into the town, bringing off fuch arms and effects of their mafters, as the night would permit, hiding in the fand what they found too heavy to carry up to the top of the mountain.

There was unfortunately then at Paita great quantities of meal, fruits, and brandy, configned to the provinces of the mountains, by the way of Piura; befides other goods depofited in the warehoufes to be fent to Panama. There was alfo no fmall quantity of gold and filver. As foon as daylight returned, the Englifh left their retreat, and feeing every place forfaken, they began to enter the houfes, houses, which are so many magazines for goods. It was not long before they met with a quantity of brandy and wine, of which, like men whose appetites are not to be governed at the sight of plenty after long distress, they made a very licentious use, and became so greatly inebriated, that the mulatoes and negro slaves, seeing their condition, abandoned their fears, and became so familiar with the English sailors as to drink with them, whilst others carried off hampers filled with the goods of their masters, together with considerable quantities of gold, which they buried in the sand. The long-boat, however, returned on-board the ship, but her chief spoils consisted of provisions; and the men employed in that service, regaled themselves with a degree of intemperance equal to those who guarded the fort.

The inhabitants of Paita, who still timorously continued on the mountain, though in want of every thing, dispatched an express to Don Juan de Vinatea y Torres, the corregidor of Piura, and a native of the Canaries, who agreeably to his known character of prudence and intrepidity, immediately assembled all the militia of that city and its dependancies, and hastened by forced marches, through a troublesome sandy road of fourteen leagues to Paita. The English had been three days masters of Paita, when discovering these succours, and being informed by the negroes and mulatoes, that the militia of Piura, headed by a famous general, were coming to dislodge them from the town, enraged at this, but wanting courage to defend what they had gained, or rather surprized, carried off whatever they could, and took their leave of the place by ungenerously setting fire to the houses; an action which could reflect but little honour on the arms of their nation; but was rather a malicious transaction, to revenge on the poor inhabitants the coming of the militia whom they did not dare to face. No body indeed imagined

imagined at that time that this proceeding was in consequence of any orders issued by the commander, and it was afterwards known that he was under great concern for such unjustifiable behaviour.

The corregidor of Piura, as he had been very active in the defence of Paita, so he lost no time in sending advice of the descent to the corregidor of Guayaquil, that he might put that city in a posture of defence; it being natural to suppose, that the English would also make an attempt there, as it had always been attacked by every enemy who before infested those seas. Accordingly the inhabitants of Guayaquil were soon in arms, and the best measures taken with the utmost expedition. But the force of the enemy being uncertain, no other ship having been seen at Paita than that which entered the port, the corregidor and magistrates applied for assistance to the president and audience of Quito; who among other measures for securing Guayaquil from the rage of the English, required us in his majesty's name, to repair immediately to that city, and take upon us the command of the troops, all the jurisdictions having received orders to send their contingences; and to direct the works to be raised, and the trenches necessary to be thrown up in the places most advantageous and most exposed.

As affairs of this nature admit of no delay, we immediately prepared for the journey, and leaving Quito the 16th of December, arrived at Guayaquil on the night of the 24th. But the passage of the mountains was inconceivably fatiguing; the natural difficulty and badness of the roads, it being the beginning of winter, having been greatly increased by the violent rains.

Having gone through all the necessary operations, and taken the most proper measures to defeat the attempts of an enemy, and such as we had the pleasure of seeing approved by the council of war
held

held in that city, our longer stay only hindered the conclusion of our grand design, and was of no further use here, especially as it was then certainly known that the enemy's squadron had sailed for Manta, the coasts of which, though in the jurisdiction of Guayaquil, are nearly twenty eight leagues N. of that city, and consequently to leeward of it. It was also known that the fleet intended to proceed from Manta to Acapulco. Impatient at the loss of time we applied to the same council of war, who were pleased to grant leave for one of us to return to Quito, in order to complete the observations still remaining, that on any subsequent exigency we might be the more disengaged; but at the same time thought it necessary that one of us should continue on the spot to act on any sudden emergency. The matter was soon agreed on between Don George Juan and myself, namely that he should remain as commandant of Guayaquil, while I returned to continue the observations at Quito. But before I proceed, it will not be amiss to give an account of the transactions of the enemy's squadron in those seas, according to the depositions of some prisoners whom they set ashore at Manta.

This squadron as its entrance into the south-sea, besides being dispersed, was in a very shattered condition; but arrived successively at the island of Juan Fernandes, to the number of four ships, from fifty to sixty guns, the Centurion and the Gloucester, a frigate between thirty six and forty guns, and a victualler. These ships came to an anchor close to the shore, their crews being very much diminished, and those which remained very sickly. Tents were pitched, a kind of village built with an hospital for the recovery of their men. They arrived at this island in the month of June, and the commander was so quick in his prosecution of hostilities, that as soon as a number of sailors sufficient to man the frigate were recovered,

covered, she was sent out on a cruize; and this being in the common tract of ships bound from Callao to the coast of Chili, they had the good fortune to take two or three, all of them richly laden, particularly the Aranzaza, one of the largest employed in these seas. Great numbers of men died on the island of Juan Fernandes, but on the recovery of the remainder, and the ships being careened, they sunk the victualler, and some time after the frigate, putting the guns and provisions on board the Aranzaza. After this the whole squadron put to sea upon fresh enterprizes, and about eight or nine vessels fell into their hands; and between Paita and the island of Lobos, they took a coast ship of great value. The sacking of Paita was the last act of hostility they committed in these parts; for the English commodore having procured intelligence of the short time requisite to alarm Guayaquil, and finding that there had been abundantly more than sufficient, prudently abandoned a design, against which he judged insuperable precautions had been taken; and indeed had he made an attempt, in all probability those spirits would have been depressed, which were so greatly elevated at their success at Paita.

After leaving Paita they steered for the coast of Manta, where they put the prisoners they had taken in the merchant ships on board a long-boat, to make the best of their way to the land; the ships keeping ten or twelve leagues from the shore; but many of the sailors, negroes, and mulattoes, who had nothing to lose, voluntarily entered with them. They now determined to sail for the Philippines, in order to intercept the galleon in her return to those islands, and which was to sail from Acapulco some time in January. This was doubtless the most advantageous scheme that could be formed in their circumstances. But in this they were disappointed by the Vice-roy of Mexico; who, from the intelligence

gence sent by the Vice-roy to Peru to all the ports on the coast of the south-sea, as well as by expresses dispatched from Guayaquil and Atacames to Panama, deferred sending the ship that year; which the enemy being apprized of, they burnt the Aranzazu, as they had before the other prizes, and continued their voyage towards the Philippines, where by a long perseverance in a most tedious cruize they accomplished their designs. For the Acapulco ship returning when all the danger was imagined to be over, fell in with the Centurion, and after a short, though smart engagement, was taken.

But to reassume the thread of the narrative, to which I hope this has been no disagreeable interruption. On the 5th of January 1742, I set out from Guayaquil for Quito, being the very worst time of the year for performing that journey; and as such I experienced it by several misfortunes. In one of the rivers we were obliged to ford, the two mules which first entered were swept away by the current, and that which carried my portmanteau was lost; and the other, on which an Indian rode and led the former, swam with great difficulty to the shore, and the Indian saved himself by holding fast by the creature's tail; in which manner they were carried near a quarter of a league below the ford. If the travelling up the mountains was not attended with such imminent danger, it was extreamly troublesome, a space of about half a league, having taken me up from seven in the morning till seven in the afternoon, the mules though light falling at every step, nor was it an easy matter to make them rise. And soon after the creatures became so fatigued, they even sunk under their own weight. At length I reached Quito on the nineteenth of the same month; but had hardly alighted from the mule with the hopes of resting myself after these dangers and fatigues, when the president informed me, me, that three days before he had sent away an exprefs, with letters from the Vice-roy, directing us to haften to Lima with all poffible expedition; and charging him in particular to provide immediately every thing neceffary that our journey might not be a moment delayed. It was therefore no time to think of reft; and acordingly after making fuch provifions as were abfolutely neceffary, I fet out on the 22d of the fame month, and a third time croffed that difficult mountain in my way to Guayaquil; where having joined Don George Juan, who was included in the orders, we travelled night and day, with a difpatch anfwerable to the governor's impatience, all the towns on the road having received orders to keep beafts in readinefs, that we might not be detained a moment; and accordingly we reached Lima the 26th of February. In the mean time the Vice-roy had ordered a fquadron of four men of war to fail from Callao to Panama, for the defence of that place, which fleet touched at Paita, in order to gain intelligence of the enemy's fhips, having orders to attack them if poffible; but, as we have already obferved, they were failed to the coaft of Acapulco. On our arrival the Vice-roy was pleafed to exprefs great fatisfaction at our difpatch, and to honour us with feveral commiffions fuitable to the exigence of affairs; giving us the command of two frigates which he had ordered to be fitted out for the fecurity of the coaft of Chili, and the ifland of Juan Fernandes, againft any reinforcement coming to the enemy. For though commodore Anfon had made no fecret of his intentions to the prifoners, and they had eagerly publifhed them, no dependance could be had on informations given out by the enemy himfelf, and which were the more fufpicious as he told them openly. Befides it was well known, that this fquadron originally confifted of more fhips; and we were apprehenfive,

that

that though the remainder had failed of reaching thefe feas, yet by perfeverance, and a fecond effort, they might fucceed.

Commodore Don Jofeph Pizarro, had alfo been difappointed in getting into thefe feas this year, though he had attempted it in a fingle fhip called the Afia; but was obliged to put back to Buenos Ayres with the lofs of one of his mafts, and another was carried away juft at the mouth of the Rio de la Plata. Thefe difappointments rendered it the more neceffary for the Vice-roy to provide for the defence of the coaft of Chili, as all fhips muft pafs near it in their courfe to Peru.

## CHAP. III.

*Voyage to the Ifland of* JUAN FERNANDES; *with an Account of the Seas and Winds in that Paffage.*

AMONG other precautions taken by the vigilant Vice-roy of Lima, for the defence of the fouth-fea, he fitted out, as we have juft mentioned, two frigates for cruizing on the coaft of Chili; and gave the command of one, called Nueftra Senora de Belen, to Don George Juan, and appointed me for the other called the Rofa: they had been both merchant fhips employed in thefe feas, all the king's fhips being fent in the Panama fquadron. They were between fix and feven hundred tons, each carried thirty guns on one deck, and three hundred and fifty men, all picked and expert failors. The fhips were alfo prime failers: fo that our force was in all refpects fufficient for the fervice on which it was employed; and, with the affiftance of providence, would doubtlefs have anfwered the Vice-roy's expectations.

On the 4th of December 1742, we got under sail intending to steer first to the island of Juan Fernandes. Our course was from S. W. one quarter westerly, to S. one quarter westerly, according as the winds permitted, which were continually between the E. S. E. and S. S. E. but not always of the same strength; sometimes short calms intervened, and at others sudden squalls, but did us no great damage. This course we continued till the 27th of the same month, when being in the latitude of 30° and a little more than 15° W. of Callao harbour, and the wind at N. W. we altered our course, steering E. S. E. and E. till we made the island without that of Juan Fernandes. This happened on the 7th of January 1743, at three in the evening; the S. point of the island bearing N. E. one quarter easterly, and the N. W. point, N. E. We now continued steering E. one quarter northerly, and the next day at eleven in the morning we had sight of the other island called de Tierra, bearing E. N. E. And in the following night having weathered the north point, we the next day came to an anchor in the bay.

During our passage from Callao to the tropic we had light winds, often interrupted with short calms; but after we had crossed the tropic, they were more settled, stronger, and squally, but not dangerous; being of short continuance. But as I have already noticed in another part, they always blow from the S. E. and never from the S. W. till you are fifteen or twenty degrees W. of the meridian of Callao. When we concluded ourselves in the proper latitude for standing towards the islands, and found the wind at N. W. we steered E. in order to reach the meridian of Juan Fernandes. The wind then shifted round from W. N. W. to W. S. W. and S. and afterwards returned to its usual rumbs of S. E. S S. E. and S. E. one quarter easterly. On the 27th of December,
the

the wind again veered to the N. W. and continued fo the whole day; the two fucceeding days at N. N. W. and N. W. but on the 30th veered to the W. N. W. On the 31ft it fhifted to S. S. W. and on the 1ft of January veered round to the S. S. S. E. and S. E. Thofe therefore who endeavour to gain fuch winds, ftand off from the coaft till they fall in with them; and this fometimes happens at a greater diftance than at others; I mean during the fummer; for in winter a different courfe is neceffary as we fhall explain in the fequel.

THE atmofphere of thefe feas is generally filled with thick vapours to a confiderable height: fo that often for four or five days fucceffively, there is no poffibility of obferving the latitude. Thefe fogs the failors call Sures pardos, and are fond of them, as they are a fure fign that the wind will be frefh and conftant, and that they fhall not be troubled with calms. At this time it is very common to fee the horizon filled with a dark cloud, but of no dangerous confequence, except frefhening the wind a little more than ufual, and a fhort fhower of rain; the weather, in four or five minutes, becoming as fair as before. The fame thing prefages the turbonada, or fhort hurricane; for the cloud is no fooner formed on the horizon, than it begins, according to the failors phrafe, *to open its eye*, i. e. the cloud breaks, and the part of the horizon where it was formed becomes clear. Thefe turbonadas are moft common after you are paffed the 17th or 18th degree of latitude.

NEAR the tropic, that is between the parallels of fourteen or fixteen and twenty eight degrees, calms greatly prevail during the months of January, February, and even March; and in fome years more than in others; but near the coaft they are not fo common, on account of the land breezes, which are always between the S. E. and E. S. E. Formerly,

and

and even till within these few years, the voyage to and from Callao to Chili, was rarely performed in less than a twelvemonth; owing to a fear of standing off to a great distance from the coast: for by tacking along the shore they made but little way; and consequently laid the ships under a necessity of putting into the intermediate harbours for water and provisions; but an European pilot making his first voyage in the usual manner, observed that the course of the currents was from the W. and S. W. whence he concluded that winds from those quarters might be found farther off at sea. Accordingly in his second voyage he stood off to a great distance, in order to fall in with those winds, and had the satisfaction to find that he was not mistaken; so that he reached Chili in little more than thirty days. This being so very far short of the usual term, he was suspected of sorcery, and ever after called Brujo, a sorcerer. From this report, and the evidence of the dates of his papers, persons of all ranks were persuaded that he failed by magic, and the inquisition caused him to be apprehended; but on examining his journals they applauded his sagacity, and were convinced that if others did not perform the same voyage with equal dispatch, it was owing to their timidity in not stretching off to a proper distance from the coast as he had done. And thus he had the honour of leading the way in that expeditious course which has ever since been followed.

In all this passage, you have an easy sea, the swell coming sometimes from the S. E. S. or E. being the points from whence the wind blows; at others from the S. W. and W. particularly after you are ten or twelve degrees from the coast. And it is only near the island of Juan Fernandes, that you meet with a hollow sea. The course of the waves is there sufficiently manifest; for on quitting the coast of Callao, to about six degrees farther to the S. their course

course is to the northwards: but from between the parallels of sixteen and twenty degrees, their course is imperceptible; while in higher latitudes they run, with some force S. and S. W. and with a greater velocity in winter than in summer; as I know from my own experience, having in my second voyage to Chili, in the year 1744, at the end of October, and beginning of November, taken the greatest care, that the distances between the knots on the log line should be 47 Paris feet and a half, for measuring the ship's way; but every day found that the observed latitude exceeded the latitude by account ten or fifteen minutes. The same observation was made by Don George Juan, in both his voyages; as well as by the captain, and officers of the French ship, in which I returned; so that the reality of the course of the sea is proved beyond exception; and in this manner it continues to the 38th or 40th degree of latitude.

In the latitude of 34° 30′ and 4° 10′ W. of Callao, you meet with a track of green water, extending N. and S. and along which you sail above thirty leagues. Probably it runs to a great distance in that sea, being found in every latitude to the coast of Guatemala; but not always under the same meridian, winding away N. W. It is also met with in a higher latitude than that of Juan Fernandes; and it has also been observed by ships in their course to Chiloe, or Baldivia.

In this passage, tho' part of it be at such a great distance from the land, we meet with a kind of birds called Pardelas, which distinguish themselves from all other species, by venturing so far from the land. They are something larger than a pigeon; their bodies long; their necks short; their tails of a proper proportion, and their wings long and slender. There are two sorts of these birds, and of different colours, one parda or brown, from whence they derive their name; the other black, and called pardela gallinera, but in

other

other circumstances they are entirely the same. A smaller bird is also seen in these seas, called Alma de Maestre; it is white spotted with black, and has a long tail; but is not so common as the Pardelas: They are most frequent in stormy weather. Within ten leagues of the islands of Juan Fernandes, are seen some balenatos, or small whales; and at near the same distance, sea-wolves; but the latter seldom go far from the shore.

Tho' this sea has not been improperly dignified with the appellation of Pacific, with regard to the interval between the tropics; yet that particular cannot with any justice be applied to it, if considered in its whole extent: tempestuous weather being equally common in the latitudes of twenty and twenty-three degrees in the south sea, as in the oceans of Europe; and in higher latitudes storms are more frequent and violent. I am inclined to think that the first Spaniards gave it the name of the pacific sea, from their being greatly pleased with its smoothness, and the gentleness of the winds in their first voyages; concluding that it was so in every part; but the fury of the winter storms, and the roughness of the sea, which are equal to those in any other parts, abundantly demonstrate, that they formed a judgment too hastily.

Along these coasts and the adjacent sea, the winter begins at the same time as at Lima; that is in the month of June, lasting till October and November; but its greatest violence is past in August or September. During the whole winter season, there is no dependance on being safe from storms, which rise with a sudden rapidity; and in all latitudes beyond forty degrees, the winter sets in considerably sooner, even at the beginning of April, and is also observed to last longer.

The winter in all latitudes beyond 30° is ushered in by northerly winds. They are not indeed fixed like those of the S. though common to the season. They always

always blow with great violence; but not always with the fame degree: being lefs ftrong in the beginning than in the depth of winter, when their rage ftrikes the moft refolute with horror, and raifes fuch enormous waves, that the atmofphere is crowded with vapours; and thefe turn to a drizzling rain which lafts as long as the ftorm continues. It often happens that thefe violent N. winds, without the leaft fign of an approaching change, fhifts round inftantly to the W. which change is called the travefia, but continues to blow with the fame force. Sometimes indeed this fudden change is indicated by the horizon clearing up a little in that quarter: but in feven or eight minutes after the appearance of this fmall gleam of light, a fecond ftorm comes on; fo that when a fhip is labouring againft the violence of a ftorm from the N. the greateft care muft be taken, on the leaft appearance, to prepare for the travefia; indeed its rapidity is often fuch as not to allow time fufficient for making the neceffary preparations, and the danger is fufficiently evident if the fhip has her fails fet, or is lying too.

In the month of April 1743, in the latitude of 40°, I had the misfortune of experiencing the fury of a ftorm at N. which lafted in its full violence from the 29th of March till the 4th of April. Twice the wind fhifted to the travefia, and veering round to the fouthward, returned in a few hours to the N. The firft time it fhifted to the W. the fhip by the vortices formed in the fea by this fudden oppofition to the courfe of its waves, was fo covered with water from head to ftern, that the officers who were on the watch concluded fhe had foundered; but fortunately we had our larboard tacks on board, and by a fmall motion of the helm, the fhip followed the change of the wind, and brought too without receiving any damage; whereas we fhould otherwife in all probability have been loft. Another circumftance in our favour was, that the wind was fome points to the weftward of the N.

For

For tho' these winds are here called nortes, they are generally between the N. and N. W. and during their season, veering in some squalls to the N. and in others to the N. W. Sudden calms also often intervene; but if these happen before the wind have passed the travesia, it returns in about half, or at least an hour with redoubled fury. These dangerous variations are however indicated by the thickness of the atmosphere, and the dense clouds in the horizon. The duration of these storms is far from being fixed or regular: tho' I well know some pilots here will have it, that the N. wind blows twenty-four hours, and then passes to the travesia; that it continues there with equal violence three or four hours, accompanied with showers, which abate its first violence; and that it then veers round till it comes to the S. W. when fair weather succeeds. I own indeed that I have in several voyages found this to be true; but at other times I experienced, that the successive changes of the wind are very different. The storm at N. I before-mentioned began March the 29th, at one in the afternoon, and lasted till the 31st at ten at night, which made fifty-seven hours; then the wind shifted to the travesia, where it continued till the 1st of April without any abatement, that is, during the space of twenty-two hours. From the W. the wind veered round to the W. S. W. and S. W. still blowing with its former violence. Hence a short calm succeeded; after which, it a second time shifted to the N. where it continued blowing with its former fury fifteen or twenty hours; then came on a second travesia; and soon after its violence abated, and the next night shifted from S. W. to S. E. Thus the whole continuance of the storm was four natural days and nine hours; and I have since met with others of the same violence and duration, as I shall mention in their proper place. What I would infer from my own experience, confirmed by the information of several pilots, is, that the duration of these ſtorms is proportional to the latitude; being between 20 and 30 degrees, neither ſo violent nor laſting as between 30 and 36; and ſtill increaſing in proportion as the latitude is greater.

THESE winds have likewiſe no regular or ſettled period, the interval betwixt them being ſometimes not above eight days; at others much longer; nor do they always blow with the ſame violence; but are moſt uncertain in the winter, riſing ſuddenly when leaſt expected, tho' not always blowing with the ſame force.

In this ſea a change of the wind from N. to N. E. is a ſure ſign of ſtormy weather; for the wind is never fixed in the N E. nor does it ever change from thence to the E., its conſtant variation being to the W. or S. W. contrary to what is ſeen in the northern hemiſphere. Indeed in both the change of the wind uſually correſponds with the courſe of the ſun; and hence it is, that as in one hemiſphere it changes from E. to S. and thence to the W. conformable to the courſe of the luminary, ſo in the other it changes, for the ſame reaſon, from the E. to N. and afterwards to W.

IT is an old obſervation among the pilots of this ſea, that a day or two before the N. wind begins to blow, there is always ſeen along the ſhores, and about the ſhips, a ſort of ſea fowl, called quebrantahueſſas, i. e. oſſirage, or break bones. Theſe birds ſeldom appear at other times. I am little inclined to believe, much leſs to propagate any vulgar report; but here I muſt declare, that after repeated obſervations, in order to diſcover the truth or falſity of this aſſertion, I always ſaw them before every ſtorm I met with here; and ſometimes even a day before, when there was not the leaſt appearance of the winds coming about to the N ; and as the winds increaſed, great numbers of them gathered about the ſhip, ſometimes flying round her, at others ſettling on the waves, but always kept near the ſhip, till fair weather returned. It is ſtill more ſingular, that they are never ſeen either on the

ſea

sea or land, except in stormy weather; nor is it known where they hide themselves when it is fair, that they should so immediately cover, as it were the sea, when their natural instinct informs them of the approach of a N. wind.

This bird exceeds the size of a large duck, has a short thick arched neck, with a large head, and a thick but short bil, a small tail, a rising back, large wings, and small legs. They are by their plumage, divided into two different kinds, one being white, spotted with dark brown, and the upper part of its wings entirely of the latter colour: the breast of the other, together with the inside of the wings, the whole head, and the lower part of the neck is white; but the back, the upper parts of the wings and neck of a very dark brown, and are hence called lamo prieto, black-backs... The last kind are, by the pilots, accounted the most certain sign, the others being often seen without any alteration of weather immediately succeeding. I well knew a pilot here, who was a native of Callao, a man of indefatigable curiosity and exactness, never omitting to insert in his journals the most minute circumstances. His name was Bernardo de Mendosa, and with him these fowls were considered as so sure a sign, that when he was in any of these ports, and his ship ready to put to sea, it was his constant custom to take a walk on the shore, to see whether he could perceive any of them in the offing; and if he did, he continued in the harbour till the tempest was over; and he assured me, that his conforming to this observation had been of the greatest advantage to him; relating, in confirmation of his opinion, that being once at Baldivia, the governor so far from regarding his apprehensions from such presages, turned them into ridicule, and insisted on his putting to sea; but was soon convinced that these omens were not chimeras, for the vessel was hardly out of the harbour when a storm at N. came on with such violence, that it was with the utmost difficulty she was saved from being wrecked in that bay; and this would infallibly at last have been the consequence had the storm continued some time longer; for even when the wind abated, they found it hardly possible to carry her into the harbour to repair the damages she had received.

OTHER observations relating to these northerly winds are, that they always blow when the sures are in their strength, in the higher latitudes, and also between the parallel of 20° and that of Panama, it being then winter in those climates; and are also found in latitudes beyond 20° but never nearer to the equinoctial. Another observation is, that during the time of the Brisas, between Panama and the equinoctial, these winds are never felt in any part of the pacific sea, the S. winds alone prevailing there. Lastly, it is observed that within thirty or forty leagues of the coast of Chili, while one part is agitated with storms at N. the S. winds freshens in another. This, however singular it may appear, is no more than what was experienced by the three ships, Esperanza, Belen, and Rosa, which being at the mouth of the bay of conception, the latter took her leave of them and bore away, with a fresh gale at S. to Valparaiso, whilst the others who steered for the islands of Juan Fernandes, were overtaken in their passage by a storm at N.

As in summer the S. winds generally shift between the S. S. E. and E. S. E. so, in winter, they continue for some time between the S. W. and S. consequently there is a necessity, in the latter season, to stand out to such a great distance from the coast in quest of them as must be done in summer.

CHAP.

## CHAP. IV.

*Account of the iflands of* JUAN FERNANDES: *Voyage from thofe Iflands to* SANTA MARIA, *and from thence to the Bay of* CONCEPTION.

THE iflands of Juan Fernandes, which, on account of their fituation, belong to the kingdom of Chili, are two in number. One as lying farther to the W. is diftinguifhed by the epithet de Afuera; and the other as nearer the land, or to the eaftward, is called la de Tierra. The former, which is fomething above a league in length, is nearly of an oval figure, and the land very high, fo that it has the appearance of a round mountain; and its fteepnefs on all fides renders it every where almoft inacceffible. Several large cafcades tumble from its fummit, and the water of one of them, after a fucceffion of long falls among the rocks on the S. W. fide of the ifland, precipitates itfelf into the fea, with fuch amazing impetuofity, that its froth may be feen at three leagues diftance. The longitude of this ifland, according to the reckoning of Don George Juan, admitting the currents to fet towards the S. W. is 3° 20′ W. from the meridian of Callao; but according to my computation, 3° 27′ By the coaft we fteered from the meridian de Afuera till we reached la de Tierra, we concluded the diftance between thofe iflands to be thirty four leagues.

THE ifland de Tierra, which is about four hundred and forty leagues to the N. of Cape Horn, is between three or four leagues from E. to W, which is its greateft length. It is for the moft part high land, but not deftitute of fome plains, though thefe are part of the mountains themfelves. Its valleys are full of trees, and fome of them of excellent timber. Here is likewife the pimento tree refembling the
Chiapa

Chiapa in new Spain. The plains and little hills produce a fort of ftraw, refembling that of oats, and growing higher than the ufual ftature of a man. The water, of which feveral ftreams fall from the eminences into the fea, is very light, creates an appetite; and, among other medicinal qualities, is excellent againft indigeftions. Here are many dogs of different fpecies, particularly of the greyhound kind; and alfo a great number of goats, which it is very difficult to come at, artfully keeping themfelves among thofe crags and precipices, where no other animal but themfelves can live. The dogs owe their origin to a colony fent thither not many years ago, by the prefident of Chili and the vice-roy of Peru, in order totally to exterminate the goats; that any pirates, or fhips of the enemy might not here be furnifhed with provifions. But this fcheme has proved ineffectual, the dogs being incapable of purfuing them among the faftneffes where they live, thefe animals leaping from one rock to another with furprifing agility. Thus far indeed it has anfwered the purpofe; for fhips cannot now fo eafily furnifh themfelves with provifions here, it being very difficult to kill even a fingle goat.

Very few birds frequent this ifland, and though we found feveral white feathers on the ground, and alfo parts of carcaffes which feemed to have been gnawed by the dogs, we faw but very few flying, and thofe wholly black. It is not indeed improbable, but thefe iflands may be the winter retreats of fome kinds of birds, which on the approach of fummer remove to another climate.

In this ifland are mountains of a great height; and the fides of thofe towards the N. are covered with trees of good timber; but few or none are feen on thofe of the S. part, except in the breaches and valleys; owing doubtlefs to the piercing violence of the S. winds, which deftroys them or checks their

growth.

CH. IV.   SOUTH AMERICA.   219

growth. On the other hand, every part is cover'd with tall grafs or ftraw, already mentioned. Among the various forts of trees with which the ifland is decorated, there are none of the American fruit trees; owing to the coldnefs of the climate, which is increafed by the violence of the winds, fo that even the heats of fummer are moderate.

In this ifland are three harbours or bays; but thofe on the W. and E. fides have only water fufficient for fmall veffels; fo that the only one proper for large fhips is that on the N. or rather N. E. fide of the ifland. The latter, which is properly called Juan Fernandes, confifts of a bay formed by the coaft, but expofed to the N. and N. E. winds; fo that in winter no fhip can lie fafely in it; and even in fummer, it is not free from danger, on account of the great depth of water; for within the diftance of a cable's length or two from the fhore, it has fifty fathom; and growing deeper as the diftance increafes. To this muft alfo be added the badnefs of the ground, which being of fand, and a tenacious mud, mixed with fhells and gravel, the cables are greatly rubbed by it; and confequently the anchorage rendered unfafe. The fhips are alfo expofed to continual fqualls caufed by the Sures, which produce a very troublefome fea: violent currents likewife fet into the bay and form dangerous eddies. Laftly, the fteepnefs of the coaft renders it very difficult to be approached on account of the dafhing of the waves againft it; and accordingly the only fhips that put into this port are fuch as belong to pirates or the enemy; this ifland being the fole refuge for them in the fouth feas. And they expofe themfelves to thefe dangers, merely through the neceffity of taking in water and wood, refrefhing their crews, and furnifhing themfelves with fifh, which is caught here in great abundance.

These foreign fhips, which in order to refrefh their crews after the fatigues of fo long a voyage,

and

and the dangers of weathering Cape Horn, make for the harbour of Juan Fernandes, are very careful to secure themseves againſt the above mentioned dangers, and therefore ſail up to the fartheſt part of the bay, where they moor with an anchor in the water, and another on the S. W. ſhore. But even this precaution is not ſometimes ſufficient to ſecure them, as appears from the wrecks of three ſhips; two of which have been long there, but the other of a more recent date.

The iſland de Afuera is every where prodigious high land, and the ſhores ſo ſteep and craggy, as to afford no convenient landing place; which, together with its having no harbour, prevents all ſhips, whether thoſe of the enemy, or the country from touching at it.

The ſea all round the iſland de Tierra may be ſaid to be filled with ſea-wolves, of which there are obſerved to be three principal ſpecies; the firſt are ſmall, not being above a yard in length, and their hair a dark brown: thoſe of the ſecond are about a toiſe and a half in length, and of a greyiſh brown colour: and thoſe of the third are in general two toiſes in length, and the hair of a pale aſh-colour. The head of theſe creatures is too ſmall in proportion to the reſt of their body, and terminates in a ſnout; which bearing a great reſemblance to that of a wolf, they have acquired the name. The mouth is proportioned to the head; but the tongue is very thick and almoſt round. They have a row of large pointed teeth in each jaw, two thirds of which are in alveoli or ſockets; but the others, being the moſt hard and ſolid, are without them. This threatening appearance is heightned by whiſkers like thoſe of cats, or rather tigers. Their eyes are ſmall; and their ears, from the root to the extremity, not above ſix or eight lines in length, and of a proportional breadth. Their

noſtrils

nostrils are also very small; and the only parts destitute of hair, these having a glandulous membrane like the same part in dogs. This creature has two fins, which serve them both for swimming in the water, and for walking on the ground. The tail, which is every where equally cartilaginous, is of a length proportional to the body, but much thicker than those of the generality of fish. They carry it horizontally; so that by inverting the last vertebræ, where the articulations are more flexible than in other parts, they form of it a kind of hind feet; and at the same time the fins helping them before, they walk without trailing the body along the ground. A remarkable particular in the formation of this amphibious creature is, that in both the fins and the extremity of the tail there are protuberances resembling fingers, they are small bones or cartilages inclosed within those callous membranes which cover the fins and tail. These fingers they can expand so as to cover the whole breadth of the fin; and thus form as it were the sole to tread upon. At the end of each is a nail of about two lines in length, and half a line in breadth.

Among the several articulations in the fins are two very remarkable, one at the junction of the Omoplata, where it forms a kind of shoulder, and the other at the extremity of the fin, where the fingers are connected. The same œconomy is observed in the tail; and thus they are adapted to an amphibious life: accordingly, tho' not with a celerity equal to that of quadrupeds, they climb up steep rocks of a height one would think them impracticable to such creatures, as they are absolutely so to men; and come down again with the same ease, notwithstanding their great bulk and fatness, which is such in the larger species, that their diameter at the fins is little short of a yard and a half.

Their organs of generation are placed at the lower
extremity

extremity of the belly, and at the time of coition, the male and female place themſelves on their tails with their faces inward, embracing each other with their fins, which, on this occaſion, ſupply the place of arms. The female brings forth and ſuckles her young in the ſame manner as terreſtrial creatures; but has never above one or two at a time.

THE largeſt ſpecies are by ſome called ſea lions, but in theſe ſeas their general name is Lobos de Aceyte, or oil wolves; becauſe when they move they appear like a ſkin full of oil, from the motion of the vaſt quantity of fat or blubber of which their enormous body conſiſts. And tho' oil is made from all the ſpecies, none yield it in proportion to theſe; indeed they conſiſt of little elſe. I was once entertained with a particular circumſtance relating to this ſpecies. A ſailor having wounded one, it immediately plunged itſelf into the ſea; but had hardly tinged the water with its blood, when it was ſurrounded in an inſtant by ſhoals of the other two ſpecies, who attacked and devoured it in a few minutes, which was not the caſe with the other ſpecies; which, when wounded, though they alſo plunged into the water, yet the ſight of their blood had no effect on others; nor were they ever attacked. They are miſchievous, and their bite the more dangerous, as they never let go their hold; but they are heavy, torpid, and ſluggiſh; nor can they turn their heads without great difficulty. They were ſo far from avoiding our men, that they were obliged to ſtrike them with ſticks to make them move out of their way. The cry of their young very nearly reſembles the bleating of a ſheep; but when they all join, as it were in concert, the noiſe is inſupportable. They are the chief food of the dogs, who after killing them, take off their ſkin with great dexterity. In their attack, they aim always at the throat; and when they have deſtroyed the creature, they tear the ſkin all round

the

the neck; then seizing it by the head, and putting their fore-feet between the skin and the flesh, they strip it entirely off, and then devour the carcase.

The largest kind, as we have already observed, are, by the sailors, called sea lions, the hair of the neck distinguishing them from the others, and has some resemblance to a mane, though not much longer than that on the other parts of the animal; but as their whole body has a greater similarity to that of the wolf, and being entirely like the other species, the name of sea wolf, seems to me more proper than that given them by the seamen.

All these kinds of sea-wolves, have so tender a sensation at the extremity of their nostrils, that tho' they will bear many wounds in other parts of the body, the slightest stroke on this dispatches them; and that they are sensible of it is evident from their making it their chief care to defend that part from any violence.

A great singularity is also observable in the dogs of this island, namely that they never bark. We caught some of them, and brought them on board; but they never made any noise till joined with some tame dogs, and then indeed they began to imitate them, but in a strange manner, as if learning a thing not natural to them.

The islands of Juan Fernandes abound greatly in fish; among which are two species, not observed in any other part of this vast sea. One is the cod, which, tho' not absolutely like that of Newfoundland, the difference is very minute, either with regard to colour, form, taste, and even the small scales observable on that fish. They are of different sizes, but the largest three or four feet in length.

The other species is a fish resembling the tollo in shape, but much more palatable. From the fore part of each of the two fins on its back, grows a kind of triangular spur, a little bent, but round near the back, and terminating in a point. It has a fine gloss, and the hardness of a bone. At the root of it

is

is a soft spongy substance. This spur or bone, for it resembles both, is such a present remedy for the toothach, that the point of it being applied to the part affected, it entirely removes the pain in half an hour. The first account I had of this singular virtue was from a Frenchman, who was my pilot; but as reason would not permit me to give credit, without experience, to a circumstance seemingly so void of probability, the asseverations of the man increased my desire of putting it to the proof, which I did several times, and always with success. I did not fail to communicate a discovery of such great benefit; and accordingly several of my acquaintance, who laboured under that excruciating pain, made trial of it, and found from it the same happy effects; with this particular circumstance, that soon after the application of the bone to the part affected, it became insensible of pain, a drowsiness succeeded, and they awaked free from the torture. I observed that the spongy substance at the root, during the operation, became gradually inflated, and softer than in its natural state, which could not be effected solely by the moisture of the mouth, the part put into it being compact, hard, and smooth as ivory. I am therefore inclined to think that it has an attractive virtue, which extracts the morbific humour, and collects it in the root. The common length of these anodyne spurs or bones is two inches and a half, of which one moiety, together with the root, is within the body of the fish. Each face of the triangle is about four lines in breadth. They are taken in the same plenty as the others.

The abundance of fish about these islands is such, that two hours fishing in the morning, and as many in the evening, with only six or eight nets, procured not only a sufficiency for all the ship's company, but a considerable quantity remained for salting. The chief kinds are cod, berrugates, the spur fish, sole, turbet, jureles, and lobsters; besides an infinite number

Ch. IV.  SOUTH AMERICA.  225

number of small fish, which covered the water: a circumstance the more surprizing, as there are such multitudes of sea wolves all along the coast, which live on nothing else. For tho' there is very little fishing near these islands, yet doubtless the constant ravages of such enormous creatures, may be thought at least equal to the capture of a large fishery.

These several species are all so delicate and palatable, that the epicure would be at a loss which to prefer. The lobsters are often half a yard in length, and are taken even with greater ease than the others. They are of an exquisite taste, tho' the meat is something hard. The berrugate is a large scaley fish.

We continued at anchor near this island till the 22d of January, during which time, we reconnoitred every part of it, and particularly visited the place where the English had erected their tents, in order to discover any private signal they might have left for the information of any other ships that should afterwards touch at this island. The president of Chili had, with the same view, sent a ship hither some months before our arrrival; but all they met with was two bottles, in each of which was a writing in cypher; and all we discovered were the piquets and poles of the tents; with their small wooden bridges for crossing the breaches, and other things of that kind. Both our frigates having taken in water and wood, we sailed at three in the afternoon for the island of Santa Maria, which we made on the 5th of February, and after carefully surveying it on all sides, continued our course till half an hour after seven of the same day, when we came to an anchor at Puerto Tome, on the E. side of the bay of Conception.

At our departure from the island of Fernandes, we steered first E. one quarter southerly, and the winds continuing between the S. and S. E. we tacked on the 23d and steered between the W. S. W. and S. S. W. but on the 27th being in the latitude of 35° 35′ 30″

33′ 30″ S. latitude, and a degree W. of the meridian de Afuera de Juan Fernandes, we obferved the winds to fhift from S. to S. W. accordingly we altered our courfe, fteered E. and E. S. E. till the 31ft day, when we found ourfelves in the latitude of 36° 23′ and about fifteen or twenty leagues N. W. of the bay of Conception. But the weather, which had been the fame alfo the day preceding, was fo hazy, that we could not fee the other frigate. Sometimes indeed we difcerned the colours, but without having any fight either of the hull or maft. This was however fufficient to affure us that they were within half a cannon fhot of each other. This, and our being fomething to leeward of the bay, obliged us to ftand to fome diftance off to fea; and thus we kept along the coaft without venturing to approach it till the 5th, when at half an hour after nine in the morning, the weather cleared up, and gave us fight of Cape Carnero, bearing S. S. E. ten or twelve leagues; and the middle part of Santa Maria, N. E. one quarter northerly. We crowded fail towards the latter, and at eleven the frigates lay to. Cape Rumena bearing S. one quarter eafterly diftance four leagues, and Cape Lavapies E. one quarter N. E. diftance two leagues. The S. point of the ifland of Santa Maria, bore N. E. four leagues diftant, the N. point of the fame ifland N. N. E. and a large rock without, N. one quarter eafterly. Here we fent our long boat with orders to go betwixt the iflands and the continent, and take a furvey of it, and then join us in Conception Bay. Accordingly the frigates got under fail at twelve at noon, with a frefh gale at S. S. E. and foon after came to an anchor in the faid bay.

Don George Juan, from his reckoning concluded that the ifland of Santa Maria, which lies in 37° 3′ S. latitude, was 7° 10′ E. of the ifland de Afuera de Juan Fernandes. Whereas I differed 14′ from him, making it only 6° 56′.

To

CH. IV.   SOUTH AMERICA.   227

To the N. W. of this ifland, at the diftance of a league and a half, is a lofty fteep rock, with feveral fmaller at its foot; and one league and a half farther to feaward, alfo on the N. W. fide of the ifland, is a fhoal, which, though we at this time faw no breakers on it, we took care to keep at a proper diftance. And in my fecond voyage in the year 1744, I had a clear view of it, for I not only faw the breakers, it being then low water, and the fea running high, but alfo a reef of rocks at the water's edge. The country pilots have affured me, that by fteering in the middle between this fhallow and the rock, there is a very fafe channel, having in moft parts fifty or fixty fathom water.

IN my fecond voyage above-mentioned, on board a French frigate called La Delivrance, in the latitude of 36° 54' and 2° 24' W. of the ifland of Santa Maria, about half an hour after making our obfervations, we unexpectedly found ourfelves in a track of thick water of a yellowifh colour; which naturally occafioning a great furprize, we ftarted from the table, being then at dinner, and haftened up to the quarter deck. It was now too late to put the fhip about; fhe being in the very center of it. This fhoal, as it appeared to us, ftretched near two leagues from N. to S. and was about fix or eight hundred toifes over from E. to W. The colour of the water was of fo deep a yellow, that after providence had happily carried us through it, we could eafily diftinguifh it at a confiderable diftance. I muft own our confternation was fuch from our concluding we were on a fhoal, as there was all the appearance of it, that we had no thoughts of bringing the frigate to, till we had got our founding line in order. In fome parts the water was of a deeper yellow, as being more fhallow. In others we could perceive rays of fea or green water, intermixed with that of the fhoal. No chart has taken any notice of it; nor was it indeed before known to any of the pilots of thefe feas, as they themfelves acknowledged, notwithftanding their repeated voyages. We fhould therefore have been guilty of a great indifference with regard to the public fafety, had we neglected to have given this account of it.

The general winds between the iflands of Juan Fernandes and this place, are the fame as thofe which reign in the gulph; and which have been already defcribed; but the currents are different, fetting N. W. and this becomes the more perceivable in proportion as you approach nearer to the coaft. From the ifland de Tierra de Juan Fernandes eaftward, the water is greenifh, and weftward bluifh. This I have myfelf obferved feveral times, even when not in fight of the ifland; and alfo that the colour of the water changes with the meridian. Between the iflands and the continent, I have frequently feen the water fpouted up by the whales; an appearance which has been often taken for breakers.

Within twenty or thirty leagues of the coaft, we met with large flights of curlews; but this diftance is the utmoft limit of their excurfions. Thefe birds are of a midling bignefs, moftly white except the breaft and upper part of the wings, which are of a rofe colour. Their heads are proportionate to their bodies, but their bill very long, flender, and crooked; and as fmall at the root as at the point. They fly in vaft troops, and confequently are eafily known.

The coafts in general of this fea from Guayaquil to the fouthward are very difficult to be feen, except in fummer time, being the whole winter covered with fuch thick fogs, that no object can be difcerned at half a league diftance. And this dangerous hazinefs extends often to the diftance of fifteen or twenty leagues off to fea. But during the night, and till about ten or eleven in the morning, the fog is only on the land. At that time it moves farther to feaward, with a prodigious denfity refembling a wall; totally concealing

every

CH. IV.   SOUTH AMERICA.   229

every object on the other side of it: And the cautious mariner forbears to make his way thro' it, being uncertain whether he shall meet with clearer weather, as he approaches nearer to the coast.

These winter fogs on the coast of Chili, seem to be occasioned by the N. winds; they being observed always to thicken when those winds blow; and tho' the atmosphere be clear when the wind shifts to that quarter, it is instantaneously filled with those vapours; which continue without any diminution, till the S. winds set in, and have blown fresh for two or three days successively. But as in winter they are usually interrupted by the winds at N. W. and S. W. these vapours, so inconvenient to commerce, are seldom totally dispersed; and it is a common phrase among the mariners of these parts, that the N. is a filthy wind on account of the disagreeable vapours, with which it is loaded, and the S. is a cleanly wind, sweeping these nuisances from the coast and country, and purifying the air. I call these winter fogs, as they are equally common all along the coast from the parallel of twenty to the equinox, where no N. winds are known. And as I have already related of * Lima, all the inhabitants of the coast, live, during the winter, in a perpetual fog.

I shall conclude this chapter, with a table of the variations of the needle observed in my second voyage, in the frigate La Delivrance, from Callao, to Conception Bay.

| South Lat. | | Long. from Callao. | | Variations and their Kinds. | | |
|---|---|---|---|---|---|---|
| Deg. | min. | Deg. | min. | Deg. | min. | |
| 22 | 13½ | 351 | 03 | 7 | 58 | E. |
| 25 | 37½ | 349 | 51 | 9 | 22 | |
| 28 | 27 | 348 | 46 | 9 | 42 | |
| 32 | 10 | 350 | 45½ | 9 | 58 | |

* Book I. Chap. VI.

| Deg. | min. | Deg. | min. | Deg. | min. |
|---|---|---|---|---|---|
| 32 | 52½ | 351 | 14½ | 9 | 06 |
| 33 | 51½ | 352 | 32 | 10 | 00 |
| 35 | 06 | 354 | 39½ | 11 | 10 |
| 36 | 57 | 000 | 47½ | 11 | 15 |

Don George Juan, who failed froom Callao, with the Delivrance, as commander of the Lys, another French frigate, made the following obfervations.

South Latitude. Long. from Callao. Variations and their Kinds.

| Deg. | min. | Deg. | min. | Deg. | min. E. |
|---|---|---|---|---|---|
| 12 | 06 | 000 | 00 | 8 | 52 |
| 12 | 50 | 359 | 00 | 7 | 48 |
| 23 | 00 | 350 | 00 | 6 | 00 |
| 25 | 30 | 349 | 15 | 5 | 00 |
| 27 | 00 | 348 | 30 | 5 | 15 |
| 30 | 45 | 349 | 00 | 6 | 00 |
| 33 | 30 | 352 | 20 | 7 | 10 |

Without the ifland of Juan Fernandes.

| | | | | | |
|---|---|---|---|---|---|
| 33 | 50 | 356 | 00 | 8 | 30 |
| 33 | 40 | 000 | 00 | 10 | 30 |
| 33 | 45 | 002 | 00 | 10 | 45 |

On the coaft of Valparaifo.

| | | | | | |
|---|---|---|---|---|---|
| 33 | 20 | 005 | 00 | 12 | 30 |

THE fenfible difference between thefe variations arofe from the difference of the needles, by which they were obferved; and the reafons for that difference have been confidered in another place.

THE difference of the Meridians between Callao and Conception, appears from the feries of obfervations made by us at Lima, and thofe by father Feville, at the fame place, to be 3° 58' which is the eaftern diftance of Conception from Callao, yet in the maps of this country it is placed eight or nine degrees to the eaftward, a miftake proceeding from a want of attention

tion in the pilots in obferving the direction of the currents; and as thefe carry the ſhip towards the S. W. the pilots, when in the offing, begin to compute their diftance from the coaſt. But this being in reality much greater than that given by the rhumb, they are afterwards under a neceffity of ſteering towards the E. and thence their reckoning makes the port farther to the eaſtward than it really is; and the currents running fometimes with a greater velocity than at others, pilots often differ in placing the meridian of Con. eption, fo that very few at firſt make the cape, tho' affiſted by that chart, which they confider are the beſt. For all thefe draughts are laid down from the falfe concluſions of erroneous journals, no allowance having been made for the fetting of the currents. The difference of latitude proves beyond contradiction the reality of the currents, and the degree of their velocity as I have already noticed.

On the 26th of January the Efperanza, a Spaniſh frigate, commanded by Don Pedro de Mendinueta, came to an anchor in the harbour of Talcaguano, after her voyage from Monte-video in the river of Buenos Ayres, round Cape Horn, which fhe had performed in fixty-fix days. On our arrival at Puerto Tome, an officer came on board the Belin, the very fame night we came to an anchor; and the day following, being the fixth of February, our two frigates joined the Efperanza, at Talcaguano, and formed a little fquadron under the command of Don Pedro de Mendinueta, according to orders from the vice-roy, who had received an account that the Efperanza lay ready at Monte-video, to proceed on her voyage that fummer into the-fouth fea, and that commodore Don Jofeph Pizarro, with other officers were travelling over land to Santiago de Chili; which he had reached at the time of our arrival.

## CHAP. V.

*Description of the City of* CONCEPTION, *in the Kingdom of* CHILI; *with an account of its commerce, and the fertility of the country.*

CONCEPTION, otherwise called Penco, was first founded by captain Pedro de Valdivia, in the year 1550. But the powerful revolts of the Indians of Arauco and Tucapel, obliged its inhabitants to remove to Santiago. They cannot, however, be charged with having quitted their settlement till they had been defeated several times by the Indians, in one of which they lost the abovementioned Pedro de Valdivia, who as governor of that kingdom, was commander in chief of the forces employed in the conquest of it. The same unhappy fate also attended Francisco de Villagra, who as Valdivia's lieutenant general had succeeded in the command. These misfortunes, and the superiority of the allied Indians, obliged the Spaniards to abandon Conception. The inhabitants however being desirous of possessing again their plantations in the neighbourhood of that city, and of which they used to make such large profits, petitioned the audience of Lima for leave to return to their original city. But had soon sufficient cause to repent of not having exerted their industry in improving the place whither they had retired, the Indians, on the first notice that the Spaniards were returned to the city, forming a powerful alliance under a daring leader, called Lautaro, took by storm a small fort, which was the whole defence of the city, and put all to the sword, except a small number who had fortunately escaped to Santiago. Some time after Don Gracia de Mendoza, son to the vice-roy de Mendoza, Marquis of Canete, arriving as governor of Chili, with a body of forces sufficient for making head against the Indians, restored the inhabitants of

Con-

Conception to their former poffeffions, with the greateft apparent fecurity. But the year 1603 gave birth to a new and more general confederacy, by which means Conception, La Imperia, and Baldivia, with fix fmaller places, were deftroyed; being the greateft part of the places in this kingdom. Conception however received frefh fuccours, the city was again repaired, and has continued ever fince.

Its latitude, according to an obfervation we made in the year 1744 at Talcaguana, which lies exactly E. and W. with the city, is 36° 43′ 15″ S. and ts longitude from the meridian of Teneriff, according to Father Fevillee, 303° 18′ 30″. The city is built on the S. W. fhore of a beautiful bay, on an uneven fandy ground, and on a fmall declivity, having a little river running through it. The city in its extent, is fcarce equal to one of the fourth clafs. The deftruction it fuffered in the dreadful earthquake of 1730, occafioned all the houfes to be built low, tho' it had before been fubject to thefe fudden convulfions of nature. This was, however, the laft of thofe remarkable for their melancholy confequences, which extended to Santiago, the capital of the kingdom, which was involved in the fame ruin. On the 8th of July at one in the morning the firft motions were felt, and the concuffions increafing, the fea retreated to a confiderable diftance; but in a fmall time returned fo impetuoufly, and with fuch a fwell, that it overflowed the whole city, and the neighbouring countries. In this fudden calamity the inhabitants had no other afylum than the neighbouring eminences. This inundation was foon fucceeded by three or four fhocks; and at about four in the morning, a little before day break, the concuffions returned with the moft tremendous violence, demolifhing the few buildings which had withftood the firft fhocks, and the rapid motion of the fea.

The houfes are all either of topias or mud walls, or adoves, unburnt bricks; but covered with tiles.
The

The churches are small and mean; the same may be said of the Francifcan, Auguftine, and Dominican convents, as well as thofe belonging to the fathers of mercy: But the college of Jefuits is not wholly deftitute of elegance, being well built and of a tolerable architecture.

THE political government of this city confifts of a corregidor nominated by the king, and who is at the head of the ordinary alcaldes and the regidores. During the vacancy of this poft, the duty is performed by the prefident of Chili, who is governor and captain general of the whole kingdom, and prefident of the audience of Santiago, on which as its capital, Conception is dependant. The court of audience was originally eftablifhed in the latter, and continued there from the year 1567, to 1574; but the danger and difturbances, occafioned by the frequent revolts of the Indians, caufed it for a while to be fupprefs'd, and afterwards to be removed to the city of Santiago. The prefident is however obliged to refide fix months of the year at Conception, that he may attend carefully to the military concerns of the frontiers, fee that the forts be in a good condition, and well provided with every thing, in order to keep the Indians of Arauco in awe, and that the military forces are in good order, and well difciplined, and always in readinefs to repel any attempts of the Indians, provided they fhould ever abandon their dread of the Spanifh troops. During the other fix months, when the governor refides at Santiago, he acts in a very different character; hearing complaints, redreffing grievances, and adminiftring juftice, that this tribunal may receive the greater dignity from his prefence. Here is alfo a chamber of finances, at the head of which is an accountant and treafurer. Befides which Conception has likewife all the other courts and offices ufual in the cities of South America.

As

## Ch. V.  SOUTH AMERICA.  235

As all the inhabitants of the towns, villages, and country, within the jurifdiction of Conception, form different bodies of militia, fome of which are in pay, and all muft be ready on any fudden alarm, there is, befides the corregidor, a Maeftra de Campo, who commands in all the military affairs without the city; but we fhall have occafion to give a farther account of his duty in the fequel.

This city at firft belonged to the diocefs of Imperial; but that being ruined by the perpetual incurfions of the Indians, the epifcopal fee was removed to Conception, and the chapter changed. It is now a fuffragan of Lima, and has a chapter confifting of a bifhop, dean, archdeacon, and two prebendaries.

The jurifdiction of Conception extends from the river Maule on the coaft N. of the city to Cape Lavapies. It has few villages; but the whole country full of feats, farms, and cottages.

The inhabitants confift of Spaniards and Meftizos, who in colour are hardly diftinguifhable from the former; both being very fair, and fome have even frefh complexions. The goodnefs of the climate, together with the fertility of the country, have drawn hither many Spanifh families, both Creoles and Europeans, who live together in that harmony and friendfhip, which fhould be an example to the other parts of thefe provinces; where the comforts of fociety are greatly leffened by the feuds arifing from a mean pride and jealoufy. The men in general are well-fhaped and robuft, and the women handfome. Their cuftoms and drefs, are a kind of compound of thofe of Lima and Quito, but more nearly refemble the latter, except that the men ufe, inftead of a cloak, a poncho, which is made in the form of a quilt, about two yards and a half or three in length, and two in breadth, having an opening in the middle juft fufficient to put their head through, the reft hanging down on all

fides.

fides. (Plate VII.) This is their drefs in all weathers, whether walking or riding. The peafants, whom they call Guafos, never pull it off but when they go to reft; tucking it up in fuch a manner, that both their arms and whole body are at full liberty either for labour or diverfion. This is an univerfal garb among all ranks when they ride on horfeback, an exercife very common here; and the women are particularly famous for their fkill in horfemanfhip.

This drefs though fo plain and uniform in itfelf, ferves to diftinguifh the rank and quality of the wearer; as its price is proportional to the work on it. Some wear it as a covering, fome for decency, and others for fhew. Accordingly if thofe of the common people coft only four or five dollars, others have ftood the owners in a hundred and fifty or two hundred. This difference arifes from the finenefs of the ftuff, or from the laces and embroidery, with which they are decorated. They are of a double woollen ftuff manufactured by the Indians, and generally of a blue colour embroidered with red or white; fometimes, indeed, the ground is white embroidered with blue, red, and other colours.

The peafants are furprizingly dextrous in managing the noofe and lance; and it is very feldom, that tho' on full fpeed they mifs their aim with the former. Accordingly thefe are their chief arms, and they will halter a wild bull with the fame agility as any other creature; nor could a man, however cautious, avoid being taken in their noofe. I fhall relate an inftance of their addrefs with regard to an Englifhman whom we knew at Lima. He was in the long boat of a privateer then lying in Conception bay, intending to land at Talcaguano, with a view of plundering the neighbouring villages; but a body of the country militia made to the fhore in order to oppofe them. Upon this the Englifh fired upon them with their mufquetry, imagining
that

that would be sufficient to put them to flight, and thus the place be open for them to land.. They had no sooner discharged their pieces, than one of the peasants, tho' the boat was at a considerable distance, threw his noose, and notwithstanding all in the boat threw themselves on their faces, he noosed the above-mentioned person, pulling him out of the boat with the greatest rapidity; whilst the others, instead of endeavouring to save him, in their fright thought of nothing but how to get out of danger as soon as possible. It was the Englishman's good fortune not to be strangled or killed by the bruises he received, the slip knot having passed from one shoulder under the opposite arm, so that he recovered in a few days.

As it is very seldom that they miss, and are obliged on haltering a creature, to draw the knot, at the same time that they throw the noose, they clap spurs to their horse, and put him on his full speed; that the creature is so far from having time to disingage itself, that it is no sooner caught than disabled. This is also one of the weapons, if I may give it that name, used in their private quarrels, defending themselves with a lance of a middling length. And their address on these occasions is so very remarkable, that very often after a long dispute in which both parties are heartily tired, they part with no other hurt than a few bruises. This is also the method they take to satisfy their revenge, endeavouring to halter the object of their hatred, either as he runs from them, or is not apprized of their intention. In this case the only resource in an open country on seeing him with his noose in his hand, is, to throw one's self on the ground, keeping the legs and arms as close to the surface as possible, that the rope may have no room to get under any part. The person may also save himself by standing close to a tree, and if in the street by placing himself against the wall. A small distance, that

is

is, under ten or fifteen paces, partly renders their dexterity ineffectual; but there is very great danger of being intangled when the diſtance is thirty or forty. The nooſes or halters, are thongs of a cow's hide cut round the ſkin, and of a proper breadth. Theſe thongs they twiſt, and work with fat, till they are of a proper degree of ſuppleneſs; but ſo ſtrong, that tho' when twiſted they are not larger than the little finger, yet they hold the wildeſt bull, when its efforts to eſcape would break a rope of hemp of much larger dimenſions.

The climate of this city is not eſſentially different from that of the greateſt part of Europe. Winter is indeed ſomething colder than in the ſouthern provinces of Spain, but milder than thoſe of the northern; and the ſummer heats proportionably. In winter the inhabitants ſeem to be little incommoded by the N. winds, and in ſummer the heats are moderated by the cooling breezes from the S. The heat is however greater in the city than in the adjacent country, occaſioned chiefly by the different diſpoſition of the ground, being interſected by various rivers, ſome of which are very large, as the Arauco and the Biobio. The latter of which, at a league above its mouth, is very near four leagues in breadth. It may however in ſummer be forded, but not without danger; in the winter it is paſſed in balzas. At the ſouthern banks of the river the territories of the wild Indians begin, and near the ſame ſhore towards that part are the chain of frontier forts, of which a farther account will be given in the ſequel. The country of this juriſdiction conſiſts principally of extenſive plains, the Cordillera being at a conſiderable diſtance to the eaſtward, and the whole ſpace between it and the ſea coaſt, one entire and uniform plain. interrupted only by a few eminences, which are an ornament to the country, and render the perſpective of it the more agreeable.

The

## Ch. V.    SOUTH AMERICA.    239

THE great affinity between this climate and that of Spain is evident from its products, though there is a remarkable difference with regard to their goodness and plenty, in both which this country has greatly the advantage. The trees and plants of all kinds have their regular seasons, embellishing the fields with their verdure, entertaining the sight with their various flowers and blossoms, and gratifying the palate with their delicious fruits. It is needless to mention that the times of the season must be opposite, consequently the winter in Spain is their summer, and the autumn of the former, the spring of the latter. In saying that this country produces the same corn and fruits as Spain, I do not mean those of the most southern parts; for neither sugar canes, oranges nor lemons thrive here. Nor is it well adapted to olive-yards, tho' some olives are produced here. But the fruits cultivated in the center of Spain, are the same with those produced here in a most astonishing plenty, wheat and other grain generally producing a hundred fold. I shall here relate an instance I myself saw and examined at Talcaguano, in a garden near the sea side, at a place called the Morro, very little more than a quarter of a league from the harbour. Among several stalks of wheat that had grown there without culture, I saw one whose stem was not more than a foot from the ground, but from its knots there afterwards sprung so many stalks, as produced thirty four ears[*], the largest of which were near three inches in length, and the least not less than two. The master of the house observing that I viewed this production of nature with astonishment, told me that it was nothing extraordinary, for tho' the grain in the ground commonly sown, did not often attain such a luxuriancy, it was com-

[*] This species of wheat is called Triticum spica multiplici, and is cultivated in Italy and Sicily.

mon

mon for each ftalk to produce five or fix ears. This information raifed my curiofity; and I met with fo many inftances afterwards, that my furprize at feeing the ftalk juft mentioned was greatly abated; as from the moifture, advantageous expofure, and richnefs of the foil, a much greater produce might naturally be expected than in the ground conftantly fown.

The great plenty of wheat here is fufficiently indicated by its price; a meafure weighing fix arobas and fix pounds, being ufually fold for eight or ten rials. Yet for want of a market, tho' at fo low a price, no more is fown than is neceffary for home confumption; and thence great part of the country lies fallow.

Here are vines of feveral kinds, and which vye with the wheat in exuberance. They are alfo, both with regard to the richnefs and flavour of their grapes, efteeemed beyond any produced in Peru. Moft of them are red. A fort of Muscadel is alfo made here, whofe flavour far exceeds any of the kind made in Spain. The grapes grow moftly in efpaliers, and not on detached vines. In this refpect alfo, as in the wheat, large tracts of ground are totally neglected. For tho' its produce is fo confiderable, the buyers are fo few, that the vineyards do not anfwer even the expence of cultivation.

The chief ufe made of thefe rich lands by the owners is, the fattening of oxen, goats and fheep. And this is the principal employment of greateft part of the inhabitants of the country of all ranks, and univerfally of the lower clafs. As foon as the horned cattle are fattened in thefe luxuriant paftures, and the proper feafon arrived, four or five hundred, and even more, according to the largenefs of the farm, are flaughtered. They take out the fat, melt it into a kind of lard, there called Graffa; and buccaneer or dry the flefh in fmoke; but the greateft profit

Vol. II.

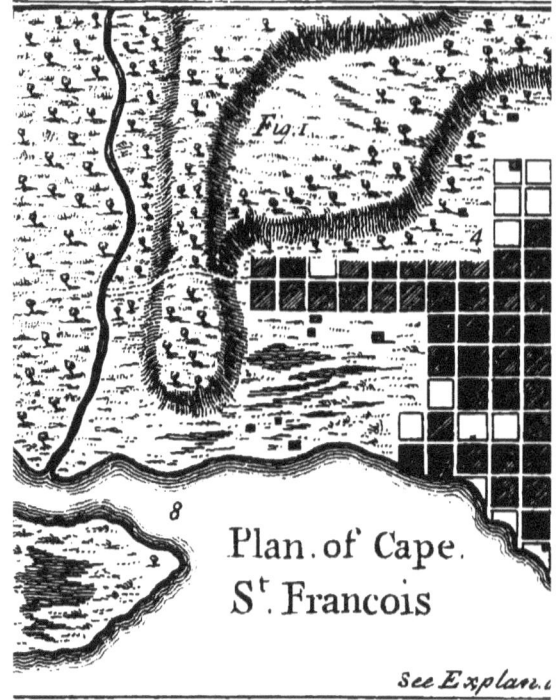

Plan of Cape St. Francois

See Explan.

Fig. 2. Men of Chili Pag. 235.

Сн.V.  SOUTH AMERICA.  241

fit arifes from the hide, the tallow, and the graffa, a fufficient proof of their prodigious fatnefs when killed. But an idea of the fertility of this country may be beft formed from the value of a live beaft, which, when fit to be killed, may be purchafed for four dollars; a price vaftly beneath that in any other part of India; and may be fufficient to remove the unjuft reproach of the poverty of this province. For were the induftry of the people equal to the fertility of the foil, this kingdom would be the moft opulent of any. in America.

THE manner of flaughtering the beafts render it a favourable diverfion to the perfons employed in performing it, and it muft be owned that their dexterity is really furprizing. The cattle intended to be killed are drove into an inclofure. At the gate are the Guafos on horfeback with their fpears two or three toifes in length, and at one end a very fharp piece of fteel in the form of a half moon, the points of which are about a foot diftant from each other. Every thing being ready, the gate of the inclofure is opened, and a beaft turned out, which naturally betakes itfelf to flight, but is immediately purfued by a Guafo, who without checking his horfe hamftrings it in one leg, and then immediately in the other. He then alights, and having difpatched his capture, fkins it, takes out the tallow, the fat for the Graffa, and cuts up the flefh for falting and drying. This done he wraps up the tallow in the hide, and loading it on his horfe, carries it to the farm; returning again for the flefh. After this he fets out on another expedition. Sometimes they turn out at once as many beafts as there are Guafos ready to kill them. And this is the daily exercife till all the cattle appointed for that year's flaughter are difpatched. An European is furprized not only at their dexterity in hamftringing the beaft, when both are on full fpeed, but alfo to fee one man alone

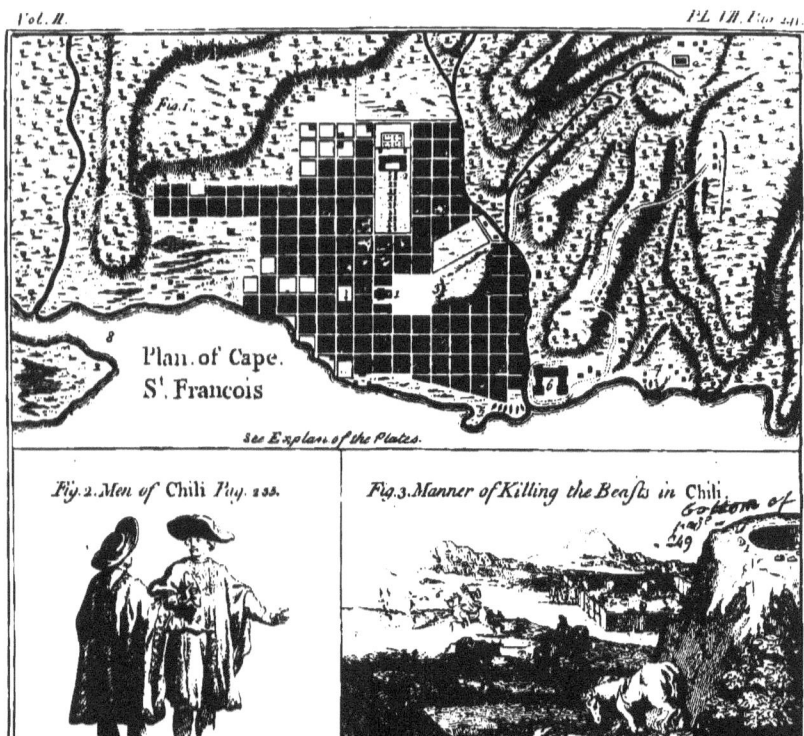

Сн.V.    SOUTH AMERICA.    241

fit arifes from the hide, the tallow, and the graffa, a fufficient proof of their prodigious fatnefs when killed. But an idea of the fertility of this country may be beft formed from the value of a live beaft, which, when fit to be killed, may be purchafed for four dollars; a price vaftly beneath that in any other part of India; and may be fufficient to remove the unjuft reproach of the poverty of this province. For were the induftry of the people equal to the fertility of the foil, this kingdom would be the moft opulent of any in America.

The manner of flaughtering the beafts render it a favourable diverfion to the perfons employed in performing it, and it muft be owned that their dexterity is really furprizing. The cattle intended to be killed are drove into an inclofure. At the gate are the Guafos on horfeback with their fpears two or three toifes in length, and at one end a very fharp piece of fteel in the form of a half moon, the points of which are about a foot diftant from each other. Every thing being ready, the gate of the inclofure is opened, and a beaft turned out, which naturally betakes itfelf to flight, but is immediately purfued by a Guafo, who without checking his horfe hamftrings it in one leg, and then immediately in the other. He then alights, and having difpatched his capture, fkins it, takes out the tallow, the fat for the Graffa, and cuts up the flefh for falting and drying. This done he wraps up the tallow in the hide, and loading it on his horfe, carries it to the farm; returning again for the flefh. After this he fets out on another expedition. Sometimes they turn out at once as many beafts as there are Guafos ready to kill them. And this is the daily exercife till all the cattle appointed for that year's flaughter are difpatched. An European is furprized not only at their dexterity in hamftringing the beaft, when both are on full fpeed, but alfo to fee one man

Vol. II.    R    alone

alone go through the whole work in such a regular method and great dispatch. If the beast be swifter than his horse, the Guaso has recourse to his noose, and halters him by throwing it either about his neck, or round one or two of his legs, according as opportunity offers, and by that means secures him. Then if a tree be near at hand he gives the end of the thong two or three turns round the trunk, and the whole difficulty of killing the beast is over.

The tallow is wrapt up in the hides, and in this manner carried to the city for sale; the Grassa is melted into bags of sheep-skins; the flesh, after being cut into thin slices, is salted, and this is what they call Tassagear; afterwards it is buccaneered or dried in the smoke, and sold. The hides they tan, and make from them a most excellent leather, especially for the soles of shoes. Goats also as we have already observed, are fattened and turn to good account. Their tallow nearly resembles that of the ox, and the Cordovan leather made of their skins surpasses every thing of that kind made in any part of the whole kingdom of Peru.

All other provisions and grain are in the same plenty, turkeys, geese, and all kinds of poultry are sold at a remarkable low price, great numbers of them being bred all over the country, with little care and no expence. Wild fowls also are very common, among which are canelones, and others described among the birds found in the desarts of Quito, tho' these are not so large, and more like the bandarrias as they are there called. Here are also wood pigeons, turtle doves, partridges, snipes, woodcocks, and royal cirapicos, &c. And with regard to these the air may be said to vie with the fertility of the earth.

Among the birds I must not omit one of a very singular kind, and found all over the country. The natives call these birds dispertadores, awakeners, from

their

their giving notice to others of the approach of any danger. On hearing the noife of the approach of any creature whether man or beaft, or feeing them within a fmall diftance, they rife from the ground, and make a loud chattering not unlike that of a magpye; continuing the noife, and flying about in the air over the object which caufed the alarm. This is underftood by the birds thereabouts, who immediately rife and by that means efcape the danger.

This bird is about the fize of a middling fowl, its plumage black and white, has a thick neck, the head fomething large, erect, and beautifully adorned with a tuft of feathers; its eyes are large, fharp and lively; its bill well proportioned, ftrong, and a little curved. On the fore part of their wings are two fpurs, about an inch in length, of a reddifh tinct towards the root, and their points refembling thofe of a cock, being very hard and fharp. Thefe are the weapons they make ufe of againft the other birds, particularly thofe of prey as hawks, and others of that kind, which probably abound the more in this country, from the great variety of prey it affords them.

Among the finging birds is the goldfinch, in every particular refembling thofe of Spain, except a fmall variation in its plumage. There are befides others proper to this country, and met with in all the cold climates, particularly the piches, which are fomething larger than fparrows. They are of a brown colour, fpotted with black, except their breaft, which is of a moft beautiful red, and fome feathers of the fame colour in their wings, intermixed with others of a bright yellow. Amidft all the fertility of this country, the only infects are the niguas or piques; and tho' fome fnakes are found in the fields and woods, their bite is not dangerous. Neither are the country peafants under any apprehenfions from ravenous beafts; fo that nature may be faid to pour her treafures on this country, without blending them with the ufual inconveniences.

The fruits which moſtly abound in Chili, are of the ſame kind as thoſe known in Europe; its cherries in particular are large, and of a fine taſte. The ſtrawberries are of two kinds, one called frutillas, and are larger than thoſe of Quito, wanting little of being equal to a hen's egg in magnitude. The other, which in ſize, colour and taſte, perfectly reſemble thoſe of Spain, grow wild, on the ſide of the eminences with which the plains are interſperſed. And here alſo grow all kind of flowers, without any other culture, than that of benign nature.

Among the remarkable herbs, of which many are medicinal, and others applied to divers uſes, is the panque, of great ſervice in tanning leather. It abounds every where, and grows to about four or five feet from the ground. The principal ſtem, which is of a ſoft ſubſtance, is betwixt four and five inches in diameter, and about two feet and a half in height, ſeparating there into ſeveral branches, bearing round, ſerrated, rough, and thick leaves, and ſo large that their diameter when full grown, is ſeldom leſs than a foot and a half, and ſometimes two feet. Before the plant is fit to be cut, when the leaves begin to turn red, the peaſants make an inciſion into the bark, and ſuck the juice which is very cooling and aſtringent; but as ſoon as ever the leaf is obſerved to turn white, an indication of decay, they cut the plant down at the root, take off the branches, and divide the ſtalk into ſhort pieces, which being dried in the ſun, make an excellent tan.

Besides this rich variety of productions, on the ſurface of the earth, the country alſo abounds with valuable mines and quarries; particularly of Lapis lazuli and loadſtone, copper equal to the beſt of Europe; beſides ſeveral of gold; but no advantage is derived from any; the inhabitants, contented with the plentiful enjoyment of all the neceſſaries of life, extend their wiſhes no farther, leaving to the curioſity and

and avarice of others the laborious search after what the earth contains in its bowels.

This kingdom of Chili seems also to have been the first country of those famous horses and mules, mentioned in the first volume. Indeed all these creatures found in America, owe their origin to some imported from Spain. At present, however, those of Chili surpass not only those of the other parts of America, but even those of Spain, from whence they are derived. The horses first brought over might possibly have been of the running kind, Spain still abounding in that sort. But it must be owned, that greater care has been taken here of preventing the breed from being mixed with others of a less generous species; and by this means they greatly exceed those of Spain; for without any other incentive than their own inclination, before they will suffer any other to get before them, they will exert their utmost strength; and at the same time their motion is so easy, that the rider is not the least fatigued. In beauty and gracefulness they are not inferior to the famous Andelusian horses, and at the same time full of spirit. Accordingly they are every where so highly valued, that a more acceptable present cannot be made to a person of the greatest distinction, than one of these beasts. Many purchase them for parade, and besides their being common all over the kingdom, they have been sent even to Quito. The great demand for them, and consequently their high price, has induced the inhabitants of several countries to attempt the breeding of them; but none are equal to those of Chili.

The commerce at Conception might be considerably increased, were the country, which is far from being the case, inhabited in any proportion to its fertility and extent; but for want of a sufficient number of hands, their commerce is at a very low ebb, consisting almost intirely in provisions, wine, &c. and this is so small, that it is chiefly carried on by by only a single ship coming once a year from Calloa to load with them, together with a few others trade-ing to Chiloe or Baldivia, and in their return touch here. Their exports are tallow, graffa, cordovan, bend leather, excellent butter, wines, and dried fruits. The goods brought hither in exchange are the several forts of woollen stuffs from Quito, and others from Europe, iron, and mercury. Very few European goods are however imported; for the people here not being remarkable for their riches, use only home made stuffs and bays, which tho' extremely good are in no great quantity. The commerce carried on between the inhabitants of Chili, and the Arauco Indians, shall be mentioned in its proper place.

## CHAP. VI.

*Description of* CONCEPTION BAY; *its roads or harbours, fish, &c. and the singular mines of shells in its neighbourhood.*

THE bay of Conception, besides its excellent bottom, is of such an extent, as not to be equalled by any on the whole coast. For from Tierra-Firma, north and south, its length is nearly three leagues and a half, and its breadth from east to west, almost three leagues, being the distance betwixt the harbour of Talcaguano, and the Cirillo virde, or little green mountain, situated near the city; from whence its breadth is contracted by the island of Quiriquina, which lying in the mouth of it, forms two entrances, of which that on the east side is the safest, being two miles in breadth, and accordingly frequented by most ships. The west entrance is between the island and Talcaguano point,

and

and is near half a league in breadth. In the principal entrance of this bay is thirty fathom water, which depth afterwards decreases to eleven and ten, till within about a mile of the shore, opposite to the entrance. The western, tho' the many rocks and breakers in it make it appear very dangerous, has a channel with water sufficient for the largest ship, the depth being at first thirty fathom, and never less than eleven; it is situated in the middle of the entrance, that is at an equal distance between the rocks which project about a quarter of a league from Talcaguano point, and Quriquina.

WITHIN the bay are three roads or harbours, where ships anchor; for tho' the bottom be every where clear, it is only in one of these three places ships can ride in safety, being no where else sheltered from the wind. The first called Puerto Tome, lies E. and W. with the N. point of Quiriquina, contiguous to the coast of Tierra Firma. The anchoring place is about half a league distant from the land, in about twelve fathom water. But this road is only used when ships come in during the night, it being difficult to reach either of the other two before day light, as several tacks must be made for that purpose.

IN this bay the principal port is that of Talcaguana. It is properly an elbow, and bears S. S. W. from the S. point of Quiriquina. This is by far the most frequented, ships in general anchoring here, having not only better ground than any other part of the bay, but are in some measure sheltered from the N. winds. Whereas at Cirillo-verde, they lie exposed, not only to these, but also to the S. winds, the land which should intercept them being low. Besides the bottom is of a loose mud, so that the anchors in a hard gale of wind, generally come home; and consequently the ships in great danger of being stranded on the coast. From these inconveniences it may be concluded, that the only ships which anchor here,

here, are such as happen to be in those parts in the midst of summer, and are in haste to take in their loading, for which this road is most convenient, as being nearest the city.

Two rivers empty themselves into this bay, one of which passing thro' the city of Conception, has thence the same name; the other is called St. Pedro. The first is the watering place for ships anchoring at Cirillo Verde; whereas those at Talcaguano, supply themselves with that necessary fluid from some streams which flow from the adjacent eminences; they easily take on board a sufficient quantity of wood, of which there is here plenty; as of all other necessaries.

SHIPS, before they enter the bay of Conception, endeavour to make the island of Santa Maria, and then coast along it, keeping at the same time, a good look out for a reef of rocks which stretches out almost three leagues from the N. W. point; thence they continue their course, keeping at a little distance from the main, there being no rocks but what are above water. After weathering the reef of rocks on the island of Santa Maria, they steer directly for Talcaguano point, at the distance of about half a league; from which seaward, is a rock called Quiebraollas, which must be the more carefully avoided at it is surrounded with shoals. There is, however, no danger, if the ship be not nearer than half a mile; indeed there is a sufficient depth of water within a cable's length. After their being abreast of this rock they steer for the N. point of Quiriquina, off which lie two rocks, but the farthest from the shore is only a quarter of a league, and may be safely approached within a stone's cast. Both these rocks swarm with sea-wolves; and as there is a sufficient depth of water all round them, there is no other danger in standing near them, than what may be seen. There is indeed a necessity for standing near them, to avoid falling to leeward of the bay. After passing

passing them, the course is continued as near as possible to the island of Quiriquina, taking care to avoid some other rocks lying along the shore.

As ships are generally obliged to make several tacks in order to get into Conception bay, care must be taken not to approach too near the island of Quiriquina, either on the E. or S. sides; for tho' the coast is bold on the N. and N. W. sides, there is a shoal on the S. extending to a considerable distance from the shore. At a third part of the distance between the road at Talcaguano, and the point of the same name, is another shoal, running about half a league to the eastward. In the middle of it is a ledge of rocks, whose tops are dry at low water. To avoid this shoal, tho' the thick water sufficiently indicates it, the best way is, at entering the mouth of the bay with a land wind, to steer directly for the middle of a spot of red earth on a mountain of a middling height, situated at the bottom of the bay, continuing this course till the ship is passed the shoal; and then steer directly for the houses at Talcaguana, till within about half a mile from the shore, which is the usual anchoring place in five or six fathom water; Cape Herradura, being covered by the island of Quiriquina. The same care is also necessary to avoid another reef of rocks, lying between the Morro and the coast of Talcaguana; nor must the Morro side be approached too near, there being a sand stretching all along from that reef of rocks to Cirillo Verde. The ships riding at Talcaguana in the manner thus prescribed, are sheltered from the N. wind; but not entirely so from the sea, which in those winds runs very high, and pours in through both entrances. The goodness of the bottom, however, secures the ship. During the force of these winds there is no possibility of landing on account of the great sea; but in fair weather, every place is convenient for going on shore.

The country round the bay, particularly that between

between Talcaguana and Conception, within four or five leagues from the shore, is noted for a very singular curiosity, namely, that at the depth of half or three quarters of a yard beneath the surface of the ground, is a stratum of shells of different kinds, two or three toises in thickness, and in some places even more, without any intermixture of earth, one large shell being joined together by smaller, and which also fill the cavities of the larger. From these shells all the lime used in building is made; and large pits are dug in the earth for taking out those shells, and calcining them. Were these strata of shells found only in low and level places, this phænomenon would be more easily accounted for by a supposition no ways improbable, namely, that these parts were formerly covered by the sea, agreeable to an observation we made in our description of Lima. But what renders it surprizing is, that the like quarries of the same kind of shells, are found on the tops of mountains in this country, fifty toises above the level of the sea. I did not indeed personally examine the quarries on the highest of those mountains; but was assured of their existence by persons who had lime kilns there; but I saw them myself on the summits of others at the height of twenty toises above the surface of the sea; and was the more pleased with the sight, as it appeared to me a convincing proof of the universality of the deluge. I am not ignorant that some have attributed this to other causes; but an unanswerable confutation of their subterfuge is, that the various sorts of shells which compose these strata both in the plains and mountains, are the very same with those found in the bay and neighbouring places. Among these shells are three species very remarkable: the first is called Choros, already mentioned in our description of Lima; the second is called Pies de Burros, asses feet; and the third Bulgados, and these to me seem to preclude all

manner

manner of doubt that they were originally produced in that sea, from whence they were carried by the waters, and deposited in the places where they are now found.

I have examined these parts with the closest attention, and found no manner of vestige of subterraneous fires. No calcinations are to be met with on the surface of the earth, nor among the shells; which, as I have already observed, are not intermixed with earth; nor are there stones, or any other heterogeneous substances found among them. Some of these shells are entire, others broken; as must naturally happen in such a close compression of them, during so long an interval of time. This circumstance, however trifling it may appear to some, may deserve the consideration of those who have advanced the notion, that shells may be formed in the earth by subterraneous fires, co-operating with the nature of the soil.

The Pie de Burro, has its name from the fish inclosed in it, resembling, when taken out, the foot of an ass. This fish is of a dark brown colour, firm and filaceous; it is an univalve, its mouth almost circular, and its diameter about three inches. The bottom of the shell is concave within, and convex without. The colour within is perfectly white, the surface very smooth; the outside scabrous and full of tubercles. Its thickness in every part is about four or five lines; and being large, compact, and heavy, is preferred to all others for making lime.

The bulgados, in the Canaries called bulgaos, are snails, not at all differing in their form from the common; but larger than those of the same name found in gardens, being from two inches, to two inches and a half in diameter. The shell is also very thick, rough on the outside, and of a dark brown colour; and, next to the preceding, makes the best lime.

All these species of shell-fish are found at the bottom of the sea in four, six, ten and twelve fathom water.

water. They are caught by drags; and what is very remarkable is, that no fhells, either the fame, or that have any refemblance to them, are feen either on the fhores continually wafhed by the fea, or on thofe tracks which have been overflowed by an extraordinary tide. They adhere to a fea plant, called Cochayuyo, (lake herb) the Indians making no nominal diftinctions between the inland lakes, and the fea, calling both cochas. This plant refembles the bejuco; its diameter is about half an inch, and from its root to its extremity of an equal thicknefs. In length is from twenty to thirty toifes, producing at every eighteen inches, or fomething more, a leaf about a yard and a half or two yards in length; but the breadth, which is in every part the fame, does not exceed two or three inches. It is remarkable fmooth, which, together with a vifcid liquor, with which it is covered, gives it a very fine glofs. The fame may be faid of the ftem, which is extreamly flexible, and ftrong. Its colour is of a pale green, but that of the leaves more vivid. This plant divides itfelf into feveral branches, equal in dimenfions to the main ftem. Thefe branches fucceffively produce others of the fame proportion; fo that the produce of one fingle root covers a prodigious fpace. At the joints where the branches fpring, are found this kind of fhell fifh, where they both receive their nourifhment, and propagate their fpecies. The extremities of thefe Cochayuyos, float on the furface, and in fome lakes, where the water has remained a long time undifturbed, form a kind of carpet. At the junction of the ftalk of every leaf with the ftem, is a berry refembling a caper, but fomething larger, fmooth and gloffy on the furface, and exactly of the fame colour with the ftem.

The feas on thefe coafts abound in excellent fifh, tho' not in fo great a degree as thofe near Juan Fernandes. Here are feen, in particular, a great number of whales, which come even into the bay; alfo

tunny-

tunny-fish, and sea-wolves. Among the amphibious creatures here is one known all along these coasts, and even at Callao. It is called Pajaro Nino, the bird-child. It in some parts resembles a goose, except that its neck and bill are not arched, and is something larger. It has a thick neck, a large head, and a strong short bill. Its legs very small, and in walking the body is in an erect position. Its wings are small, cartilaginous, and nearly resemble the fins of the seal. Its tail is so small as hardly to be distinguished; its wings and whole body are covered with a short brown hair like that of the sea-wolves, and generally full of white spots, tho' some are of other colours. So that upon the whole, the bird makes no disagreeable appearance. It lives promiscuously either in the water or on the land; on the latter it is easily taken, being very slow in its motions; but when attacked, bites severely, tho' it is observed never to be the first aggressor.

## CHAP. VII.

*Description of the City of* SANTIAGO, *the Capital of the Kingdom of* CHILI.

AFTER giving an account of all the cities and places of note, thro' which we passed, I must not omit the capital of the kingdom of Chili. We had not indeed occasion to visit it personally; but by the informations we received from persons best qualified to answer our inquiries, in the ports of its jurisdiction, to which our affairs called us more than once, we are enabled to gratify the curiosity of a rational reader.

The city of Santiago, originally called Santiago de la Nuestra Estremadura, was founded by captain Pedro de Valdivia, who began the foundation on the 24th of February 1541, in the valley of Mapocho, near that of Chili, which gives its name to the whole kingdom. It has not been subject to the revolutions of other places, but still stands on its original spot, which is nearly in 33° 40′ south latitude, and about twenty leagues from the harbour of Valparaiso, the nearest port to it in the south seas. Its situation is one of the most convenient and delightful that can be imagined, standing in a delightful plain of twenty-four leagues in extent, watered by a river flowing in meanders thro' the middle of it, and called by the same name of Mapocho. This river runs so near the city, that by means of conduits, the water is conveyed from it thro' the streets, and also supplies the gardens, which few houses here are without, and hence the delightful situation of the place, and the pleasure of the inhabitants are greatly heightned.

The city is a thousand toises in length from E. to W. and six hundred in breadth from N. to S. On the side opposite the river, which washes the N. part of it, is a large suburb, called Chimba; and on the E. side, almost contiguous to the houses, is a mountain of a middling height, called Santa Lucia. The streets are all of a handsome breadth, paved and streight; some run exactly in an E. and W. direction, and are crossed by others, lying exactly N. and S. Near the middle of the city is the grand piazza, which, like that of Lima, is square, with a very beautiful fountain in the center. On the N. side are the palace of the royal audience, where the presidents have their appartments, the town-house, and the public prison. The W. side is taken up by the cathedral and the bishop's palace. The S. side consists of shops, each decorated with an arch; and the E. is a row of private houses. The other parts of the city are divided into insulated squares of houses, regular, and of the same dimensions with those of Lima.

The houses here are built of adoves, or unburnt bricks, and very low; this necessary caution against
the

the terrible devaſtation of earthquakes being equally neceſſary here as in all other towns of Peru, calamities with which this city has been often viſited; but the moſt remarkable are the following.

1. In the year 1570, an earthquake happened, which overflowed ſeveral mountains in this kingdom; many villages were entirely deſtroyed, and great part of the inhabitants buried in their ruins.

2. In the year 1647, on the 13th of May, many of the houſes and churches of this city were ruined by another ſhock.

3. In 1657, on the 15th of March, the earth was obſerved to have a tremulous motion for the ſpace of a quarter of an hour, and few of the buildings in the city were left ſtanding.

4. In 1722, on the 24th of May, great part of the houſes were damaged by another earthquake.

5. In the year 1730, on the 8th of July, happened that tremendous earthquake already mentioned in our account of Conception. This ſhock not only ruined the greateſt part of the city, but concuſſions were often felt for many months afterwards; and this cataſtrophe was ſucceeded by an epidemical diſtemper, which ſwept away even greater numbers than had before periſhed by the earthquake.

Notwithstanding the houſes are low, they make a handſome appearance, and are well contrived both for pleaſure and convenience.

Besides the cathedral and the pariſh church of the Sagrario, here are two others, namely, that of St. Anne, and St. Iſadoro. There are alſo three convents of St. Franciſco, San Diego, a college for ſtudents, and, without the city, a convent of recollects; two of Auguſtines, one of Dominicans, one of the fathers of mercy, one of St. Juan de Dios, and five colleges of Jeſuits, namely, St. Michael, the Noviciate, St. Paul, St. Xavier, a college for ſtudents, who wear a brown cloak, and a red ſcarf, and the college, called La

Olleria,

Olleria, for the exercifes of St. Ignatius. Here are alfo four nunneries, two of St. Clare, two of Auguftines, and one of Carmelites, and a religious fifterhood, under the rules of St. Auguftine. All which have a large number of reclufes, as is common in all the cities of Peru. The churches of the convents, befides being very fpacious, are built either of brick or ftone, and thofe of the Jefuits are diftinguifhed by the beauty of their architecture. The parifh churches are in every refpect greatly inferior to them.

The inhabitants of Santiago are computed at about four thoufand families, and of thefe nearly one half are Spaniards of all degrees; and among them fome very eminent both for rank and opulence. The other moiety confifts of Cafts and Indians, but chiefly of the latter.

The cuftoms here differ very little from thofe already mentioned in our account of large cities. They are not fo negligent in their care of their apparel as at Conception; and inftead of the oftentation of Lima, they follow the modeft decency of Quito. The men, except on fome particular ceremonies, generally wear ponchos, and all the families who can any way afford it, keep a calafh for driving about the city. The men are robuft, of a proper ftature, well-fhaped, and of a good air. The women have all the charms of thofe of Peru, and are rather more remarkable for the delicacy of their features, and the finenefs of their complections; but they disfigure their natural beauty by a mifplaced art, painting themfelves in fuch a prepofterous manner, as not only to fpoil the natural delicacy of their fkin, but even their teeth; fo that it is very rare to fee a woman here of any age with a good fet.

In this city is a royal audience, removed hither from Conception. It confifts of a prefident, four auditors, and a fifcal, together with another officer dignified with the indearing title of patron of the Indians.

Indians. The determinations of this court are without appeal except to the fupreme council of the Indies, and this only in matters of notorious injuftice, or denial of redrefs.

The prefident, tho' in fome particulars fubordinate to the vice-roy of Lima, is alfo governor and captain general of the whole kingdom of Chili; and, as fuch, he is to refide one half of the year at Conception, and the other at Santiago. During his abfence from the laft city, the corregidor acts as his reprefentative; and his jurifdiction, on this occafion, extends to all the other towns, except the military governments.

The magiftracy, at the head of which is the corregidor, confifts of regidores, and two ordinary alcaldes. In thefe are lodged the police, and civil government of the city; and during the time the prefident refides here, the jurifdiction of the corregidor is limited to the liberties of Santiago.

The office for the royal revenue, is directed by an accountant and treafurer; where are paid the tributes of the Indians, and other parts of the revenue; the falaries of officers within its department, and other affignments.

The chapter of the cathedral confifts of the bifhop, dean, archdeacon, chantor, four canons; and other fubordinate ecclefiaftics.

Here is alfo a tribunal of Croifade, the members of which are a fubdelegate commiffary, an accountant and treafurer. Likewife a commiffion of inquifition, all the officers of which are appointed by the tribunal of inquifition at Lima.

The temperature of the air at Santiago is nearly the fame with that of Conception. The luxuriancy of foil, and exuberance of all kinds of provifions, the commerce, and other neceffary particulars, I fhall mention in the following account of the kingdom of Chili.

## CHAP. VIII.

*Account of that part of* CHILI *within the jurisdiction of the audience of* SANTIAGO.

THE kingdom of Chili extends from the frontiers of Peru to the streights of Magellan, the distance being five hundred and thirty leagues. These two kingdoms, as I have mentioned in another place, are separated by the desart of Atacamo, which extends eighty leagues between the province of the same name, being the last of Peru, and the valley of Copoyapu, now corruptly called Copiapo, the first in Chili, and in every particular resembles the desart of Sectura. Eastward, some parts of this kingdom terminates on the frontiers of Paraguay, tho' some uninhabited desarts intervene; and others border on the government of Buenos Ayres. Tho' between these are the Pampas or extensive and level plains. Its western boundary is the south-sea, extending from 27 deg. nearly, the latitude of Copiapo, to 53° 30′ S. But to confine ourselves to the true extent of this kingdom, as inhabited by the Spaniards, it begins at Copiapo, and terminates at the large island of Chiloe, the southern extremity of which is in 34° of S. latitude; and its extent from W. to E. is the distance between the Cordillera, which is here of a stupendous height, and the coast of the south-sea; that is, about thirty leagues.

PART of the country which at present composes the kingdom of Chili, was subjected to the empire of the Yncas by Yupanqui, the tenth emperor; who, incited by the inchanting account given of these provinces, undertook the conquest of them; and prosecuted the enterprize with such success, that he subdued the several nations inhabiting the valleys of Copoyapu or Copiapo, Coquimpu, or Coquimbo, and
Chili.

Chili. But in his intended career southward, the victorious Ynca met with an unsurmountable difficulty from the Purumauco Indians, and other nations, whom the rapidity of his conquests had induced to oppose him by a general confederacy. Thus he found himself under a necessity of desisting, after having carried his arms as far as the river Mauli, which is in the latude of 34° 30′.

AFTER the Spaniards had undertaken a descent in Peru, and made themselves masters of its several provinces, the marshal Don Diego de Almagro, was commissioned for the conquest of Chili. Accordingly he marched from Cusco at the beginning of the year 1535, and after losing the greatest part of his Indians, and a considerable number of Spaniards, who perished with cold in passing over the cordillera nevada, he arrived at Copiapo, where the Indians, without trying the chance of war, submitted. Animated with such unexpected pusillanimity, he proceeded to the conquest of other nations; even such as never had acknowledged the Yncas. And tho' he here met with a more warlike people, who were determined to sell their liberty dear, he carried on the war prosperously. But his majesty, in consideration of his great services, performed with so much hazard, having conferred on him the government of a territory a hundred leagues in length, south of that which belonged to the marquis Don Francisco Pizarro, a difference arose between these two great men, with regard to the boundaries of their respective governments. Almagro, impatient to take possession, and pretending that the city of Cusco ought to be included in his government, the conquest was suspended, and he himself hastened to that city, where instead of being invested with the chief command, he fell a sacrifice to the jealousy of Hernando Pizarro, who endeavoured to conceal his irregular proceedings under the veil of juſtice.

In the year 1541, the conqueſt of Chili was again ſet on foot, and the marquis Pizarro conferred the command on Pedro de Valdivia, together with the title of general. Accordingly he marched into the country, and founded moſt of the principal towns, and villages in it. So that in the year 1548, he was promoted to the government of it, by the preſident of Peru. In the profecution of the conqueſt of theſe provinces, he had many ſharp ſkirmiſhes with the natives, till at laſt, in the year 1553, bravely oppoſing a general revolt, with a very inferior force, he fell fighting with the greateſt intrepidity at the head of his troops, the greateſt part of whom, enraged at loſing ſo brave a man, choſe to periſh with him rather than ſave themſelves by flight. His name, beſides the figure it makes in hiſtory, is ſtill preſerved in this country in the town of Valdivia, which he founded.

The martial genius of the Indians of this kingdom, conſiderably retarded the reduction of it; and has always been the chief cauſe why the Spaniſh ſettlements here, are ſo little proportional to the extent, fertility and riches of the country. Accordingly the captain-generalſhip of this vaſt kingdom has only four particular governments, and eleven juriſdictions; which are the following.

Particular governments in the kingdom of Chili.

I. The major-generalſhip of the kingdom of Chili.
II. Valparaiſo.
III. Valdivia.
IV. Chiloe.

Juriſdictions in the kingdom of Chili.
I. Santiago.
II. Rancagua,
III. Colchagua.
IV. Chillan.
V. Aconcagua.
VI. Melipilla.
VII. Quillota.
VIII. Coquimbo.

IX. Copiapo,

IX Copiapo, & Guafco.   X. Mendoza.
XI. La Conception.

I. To the majorgeneralfhip of the kingdom of Chili, belongs the military government of the frontier towns and fortreffes. Thefe are Arauco, the ftated refidence of the general, Santajuana, Puren, Los Angeles, Tucapel, and Yumbel. It will be here neceffary to obferve, that not above five leagues fouth of Conception bay, the fea receives a river called Biobio, both the fouth banks and head of which are inhabited by wild Indians: and to prevent their incurfions, ftrong forts have been erected along the banks, and are always well garrifoned and furnifhed with all kinds of military ftores. Among thefe on the fouth banks of the river is the fort of Arauco, and the others at a proper diftance eaftward to the mountain of Tucapel. Thus all attempts from thefe Indians is precluded, and the Spanifh fettlements protected from their depredations. The general is obliged to vifit thefe forts from time to time, carefully infpecting into their condition, and, in cafe of neceffity, to haften to their relief. During his abfence, the commanding officer of each is the captain of the garrifon, which ufually confifting both of horfe and foot with their officers, the perfon on whom the command devolves is previoufly nominated. This important poft is in the difpofal of the prefident, as fuppofed to be beft acquainted with the merits of the feveral competitors when a vacancy happens; and that the fafety of his government will induce him to prefer the moft deferving. Accordingly whoever intends to offer himfelf a candidate for this poft, fhould folicit to be employed in the frontier fervice, procure a competent knowledge of the ftratagems of the Indians, and be very attentive to diftinguifh himfelf on any alarm, or encounter. It is indeed expreffed in the royal commiffion, that the corregidor of Conception,

ception, shall be the military commander in chief; and, consequently, it is to him that the appointment of the general properly belongs; but this, from very powerful reasons, is dispensed with, the proper discharge of these two posts, being utterly incompatible; and the civil and military requisite here very rarely meeting in the same person. But when this obstacle does not exist, and the corregidor is one of these extraordinary persons, the president, agreeable to the royal expression, confers the post of Maestre de campo on the corregidor of la Conception.

II. VALPARAISO is the second military government. But the particular account of it, I shall reserve for a more proper place.

III. VALDIVIA has a military governor nominated by the king. Here is also a good body of troops, both for garrisoning the place, and the forts built to defend the entrance of the river and harbours in it. Close to the river stands the town, the inhabitants of which are chiefly whites or Mestizos; but a village forming a kind of suburb is inhabited by friendly Indians. This government has undergone some vicissitudes in point of subordination, being sometimes independent of the presidents of Chili, and immediately subject to the vice-roy of Lima; and at other times a part of the former. At last, on weighing the difficulties for providing for any sudden exigence, or having a watchful eye over its necessary concerns at so great a distance as Lima, it was annexed to the jurisdiction of the president of Chili, as being nearer at hand to see that the forces are always on a good footing, and constantly in a proper posture of defence.

IV. CHILOE has a military governor, who resides at Chacao, the principal harbour of the island, being well fortified and capable of making a good defence. Besides Chacas, which has the title of a city, is another place much larger, called Calbuco,

where

where refides a corregidor, who is nominated by the prefident of Chili. It has alfo regidores and alcaldes chofen annually. Befides the parifh church here is a convent of Francifcans, another of the fathers of mercy, and a college of Jefuits. The ifland is every where well peopled with Spaniards, Meftizos, and chriftian Indians.

The kingdom of Chili has continually a body of regular troops, confifting of five hundred men, for garrifoning Valparaifo, a fort at Conception, and thofe on the frontiers. One half of this body is infantry and the other cavalry. Under the major general who commands in chief is a ferjeant major, whofe duty it is to render them expert in all the various parts of military exercife; and that he may more conveniently render them ready at their feveral evolutions, he refides at the fort of Jumbal, which lies in the center of the others. To thefe alfo belong a commiffary general of the horfe, whofe poft is at Arauco, and in the abfence of the general has the command. Thefe troops have alfo a mufter-mafter general, who refides at Conception. The ftanding forces of Chili, till the beginning of this century, confifted of two thoufand men; but the great charge of fupporting fuch a body of troops, occafioned them to be reduced to the prefent number.

The produce of the revenue offices at Santiago and Conception, not being fufficient to defray the expences of even this fmall body, a remittance of 100,000 dollars, is every year fent from Lima, half in fpecie, and half in cloaths, and other goods. But fix or eight thoufand is annually deducted out of this fum for repairing the forts of the frontiers, and making prefents to the deputies of the Indians who attend at conferences, or to fatisfy thofe who complain to the prefident of injuries received.

Valdivia alfo receives from the treafury of Lima, an annual fupply of 70,000 dollars, 30,000 in fpecie, the value of thirty thoufand in clothes for the foldiers, and 10,000 in fpecie, which is paid to the king's officers at Santiago, in order to purchafe flour, charqui, graffa, and other neceffaries for the garrifon at Valdivia. Thefe remittances are conveyed in fhips which fail from Valparaifo.

I. THE jurifdiction of Santiago we have already obferved to be limited to its boundaries.

II. RANCAGUA is a jurifdiction in the country, and owes its name from the inhabitants living in fingle houfes, without the appearance of a village, every family in their lonely cottage four, fix or more leagues from each other. It is not, however, without a kind of capital, confifting of about fifty houfes, and between fifty and fixty families, moft of them Meftizos, tho' their cafts is not at all perceivable by their complection. The whole jurifdiction may contain about a thoufand families, Spaniards, Meftizos, and Indians.

III. COLCHAGUA refembles in every circumftance the former, except its being better peopled; its inhahabitants according to the beft computations, amounting to fifteen hundred families.

IV. CHILLAN is a fmall place, but has the title of city, the number of families, by an accurate calculation not exceeding two or three hundred, and having few Spaniards among them.

V. ACONCAGUA is a very fmall place at the foot of the mountains, but the country is interfperfed with a great number of fingle houfes. The valley of the fame name is fo delightful, that a town called Phelipe le Real, was built in it in 1741.

VI. MELIPILLA made no better figure than the foregoing jurifdictions, till the year 1742, when a town was erected in it by the name of St. Jofeph de Longronno.

VII QUILLOTA. The town of this name does not
contain

contain above a hundred families; but thofe fcattered over the country exceed a thoufand.

VIII. Coquimbo, or la Serena, according to father Fevillee, ftands in 24° 54' 10" fouth latitude. This was the fecond town built in the kingdom of Chili, in 1544, by Pedro de Valdivia, with a view of fecuring the intercourfe between Peru and Chili, for the more convenient fupply of what fuccours might be wanted; and at the fame time, for fecuring the fidelity of the Indians who lived in that valley. This place is fituated in the valley of Cuquimpo, from whence it received its original name; but Valdivia gave it that of la Serena, from an affection to the province of that name in Spain, and of which he was a native. It ftands about a quarter of a league from the coaft of the fouth-fea in a moft delightful fituation, having an extenfive profpect of the fea, the river, and the country, which prefents the fight with a charming variety of fields of different kinds of grain, and woods of a lively verdure.

This town is of itfelf large, but not proportionally peopled; the number of families not amounting to above four or five hundred, confifting of Spaniards, Meftizos, and a few Indians. The ftreets are ftrait and of a convenient breadth, fome of which lying N. and S. and others interfecting from E. to W. the town confifts of fquares of buildings, like Santiago, and other places of note in this part of America. The houfes are all of mud walls, and covered with leaves; but none are without a large garden, well planted with fruit trees and efculent vegetables, both thofe of America and Spain; for the climate is happily adapted to a variety of both kinds, the heats not being exceffive, nor the cold fevere; fo that both in the fertility of the earth, and the chearful appearance of the country, the whole year wears an afpect of one perpetual fpring. The ftreets, though regular and convenient as abovementioned, are not entirely formed

by

by the houses, parts of the intervals between the several squares being filled up with gardens; and most of them have so charming an appearance, as to attone for the mean aspect of the houses.

Besides parish churches, here is a Francifcan, a Dominican, and an Auguftine convent; one belonging to the fathers of mercy, another to St. Juan de Dios; and a college of Jefuits. The churches of thefe religious fraternities are large and decent. The parish church occupies part of one fide of the great fquare; and oppofite is the town-house, where the alcaldes and regidores meet, who with the corregidor form the corporation.

On the N. fide of Coquimbo runs the river, after flowing in various meanders thro' the whole valley of the fame name; and by canals cut from it, furnifhes the town with water, one great ufe of which is to preferve the beauty of their gardens.

IX. Copiapo is about twelve leagues from the fea-coaft, very irregularly built, but contains between three and four hundred families. The fea-port neareft to it is that known by the fame name. There is indeed another port in this jurifdiction; but it lies thirty leagues farther to the S. and confifts only of a few huts.

X. Mendosa. The town of this name is fituated on the eaftern fide of the cordillera, at the diftance of about fifty leagues from Santiago. It ftands on a plain, and is decorated with gardens in the fame manner as Coquimbo, and the place being well fupplied with water by means of canals, no care is wanting to keep them in their greateft beauty. The town confifts of about an hundred families, half Spaniards or whites, and the other half cafts. It has befides a decent parifh church, a Francifcan, Dominican and Auguftine convent, together with a college of Jefuits. This jurifdiction has alfo two other towns, that of St. Juan de la Frontera, likewife

wife to the eastward of the cordillera, and about thirty leagues N. of Mendoza, and St. Luis de Loyola, about fifty leagues eastward of Mendoza. The latter however is mean and small, not containing above twenty five houses, and fifty or sixty families, Spanish and casts; tho' many more are scattered up and down the neighbouring country. In such a small place it is something remarkable to see a parish church, a dominican convent, and a college of Jesuits. Here the presidents of Chili are received as governors of it, in their way to Chili from Buenos Ayres, this being the first place in their government on that side. The town of St. Juan de la Frontera is, in every respect equal to Mendoza itself.

XI. The jurisdiction of Conception is the last; but having already given an account of it, I shall proceed to consider the commerce carried on by the kingdom of Chili with Peru, Buenos Ayres, Paraguay, and its own towns; and subjoin an account of that carried on with the wild Indians bordering on it, with the manner of maintaining a harmony with these savage people. In the mean time I shall conclude this chapter with observing, that the corregidors of the whole jurisdiction are nominated by the king, except those of Rancagua, Melepilla, and Quillota, who are appointed by the president of Chili. This is indeed the case of all the others, when a corregidor happens to die, before a person is nominated to succeed him; but the office of these corregidors being only for five years, the prolongation must be by his majesty's express order. The inhabitants are formed into companies of militia, and every one knows the place of arms to which he is to repair on any alarm. Thus to Valparaiso belongs the companies of militia of Santiago, Quillota, Melipilla, Aconcagua, and Rancagua; and these in all amount to between two or three thousand men, and are formed into troops and companies.

nies. Rancagua, when Santiago and Colchagua are threatned, is alſo to ſend ſuccours thither; and the ſame duty lies on Chillan with regard to Conception. In theſe caſes notice is conveyed with ſuch diſpatch, that they are ſpeedily at their rendezvous, all they have to do, being to mount their horſes and repair to their ſtation with the uſual pace uſed in that country, which is always a gallop; and thus the militia of this country may be ſaid to ride poſt to the parts where danger calls them.

## CHAP. IX.
*Commerce of* CHILI. *Methods uſed to keep up a good Harmony with the wild Indians.*

IN my deſcription of the city of Conception, I mentioned the inchanting beauties of the neighbouring countries; and the exuberant returns of nature for the huſbandman's toil. The like profuſion of natural productions is ſeen all over this kingdom. Its plains, eminences, valleys, in ſhort the whole country to the ſmalleſt portion of ground is an object of admiration. Every particle of earth, in this amazing fertility, ſeems transformed in feed. The country round Santiago, as it is not inferior in pleaſantneſs and fertility to that of Conception; ſo alſo from the great affinity to the climates, its products are nearly the ſame. Accordingly ſome farmers wholly apply themſelves to corn, others to fattening of cattle; ſome confine themſelves to the breeding of horſes, and others to the culture of vines and fruit trees. The firſt find their account in plentiful harveſts of wheat, barley, and particularly in hemp, which thrives here ſurprizingly, and ſurpaſſes thoſe of the former. The ſecond at their large ſlaughters, have great quantities of tallow, graſſa, charqui, and

ſole

sole leather tanned. Of the goat skins is made Cordovan leather; some tallow is also procured from those creatures. Wines are made here of several sorts, and tho' not so excellent as those of Conception, they are very palatable and of a good body; brandy is also distilled from them. These are the principal articles of the active commerce of this kingdom with Peru, which it supplies with wheat, tallow, and cordage; and by the most careful estimate, the quantity of wheat sent annually from Santiago to Callao, amounts to 140,000 Tanegas, each weighing one hundred and fifty six pounds; about eight thousand quintals of cordage; and between sixteen and twenty thousand quintals of tallow: besides sole leather, nuts, filberts, figs, pears, and apples; Grassa, Charqui, and neat tongues: the three last being no inconsiderable articles.

The more northern parts of the kingdom, as Coquimbo, produce olives, the oil of which is preferable to that of many parts of Peru; but being a natural commodity of that kingdom, and consequently, not an article of exportation, is consumed at home. The country about Santiago, likewise, produces good olives; but in no great quantity, the genius of the inhabitants having not hitherto led them to make large plantations of those trees.

Besides the commerce carried on with Peru in provisions, there is that of metals, this kingdom abounding in mines of all kinds, but principally of gold and copper, which we shall briefly consider.

The most famous gold mine known in Chili, is called Petorca, and lies in a country E. of Santiago. This gold was formerly highly esteemed, and found in great plenty; but now on account of a whitish tinge, the value of it is considerably diminished. This mine for the length of time it has been worked, is equal to the most celebrated in Peru.

In the country of Yapel, which is situated in the same

same quarter, but farther to the northward along the cordillera, are also rich gold mines; and the metal twenty-three carats fine. In 1710, in the mountains of Lumpanqui near the cordillera, were difcovered mines of gold, filver, copper, lead, tin, and iron, the gold between twenty one and twenty two carats fine; but the working from the hardnefs of the ftone, where, according to the miner's phrafe, " the metal arms," was very difficult and laborious. This inconvenience does not however occur in the mountain Llaoin, where the ftone is foft, and not lefs rich in metal, equal in finenefs to the former. Befides thefe there are other gold mines, worked with good fuccefs at Tiltil, near Santiago.

BETWIXT Quillota and Valparaifo, in a part called Ligua, is a very rich gold mine, and the metal greatly efteemed. Coquimbo, Capiapo, and Guafco, have alfo gold mines, and the metal found in the two laft, is, by way of pre-eminence, called Oro Capote, being the moft valuable of any yet difcovered. Another kind of mines of the fame metal has alfo been found in this kingdom; but thefe were exhaufted almoft as foon as they were opened. Mines of this kind are very common, as well as another kind called Lavaderos *, moft of which are between Valparaifo and Las Pennuelas, and about a league from the former. Some of them are alfo found at Yapel, on the frontiers of the wild Indians, and near Conception. Thefe, together with the others known in this kingdom, yield gold duft. Sometimes indeed lumps of gold of confiderable magnitude are found; and the hopes of difcovering thefe animate many to work the mines.

* Thefe Lavaderos are pits dug in the angles of ravins or trenches made by rain, and in which it is imagined there may be gold; and in order to difcover the metal, a ftream of water is turned through it, and the earth briskly fpread, that the gold may be carried down with the current, and depofited in the pits.

ALL

CH. XI.    SOUTH AMERICA.    271

ALL the gold thus collected in Chili is bought up in the country, and sent to Lima to be coined, there being no mint in Chili; and by the accounts constantly taken, it amounts one year with another to six hundred thousand dollars; but that clandestinely sent by way of the cordillera is said to be nearly four hundred thousand. Consequently the whole must be at least a million. In the countries of Coquimbo and Guasco mines of all kinds of metals are so very common, that the whole earth seems wholly composed of minerals; and it is here those of copper are worked, and from them all Peru and the kingdom of Chili are furnished with that metal. But though this copper exceeds every thing of the kind hitherto known, the mines are worked with great caution, and no more metal extracted than is sufficient to answer the usual demand; and other mines, though known to be equally rich, are left untouched.

IN exchange for the grain, fruits, provisions, and metals, which Chili sends to Peru, it receives iron, cloth, and linen made at Quito, hats, bays, though not many of the latter, there being manufactures of the same kind in Chili, sugar, cacao, sweetmeats, pickles, tobacco, oil, earthen ware, and all kinds of European goods. A small commerce is also carried on between the kingdom of Chili, Paraguay and Buenos Ayres, of which the latter is the staple. The products of Paraguay, which indeed consist only in its herb and wax, are carried thither, then forwarded to Chili, whence the herb is exported to Peru. Large quantities of tallow are also sent to Mendoza for making of soap. In exchange for these commodities Chili sends to Buenos Ayres linen and woollen stuffs, some of which are imported from Peru, and others manufactured in the country: also Ponchos, sugar, snuff, wine and brandy, the two last the traders chiefly buy at San Juan, as most

con-

convenient for tranfportation. During the affiento for negroes, they are ufually brought to Chili from the factory at Buenos Ayres, the way of Peru being attended with great inconveniences; as in their journey from Panama, they take an opportunity of concealing themfelves among the farm-houfes; fo that what with the great expence, and the numbers who die during their long rout, by the variety of climates, their purchafe muft confequently be very high.

THE home commerce of Chili, or that carried on within itfelf, chiefly confifts in the provifions fent to Valdivia to the amount of ten thoufand dollars, which as the deducted part of its remittance are fent from Lima to Santiago for that purpofe. Valdivia furnifhes the reft of the places with cedar. Chiloe purchafe from the other parts brandy, wine, honey, fugar, the Paraguay herb, falt and Guinea-pepper; and returns to Valparaifo and Conception, feveral kinds of fine wood, in which the ifland abounds; alfo woollen ftuffs of the country manufacture, made into ponchos, cloaks, quilts, and the like; together with hams, which from the particular delicacy of the flavour are in great requeft even in Peru, and dried pilchards, the bay and coaft of that ifland being the only places in the fouth-fea where the fifh are caught.

COQUIMBO fends copper to Valparaifo; for tho' all parts of the Cordillera, towards Santiago and Conception, abound in mines of that metal, and particularly a place called Payen, where feveral were formerly worked, and where maffes of fifty or a hundred quintals of pure copper have been found, yet as thefe mines are now no longer worked, the whole country is under a neceffity of receiving their copper from the Coquimbo and Guafco mines; fending thither in exchange cordovan leather and foap, made at Mendoza, from whence it is carried to Santiago, and thence fold to different parts of the kingdom.

HAVING thus confidered the trade of Chili in both
par-

particulars, I shall next proceed to mention that carried on with the wild Indians, and this consists in selling them hard ware, as bits, spurs, and edge tools; also toys, and some wine. All this is done by barter; for though the countries they inhabit are not destitute of gold, the Indians cannot be prevailed upon to open the mines; so that the returns consist in Ponchos, horned cattle, horses of their own breeding, and Indian children of both sexes, which are sold even by their own parents for such trifles; and this particular kind of traffick, they call rescatar, ransoming. But no Spaniard of any character will be concerned in such barbarous exchanges, being carried on only by the Guasos, and the meanest class of Spaniards settled in Chili. These boldly venture into the parts inhabited by the Indians, and address themselves to the heads of the several families.

The Indians of Arauco, and those parts, are not governed by Caciques, or Curacas, like those of Peru, the only subordination known among them being with regard to age, so that the oldest person of the family is respected as its governor. The Spaniard begins his negociation with offering the chief of the family a cup of his wine. After this he displays his wares, that the Indian may make choice of what best pleases him; mentioning at the same time the return he expects. If they agree, the Spaniard makes him a present of a little wine; and the Indian chief informs the community that they are at liberty to trade with that Spaniard as his friend. Relying on this protection, the Spaniard goes from hut to hut, recommending himself at first by giving the head of every family a taste of his wine. After this they enter upon business, and the Indian having taken what he wanted, the trader goes away without receiving any equivalent at that time, and visits the other huts, as they lie dispersed all over the country, till he has disposed of his stock. He then returns to the cottage of the chief, calling on his cuftomers in his way, and acquainting them that he is on his return home. Upon this fummons, not one fails of bringing him to the chief's hut, what had been agreed on. Here they take their leave of him, with all the appearance of a fincere friendfhip, and the chief even orders fome Indians to efcort him to the frontiers, and affift him in driving the cattle he has received in exchange for his goods.

FORMERLY, and even till the year 1724, thefe traders carried large quantities of wine, of which, as well as of all other inebriating liquors, the Indians are immoderately fond; but on account of the tumults and wars that arofe from the intemperate ufe of fpirituous liquors, this branch of trade has been fuppreffed, and no more wine allowed to be carried into the Indian territories, than what fhall be judged neceffary to give the mafters of families a cup by way of compliment, and a very fmall quantity for trading. The happy effects of this prohibition are felt on both fides; the Spaniards live in fafety, and the Indians in peace and tranquility. They are very fair dealers, never receding from what has been agreed on, and punctual in their payments. It is indeed furprizing that a whole people, who are almoft ftrangers to government, and favage in their manners, fhould, amidft the uncontrouled gratification of the moft enormous vices, have fo delicate a fenfe of juftice, as to obferve it in the moft irreproachable manner in their dealings.

ALL the Indians of Arauco, Tucapel, and others inhabiting the more fouthern parts of the banks of the river Biobio, and alfo thofe who live near the cordillera, have hitherto fruftrated all attempts made for reducing them under the Spanifh government. For in this boundlefs country, as it may be called, when ftrongly pufhed, they abandon their huts, and retire into the more diftant parts of the kingdom, where

being

being joined by other nations, they return in such numbers, that all resistance would be temerity, and again take possession of their former habitations. Thus Chili has always been exposed to their insults; and if a very few only call for a war against the Spaniards, the flame immediately spreads, and their measures are taken with such secrecy, that the first declaration of it is, the murder of those who happen to be among them, and the ravages of the neighbouring villages. Their first step, when a war is agreed on, is, to give notice to the nations for assembling; and this they call Correa la Fletcha, to shoot the dart, the summons being sent from village to village, with the utmost silence and rapidity. In these notices they specify the night when the irruption is to be made, and tho' advice of it is sent to the Indians who reside in the Spanish territories, nothing transpires: nor is there a single instance, among all the Indians that have been taken up on suspicion, that one ever made any discovery. And as no great armaments are necessary in this kind of war, their designs continue impenetrable till the terrible executions withdraw the veil.

The Indians of the several nations being assembled, a general is chosen, with the title of Toqui; and when the nights fixed on for executing their designs arrives, the Indians who live among the Spaniards, rise and massacre them. After which they divide themselves into small parties, and destroy the seats, farm-houses and villages, murdering all without the least regard to youth or age. These parties afterwards unite, and in a body attack the larger settlements of the Spaniards, besiege the forts, and commit every kind of hostility; and their vast numbers, rather than any discipline, have enabled them, on several occasions, to carry on their enterprizes with success, notwithstanding all the measures taken by the Spanish governors to prevent them. For tho' multitudes of them fall on these occasions, their army continually receives larger reinforcements. If at any time the Spaniards gain the superiority, the Indians retire to the distance of several leagues, where after concealing themselves a few days, they suddenly fall on a different part from that where they were encamped, endavouring to carry the place by a sudden assault, unless the commandant's vigilance has provided against any sudden surprize; when, by the advantage of the Spanish discipline, they are generally repulsed with great slaughter.

These Indian wars against the Spaniards usually continue some years, being of little detriment to the Indians; for most of their occupations which consist in the culture of a small spot of ground, and weaving ponchos and cloaks for apparel, are carried on by the women. Their huts are built in a day or two, and their food consists of roots, maize, and other grain. War therefore, is no impediment or loss to them; indeed they rather consider it as a desirable occupation, their hours at other times being spent in idleness, or carousals, in which they drink chicha, a liquor common among them, and made from apples.

The first advances towards a treaty of peace with these Indians are generally made by the Spaniards; and as soon as the proposals are agreed to, a congress is held, at which the governor, major-general of Chili, and the principal officers, the bishop of Conception, and other persons of eminence assist. On the part of the Indians the toqui, or generalissimo, and the captains of his army, as representatives of the communities, repair to the congress. The last inroad made by these savage enemies, was in the year 1720, during the government of Don Gabriel Cano, lieutenant general of his majesty's forces, who managed the war against them with such vigour and address; that they were obliged to solicit a peace; and their preliminaries were so submissive, that at a congress held in 1724, the peace was concluded, whereby they were left in possession of all the country south of the river Biobio;

and

and the Capitanes de Paz were suppressed. These were Spaniards residing in the villages of the converted Indians, and by their exactions had been the principal cause of the revolt.

Besides the congresses held with these Indians, for concluding a treaty of peace, others are held on the arrival of a new president, and the same ceremonies observed in both; so that an account of the one will be sufficient to give a just idea of the other.

On the holding a congress, the president sends notice to the frontier Indians of the day and place, whither he repairs with the abovementioned persons; and on the part of the Indians, the heads of their several communities; and both, for the greater splendor of the interview, are accompanied by an escort consisting of a certain number previously agreed on. The president and his company lodge in tents, and the Indians incamp at a small distance. The elders or chiefs of the neighbouring nations pay the first visit to the president, who receives them very courteously, drinks their healths in wine, and himself gives them the glass to do the like. This politeness, with which they are highly pleased, is succeeded by a present of knives, scissars, and different sorts of toys, on which they place the greatest value. The treaty of peace is then brought on the carpet, and the manner of observing the several articles is settled: after which they return to their camp, and the president returns the visit, carrying with him a quantity of wine sufficient for a moderate regale.

Now all the chiefs of the other communities, who were not present at the first visit, go in a body to pay their respects to the president. At the rising of the congress, the president makes each a small present of wine, which the Indians liberally return in calves, oxen, horses, and fowls. After these reciprocal tokens of friendship, both parties return to their respective habitations.

In order to gain more effectually the hearts of these Indians, who, tho' in our esteem wretchedly poor, conceal the most stubborn pride, which can only be softened by compliments and favours, it is a maxim with the presidents to admit to their table those who are apparently of the best dispositions, and during the three or four days of the congress, neglects no means of ingratiating himself with the whole body. On these occasions a kind of fair is held at both camps, great numbers of Spaniards repairing thither with such goods as they know will please the Indians, who also come with their ponchos and cattle. Both parties deal by exchange, and never fail of selling their whole stocks; and of observing in their dealings the most exact candour and regularity, as a specimen in which all future commerce is to be conducted.

Tho' these Indians have shewn such a determined aversion to submitting to the Spanish monarchs, their behaviour has been very different to the missionaries, whom they voluntarily permitted to come among them; and many have even shewed the greatest joy at being baptized. But it is extreanly difficult to prevail on them to quit their free manner of living; which being productive of vice and savageness, prepossess the mind against the precepts of the christian religion. Before the war of the year 1723, the missionaries, by their indefatigable zeal, had formed several villages, hoping by that means to induce their converts to practise the doctrines of the christian faith. These villages were called St. Christover, Santo Fè, Santa Juana, St. Pedro, and La Mocha, all of them being under the inspection of the Jesuits. The chaplains also of the forts on the frontiers had an additional salary for instructing a certain number of Indians. But on that general insurrection, their innate savageness returned, all these converts abandoned the missionaries and joined their countrymen. On the re-establishment of the peace, they again follicited

the

the missionaries to come among them; and some communities have been since formed; but they are far short of their former promising state, it being very difficult to bring even this small number to embrace a social life.

AMIDST all the sanguinary rage of these Indians in their hostilities against the Spaniards, they generally spare the white women, carrying them to their huts, and using them as their own. And hence it is, that many Indians of those nations have the complexions of the Spaniards born in that country. In time of peace many of them come into the Spanish territories, hiring themselves for a certain time to work at the farm houses, and at the expiration of the term return home, after laying out their wages in the purchase of such goods as are valued in their country. All of them, both men and women, wear the poncho and manta, which they weave of wool, and tho' it cannot properly be called a dress, is abundantly sufficient for decency; whereas the Indians at a greater distance from the Spanish frontiers, as those who inhabit the countries south of Valdivia, and the Chonos, who live on the continent near Chiloe, use no sort of apparel. The Indians of Arauco, Tucapel and other tribes near the river Biobio, take great delight in riding, and their armies have some bodies of horse. Their weapons are large spears, javelins, &c. in the use of which they are very dextrous.

---

CHAP. X.

*Voyage from* CONCEPTION *to the Island of* JUAN FERNANDES; *and from thence to* VALPARAISO.

THE ships being come to an anchor in the port of Talcaguano, we waited on Don Pedro de Mendinueta, at the city of Conception, who informed us us that the commodore Don Jofeph Pizarro, together with the land and fea officers, were arrived at Santiago, and that he intended to fet out for Valparaifo, in order to hoift his flag on board the Efperanza, and take upon him the command of that fquadron. On receiving this intelligence, and having no orders to continue at Conception, we put to fea on the fixth of February, and fteering for the place of our deftination, made, on the 20th, the ifland de Tierra de Juan Fernandes, and at half an hour after ten, as we were plying to windward along the coaft, and ftanding towards the ifland which then bore two leagues weft from us, we faw on the top of one of the mountains a bright light, which furprized us the more, as on the following day we faw no traces of any fhip's being in the port fince we left it. I had a clear view of it from the inftant it began, and obferved that at firft it was very fmall, and increafed, fo as to form a flame like that of a flambeau. The full vigour of its light lafted about three or four minutes, when it diminifhed in the fame gradual manner it had increafed. It did not appear again all the next night, nor had we during the whole time we were at an anchor in the port, any view of fuch a phænomenon. We fent fome of our people on fhore to examine all the mountains, and other parts of the ifland, and they fpent feveral nights on that and the adjacent mountains, but could not difcover the leaft veftige of any fire. As I knew the ifland to be abfolutely deftitute, the fanguine colour of the flame, inclined me to think there might be fome volcano; but having never feen any thing of that kind before, nor heard from others that there was ever any eruption, I was far from being tenacious of my opinion. We had indeed all our conjectures; but the difficulty was not cleared up till my fifth and laft voyage to this ifland, when Don Jofeph Pizarro, fent fome people on fhore to take an accurate furvey of this place, and the ground was found to be burnt, full of fiffures and hot, which verified my firſt opinion of a volcano.

On the 21ſt after coaſting along this iſland, we continued our courſe for Valparaiſo. where our little ſquadron came to an anchor on the 24th, and were the more pleaſed as we found there the preſident of Santiago, Don Joſeph Manſo, and our commodore; and in the harbour, beſides the Callao fleet, three French ſhips, called the Louis Eraſme, Notre Dame de la Delivrance, and the Lys, which had been freighted by four merchants as regiſter ſhips; and Valparaiſo was the firſt port they had touched at, for vending their cargoes.

From ſeveral obſervations made in this harbour by Don George Juan, in the laſt voyage of 1744, its latitude appears to be 33° 02′ 36″ 30‴ and father Fevillee ſettled its longitude at 304° 11′ 45″ from the meridian of Teneriff. This town was at firſt very mean, conſiſting only of a few warehouſes built by the inhabitants of Santiago for laying up their goods till ſhipped off for Callao, the harbour of Valparaiſo being the neareſt port to that city, from which it is only twenty leagues diſtant, tho' the natives will have it to be more. The only inhabitants at that time were the few ſervants left by their reſpective maſters for taking care of the warehouſes, and managing their mercantile affairs. But in proceſs of time, the merchants themſelves, together with ſeveral other families, removed from Santiago, in order to be more conveniently ſituated for trade; ſince which it has gradually increaſed, ſo that at preſent it is both large and populous; and would be ſtill larger were it not for its inconvenient ſituation, ſtanding ſo near the foot of a mountain, that a great part of the houſes are built on its acclivity, or in its breaches. The broadeſt and moſt convenient part is that along the coaſt; but this is very unpleaſant in winter, being ſo expoſed to the N. winds, that the waves beat againſt the walls of the houſes,

houſes, ſome of which are built of unburnt bricks, ſome of chalk and pebbles, and others of bajareques.

VALPARAISO, beſides its pariſh church, has a convent of Franciſcans, and another of Auguſtines; but very few religious, and the churches belonging to them ſmall and mean. It is inhabited by families of Spaniards, and Caſts, both Mulattoes, and Meſtizos. In its neighbourhood are ſeveral villages, and the great number of farm houſes give the country a chearful appearance. Here is a military governor nominated by the king, who having the command of the garriſons in the ſeveral ports, and of the militia of the place and its dependences, is to take care that they are properly diſciplined.

THE proximity of this port to Santiago has drawn hither all the commerce formerly carried on at that city. To this it owes its foundation, increaſe, and preſent proſperity. At preſent all the Callao ſhips which carry on the commerce between the two kingdoms come hither. The cargoes they bring are indeed but ſmall, conſiſting only of the goods already mentioned, as not produced in Chili. But in this port they take in wheat, tallow, cordovan leather, cordage, and dried fruits, and with theſe return to Callao; and a ſhip has been known to make three voyages in one ſummer, namely, between November and June, during which interval, the droves of mules and carriages from all the farm houſes in the juriſdiction of Santiago, bring freſh ſupplies to the warehouſes, that trade is carried on both by land and ſea. The maſters of ſhips, who generally reſide at Lima or Callao, enter into partnerſhip with the landed gentlemen of Chili, that the cargo of every ſhip generally belongs in part to the maſter; tho' ſome ſhips are freighted, and if the loading be wheat, greatly augments its value; for the fanega coſts here only ten or twelve rials, or two dollars, and the freight is from twelve rials to two piaſters. Another circumſtance which raiſes

the

the price of wheat at Callao, where it is fold for twenty-four or thirty rials is, that the fanega is there only five arobas, and five pounds, whereas at Chili the fanega is fix arobas and fix pounds.

This commerce being carried on only in fummer, that feafon may be termed the fair of Valparaifo; but on the approach of winter the place becomes as remarkably defolate, the crowd of traders repairing to Santiago, thofe only continuing at Valparaifo, who cannot afford to remove.

Valparaiso is abundantly fupplied with provifions from Santiago, and other places in its neighbourhood; but fhips do not victual here fo cheap as at Conception. The fruits cannot be viewed without admiration, both with regard to their beauty and fize, particularly a fort of apples called Quillota, being brought from that place; they prodigioufly exceed the largeft in Spain, and befides their exquifite flavour, are fo lufcious that they melt in the mouth.

Among the feveral kinds of game, there is here fuch a plenty of partridges in their feafon, which begins at March and lafts feveral fucceeding months, that the Santiago muliteers knock them down with fticks without going out of the road, and bring great numbers of them to Valparaifo. But few of thefe or any other birds are feen near the town. It is the fame with regard to fifh, very little being to be caught either in the harbour or along the coaft, in comparifon of what may be taken in the other parts.

The coaft of Valparaifo forms a bay, lying N. E. and S. W. three leagues in length, and having two capes called Concon, and Valparaifo. In the S. W. part of this bay is the harbour, of a convenient fize, and running above a league farther up the country. The bottom is a firm tenacious mud. At the diftance of a cable's length and a half from the fhore, is from fourteen to fixteen fathom water, which increafes in depth proportional to the diftance, that at the diftance of half a league there is thirty-fix or forty fathom. The harbour is every where free from rocks and shoals, except to the N. E. of the breach de los Angeles, where, about a cable's length or two from the land is a rock, which muft be the more carefully avoided, as it never appears above water, but fometimes has not a depth fufficient for a fhip of any burden to pafs over it. The courfe into this harbour is to keep near the point of Valparaifo, within a quarter of a league from the fhore, where there is twenty, eighteen, and fixteen fathom water. After getting round the point you muft ftand nearer to the fhore, in order to avoid a bank, which lies thereabouts. Not, that it can be attended with any danger, for the fide of it is fo bold, that if the fhip fhould touch it little damage could enfue. This bank is always above water, and there is a neceffity for paffing fo near it, in order to keep to windward, as otherwife it would be difficult to fetch the harbour. Regard muft alfo be had to the time proper for entering the port of Valparaifo ; for it is by no means proper to attempt it in the morning, as the wind tho' blowing frefh without does not then extend fo far into the bay, and thus the fhip, by having very little way, and, confequently not anfwering her helm, might drive upon the bank; and to let go your anchor in fifty fathom water, which is the depth clofe to the fand, will be very inconvenient. The common method therefore is, to keep in the offing till about noon, or fomething after, when the wind ufually continues to the bottom of the harbour; and then by obferving the abovementioned rules, the fhip will fall into her ftation without any difficulty. Or you may run into the bay and there come to an anchor, till the day following, and then weigh early and go in with the land breeze, here called Concon, as blowing from that point ; and this breeze may be depended on every day at a certain hour, except dur-

ing

ing the time of the N. winds, which caufe fome alteration in it.

The fafeft method of mooring fhips is lying one anchor on the fhore towards the S. S. W. and another in the channel towards the N. N. W. The former muft be well fecured, as the refource againft the S. and S. W. winds; for though they come over the land, they are often fo violent, and the fhore of the harbour fo floping, that the fhips would otherwife drive.

As foon as the north winds fet in, which happens in the month of April and May, the veffels in the harbour are expofed to their whole violence, which alfo caufes a very high fea. In this exigence, the whole fecurity of the fhips depends on the anchor and cable towards the N. N. E. it will therefore be very proper to lay another in the fame direction; for if it fhould give way, it would be impoffible to hinder the fhip from ftriking on the rocks near the fhore. The only favourable circumftance here is, that the bottom being very firm, and rifing towards the fhore, the anchor has good hold; and confequently the whole depends on the ftrength of the cable.

## CHAP. XI.

*Voyage from* VALPARAISO *to* CALLAO; *fecond return to* QUITO *to finifh the obfervations; third Journey to* LIMA, *in order to return to* SPAIN *by the way of* CAPE HORN.

THE fervice our fquadron was employed on, being that of cruifing in thofe feas, in queft of the enemy as long as it fhould be thought requifite, the commodore, without ftaying any longer than was abfolutely neceffary, came on board, and we immediately

diately put to fea, and feveral times vifited the iflands of Juan Fernandes, till the 24th of June, 1743, when we fhaped our courfe for Callao, which port we entered on the 6th of July. The day following the commodore and principal officers went on fhore, and were received by Don Jofeph de Llamas, general of the forces in Peru, and governor of Callao; who, on account of the firft employment, refides at Lima, but was come to Callao to compliment the commodore. He attended him to Lima, and introduced him to the vice-roy, who expreffed his great fatisfaction at his fafe arrival after fuch long expectations. He was alfo met on the road by the principal perfons of the city.

AFTER taking our departure from the ifland de Tierra de Juan Fernandes, we fteered the three firft days N. N. E. and N. E. one quarter northerly, having frefh gales at W. and a heavy fea from the S. W. When we came into the latitude of 28°, 30' we fteered N. fix or feven degrees eafterly, till the third day at nine in the morning, when being in the latitude of 16°, 28', we made the land on the coaft of Chala; and the day following, being the 4th, the ifland of Sangallan, which at noon bore E. N. E. diftance fix leagues. We then coafted along the fhore; and on the 5th at noon we faw the ifle of Afia, bearing E. N. E. fix leagues diftant; and on the 6th as before mentioned, the fquadron came to an anchor at half an hour after one in the afternoon, in Callao harbour.

HENCE it appears, that till we were in the latitude of 28°, 30', the wind was at S. W. which agrees with my obfervations mentioned Chap. III. relating to this fea; and if no other circumftance concurred to verify them, it muft be imputed to the feafon of the year, it being the beginning of winter when we returned to Callao. But as during the firft three days, the ftrength of the wind had driven us near the coaft; fo from the latitude we found it farther to the

fouth;

south; between 25 and 21, began to incline towards the S. E. and from the latitude of 20°, when we found ourselves near the land, till our arrival at Callao, we had the wind S. S. E. and E. S. E. It was the same with regard to the sea coming from the S. W. for it gradually diminished as we approached the coast: so that from 25 it was not at all troublesome, and after we were passed 21° became imperceptible. But it was very different with regard to the current, which from the parallel of 20 or 21°, we perceived to set towards the N. W. parallel to the direction of the coast, and became much more sensible after we had sight of the land, its velocity increasing, as latitude decreased.

I would recommend two precautions to be used in the voyage from Chili to Callao. The first is not to make the land in the bay of Arica, the many eddies of the current there rendering it very difficult to get again clear of the coast; which must be done by keeping along shore; as by standing out to sea, you will be in danger of not reaching the harbour: for the current setting N. W. on standing in for the land, you will probably find yourself to leeward of the harbour; in which case it will be far from easy to work up against the wind and strong current. The second flows from the former, and is to make the land somewhere between Nasca and Sangallan, as the coast may be then kept at a proper distance, and the danger of falling to leeward of the port avoided: a misfortune which has happened to many, who have been carried farther out than they expected; so that after a long look out for land, they find themselves on its first appearance to leeward of their port.

In winter, especially, too much care cannot be taken, as from the continual thickness of the atmosphere, observations cannot be made so often as requisite; sometimes not for five or six days successively; at the same time

time the fight of land is entirely intercepted by the denfity of the fog. This we experienced; for after we were anchored in Callao at only a quarter of a league diftant from the land, the people on the fhore had no fight of the fhips: and it was owing to our being very near the coaft that we made the harbour; for had we been at a diftance, we fhould have been far to leeward, when the weather cleared up.

On the 25th of June, being the fecond day after our departure from the ifland de Tierra de Juan Fernandes, we faw a meteor like that we had before feen at Quito, namely, a globe of fire, or large globe of inflammable exhalations. It firft appeared in the weft, at half an hour after three in the morning, and moved with great velocity for a confiderable fpace towards the eaft, as if carried by the wind. The light of this meteor was fuch, that the watch on the quarter-deck could plainly diftinguifh every perfon on the fore-caftle; and both were not a little terrified. The phænomenon lafted between three and four minutes, and half an hour after we felt two violent fhocks, at an interval of about a minute and a half betwixt them, fo that all apprehended the fhip had ftruck on fome fhoal; but on reflection we concluded it to be the effect of an earthquake.

The fquadron being fafely arrived at Callao, with the commander in chief of the fouth-fea, a title given to Don Jofeph Pizarro, and a fufficient number of officers of fuch diftinguifhed zeal and experience, that they might well fupply our place without detriment to the fervice; and, at the fame time, we being willing to put the finifhing hand to our principal work, we afked the vice-roy's leave to return to Quito; but his excellency was defirous that we fhould firft compleat fome particulars he had commited to our care. Accordingly we applied ourfelves affiduoufly to our work; and Don George Juan, having finifhed his part firft, left Callao on the 14th of November, propofing posing to make all the necessary preparatives against my arrival, that the proper observations might be made without delay. On the 27th of January, 1744, I reach'd Quito, where I found Don George Juan had, by his extraordinary care, nearly finished every thing necessary for the continuation of our work; and whilst the remainder was performing, we had an opportunity, in conjunction with Mr. Godin, the only French academician now remaining in this province, of observing the comet which appeared this year.

Though the comet might have been seen on the 2d and 3d of February, the atmosphere of Quito being so unfavourable to astronomical observations on account of the clouds, it was the 6th before we could observe it. The comet was then near the western part of the horizon, and being behind the mountain of Pichinca, its altitude concealed it from our sight, so that we could not observe it after seven or eight at night. On the 6th, at seven in the evening, we found its altitude above the horizon to be 15 degrees, and its azimuth from the N. 72 degrees; Mr. Godin and Don George Juan judged its nucleus to be oblong, to me it appeared perfectly circular; but we all agreed that it was larger than Jupiter. The tail, which we discerned through some light clouds, seemed to extend two degrees, and to form with the verticle circle, an angle of near thirty degrees.

On the 7th, at eight minutes after seven in the evening, on repeating our observations, we found its altitude to be 11°, 11', and its azimuth from the north 72°, 45'. From this second observation, which we considered as more accurate than the former, having made proper allowances for refraction, we concluded that the right ascension of the comet was 332°, 50', and that its northern declination was 20°, 5'. Whence we inferred, that its trajectory was the same with that observed in 1681 by Cassini, and by Tycho Brahe in 1577, and that, in all probability

bability it was the same; for though the periods do not agree, it might have appeared twice in the firſt interval. After this we were hindered from proſecuting our obſervations by the cloudineſs of the nights: and ſome days afterwards we were aſſured by ſeveral, that they had ſeen it in the morning.

As all the triangles on the north ſide from Pambamarca, to the place where Mr. Godin had made his ſecond aſtronomical obſervations were not compleated, and the inſtrument conſtructed for that purpoſe kept in readineſs, we made that our firſt taſk; Mr. Godin not having then gone through them all. After finiſhing every thing here, we repaired on the 22d of March to the obſervatory de Pueblo Viejo de Mira, where meeting with the ſame difficulties from the thickneſs of the atmoſphere, as we had before experienced during the whole courſe of our operations, we were obliged to continue there till the 22d of May, when being ſatisfied with the accuracy of the obſervations made during this long interval, we returned to Quito, with the pleaſing expectation, that our perſeverance againſt the conſtant difficulties we met with from the clouds was at laſt come to a period; and that we ſhould now reſt from the toils and hardſhips of living on frozen deſarts; a repoſe the more pleaſing, as it was accompanied with a conſcioufneſs that no inconveniences had occaſioned us to omit the leaſt part of our duty.

During our ſtay at Mira, Don George Juan applied himſelf to obſerve the variation of the magnetic needle, and by four obſervations nearly coincident, he concluded to be nearly $8^{\circ}$, $47'$, eaſterly.

We now began to deliberate on our return upon the favourable opportunity of the above-mentioned French ſhips, which were preparing to ſail for Spain; as we ſhould then paſs round Cape Horn, and not only complete from our own experience, an account of the ſouth-ſea, but be enabled to make obſervations on the whole.

whole courfe. Another, and indeed our principal motive was, the fafety of our papers, concluding there could be no danger in a neutral fhip, as we then imagined thofe to be. The concurrence of fo many advantages immediately determined us; and leaving Quito we fet out for Lima, where I arrived firft, Don George Juan having fome days been detained at Guayaquil by a frefh commiffion by the vice-roy. Thefe fhips, not failing fo foon as expected, I employed the interval in drawing up an extract of all interefting obfervations and remarks, and prefented it to the vice-roy, who was pleafed to order the papers to be preferved in the fecretary's office, that if any misfortune fhould happen to us in the voyage, our fovereign might not be totally difappointed in his generous views of promoting the ufeful fciences of geography and navigation.

WHILE we were employed in finifhing our obfervations at Mira, the univerfity of Lima gave a remarkable teftimony of their fenfe of Mr. Godin's eminent talents, by chufing him profeffor of mathematics, in the room of Don Pedro de Peralta, deceafed; which he accepted of with the greater fatisfaction, as fome indifpenfable affairs of his company would not permit him to gratify his defires of returning to Europe. Accordingly he propofed to fpend this interval in making frefh obfervations and experiments, concluding that the atmofphere of Lima, during the fummer feafon, would be more favourable to his defigns than that of Quito or the mountains. On his arrival at that city, the vice-roy, who was no ftranger to his great abilities, and pleafed with the prudent choice of the univerfity, conferred on him, at the fame time of his being invefted with the profefforfhip, the poft of cofmographer to his majefty; with other advantages annexed to it. But this gentleman was far from propofing to make any longer ftay there than what thefe affairs required; no advantages or honours being sufficient to make him forget the obligations he was under of giving an account of his voyage and obfervations to his fovereign and the academy, efpecially as being the eldeft of the three academicians; fo that all the teftimonies of efteem could not fupprefs his uneafinefs at the delay.

M. de Juffieu, tho' with the fame regret as the former, determined to continue fome time at Quito, with M. Hugot, till he faw what turn the war would take, that he might efcape, in his return to Europe, thofe dangers then fo common at fea. M. Verguin chofe to go by the way of Panama: and the others, except the two who died in the country, one at Cayambe, and Cuenca, were difperfed; one fettling in Quito. Thus, the whole French company feparated: and it muft be confidered, as a fingular happinefs, that after fuch a fcene of labours, hardfhips, and dangers, in fuch a variety of climates, and amidft fuch inhofpitable defarts and precipices, our operations were accurately performed: and we capable of entering on a new fcene of dangers and difficulties, which it was our fortune to experience before we were in a condition of prefenting this work to the publick.

BOOK

# BOOK III.

*Voyage from* CALLAO *to* EUROPE; *with an Account of the Voyage from* CONCEPTION *in* CHILI *to the island of* FERNANDO DE NORONA, CAPE BRETON, NEWFOUNDLAND, *and* PORTSMOUTH *in* ENGLAND: *and from the same Harbour in the South-sea to* CAPE FRANCOIS *in* St. DOMINGO, *and from thence to* BREST *in* FRANCE.

## CHAP. I.

*Departure from* CALLAO. *Arrival at the Bay of* CONCEPTION. *Voyage from thence to* FERNANDO DE NORONA.

HAVING, as I have already observed, determined on the voyage for returning to Spain; on our arrival at Lima, in the year 1744, we were informed that two of the French frigates, Notre Dame de la Delivrance and the Lys, lay at Callao, and were soon to sail. Such a favourable opportunity was not to be missed, and accordingly Don George Juan and myself agreed for our passage, and also to make the voyage in separate ships, that one at least might escape the dangers to be apprehended in so long a voyage; there being thus the greater probability that one might reach his country, and there give an account of our proceedings with regard to the commission with which we had been honoured.

THE vice-roy had given us leave to return with the greatest marks of esteem; and the ships being ready we embarked on the 22d of October; and the same day

day put to fea, fteering our courfe for Chili. The two frigates kept company till the 11th of November, when they feparated in the latitude of 33°, 40', the Lys being obliged to touch at Valparaifo, whilft the Delivrance continued her courfe for Conception bay; where fhe came to an anchor on the 21ft of November. This voyage was remarkably fhort, being performed in twenty-nine natural days. What greatly contributed to this expedition was, that having put to fea at the end of winter, we fell in with fome breezes at N. which carried us to the fouthward, and faved us the trouble of ftanding fo far out to fea, as muft be done when the fummer is advanced.

In this bay we found the Louis Erafme frigate, which had waited there fome time, in order to fail in company with us; and on the 6th of January, 1745, we were joined by the Lys, accompanied with another French fhip, called la Marquis d' Antin, which having come hither as a regifter fhip, had taken in a loading of cacao at Guayaquil, and was in her return to Europe. The feafon being far advanced, our little fquadron put to fea the firft fair wind; which happened on the 27th of January, when about ten in the morning we all got under fail, fteering W. and W. one quarter northerly, according as the winds would permit, which were continually varying from S. W. to S. S. E. On the fourth of February we found ourfelves in the latitude of 35°, 21', and 9°, 38', weft of the meridian of Conception; when the wind blowing frefh at S. W. by W, we tacked in order to ftand to the fouthward. The next day we were informed that a very dangerous leak had been difcovered in the head of the Lys, and that it was fo far under water as not to be ftopped without going into fome harbour and lightening the fhip; which had determined the captain to run into fome of the harbours of Chili in order to ftop the leak; accordingly he left the reft of the fleet the fame day. The Delivrance, on board of which I embarked,

was

Ch. I.   SOUTH AMERICA.   295

was in little better condition, making daily a great deal of water ever since our departure from Conception. But the captain, unwilling to lose the benefit of sailing in company, and, at the same time, fearful that his men would leave the ship, determined to keep the sea. He also apprehended, that as the ship's hull was very old, and greatly shattered by her late voyage, on being searched, the necessary repairs would require a considerable time; and thence, besides the costs, he would find it difficult to get round the cape that year. These considerations determined him to continue his voyage, without acquainting the other ships of the bad condition of his vessel. But this prudence had nearly proved fatal to all on board, as the defects were greatly increased during the course of the voyage.

Till the 6th the winds were variable, sometimes fresh, then dying away; the sea proportionable, running high in a fresh gale, and abating with the wind.

From the latitude of 35°, 21', we steer'd between the S. E. and S; and on the 12th, being in the latitude of 41°, 20', we were obliged again to steer between S. W. and W. till the eighteenth; when we found ourselves in the latitude of 45°, 20'. The winds were first at W. afterwards N. N. E. from which they changed to the E. N. E. and N. E. and varying continually, at last shifted to the S. E. S. and E. During this interval, every change of the winds was attended with calms and violent showers; and at other times the sea was covered with fogs, or the atmosphere so clouded with vapours as to intercept the rays of the sun.

From the time we left Conception till the 7th of February, being then in 36°, 12', and 9°, 20', west of the meridian of Conception, we always saw that kind of birds called Pardelas, but here they left us. On the 11th, in the latitude of 40°, 45', and something more to the westward than on the 7th, we saw a number of small black birds, flying singly, and against the current of the water. On the 15th, the weather being fair, but the wind blowing fresh at W. S. W. we saw a Quebrantahueſſos, or offifrage; and on the 16th, being in the latitude of 44°, 31', and 11°, 24', west of the meridian of Conception, we saw several flights of Curlews and Pardelas; and the Quebrantahueſſos kept continually in sight of the ship: soon after the wind came about to the S. W. and blew so strong, that the frigates were obliged to hand all their sails except their courses. On the 18th the wind abated, the sea, which ran exceeding high, became tolerably smooth, and the Quebrantahueſſos disappeared at the beginning of this welcome change of weather.

FROM the 18th to the 26th our course was east, one quarter southerly, and S. E. one quarter easterly; the winds being variable between the S. S. W. and W. S. W. with some short transitions to N. W. From the 26th to the 3d of March we steered E. S. E. and E. with the same winds, but so very variable, that from W. they shifted to the S. W. and from thence flew about to the E; so that in this interval they blew from every point of the compass, but rarely continued a single day in one direction. Sometimes for three or four hours we had a fresh gale, this soon died away, and was often succeeded by calms, being regular only in inconstancy.

ON the 20th of February we had a strong gale of wind at W. S. W. which obliged us to double reef our topsails. We were then in 48°, 2', latitude. On the 21st the wind abated, and continued so all the morning with an easy sea. At noon the wind freshened, and a storm came on at W. N. W. W. and W. S. W. so that we could carry only our reefed courses. The storm continued till the 23d about sun-set, when we let out the reefs in our courses, and set our topsails, after reefing them. During the whole time we

had

had a very hollow sea, and at the same time the atmosphere so hazy, that sometimes we lost sight of the other ships. This fog precipitated itself in a mizzling rain, which continued incessantly two days after the storm was over.

On the 20th we were amused with the sight of a great number of birds of all sizes, and among them one larger than a goose, and entirely black. On the 21st their numbers increased, some of which were larger than the Quebrantahuessos, but seemed to be of the same species. All the feathers of this bird were white, except those on the upper part of its wings, which were brown. Its wings were long, slender, and something curved. On the 22d when we were in the latitude of 51°, 2′, and 9°, 35′ west of the meridian of Conception, they continued with us in the same numbers. On the 23d they increased, and among them were several gulls. The feathers on the bodies of the latter were white, their tails short and broad, their necks large but well proportioned, and their heads and beaks answerable: on the upper parts of their wings the feathers were black, and white underneath; the wings very disproportionate in length, and considerably crooked at the middle articulation. This bird flies very swift, sometimes just above the surface of the water, then mounts into the air; and after taking two or three gyrations, they again dart down near the waters edge. On the 25th, the weather being foggy, with a mizzling rain, in the latitude 55°, 6′, and 6°, 42′, west of the meridian of Conception, we saw great numbers of birds, and among them the Quebrantahuessos of both the kinds already mentioned, and on the 26th several Toninas, a kind of wild ducks.

On the 27th we had little or no wind, with snow and hail. The birds shewed themselves in greater numbers and variety than before; but the most numerous were gulls, like those already described, but the colours something different; some being of an ash colour,

colour, others had their whole bodies white, and their wings black, and others the reverfe. Some, though very few, were entirely black, without the leaft fpot of white. We alfo faw among them the Toninas, with their white bellies and brown backs.

On the 1ft on March, being in the latitude of 57°, 50′ and 0°. 3′ eaft of the meridian of Conception, we faw fome whales, but the number of birds were confiderably diminifhed : the fnow and hail ftill continued; the denfe clouds, which were continually forming in that part of the horizon whence the winds blow, precipitating themfelves in thefe meteors; and though the winds were moderate, the clouds were conftantly gathering. On the 3d we had thick weather; the cold became extreme, and a great deal of fnow fell. The birds, alfo, returned in their former numbers; principally of the larger fort.

On the fame day, at noon, in the latitude of 58° 40′, and 4° 13′ E. of the meridian of Conception, a little W. of the meridian of Cape Horn, and 60 leagues to the fouthward of it; we altered our courfe, fteering E. N. E. and continued failing between that and the N. E. till the 28th of the fame month. But the winds were fo variable and unfettled, that there was fcarce a day in which they did not blow from two different quarters, and fometimes from points almoft oppofite.

On the 4th we had fair weather, with the wind at N. N. E. and W; on the 5th at S. E. and W; on the 6th S. and S. W. changing round the whole compafs, and fcarce ever continuing a day in one point, till the 8th, when we found ourfelves in the latitude of 55° 16′ and 14° 30′ E. of the meridian of Conception, having weathered both Cape Horn, and Staten Land. It fnowed and hailed continually, fo that it was fix inches deep on the deck : but now it began to diminifh, and with it the cold. The birds likewife no longer appeared in fuch vaft flocks :

and

and on the seventh we saw a new species of a dark brown colour, greatly resembling geese, and, like them, keep swimming on the water for a long time. On the 8th we saw birds of a brown and white colour, in small flocks, of ten or fifteen in each. These also swam on the water, and when flying, kept always near the surface. On the 9th being in the latitude of 54° 21' and 16° 10' E. of the meridian of Conception, besides the same flocks of birds, we also saw Pardelas, but of a less size than those in the south sea. On the 10th in the latitude of 54° 1', and 17° 38' E. of Conecption, the winds were very variable between the N. N. E. and S. W. with so thick a fog, that the ships fired guns to avoid running foul of one another; for each had kept two guns mounted for making signals. We had also heavy showers, and in the evening saw flocks of birds, most of them of middling size, with dark brown feathers, and slender crooked wings. The whole difference between them consisted in the size, their form and colour being perfectly alike; and tho' we saw them during the whole day, they were in the greatest numbers from four to six in the evening. On the 11th being in the latitude of 52° 15', and 18° 9' E. of Conception, we observed that the colour of the water was changed, it being now greenish; but another days sailing brought us into water of its usual colour. On the 12th and 13th the wind blew fresh at N. W. and W. accompanied with heavy showers, but of no long continuance, nor attended with any bad consequences. Among the birds seen these two days, and which were more numerous than before, two species in particular engaged my attention; one large, resembling vultures, with black wings, and their bodies of a light brown spotted with white: the other, tho' little different in colour from the former, did not exceed the Pardelas in size: both sorts kept near the ship; and our men told us

they

they had seen a shoal of fish, which had probably drawn such numbers together.

On the 14th the wind variable betwixt the W. N. W. and S. W. and our latitude 48° 12', we began to be sensible of an agreeable change in the temperature of the air; in the day time it was not cold upon deck, and at night the cabins were warm. On the 15th we had a fresh gale at W. N. W. and N. W. with a hollow sea, which continued the two following days being the 16th and 17th, the weather was very hazy, sudden showers frequent, and the same number of birds still continued. On the 16th the marquis d'Antin came along side and told us, that the ship had sprung a leak, and that they had laboured the whole night to stop it, having, after a long search, found it to proceed from a hole made by the rats in one of her quarters near the water's edge. This obliged them to heel the ship in order to stop it, and the other two slackened sail that she might come up with them. On the 17th we saw many large whales, several of which played round the ship for a considerable time.

The wind during the last day was at S. E. and at S. S. E. but moderate; the sea smooth, with showers of rain; when we found ourselves in the latitude of 44° 30' and 25° 13' E. of Conception, and saw several flights of birds both of the large and small species, but different in colour from any we had seen before, being intirely white.

The water now increased so prodigiously in our ship, that for some days our men had been almost continually labouring at the pump, which quite exhausted their spirits; and all of us under the greatest apprehensions of perishing. Nor was this a sudden pannic, the water sometimes increasing so suddenly, that notwithstaneing all our efforts it seemed to gain upon us. We observed that the principal leaks were at the head and stern, and the 19th proving a fine day,

we

we hoisted out our boat, for the carpenters to nail sheet lead over the seams; but the sea ran too high for them to execute it.

On the 20th the wind blowing strong at N. and N.E. one quarter northerly, and the sea running high, we laid to, under our mainsail; but rain coming on, we had, next day, moderate weather. The wind continued in the same quarter till the 25th, but little of it, with fogs and showers. We were now in the latitude of 39° 14' and 30° 5' E. of the meridian of Conception. During these days we saw several birds, but in much less numbers than before; some of them very different, as black pardelas, and others of the same colour, but of an unknown species.

The water in our ship was now so greatly increased, and our men so spent with continually labouring at the pump, that we had thoughts of quitting her; and doubtless this would have been done some days before had it not been for her valuable cargo; having on board near two millions of Peruvian dollars, a million and a half of which was in gold and silver, and stowed under the cacao she had taken in at Guayaquil. In order therefore in some measure to keep out the water, a sail quilted with oakum, and shot fastened to the clues to sink it, was lowered into the water from the head of the ship; but this expedient had little effect. For tho' at first the water did not seem to enter with the rapidity as before, yet the oakum which prevented it, was soon carried away, when our condition was not mended in the least.

From the 29th, when we were in the latitude of 35° 38' and 33° 27' E. of the meridian of Conception, our course was W. N. W. till the 4th of April, when till the 20th we steered between the N. E. and E. N. E. with the same variable weather, showers, hard gales, and calms. So that during this long interval of twenty nine days, our latitude diminished little

more

more than nine degrees and a half, finding ourfelves in the latitude of 25° 55'; and between the twenty eight and twenty ninth degree we were detained from the 7th to the 15th without being able to make better way. On the 29th of March we faw Pardelas and the other kind of black birds. On the 30th we took down our weather boards, and got our top-gallant-mafts up. During this time the birds feemed to have entirely forfaken us; but on the 3d of April, we faw great numbers; and on the 5th and 6th we faw a new fpecies, refembling a lark in fhape and fize. Here we had alfo a firft fight of the Dorados; but from hence we never miffed feeing that fifh and alfo the bonito. On the 8th in the latitude of 28° 58', we began to meet with very thick fogs, violent and frequent fqualls of wind and rain, which continued with little or no inter-miffion to the 13th, but that day proving fair, we made ufe of it in getting up and mounting our guns. The carpenters and caulkers were ordered into the boat, to endeavour to ftop the leaks at the water's edge; for tho' they had nailed fheet lead over the feams, it did not anfwer the purpofe, the water nearly iffuing with the fame rapidity. On the 18th being in the latitude of 26° 52', we firft faw the fly-ing-fifh, and Taburones, but afterwards we had continual fight of them, their numbers increafing in proportion as we leffened our latitude.

In the latitude of 39° 14' on the 25th of March, Don Pedro de Arriago, freighter both of the Louis Erafme, and la Delivrance, made an offer to the captains, that if they thought it neceffary, provifions and water growing fcarce, they might put into the harbour of Monte Video, where they might not only refit the fhips and provide them with all neceffaries, but alfo take the benefit of a convoy, the Afia man of war being to fail for Spain about that time, with commodore Don Jofeph Pizarro;

adding

adding that it was the more adviseable to embrace this opportunity, advice having been received from Europe, three or four days before their departure from Conception, that France and England were at war. But the captains from selfish motives rejected this salutary proposal, tho' at the same time they must be sensible that the want of water and provisions, together with the bad condition of our frigate, would unavoidably oblige them to put into some harbour. And this, in opposition to the worthy merchant's advice, they determined should be the desart island of Fernando de Norona; for tho' the Portuguese of Brasil had some time since sent a colony thither, it was abandoned on account of its sterility. The French India company also had for some time a settlement there, but were obliged, on the same account, to leave it; and during the time of that settlement, the captain of the marquis d'Antin had been there, and thence knew that it abounded with water and wood, the two articles mostly wanted. Don Pedro Arriago adhered to his first proposal, and it had doubtless been complied with by the two frigates freighted by him, had not the marquis d'Antin been in company, the captain of which made use of such plausible reasons in support of his opinion, that it prevailed, and we accordingly steered for the harbour of Fernando de Norona.

From the 20th to the 26th of April, we had calms and squalls, and from thence to the 8th of May, when we found ourselves in the latitude of 16 deg. 58 min. we had little wind, and variable between the N. and E. but mostly at N. E. nearly. On the 8th the wind began to freshen, and tho' for several days it was at E. and E. N. E. we had it generally at E. S. E. till our arrival at Fernando de Norona. Our course from the 20th of April, was as the winds would permit, sometimes N. N. W. N. W. one quarter northerly, and W. N. W. but from the 7th of May,

May, when the wind settled to the eastward, we steered N. and N. one quarter easterly to the 15th, when finding ourselves in the latitude of 4 deg. S. being nearly the same with that of Fernando de Norona, we stood directly W. and having sight of it at half an hour after nine in the morning of the 21st of May, all the frigates at half an hour after three in the evening, came to an anchor in the road; to our no small joy. This voyage had continued an hundred and fifty days, and been attended with great fatigue and anxiety, on account of the bad condition of our frigate. For more than once, we had the greatest reason to apprehend she would founder, before we had time to provide for our safety.

From the 6th of April, we saw no birds till the second of May, when being in the latitude of 20° 18', we saw an Rabiahorcado, which the French call Tailleur, the taylor, from the form and motion of its tail. This bird is about the size of a wood pigeon, with a short neck, a proportionate bill, and its wings very long, broad and curved. The tail seemed to be composed of very few feathers, and these dividing at the root, so as to represent a pair of scissars opened; but when it is on the wing, it shuts and opens them at pleasure, representing the manner of using that instrument. The two blades, of which the tail consists, are very long in proportion to the body of the bird; and together with the whole plumage are of a fine glossy black, except the breast, which is a sort of very pale ash colour. It flies very swiftly, and generally high, never being seen low, but when hovering about a ship, as if intending to settle on it.

On the 4th of May we saw a pardela as large as a wood pigeon; the feathers on its belly, breast, and under the wings, were an ash colour; and those on the neck, head, and upper part of the wings, of a dark brown. From this day, when in the latitude of 19° 40', till the twelfth, when we came into ten degrees, we constantly saw some

though

though few of the two laſt mentioned kinds of birds; but from that time we had no more ſight of them till the evening of the 16th, when in the latitude of 4°, 30', nearly, we ſaw a different kind larger than the pardelas; but from the ſlow motion of its wings we concluded it to be a land bird. It was at too great a diſtance for us clearly to diſtinguiſh its colours and form. We were, however, notwithſtanding this ſignal, under a neceſſity of ſteering W. when after a run of 102 leagues we made the iſland. The following days we never failed of ſeeing a few of the ſame ſpecies; but on the 19th their numbers increaſed. They were wholly black, except a few brown feathers on the wings. Among theſe birds we obſerved one larger than the reſt, with a long neck, a prominent body, and its whole plumage of a dark brown: it moved its wings ſlowly, and every way reſembled a cormorant. We ſaw him ſeveral times dart down with great rapidity to catch fiſh; and on the 29th in the morning we were entertained with the ſight of great numbers of them, whom hunger rendered very alert in the ſame exerciſe. From the time of ſeeing the firſt, till we were directly S. of the iſland, we ſailed 33 leagues, the greateſt diſtance theſe birds are known to venture out to ſea. On the 20th in the evening, being betwixt ten and eleven leagues from the iſland, we ſaw ſeveral birds reſembling the guanaes already deſcribed; and at ſun-ſet great flocks of them were flying towards the W; whence we concluded that we were not far from the iſland. Theſe birds, which the French call Fou, and the Engliſh Booby, are about the ſize of a gooſe, have a large and curved wing, all over of a dark brown, and in flying uſe a great deal of motion with their wings; but when they attempt to catch a fiſh, they dive with the ſame rapidity as the guanaes.

About two hours before we made the iſland, we ſaw ſeveral Rabijuncos, a bird, which by always keeping near the ſhore, indicates its proximity. They are about the ſize of a wood pigeon, with a ſhort thick neck, a ſmall head, the whole plumage white, and a long tail in the form of a rabijunco or ruſh, half an inch diameter near the body, tapering its whole length till it terminates in a point, whence it was called Rabijuncos. Theſe birds are never ſeen above eight or ten leagues from the ſhore.

From the time we firſt ſaw the Dorado and Bonito, the laſt increaſed in numbers as our latitude diminiſhed. We now alſo ſaw the Tunny, and a great many flying fiſh. We caught ſome of all kinds; and here it is not unworthy notice, that the Bonitos and tunny-fiſh bite only from day-break till about ſeven in the morning, and again in the evening from ſun-ſet till dark.

## CHAP. II.

*Nautical Obſervations and Remarks on the Voyage round* CAPE HORN.

FROM the time of our ſteering weſt, being in the latitude of the iſland, till we were under its meridian, we ſailed 5 deg. 4 min. and a half, tho' all on board, who had kept an account of the ſhip's way, imagined we were to the weſtward of it; but the variation of the needle convinced us, that our reckoning was not to be depended on, and that the ſhip was much farther to the eaſtward than we imagined: an error owing principally to the motion of the currents, which had drawn us at ſuch a great diſtance from the land; all the French pilots on board the Delivrance agreed in this particular; and ſome related, that when they thought themſelves near the land, they had often found the ſhip above three hundred leagues to the eaſtward of their reckoning. I did not, however, make any correction in my journal on

this

this account; for which I had two reasons. The first, that I might be able to judge of the distance the currents had carried us to the eastward. The second, was an unwillingness to commit a fresh error by making an uncertain correction, as I was not satisfied that there were any currents; and consequently unable to guess at their velocity; some affirming they had found them very violent; and others as positively asserting, that they had never met with any. This was the case of the three frigates when they entered the south-sea: and the captain of the Delivrance informed me, that without attending to the currents in going round the cape, in the latitude of 62 degrees, his reckoning perfectly agreed with the time of making land; and that several Frenchmen had done the like: but, on the other hand, it has happened to some, that when they imagined themselves in the south-sea by the place of the ship according to their reckoning, steered N. E. till from the disappointment of not falling in with the land, at the time expected, had convinced them that they had not weathered the cape; and accordingly steering towards the W. they have found their suspicions confirmed by making the coast of Brasil, or Buenos Ayres.

On the 21st of May, at one in the afternoon, we were under the meridian of Fernando de Norona, and at above three quarters of a league distant to the northward of it. Whereas according to my computation, the frigate was only $29° 56'$ E of the meridian of Conception; but by the modern French map, laid down from the observations sent to the academy of sciences, in which the longitudes of all places are marked with all the accuracy which distinguishes the works of that learned body, this island lies no less than $42°, 32', 30''$, E. of the meridian of Conception; consequently the difference between my reckoning, and the true longitude of the island, being $12° 36', 30''$, is the distance which the currents carried our frigate to the eastward, exclusive of her lee-way.

ON the 15th of May, namely, before he began to steer W. we spoke with the marquis d'Antin, and her captain gave us to understand, that according to his reckoning, the ship was then 45°, 3', E. of the meridian of Conception. Whereas the distance, according to my account was only 34°, 19'. Thus the ship, according to his computation, was 10°, 44', further to the eastward than by mine, and the difference on the ship's arrival at the island, will be 2° the distance the currents had carried him to the eastward beyond what he had judged. The captain of the Delivrance, on the same day, made the ship 39°, 15', east of the meridian of Conception; that is 4°, 56', more than I; and consequently on reaching the island, his account was 7°, 40', further to the westward than the ship. Others, who kept a journal on board the Delivrance, differed as much; some nearly agreeing with me, namely, those who had made no allowance for the currents; whilst others approached nearer to the account of the captain of the Marquis d'Antin, having used an equation in respect to the currents. But every one, at making the island, found their reckoning erroneous; the ship, according to their accounts, being farther to the westward than she really was; but differed in the quantity of that error, according to the different allowances they had made for the setting of the currents.

THE difference betwixt my account and that of the captain of the Marquis d'Antin, who was one of those who made the ship fartheft to the eastward, proceeded from the captain's knowing by observing the variation of the needle, that the frigates made more way than the reckoning allowed of, and therefore concluded that a correction was necessary, which he performed by adding a proper distance, from the journals of others, and thence inferred that the velocity of the currents was considerable; but as that really exceeded the allowance he made for it, his ship was always to the eastward of his reckoning. The captain of the Louis Erasme found the difference nearly the same as the captain of the Marquis d'Antin, who made use of an equation. Both, as I have already observed, founded their corrections on the variations; differing very considerably from that delineated on the charts.

The great variety of currents met with in sailing round Cape Horn, being sometimes strong, sometimes moderate, and at others scarce perceivable, induces me to think that they were not considerable in correcting the account. For their velocity being uncertain, it is in fact only committing a voluntary error; and as the variations enable us to guess at our longitude within two or three degrees; and as after making use of the equation, the place of the ship cannot be known nearer the truth, the correction is entirely useless; and the inference drawn from observing the variation, is abundantly sufficient for security. I say, that the place of the ship may be known so within two or three degrees; and a more exact conformity between the corrected reckoning and the time of making land would be rather fortuitous than the effect of accuracy, in making the correction. The difference of one or two degrees in the variations, an error unavoidable, may produce in the longitude an error of three or four degrees, or even more, according to the place of the ship. Every one on board the three frigates, found their reckoning to the westward of the ship's true place; though they had made an allowance for the currents; and the difference between some of their accounts was not small, as I have already noticed. This was owing to the like uncertainty in the journals of other voyages they had with them; for the currents being stronger at sometimes than others, they who followed the former made a much larger allowance than those who regulated their corrections by the latter; and confequently their reckonings muft have been very different. The currents therefore being uncertain, and the journals of thofe voyages very variable with regard to their velocity, there is no more fecurity in following one than another, and even if we take a medium between them, there would be no more fafety in relying upon it, than blindly to follow that which was thought the beft. However, their utility and even importance cannot be denied, as they inform the navigator of the parts where he muft expect to meet with currents, and at the fame time warn him of their variety.

ONE caufe of the little knowledge we have of thefe currents is, that this voyage is feldom made, and lefs by the Spaniards than by any other maritime nation; and though fince the year 1716 feveral French fhips have failed into thofe feas, they have not yet been able to remove this difficulty, and fettle the times of the feveral degrees of velocity of the currents in the different latitudes paffed thro' in weathering the Cape. This is indeed only to be expected from long experience and repeated voyages; and in order to this navigators fhould not make any allowance for their currents in correcting their days works; for the diftance between the knots on the log-line being truly adjufted as ours was at forty feven Paris feet and one third, and the half-minute glafs carefully attended to, the error in the diftance will be very inconfiderable, and confequently the drift of the current, on making land, known very near the truth; and this muft be added to or deducted from the reckoning by account. By purfuing this method we fhall advance one ftep towards a more certain knowledge of them.

THOUGH we are not yet able to determine the velocity of the currents, nor the times of their fetting, yet we can advance one ftep towards it, namely, that they always fet towards the E. nor is there a fingle instance to the contrary, unless very near the land on the W. side of America near Cape Horn; the proximity of the coast causing there a great variety of eddies, and Terra del Fuego, being composed of a cluster of islands, forming as many channels, the course of the current is altered according to their disposition; and at a small distance from them the meeting of these currents is plainly distinguishable.

In the account of Don George Juan's voyage inserted in the sequel, tho' his course in weathering Cape Horn, was nearly in the same latitude as ours, but a month later as to time, and the weather and winds very different, yet no current was perceivable; which confirms what I have already observed.

Though the general winds here are towards the W. and S. W. those from the E. are sometimes known, as we experienced in passing between the 57th and 58th degree of latitude, and for three or four days after we lessened our latitude. This, however, seldom happens; and therefore a ship bound into the south-seas when in the latitude of Cape Horn, should keep as near the wind as possible, if it be at N. W. or any other intermediate point between the S. W. these being the reigning winds in all seasons, taking advantage of the first in order to gain the necessary latitude, which should be something above 60 deg. that if she should be obliged to tack with the wind at S. W. she may have sufficient sea-room in weathering the Cape; for otherwise if the wind should take her short, after two or three days, it would be necessary to return again to a higher latitude; and this is, at all times, attended with great fatigue and hardship, both on account of the rigour of the climate, and the frequency of storms, attended with the most terrible seas. It was the middle of summer when we came round the Cape, yet the snow and hail fell very thick, and the cold was proportional. And tho' when we were between the 57th and 58th degree, there was very little

little wind, yet we had, to the great fatigue of the feamen, a very heavy fea from the S. W. and W. and fometimes the fea run in two or three different directions.

From our leaving the bay of Conception, till 17th Feb. when we were in the latitude of 45° 17′ the differences either with regard to excefs or deficiency between the latitude by account, and that obtained by obfervation, were inconfiderable: But from that day, the latter was always greater than the former, as will appear from the following feries. From the 15th of the fame month to the 17th, the latitude by obfervation exceeded that by account 18 min. from the 17th to the 20th, 32 min. from the 20th to the 23d, 37 minutes and a half, from the 23d to the 27th, 33 min. from the 27th, to the fecond of March, 43 min. and from the 2d of March to the 6th, 20 min. and a half. We were now according to my computation, 12° 6′ E. of the meridian of Conception, and in the latitude of 56° 44′. After this the difference between the latitudes by account and obfervation began to decreafe; but fometimes the latitude by obfervation exceeded that by account, and at other times was lefs. From the fixth to the feventh the difference was 4. min. and a half; nor did it exceed five or fix at the end of three or four days in which we had no obfervation. This evidently fhews that from the above latitude of 45° 17′ the currents began to fet to the fouthward, and when the land parallel to their courfe failed, they ran towards the eaft, when it was impoffible to diftinguifh them. But that there were ftill currents, and very ftrong ones too, feems to me beyond doubt; and it is much more natural to think, that the prodigious volume of water which ran towards the fouth, when there was no longer any land to obftruct its courfe, fhould incline towards the E. rather than towards the W. the latter being the quarter from whence the wind proceeded. On

On the 30th of March, being in the latitude of 34° 27' S. and, according to my account 32° 47' E. of the meridian of Conception, we came into a current, which seemed to set S. E. the latitude by obfervation exceeded that by account by 10 or 11 min. But from the 21st of April, being in the latitude of 25° 9', and 36° 15' E. of Conception; the two latitudes agreed, and thus continued till we reached the island of Fernando de Norona.

THE variation, of which we shall soon give a catalogue, gave us to understand from the time we were under the meridian of Cape Horn, that the currents carried our ships towards the E. founding our judgment on the difference between those observed, and those given us in the journals of other voyages, conformable to the places where we made our observations. And as they may be serviceable to others in making the same voyage, in order to render them still more useful than if I had adapted them to the longitude from my account, as that was not the real place where the observations were made, I have corrected the longitude in the manner I am going to explain.

IT being certain from what has been said concerning the currents, that their effects became sensible from 45° south-latitude in a S. E. direction to the latitude of 56, or 57 degrees; that from thence they continued to run directly E. till we were in the latitude of 34° 27', and 32° 47' E. of the meridian of Conception: where their course turned to the S. E. and continued to run in that direction till we came into the latitude of 25° 9', and 36° 15' E. of Conception, where they ceased. It will therefore be necessary to divide, in all journals the 12° 36' 30", which the ship was to the eastward of my reckoning, in a proportion agreeably to the interval of time between their beginning and cessation, regard being had to their velocity in those parts when they were

most

moſt evident by the difference between the latitudes by account and obſervation, and this will give the true place of the ſhip correſponding to the different obſervations.

THE obſervations having been made either at ſun-riſing or ſun-ſetting, and the daily reckoning not been adjuſted till noon, according to the common practice at ſea, occaſions, between the longitude determined that day, and that in which the ſhip really was at the time the variation was obſerved, a difference, which ſometimes amounts to a degree or more, I have therefore taken care in the following table to ſettle the longitude and latitude agreeable to the hour when the variation was obſerved.

A TABLE of the VARIATIONS obſerved in the Voyage from the BAY of CONCEPTION to the Iſland of FERNANDO DE NORONA, in different latitudes and longitudes, the latter being reckoned from the meridian of CONCEPTION.

| Days. | Lat. South Deg. Min. | Long. from the Mer. of Concep. Deg. Min. | Variations. Deg. Min. | Times of making the Obſervation. |
|---|---|---|---|---|
| 28 Jan. | 36 16½ | 1 8 W. | *13 17 E. | Evening. |
| 7 Feb. | 36 23 | 9 25 W. | 10 45 | |
| 28 | 57 41 | 0 10 E. | 23 20 | |
| 2 Mar. | 58 32 | 4 1 | 22 14 | |
| 8 | 55 28 | 16 24 | *26 44 | Morning. |
| 9 | 54 57 | 18 32 | 20 00 | |
| 11 | 52 42 | 19 59 | 18 50 | |
| 12 | 50 57 | 22 12 | 18 44 | Evening. |
| 13 | 49 22 | 23 35 | 18 32 | |
| 14 | 47 52 | 24 24 | 18 42 | |
| 26 | 38 36 | 34 41 | 9 0 | Morning. |
| 27 | 37 46 | 35 49 | 10 30 | |
| 30 | 34 27 | 37 11 | 6 23 | Evening. |
| 1 April | 33 06 | 35 19 | 5 55 | Morning. |
| 1 | 32 42½ | 34 39 | 5 45 | Evening. |
| 2 | 32 15 | 34 27 | 5 10 | Morning. |
| 4 | 31 30 | 34 02 | 6 0 | Evening. |
| 8 | 29 4 | 37 48 | 4 0 | Morning. |
| 16 | 27 16 | 46 0 | *2 5 W. | Evening |
| 18 | 26 48 | 48 18 | *2 15 E. | |

## CH. II.  SOUTH AMERICA.  315

| Days. | Lat. South. Deg. Min. | | Long. from the Mer. of Concep. Deg. Min. | | Variations. Deg. Min. | | Times of making the Observation. |
|---|---|---|---|---|---|---|---|
| 19 | 26 | 49 | 49 | 1 | 0 | 40 W. | |
| 20 | 26 | 7 | 48 | 57 | 0 | 30 | |
| Ditto | 25 | 44 | 48 | 46 | 0 | 15 | |
| 22 | 25 | 01 | 48 | 47 | 1 | 30 | |
| 22 | 24 | 55 | 48 | 47 | 1 | 18 | Evening. |
| 24 | 24 | 43 | 48 | 44 | 0 | 45 E. | |
| 26 | 24 | 00 | 48 | 48 | 0 | 08 | |
| 27 | 23 | 04 | 48 | 14 | 0 | 00 | |
| 29 | 21 | 30 | 47 | 10 | 0 | 15 E. | |
| 1 May | 20 | 24 | 46 | 56 | 0 | 30 | |
| 2 | 20 | 15 | 47 | 10 | 0 | 05 | |
| 3 | 20 | 00 | 47 | 05 | 1 | 50 W. | Morning. |
| 3 | 19 | 51 | 46 | 45 | 0 | 20 E. | Evening. |
| 4 | 19 | 34 | 45 | 43 | *3 | 00 | |
| 5 | 19 | 23 | 45 | 06 | 0 | 20 W. | Morning. |
| 7 | 18 | 21 | 45 | 02 | 1 | 30 E. | |
| 9 | 15 | 49 | 45 | 11 | 2 | 00 | |
| 10 | 13 | 16 | 45 | 20 | 0 | 50 | Evening. |
| 12 | 9 | 34 | 45 | 57 | 0 | 05 | |
| 17 | 4 | 10 | 45 | 29 | 0 | 22 W. | Morning. |
| 19 | 4 | 17 | 43 | 55 | 1 | 41 E. | |
| 19 | 4 | 18 | 43 | 40 | 3 | 25 | Evening. |
| 22 | 3 | 53 | 42 | 32 | 2 | 47 | |
| 31 | 3 | 53 | 42 | 32 | 1 | 33 | |

The two last observations were taken in the harbour of Fernando de Norona; and those marked with an * were not determined with the desired accuracy, some accident intervening at the time of the observation.

It will be proper, for mariners unacquainted with the precautions customary in a voyage little frequented, to observe, that in this part of the passage they may expect to meet with very tempestuous seas, continual squalls of wind and fogs; so that it is absolutely necessary in the night and in hazy days to keep a very careful look out against the ice, large islands of which, breaking from the shore, are driven by the wind beyond the latitude of 64°, and ships too often meet with them from 55°.

55° upwards. They are ufually nearer the fhore towards the end of winter than in fummer, when beginning to loofen themfelves from the land, they gradually move from it; and not diffolving by reafon of the continuance of the coldnefs of the air, they are always feen at higher latitudes than that of 60 degr. The Hector, a regifter fhip in her paffage from Cadiz to the fouth-fea was loft on one of thefe iflands of ice: and many others have narrowly efcaped the like misfortune.

These maffes of ice and the many eddies of the currents render it advifeable to keep a good offing at weathering the Cape in the return from the fouth-fea, efpecially as there are fome iflands at a little diftance from the coaft, reaching to 56 deg. at leaft. Thefe are at all times dangerous, both from the difficulty of determining with certainty, on account of the currents, the place of the fhip; and likewife from fogs which are there fo common and thick, that the whole day is as it were turned to night, and the darknefs fuch that thofe on the poop cannot fee the men on the forecaftle. Thefe dangers render it therefore advifeable, that the fhip in returning to Europe, fhould always ftand into the latitude of 58 or 60 degr.

In paffing into the fouth-fea, a larger latitude even from 60 to 63 or 64 degr. as the wind will admit, and then fteering W. 60 or 80 leagues beyond what may feem neceffary by account, will be advifeable; becaufe if the fhip fhould have met with currents, fufficient allowance would be made for them; and confequently the great inconvenience prevented of not weathering the cape; which might be the cafe without the allowance of thefe 60 or 80 leagues. This weftern diftance, after it appears, by the reckoning that the fhip has weathered the cape, will be of little confequence, if we confider the great advantages gained thereby; it is always better

for

Ch. II.   SOUTH AMERICA.   317

for the ship to be obliged to sail 100 leagues eastward, till she makes the western coast of America, than to want but one of being to windward of it; for to gain only this one league, the ship must go a great way back to the southward, before she will be able to get round the cape; especially as there is little chance of having a fair wind. In a subsequent chapter, 1 shall more fully consider this subject, and specify other precautions necessary to be observed in sailing on that ocean.

## CHAP. III.

*Arrival at* FERNANDO DE NORONA; *and Description of that Island.*

WE now from our reckonings and other signs concluded that we could not be at any great distance from the island we were searching for; and accordingly on the 20th of May, when a fog came on with rain, we laid to under our top-sails, rather from an apprehension of overshooting the island than of losing company or running foul of each other. On the 21st, having an appearance of fair weather, the frigates made sail, and at half an hour after nine, the Louis Erasme discovered the island bearing west one quarter southerly, distance nine leagues, as was afterwards verified by the log-line.

This island we imagined to be totally desart; but from a supposition that for the conveniency of its harbour, ships of any nation returning from the East-Indies might, either for water, or on any other necessary occasion put in there, it was agreed by the captains of the French frigates to go in under English colours; in order the better to conceal their course, and in case we found any ships of the enemy, to take the best precautions in their power for defence.

fence. But to our great satisfaction, we saw, on our approach, two forts with the Portuguese flag flying, and a brigantine with an ensign and long pennant of the same nation. We were the more surprized at this, as according to all the accounts we had received, the island was a desart, having been forsaken by the Portuguese as not susceptible of tillage: but on our arrival we were informed, that the French East India company had made a settlement on it as a convenient place for their ships to put in at for refreshments: but the court of Portugal being unwilling that either the French or any other nation should have a settlement so near the coast of Brazil, obliged them to evacuate it. This resolution was taken about seven years ago, since which these and other forts have been erected, and a colony settled on the island.

We now began to consider whether it was possible to procure any true account of the state of affairs in Europe; or whether Portugal, in the present war, might have gone farther than a neutrality. But as this could not be immediately determined, it was thought adviseable for the three frigates to agree on signals of certain import to be made at going into this harbour. In order to get in it is necessary to weather the island on the north side, as the force of the current to the southward is such, that it cannot be done at least under four or five days or more, beating to windward up to that part where the currents do not obstruct the entrance. Having been previously informed of this, when we found ourselves to the southward, and so near as I have mentioned, we steered S. W. 5 deg. westerly, and after sailing near a league till we weather'd the island, we stood S. $\frac{1}{4}$ southerly, with the ship's head directly towards a large mountain, betwixt two others plainly distinguishable; but that on the E. side was larger than that in the middle, and the other on the W. a high

rocky

## Ch. III.  SOUTH AMERICA.  319

rocky peak, that looks as it were falling towards the E. and on account of its height and figure called the Companario, or the belfrey. The currents here set so strongly to the westward, that after several tacks, instead of gaining ground, we found ourselves carried further from the island; so that in order to avoid any further inconveniency, we came to an anchor at some distance from the proper anchoring-place, in twenty five fathoms water, the bottom mud mixed with shells and gravel; about a league and a quarter from the shore, fort Remedios, the largest of those built for the defence of the harbour, bearing S. S. E. The prodigious sea here occasioned by the violence of the wind, and the strength of the current causing our frigates to strain on their cables, obliged us to weigh, and stand farther into the usual anchoring-place, beyond which no ships are permitted. This is about $\frac{1}{3}$ of a league from the shore: and here on the 23d of March, the Louis Erasme anchor'd in thirteen fathom water, the bottom of a fine white and black sand; fort San Antonio bearing E. 5 deg. southerly, Remedios, S. $\frac{1}{4}$ westerly. Conception S. S. W. 4. deg. westerly, and Campanario peak S. W. 3. deg. southerly.

This island has two harbours capable of receiving ships of the greatest burthen: one is on the N. side, and the other on the N. W. The former is in every respect the principal both for shelter, capacity, and the goodness of its bottom. But both are entirely exposed to the N. and W. tho' these winds, particularly the N. are periodical, and of no long continuance. These harbours, however, when these winds do prevail, are both impracticable, the ships being in danger, and all communication with the shore entirely precluded by the agitations and violence of the surface; for the coast being every where lined with rocks, no boat or vessel can come near it without the greatest danger of being beat to pieces.

And

And even in the feafon of the eafterly winds, you cannot land without fome danger. This interval indeed affords fome days when the agitation of the fea is greatly abated, but even in thefe the landing muft be done with great circumfpection; and at other times the violence of the fea, and the rocks on all fides render it utterly impracticable. Thus throughout the whole year this harbour is by no means a defirable retreat; but happily ferves on an urgent neceffity of making land, notwithftanding the danger or inconveniency that may attend it.

AFTER the Portuguefe had caufed the French Eaft India company to remove from this ifland, they fecured it to themfelves by fortifications; for befides the three forts which defend the N. harbour, it has two others for the defence of the N. W. and two in the E. part of the ifland in a fmall bay, though fit only for fmall barks, and difficult even to thefe. The forts are all of ftone, fpacious and well provided with large artillery. Thus though the whole length of the ifland is fcarce two leagues, and it does not yield wherewithal to fupport the garrifon, and the few other inhabitants, it has no lefs than feven elegant forts. It is under the government of Fernambuco, from whence it is fupplied with provifions and other neceffaries. But the jealoufy of the Portuguefe, leaft any other nation fhould get footing on it, and make that the fountain of farther pretenfions, has induced them to fpare no expence for keeping the forts in a condition to affert their fovereign right againft any intruders.

THE principal fort ftands on an high fteep rock wafhed by the fea, at the foot of which is a cavern, where vaft quantities of water are continually pouring in without any fenfible outlet. In this place are heard at fhort intervals, very dreadful eructations of the wind, which being compreffed ftruggles for a vent againft the torrent of the water, and by

filling

filling the whole mouth of the cave in its afcent, leaves a large vacuity after its difcharge, which is done with a noife refembling that of a volcano: but neither on the oppofite fide of the ifland, nor throughout its whole circuit, is there any place or mark which affords the leaft room for conjecture, with regard to the other mouth of this cavern; fo that it is fuppofed to be at a great diftance from it in the fea.

The barrennefs of the ifland does not proceed from any defect in its foil, which produces every fpecies of grain, and fruits common in hot climates, as experience has fufficiently demonftrated; but from the want of moifture: for befides two or three years often pafs without any rain, there is not the leaft drop of water to be found throughout the ifland except in fome brooks; and by reafon of this fcarcity the plants wither and die away in their growth. The moft fruitful parts of the ifland unlefs when foften'd by moifture from the clouds, becomes as arid and barren as rocks. At the time we were there it was two years fince they had any rain; but on the 19th of May came on violent fhowers, which continued the whole time we remained near the ifland. The inhabitants ufe the water which they fave in pits refembling cifterns, but this as well as the waters of the brooks on its beginning to rain, grow thick and brackifh. The Portuguefe indeed fay that in the inward parts of the ifland where thefe brooks have their origin, water is never wanting; and that it is clear and wholefome.

In the inland part of the ifland is a Portuguefe town, in which refide the parifh-prieft and a governor, who on advice of any fhips being in fight repair to the forts, which are all well garrifon'd, there being only in fort Remedios, while we were there, near 1000 men, partly regulars fent from Fernambuco, which are relieved every fix months, and partly tranſports, from all that coaſt of Braſil: and ſome, though few, which are ſettled here with their families, all being poor people and Meſtizos. Here are alſo ſome Indians who are ſent to work on the fortifications, and likewiſe to ſerve the governor and other officers in the iſland. Among theſe are an Almojarife or treaſurer and a proveditore, who controuls the payments and iſſues of proviſions to the troops and others: which is done with an equity and exactneſs worthy the imitation of Europeans.

The common food of the inhabitants of all ranks, both here and throughout Brazil, is the farina de Pau or wood-meal, which is univerſally eaten inſtead of bread. It is made of the root called Moniato, of which I have given an account in the deſcription of Carthagena; as well as of thoſe of Name and Yuca. They firſt cleanſe it and then macerate it in water, till the ſtrong and noxious juice in it be entirely extracted: then grate or grind it into meal; which having again ſoaked in ſeveral waters, they dry, and then eat it with a ſpoon or mix it with other foods. They are ſo habituated to it, that even at a table where they have wheat bread at command, with every mouthful of it they take a little of this meal. Beſides this flour, which is in fact, nothing more than wood-meal or ſaw-duſt, both with regard to taſte and ſmell, they eat a great deal of rice and ſugar-cane, brought from Fernambuco. Here are two tranſports belonging to the king of Portugal, for bringing proviſions and ſoldiers, the latter of which is done ſo methodically, that the time when they are to leave Brazil is ſettled: and thus while one is coming towards the iſland, the other is returning with the late garriſon.

After the ſecond ſettlement of the Portugueſe here, beſides the little plantations which was one of their firſt cares, they alſo brought over cows, hogs, and ſheep, in order to breed thoſe uſeful creatures; and as a small quantity of flesh serves the Portuguese, they are, even in this barren soil so greatly increased, that during our stay here we had the pleasure of victualling our crews with fresh provisions; and at our departure took on board a quantity sufficient to last us for several days.

THESE harbours or roads abound in fish of five or six different species: and among these are lampreys and Morenos; the last are of an enormous size, but neither of them palatable. At the bottom of this harbour is taken a fish called cope, from its triangular figure. It has a snout not unlike that of a hog; and its whole body inclosed in one bone resembling horn, within which is the flesh, intrails and other parts. On the two upper superficies it is covered with green scales, and underneath with white. It has two small fins like other fishes, and its tail which is horizontal, is also small. On being taken out of the water it immediately emits from its mouth a greenish froth of an insupportable smell, and which continues for a considerable time. Some of our people who had seen this fish in other parts affirmed, that its flesh is of such a poisonous nature as to cause the bodies of those who eat, tho' but moderately of it, to swell till they burst. But the people on this island were as positive to the contrary, and affirmed it from their own experience. They however make use of this precaution before they eat it, namely, of laying a great weight on it, that all the malignant particles might the better ooze out in the foam: and after keeping it a whole day in this manner, they open the hard shell within which it is inclosed, boil it till about half ready, and then shift it into another water. By these precautions they affirm that all the noxious particles are extracted. But, in my opinion, this troublesome process is thrown away, the taste of its flesh not being at all answerable: and were it even in any degree palatable, furely the remembrance of its fetid fmell muft difguft the ftomach.

DURING the feafon in which the turtles lay their eggs, namely from December to April, the fhores of the whole ifland are covered with them; after which retiring into the fea they difappear, as was the cafe when we were at Norona. In thefe months the winds are at N. and N. W; and from May forward they fhift to the E. fometimes inclining to the S. E. and at others to the N. E. The latitude of this ifland, as taken by feveral French pilots, at the time it was in poffeffion of that nation, is 3° 53' S. and thus it ftands in the new French map; and lies 33° W. of the obfervatory at Paris. Its diftance from the coaft of Brafil is betwixt 60 and 80 leagues; but this is not precifely determined, the French map placing it 60 leagues E. of it, whilft the Portuguefe pilots belonging to the tranfports, and who confequently, fhould be well acquainted with the paffage, judge it to be 80 leagues. By taking a medium betwixt the two, the diftance will be 70.

ON the frigates coming to an anchor in the bay, and all our apprehenfions diffipated by a certainty that the Portuguefe poffeffed this ifland, we took in our Englifh colours, and hoifted French; and fucceffively faluted the Portuguefe flag, which was anfwered by all the three forts in the bay. Afterwards an officer of the marquis d'Antin was fent afhore with compliments to the governor, in the name of the captains and mafters of the frigates. After a very polite reception, the governor fignified to the officer that his duty obliged him to be fully informed what frigates they were, whence they came, and whither they were bound; and that he defired the captains would fend him a written account, together with their commiffions, invoyances and clearances. And this indifpenfible demand being complied with, they might depend on all the friendly offices within his

power.

power. This was immediately done: and on his part, after an attentive perusal of the several papers, being satisfy'd with their contents, he wrote a very obliging letter to the captains, offering them whatever the island afforded: for besides his own personal disposition to act up to the laws of hospitality towards all who stood in need of succour, he and all the governors of Brasil had express orders in their commissions from their sovereign to shew all manner of friendship to any ships belonging to other states, which might put in to their ports; and likewise to furnish them all equally with whatever they wanted, provided it was not detrimental to his people or vessels, nor give just cause or complaint to any other nation at war. The French captains were not wanting to shew their sense of such humane and prudent expressions; and the generous governor soon shewed they were sincere, by furnishing whatever provisions we required as necessary, ordering a number of Indians to assist us in watering, and the transport to receive on board so much of the cargo of the Delivrance as was necessary to lighten her, in order to her being caulked and careen'd, that she might perform the remainder of the voyage with safety and dispatch.

Notwithstanding all the civility and friendship of the governor in every particular, we were in the same condition in the island, with regard to recreation and amusements, as if we had been at sea; being hardly permitted to go a-shore; the Portuguese from their natural suspicion and jealousy observed their orders with such precise strictness, that to go from the shore to the principal fort where the governor of the island resided, was the only walk allowed: and in this he who went a-shore was attended with three or four soldiers, who never left him, till he returned to the boat, which was immediately ordered to be put off. Guards were placed in all quarters of the harbour; and on seeing any boat, they immediately ran to the place they supposed she intended to land, in order to accompany the passengers. These disagreeable precautions, however, are to be imputed to the abrupt settlement made on this island by the French East India company, when the Portuguese retired from it; and now thinking it a place of great importance to the French, they preclude them from any acquaintance with the inland parts of the island, least such a knowledge might facilitate the execution of their supposed designs, namely of taking it from the Portuguese, and fortifying themselves in such a manner as not to be easily dislodged.

## CHAP. IV.

*Voyage from* FERNANDO DE NORONA. *Engagement with two English privateers.*

ON our arrival in the harbour of this island, our first care was to repair the Delivrance; but upon examination, her condition was found so bad, that to have entirely compleated her would have occasioned too great a delay. It was therefore thought proper to repair her only so far, as was necessary against the danger and fatigue of being continually at the pump; and accordingly, when we came to sea we found, that instead of repeating that fatiguing operation every half hour, once in an hour was now sufficient.

HAVING taken in the necessary supplies of wood and water, with some calves and hogs, it was determin'd to put to sea with all expedition, in order to retrieve in some measure, the delay which the repairs, however slight, of the Delivrance had occasioned.

June

CH. IV.   SOUTH AMERICA.   327

June the 10th at ten in the morning the frigates got under fail, and steered N. ¼ easterly till June the 18th, when they were in the latitude of 8 deg. 12 min. N. and 43 deg. 27 min. E. of Conception, having crols'd the line on the 12th under the meridian of 42 deg. 45 min. E. of that city, and 32 deg. 47 min. W. of Paris. We had fresh gales at S. till we came into the latitude of 6 deg. N. where the wind abated and became variable; sometimes N. N. E. and N. E; and at other times E. S. E. and E. N. E. but never blowing with any strength till the 8th of July, when, having steered N. E and N. we found ourselves in 34 deg. 31 min N. lat and 31 deg. 23 min. E. of Conception, where what little wind we had shifted to S. S. W. and S. W. From the 8th to the 31st of July we steered N. E. and N. E. ¼ northerly, except three days, when we ran E. N. E. and one day N. W. ¼ northerly, being forced to alter our true course by the winds, which veered to the N. and N. E.

On the 2d day after leaving the island, we lost sight of all birds of any kind, but saw great numbers of flying fish and bonitos. On the 13th of June in a clear night and settled breeze at S. E. without the least appearance of any disagreeable change, we were surpriz'd by a storm of wind and rain, that all we could do was to bear up under our courses. It was indeed too violent to last; and accordingly about an hour after the weather cleared up. On the 15th we began again to see Tunny fish in large shoals; and the 16th it was calm intermix'd with gentle breezes and showers, till the 17th. The same weather continued the 18th and 19th, with now and then thick clouds in the horizon, which we observed afterwards to go off in violent showers.

On the 20th of June in the lat. of 9 deg 28 min. N. we saw a bird, the only one which had appeared since our departure from the island. It was something larger than the Pardela, of a dark brown colour, except the breaſt and lower parts of the body, and the wings remarkably long. On the 22d ſqualls and ſhowers. On the 24th we ſaw great numbers of Tunnies, flying fiſh and cavallas, a fiſh not unlike a mackrel; and a bird of the ſame kind as that we ſaw on the 21ſt.

On the 27th, being in 17 deg. 57 min. N lat. the ſea was covered with a kind of weed called Sargaſo, which pickled, is by many thought equal to Samphire: and along this verdant ſurface our courſe continued till the 7th of July, that is, till we were in the lat. of 33 deg. 31 min. when little of it was to be ſeen. Whereas for ſome days before the whole ocean within ſight was, as it were, covered with it. During this time we alſo ſaw ſome birds; but particularly in the afternoon of the 29th of June, and on the 30th in the morning. Some of theſe were of a middling ſize and of a dark brown colour; alſo ſome black Rabiahorcados; and on the morning of the laſt day we alſo ſaw ſeveral rabijuncos. On the 1ſt of July we again had ſight of the abovementioned brown birds, but without any of the other two ſpecies: and on the 3d, being in 27 deg. 34 min. latitude, and 32 deg. 27 min. E. of Conception, we ſaw no kind of large fiſh, tho' abundance of the flying fiſh.

On the 8th being in 34 deg. 31 min. latitude, we again had ſight of the Dorados; and likewiſe ſaw a middle-ſized bird all black, which for a long time continued hovering about the ſhips. On the 9th in the evening, we were ſurprized with the appearance of a ſmall whale; and on the 10th in the morning, being in the latitude 36 deg. 57 min. and 32 deg. 6 min. E. of Conception, we ſaw ſeveral birds of a middling ſize, with long and broad wings, the neck, head and tail black, and the other parts of the body white.

## Ch. IV. SOUTH AMERICA.

On the 10th, being in 36 deg. 57 min. latitude, and 32 deg. 6. min. eaſt. of Conception, by my reckoning, according to which, and likewiſe in the Dutch and common French chart, the iſland of Flores, one of the Azores, lay E.N.E. 2 degrees N. diſtance 112 leagues. In the French chart are ſet down ſome iſlands, which, as being of later diſcovery, do not occur in the Dutch: among theſe is Santa Ana bearing weſtward five leagues; but by the new French chart, the iſland of Flores lay E.N.E. 5 deg. eaſterly and at the diſtance of 167 leagues. All this morning we had a cockling ſea coming from the N.W. and by W. which we conjectured might proceed from the proximity of the iſland of Santa Ana, as by our reckoning it muſt have been very near us.

On the 17th being in 41 deg. 49 min. latitude, and 36 deg. 48 min E. of Conception, we were amuſed with the ſight of vaſt flights of birds, of a middling bigneſs, and of a brown colour intermixed with black, reſembling on the whole the Cormorant. On the 18th we alſo ſaw great numbers of the ſame birds; but from the 19th when we were in 42 deg. 53 min. latitude, and 39 deg. 23 min. E. of Conception, they gradually decreaſed ſo that we ſaw very few of them.

From the time of our leaving the iſland of Fernando de Norona, till we reach'd the equinoctial, the S. latitude by obſervation every day exceeded that by account ten or eleven minutes, that is, the ſhip did not in reality, make ſo much way as ſhe ſeemed to do by the log-line. But after paſſing the equator, the latitude by obſervation continued ſtill to exceed that of the reckoning taken from the log-line: and as we ſtood directly north, it appeared that the ſhip's real way exceeded the diſtance meaſured; whence this corollary may be deduced, that in the ſouthern hemiſphere near the equinoctial, the

waters

waters tend fouthward; and that, on the contrary, in the northern hemifphere the current runs northward; which agrees with the accounts given of thofe, who in the voyages to the Eaft Indies have feveral times had occafion to crofs the line. Till the 24th of June the courfe of the waters continued northward 10 or 11 min. a day; but when we reached 14 deg. 22 min. the latitude by obfervation began to correfpond with that by account.

THE differences between the latitudes by account and obfervation can only be attributed to the courfe of the water in the two hemifpheres; and not to any defect n the meafurement by the log-line: for were that the cafe, how can it be reconciled with this known circumftance, that the way of the fhip whilft in the fouthern hemifphere was in reality lefs than it appeared by the log-line: and on coming into the northern hemifphere, it was quite the reverfe. As little can it be charged on any defect in the inftruments; for befides the daily agreement of all concerning the difference, when we were got out of thefe oppofite courfes of the water, the latitude by obfervation agreed with that by account. The preceding reafons alfo fhew, that the perfon who tended the log line was not carelefs; for if any error had been committed here, the difference would have continued, the management of it having on all occafions been entrufted to the fame perfon, who befides his fobriety and attention, was a complete artift. But the above caufe is further evident from the continual uniformity of the diftance, never exceeding ten or twelve minutes; or decreafing betwixt ten and twelve minutes every day: and that if on any day the latitude had not been obferved, on the day following the difference was found double; a circumftance that not only proves the reality of the currents here, but likewife confirms what we have faid in chapter 2d, concerning thofe in our paffage from Conception to this
ifland,

## CH. IV. SOUTH AMERICA.

island, exclusive of those which will be mentioned in the sequel.

On the 7th of June, being in 33 deg. 31 min. latitude, and 31 deg. 37 min. east of the meridian of Conception, we suddenly felt a strong motion of a current, which the more surpriz'd us, as we perceived nothing of that kind the day before, tho' in the same latitude. However, we were confirmed that we were not mistaken by our reckoning the following days, till the 11th, the latitude by observation daily exceeding by 13 or 15 min. that by account; but on the eleventh they again agreed. On the 12th in 39 deg. 44 min. latitude, that by observation again proved different to that by account, the former being less than the latter, by 13 min. And on the 13th the difference continued to be the same. Thus the course of the current continued lessening the ship's way, by carrying us southward till the 15th and 16th, when the difference became greater, but in an opposite direction; that is, the currents carried us northward. On the 17th they continued the same course, but on the 18th, we found 27 min. difference; having suddenly entered into waters of a different course, that is, they again carried us southward. Had this variety of differences been reported only by a single person, doubtless from the strangeness of the phænomenon, it would have been looked upon as a mistake in the observation; but the reality of these dangers does not now admit of any rational doubt. The observations were taken by seven persons, each with a different instrument, one of which was a quadrant invented by the celebrated Mr. Hadley, and all agreed in the differences. From the 18th day of the month to the 20th the difference betwixt the latitudes by observation, and that by account, proved to be 40 min. which was near double of that which had appeared in the course of the 18: and on the 20th we were in the latitude of

43 deg. 8 min. and 38 deg. 57 min. E. of the meridian of Conception.

Notice has already been taken of the indifferent condition of the Delivrance at our departure from the iſland of Fernando de Norona. And thus it continued till the 16th, when, whether it proceeded from the working of the ſhip or any other cauſe, the water increaſed ſo faſt that the ſhip was reduced to that diſtreſs, which had beeen the chief occaſion of our puttiug into the above iſland, and of our long ſtay there. On the 20th it increaſed upon us in ſuch a manner that the pumps were kept continually going the whole night; but on the 21ſt it ſuddenly abated to near a fourth part of what it had been the day before; a moſt ſeaſonable relief to the ſhip's company ſpent with a fatigue, which their fears rendered ſtill more painful. We obſerved that the water continued to decreaſe from the time of our getting into the ſargaſo or weeds, ſo that on the 27th the ſhip ſcarce made an eighth part of the water as on the 20th. This happy change could be attributed only to the ſargaſo ſuck'd into ſuch ſeams as were open: and this farther appear'd by ſeveral pieces of it thrown out by the pump; beſides a conſiderable quantity of the weed was ſeen ſticking to the outſide of the ſhip's bottom. But on the 29th the water began again to encreaſe, and ſoon after abated; in ſuch variations it continued during the whole voyage. And we according to its ſtate, fluctuating betwixt hope and fear.

On the 21ſt of July, about ſix in the morning, being in 43 deg. 57 min. latitude, and 39 deg. 44 min. E. of Conception, we diſcovered two ſail within three leagues of us; bearing E. N. E. The rays of the ſun had hinder'd us getting ſight of them ſooner. They ſtood to the S. W. and our three ſhips kept on together N E. without altering their courſe till ſeven in the morning, when being within little more than

cannon

CH. IV.   SOUTH AMERICA.   333

cannon-ſhot of each other, the largeſt of the two fired a gun with ſhot, and at the ſame time both hoiſted Engliſh colours, our frigates alſo formed a line, tho' little in a condition for fighting; for beſides being weakly mann'd, and the want of arms and ammunition, they had no nettings for ſecuring the men, ſo that both the quarter deck and forecaſtle were expoſed.

WE, however, after the enemy had hoiſted their colours, continued ſailing in a line, but ſtill in our proper courſes, till the ſmalleſt of the Engliſh ſhips bore down upon us, and fired ſeveral ſhot to oblige us to hoiſt our colours; on which at half an hour after ſeven a fire both of great guns and muſketry began on both ſides; and at eight o'clock the ſhips were within piſtol ſhot of each other.

THE force of the three French frigates was this, the Louis Eraſme carried twenty guns; eight on the quarter deck of eight pounders, and the twelve on the fore-caſtle ſix pounders, and had betwixt ſeventy and eighty perſons on board ſeamen, paſſengers and boys. The marquis d'Antin alſo carried ten guns on a ſide, the five aftermoſt of ſix pounders, and the five forward of four; and had aboard about fifty or fifty five perſons. La Delivrance was ſtill ſmaller than the other two, having only ſeven four pounders on a ſide, and all the perſons on board did not exceed fifty one.

THE enemy who afterwards proved privateers, were conſiderably ſuperior in force. The largeſt of them called the Prince Frederick, commanded by captain James Talbot, carried thirty guns, twenty four of them being twelve pounders, beſides croſsbar ſhots which ſtuck in our maſts and ſides, and ſix ſix pounders on the quarter deck. The name of the ſmalleſt privater was the Duke, captain Morecock, had ten guns on a ſide, and theſe likewiſe twelve pounders, beſides paderevos on both, which did great execution

on

on our rigging. The Prince Frederick to all appearance keeping a continual fire both with the great guns and small arms, could not carry less than two hundred or two hundred and fifty men, and the complement of the Duke from the like circumstances we concluded to be about one hundred and fifty or two hundred.

THE fight was maintain'd with great resolution and alacrity on both sides, though under this considerable disadvantage to the French, that one broad side from the enemy did twice the execution of one from their ships: and as for musketry, with which the English were well furnished, and kept an incessant fire, all that the French could use, was about twelve or fourteen on board each ship, it being present death for any one to shew himself on the forecastle, and a musket was what very few on board knew how to make use of. At length about half an hour after ten the marquis d'Antin, which was in our rear struck to the largest of the enemy, with which she was engaged, after losing her captain, who died encouraging his men with the same vigour that he had begun the action. And however reluctant they who survived were to the surrender, it was now become of absolute necessity, the ship having received so many shot betwixt wind and water, that she was on the point of sinking.

THE captain of the Delivrance, which was the headmost ship, seeing one of our company taken, and judging from this diminution of our force, there was still less hope of a successful event, he prudently crowded sail, that whilst the enemy's ships were taken up with their prize, that he might get from them; for no sooner had the marquis d'Antin struck her colours, than the least of the enemy's ships withdrew from the action which she had alternately maintain'd with the other two, in order to secure the prize, whilst the larger was to renew the fight.

It

It was half an hour after eleven when the Delivrance thus began to seek her safety in flight: the Louis Erasme could not hesitate to follow her example, but the largest of the English privateers was not long in coming up with her, and by the superiority of their force, and the vigour with which they exerted it, soon laid her under a necessity of surrendering, though not till the worthy captain had been wounded, so that he died the following day. The two privateers being now taken up each with its prize, and the S. E. wind freshening, favoured the escape of the Delivrance, which stood N. E. and at four in the evening got quite out of sight both of privateers and prizes.

The cargoes of the marquis d'Antin and the Louis Erasme, thus taken, were valued at three millions of dollars, two in coin, gold and silver, and ingots, or wrought plate. The other consisted in cacao, which was the principal part of her lading; some Quinquina and Vigonia wool.

## CHAP. V.

*Voyage of the* Delivrance *to* LOUISBURGH *in l' Isle* ROYALE *or* CAPE BRITON, *where she was also taken.*

THE captain of the Delivrance, after this, in all appearance, fortunate escape, consulted with his officers what course was most adviseable to steer. Among them was one who had often been at Louisburgh in the island of Cape Breton, near Newfoundland; and had a perfect knowledge of the situation and nature of the place. He likewise informed us, that in the beginning of the summer, two men of war were every year sent thither, to carry money and troops

troops for that place and Canada; and likewife to
protect the cod-fifhery.

As this was the conftant practice in time of the
moft profound peace, it was natural to fuppofe, that
in a war with a maritime power, the number of fhips
would be increafed: at leaft, this precaution had
never been omitted in the laft war under Lewis XIV,
the place being of the utmoft importance to France,
as the key of Canada, the moft fecure port for the
fifhery, and carrying on a very confiderable commerce
with the iflands of St. Domingo and Martinico.
Thefe reafons and this courfe appearing lefs dangerous
than that towards the coaft of Spain, determined
the captain to purfue what he thought
the fafeft method, and make for Cape Breton: befides,
the condition of our fhip fcarce permitted any
choice, as affording little hopes that fhe ever would
be able to reach any port in Spain. We had likewife
been informed at Conception, a little before
our departure, that a company had been formed in
London for fitting out thirty privateers from twenty
to thirty guns, and to be ftationed fo as to intercept
all fhips coming from the Indies. Though this
was in fact a falfe alarm, the misfortune of meeting
the two abovementioned of a force agreeing with
the report, gave it to us all the appearance of truth;
and we concluded that there muft be many more
cruifing in proper ftations nearer the coafts. This
opinion was very natural to us, who for above two
years had received no other accounts; and after
what had happened, it would have feemed an inexcufable
ftep, to have expofed fuch a valuable cargo,
as that of the Delivrance, in fuch a heavy veffel, as
muft unqueftionably have fallen into the hands of the
firft enemy that fhould give her chace. All her force
confifted in fourteen four-pounders, and about fifteen
mufkets; befides nine of our people had been difabled
in the laft action: and what was ftill worfe, we
had

had little or no powder. Another bad circumstance was, that from the damage the ship had received in the action, she made so much water, that though we began to pump immediately on the conclusion of it, it was midnight before we could free the ship; and every one who had received no hurt in the action, without distinction, voluntarily took his turn in the labour. Weighty as these reasons were, that the captain and his officers might not be charged with taking such an important step of themselves, a representation was also made to the passengers, who all readily approving of it as the best resource in our present exigency, the very same evening our course was altered; and we began to steer for Louisbourg as a port of safety.

The place where the action happened, according to my reckoning and the new French chart, was 96 leagues N.W. 5 degrees westerly from the island of Flores.

After changing our course we steered N.W. one quarter westerly, and W. one quarter northerly, till the 28th, when by observation we found ourselves in the latitude of 46 degrees, 18 minutes, and 23 degrees, 45 minutes east of Conception, the winds generally being S.S.W. and W.S.W. One day only we had them at N.W. and W.N.W. and this was on the 23d after a very violent storm, which began at twelve in the night of the 22d, at E.S.E. whence at six in the morning the wind flew about to the S. and S. one quarter westerly, whilst we lay to under our mainsail; and, when the wind offered, made way under that and a topsail with a reef in both; besides the high seas which such a storm naturally occasioned, we had also fogs and rains.

From the 46th degree we continued steering W: sometimes a little towards the S. or N. endeavouring always to keep that latitude, though sometimes the winds obliged us to alter our course: for though they were generally S.S.W. and S.W. though oftner in the firſt than the ſecond; they ſometimes came about to the N. E. E. and S. E. and theſe changes were always attended with hurricanes.

On the 5th of Auguſt we found ourſelves in the latitude of 45°, 14′, and 24°, 16′ E. of the meridian of Conception; the wind, which till ſix in the evening of the foregoing day had been S. now became calm; and at two in the morning, we had it at W. N. W. and N. W. from whence it veered N. about to the E. and from thence again returned back to the N. E. freſhening more than it had done before. Afterwards it began to blow in ſqualls, and again ſhifted to the N. On the 6th, at eight in the evening, it veered to the E. and two hours after to E. S. E. where it continued till ſix in the morning of the ſeventh, when it ſettled in the S. E. and abated; tho' its greateſt force here had never been ſuch as to render it neceſſary for us to lay to, as had been the caſe before, and was again afterwards.

On the 7th, being in the latitude of 45°, 17′, and the wind at S. at two in the afternoon it ſuddenly flew about to the W. where its extreme violence obliged us to furl every ſail, and lie to. We had alſo here a very high ſea to encounter with, but in two hours our apprehenſions were relieved, the wind ſhifting to the N. W. and abating conſiderably; and two hours after it again returned to the N. whence at ten at night it veered to W. one quarter ſoutherly, and became ſo moderate that we could carry our top-ſails. Here it ſettled, and the weather became fair and eaſy; but theſe variations, by forcing us out of our true courſe, were of great detriment to us, as will be ſeen in the ſequel.

On the 10th, being in the latitude of 45°, 14′, and 17°, 25′ E. of Conception, with the wind at S. it began to blow, and at five in the morning we were obliged to take in all the reefs in our top ſails; it

then

then shifted to the S. S. W. with a prodigious sea; so that at three in the afternoon we were obliged to lie to under a reefed mainsail. At ten o'clock it shifted to the S. W. and S. W. one quarter westerly; when abating a little on the 11th, at six in the morning, we made way under our foresail and topsails all reef'd; and the wind continued for some time in this rhomb.

The usual inclination of the wind in these seas, and common to all parts of the northern hemisphere, is to follow the sun from E. to S. S. S. W. and N. something like what has been observed in the chapters which treat of the South-sea. And thus when it has blown a storm, instead of continuing its inclination, it returns; and tho' with all the appearance of a calm, within a day or two it rises again with redoubled fury. This is a difficulty not easily solved, for among the great number of persons, otherwise doubtless respectable for their eminent talents, who have applied themselves to investigate the causes and origin of winds, not one of them has accounted for their irregularities and gradations, both with regard to their variations, impulse, and direction.

In this passage to the Newfoundland seas, storms are very frequent, yet they differ according to the seasons of the year. We have already seen that they most usually happen when the wind is at S. and tho' the northern winds are very strong, yet they do not equal those of the former quarters. On attending to this particular, a certain conformity will be found betwixt the two opposite hemispheres; as in each, besides the circulation of the winds, the storms happen when they blow from that part of the pole opposite to that which is nearest each hemisphere. In the south sea the storms generally rise from the N. and W. winds; and in that of the N. they are occasioned by the S. and W. winds.

The hard gales which are met with in fummer in the paffage to Newfoundland, are of no long continuance, like the two with which we were furprized in this voyage; but they are more fudden and violent than in winter; for from their beginning to the very height of their violence is fcarce half an hour; and though in this feafon they are not very frequent, yet it never paffes without fome: but in winter they continue three or four days fucceffively, and with no fmall force. Thefe of both feafons are more or lefs accompanied with fogs and fhowers.

JULY the 31ft, according to my account, at eight in the morning, being in 45 degrees, 57 minutes latitude, and 27 degrees, 3 minutes E. of Conception, we found by the whitifh tinge of the water, that we had entered on the bank; and on founding found 55 fathom, and the bottom, fand mixed with fmall fhells. On comparing the founding and the bottom with the new French map, my reckoning of the courfe was fix or feven leagues too forward; that is, we had that diftance to fail before we came to a bottom of that kind. On the evening we tack'd with an intent of leffening our latitude, as well to keep at a diftance from Placentia, as to avoid fome fhoals lying at the weft end of the bank in the latitude of 46 deg. and on this account we again ftood from it.

ON the 2d of Auguft being in the latitude of 45 deg. 30 min. 30 fec. 27 deg. 2 min. E. of Conception, we founded, and found 70 fathom water, and the bottom rocky. We continued our foundings every day, and found the bottom as fpecified in the following table:

Days

## Ch. V.   SOUTH AMERICA.

| Days | Latitude | Long. from Merid. of Conception | Fathom of Water. | Bottom | Colour of the Water. |
|---|---|---|---|---|---|
| 4 Aug. | 45 14 | 24 38 | 40 | small gravel | green |
| 5 | 45 12 | 23 50 | 48 | brown gravel | whitish |
| 6 | 45 8 | 22 56 | 48 | stony | sea blue |
| 6 | 45 9 | 22 30 | 50 | ditto | ditto |
| 6 | 45 11 | 21 51 | 55 | small gravel and sand of different colours | light blue |
| 7 | 45 18 | 19 53 | 35 | coarse white sand and small gravel | dark blue |
| 8 | 45 23 | 20 12 | 45 | coarse sand of all colours and small gravel | whitish green |
| 8 | 45 26 | 20 7 | no bottom at 80 fathom | | ditto |
| 9 | 45 20 | 19 12 | ditto | | light blue |
| 10 | 45 16 | 17 14 | 45 | stony | of a blueish green |
| | 45 19 | 16 32 | no bottom at 80 fathom | | dark green |

July the 27th, in the latitude of 45 deg. 54. min. and 32 deg. 6 min. E. of Conception, we saw some birds as it were sporting on the water. The size of them was something less than a wood-pigeon, and all over black except the tail which was white. They who are conversant in these voyages say, that they are seen at a great distance from the bank; and thus we found it, being obliged to lessen our longitude 5 deg. to return to our first soundings. We also saw two birds of that kind called Penguins, of which there are great numbers on the bank: and tho' in the common opinion these birds never fly to any great distance from it, we found it otherwise. These penguins are of the bigness and shape of a goose, also with little or no tail. They fly against the course of the water; their plumage on their breast and belly is white, but their back, the upper part of their wings and all their neck brown. As fish is their whole subsistence, they dart down into the water with prodigious celerity, and continue a long time under it in pursuit of their prey.

On the 30th, in the latitude of 45 deg. 54 min. and 28 deg. deg. 43 min. E. of Conception, we again saw some

some of the same birds as on the 27th, besides some small whales near the ship. During the whole remainder of the voyage we had always sight of these kind of birds, and another very nearly resembling the Penguin; but the bill was black, very large, and of a square form. Both kinds swarm on the bank, but without it they are not so frequent. On our approach to the bank we also saw great numbers of cavallas, which abound all along the coasts. We likewise saw some shoals of tunny fish. About the edge of the bank there is always a great swell: but on coming within the soundings, even in a hard gale of wind, tho' attended with a high sea, it does not continue any longer than the wind; the one subsiding as the other abates.

IF I have been so very circumstantial in my account of the voyage from Conception, and given a detail not only of the winds and times of the year, but also of the agitation of the sea, in storms and hard gales, the course, the colour of the water, and the signs of birds and fishes, I hope it will be attributed to my zeal for the improvement of navigation, and my desire that mariners who are strangers to this voyage, might be acquainted with these things which are certainly of real utility; as by thus acquiring a knowledge of the latitudes and longitudes, which are punctually set down at every sign or an extraordinary occurrence, they might be acquainted with the particulars of every part; and consequently the better enabled to take the most proper measures; and that nothing may be wanting for their information in the particulars of this last voyage, I shall postpone the account of our misfortune at Louisbourg, to insert here

A table of variations of the needle as observed in our passage, from Fernando de Norona, to Cape Breton, according to the latitudes, and longitudes

from

## CH. V.　SOUTH AMERICA.

from the island of Conception, in which the observations were made.

| Days of the Month. | Lat. D. M. | Long. D. M. | Variations D. M. | Time of making Observation. |
|---|---|---|---|---|
| June 11 | 1 24 S. | 42 35 | 2 39 E. | Evening. |
| 12 | 0 16 N. | 42 50 | 2 43 E. | Ditto. |
| 17 | 7 14 | 43 32 | 0 38 W. | Ditto. |
| 19 | 8 17 | 43 21 | 1 40 | Morning. |
| 27 | 18 16 | 35 46 | 1 15 | Ditto. |
| July 3 | 27 11 | 32 34 | 0 10 | Ditto. |
| 3 | 27 58 | 32 24 | 1 20 | Evening. |
| 4 | 28 47 | 32 17 | 1 20 | Morning. |
| 6 | 32 44 | 31 58 | 6 50 | Evening. |
| 7 | 33 16 | 31 44 | 6 55 | Morning. |
| 9 | 35 47 | 31 46 | 7 0 | Evening. |
| 12 | 40 10 | 32 58 | 8 5 | Morning. |
| 13 | 40 22 | 34 17 | 10 55 | Evening. |
| 17 | 41 35 | 36 16 | 11 0 | Morning. |
| 20 | 43 24 | 38 41 | 11 0 | Evening. |
| 25 | 45 7 | 34 29 | 15 50 | Ditto. |
| 29 | 46 7 | 28 10 | 14 30 | Ditto. |
| 30 | 45 59 | 28 16 | 13 10 | Morning. |
| Aug. 5 | 45 12 | 23 41 | 20 15 | Evening. |
| 8 | 45 22 | 20 12 | 13 20 | Morning. |
| 8 | 45 27 | 19 45 | 13 0 | Evening. |
| 9 | 45 22 | 18 39 | 15 15 | Morning. |

On the 24th of July, in the latitude of 44 deg. 52 min. by observation, which was 25 min. less than that by account, and according to my estimate 36 deg. 6 min. east of Conception; no observation had been taken since the 20th. But we found that the currents had in each days sailing carried the ship 6 min. S. On the 25th in the latitude of 45 deg. 6 min. and 34 deg. 47 min. east of the same meridian, we again found the latitude by observation to be 8 min. less than that by account. But afterwards they agreed till we had pass'd the bank, when on the 12th of August, 16 deg. 2 min. east of Conception, our latitude by observation, was 45 deg. 58 min. an excess of just 30 min. beyond that by the reckoning; and this great difference had commenced on the 9th, when we were in 45 deg. 22 min. latitude, and 19 deg. 1 min. eaſt of Conception.

FROM this difference it is manifeſt that, on the weſt ſide of the bank, betwixt it and Cape Breton, that is under the meridian of Placentia, the currents ſet to the northward, agreeably to the opinion of the pilots in thoſe ſeas, who all declare that the ſea ſets into the gulph of Canada by the ſtreight betwixt cape Roze, the moſt weſtern point of the iſland of Newfoundland, and the north cape in the iſle royale; and diſcharges itſelf by the ſtreight of Beliſle, formed by the main land and the north point of Newfoundland: and we ſenſibly found on making the coaſt, that the waters carried the ſhip northward.

ON the 12th of Auguſt in the morning, we ſaw a great number of thoſe kinds of ſea-fowl which always keep near the ſhore, and particularly ſeveral gulls, from which with the courſe we had ſteered from the time of our coming into ſoundings on the 2d of Auguſt, we concluded ourſelves to be not far from land, having alſo diminiſhed our longitude exactly 11 deg. In this conjecture we were ſoon confirmed by weeds, pieces of wood and boughs floating on the water, and at twelve o'clock we actually made the land, tho' at a great diſtance. At four o'clock in the afternoon we had a plain ſight of it; but being low and level we were obliged to ſhorten ſail and lie to, till the following day, when at half an hour after ſix in the morning, we ſaw the iſland of Eſcatari, which lies about five leagues north of Louiſburgh: but the wind continuing S.W. and the current ſetting the ſhip northward, we were obliged to work up towards the harbour.

ON the 13th, at ſix in the morning, we ſaw a brigantine plying along the coaſt for Louiſbourg; the Delivrance on this hoiſted a French enſign, which was anſwered by the other, firing two or three guns. This gave us no manner of uneaſineſs; con-

concluding that the brigantine suspecting some deceit in our colours, had fired those guns as a warning to the fishing barks without, to get into the harbour; and they put the same construction on this firing, immediately shewing the greatest hurry in making for a place of safety. An hour afterwards, being near eight o'clock, we saw coming out of Louisburgh two men of war, which we immediately took for ships belonging to a French squadron station'd there for the security of that important place, and that they had come out on the signal from the brigantine, that a ship had appeared in sight, lest it might be some Boston privateer, with a design on the fishery. Thus we were under no manner of anxiety, especially as they came out with French colours, and one of them had a pennant. All the forts of Louisbourg, as well as all the ships in the harbour, which we could now plainly distinguish, wore the like disguise. Here I must refer to the reader's imagination the complacency and joy which swell'd every heart, imagining that we now saw the end of all our fears and disasters; a place of safe repose after a voyage of danger and fatigue. Then let the reader be pleased to think what an edge the melancholy disappointment gave to our astonishment and dejection, when amidst the indulgence of such pleasing ideas, we found our hopes destroyed, and all our visionary schemes of delight, ending in the real miseries of captivity.

We were now so near the two ships which were coming out of the harbour, that orders had been given for hoisting the boat out to go with an officer on board that which seemed to be the commodore; and we unloaded our guns of their shot to salute them. The smallest which carried fifty guns leading the way, came along side of us; then indeed from what we both heard and saw, our fatal disappointment became too evident, and our misfortune was

was immediately confirmed to us, the ſhip hoiſting its national colours, and firing into us carried away the foretopſail halliards, that the ſail drop'd down, and at the ſame time the larger ſhip came up on the ſtar-board ſide of us. Betwixt two ſuch enemies no reaſonable perſon will offer to charge the captain of the Delivrance with cowardice, that without offering any reſiſtance, which would have been a wild temerity, he immediately ſtruck his colours. The boat from the ſmalleſt ſhip came aboard and took poſſeſſion of us, having as ſhe advanced been hoiſted out for that purpoſe: and thus after firing only one gun, return'd into the harbour with a very rich prize.

This accident gave a total change to our flattering expectations; brought ruin on our fortunes: overthrew all our ideas of the uſe and improvement of them. Our joy was ſtifled in its birth; and inſtead of our anticipated repoſe, we entered on a new ſcene of troubles and diſtreſs, aggravated by the loſs of our ſubſtance and liberty, where we had promis'd ourſelves recreation and enjoyment.

These two Engliſh men of war were the Sunderland, captain John Brett, of ſixty guns, and the Cheſter, captain Philip Durell, of fifty: and it was to the latter that the Delivrance ſtruck. The officers, captain Durell, for their better accommodation, ſent to the houſe which had been aſſigned him, when, purſuant to the articles of capitulation at the taking of Louiſbourg, the inhabitants were ſent back to France. This houſe he made but little uſe of, living continually aboard the ſhip.

As to my papers, on our departure from Fernando de Norona, I had made a packet of all the plans and relations which might have been of ſervice to the enemy; alſo the vice-roy's letters and other papers committed to my care, that on an exigency they might be ready to be ſunk. I had alſo deſired of the captain, the ſupercargo and other officers, that in

caſe

case it was my fate suddenly to fall in the action, they would do me that kind office. Accordingly when I saw that there was no possibility either of opposing or getting clear of the enemy, I threw them into the water, with some bullets fasten'd to them, to disappoint the alertness of the enemy, who otherwise would unquestionably have been for laying hold of them; but my papers relating to the mensuration of the degrees of the meridian, together with the physical and astronomical observations and historical narratives, I kept by me, the contents being of universal concern, and no detriment could result from the enemy's knowledge of them: but as among men who seem'd to mind nothing but what was silver or gold, they would have ran a great risk of being abused or confounded among a multitude of others, I thought proper to acquaint the captains on what service I had been, and as those papers tended to the improvement of navigation, took the liberty of recommending them to their favour: upon which, after having looked on them with some attention, they laid them aside, and carried them afterwards to the commander of the squadron, with whom they remain'd, till, together with myself, they were sent to England.

## CHAP. VI.

*Don* GEORGE JUAN's *Voyage from* LA CONCEPTION *to* GUARICO *in the Island of* SAN DOMINGO; *and from thence to* BREST *in* FRANCE, *together with his return to* MADRID.

THE frigate la Lys, having on the 5th of February, parted company from the three others, on account of her making six inches water every hour,

hour, which would naturally increase by the working of the ship, steered directly for Valparaiso, where making all possible dispatch in careening and watering, on the 1st of March she was ready to put to sea. The winds, as is usual at that season, being at S. and S.W. the Lys was obliged to stand to the northward of the island of Juan Fernandes; and drive till she was in the latitude of 32 deg. 18. min. where she fell in with a wind at S. E. which carried her to the latitude of 35 deg. and 11 deg. W. of the meridian of Valparaiso; here it shifted to the S. W. and thence along the N. W. quarter to the N. in which time the Lys only got into the latitude of 36° 30′ being the 17th day of the month. Here the wind veered to the S. and S. W. blowing very hard, which caused such a sea that they were obliged to lie to under their mainsail. On the 18th, tho' the violence of the wind abated, it continued in the same point: afterwards it changed to the W. and N. W. where it continued till the ship came into 40° 30′ latitude, still keeping the same longitude of 11°. Here she met with a second hard gale at south, which they weathered in the same manner, till it abated, shifting immediately to the S.W. west, and N.W.

On the 25th, in the latitude of 46° they met with a storm at W. which obliged them to lie to under a reefed mainsail. After its greatest violence was spent, till the fourth of April, when they found themselves in 58° latitude and 1 E. long. from Valparaiso, the first meridian for the course of the voyage, the wind shifted from S. to S.W. W. and N. varying also in its force; and the ship carrying sail accordingly.

On the 10th in the lat. of 55 and 18° east of Valparaiso, they were surprized with a hard gale of wind at S. and S. E; which obliged them to run under their courses. The force of the wind indeed was not so great as in the two gales beforementioned;

tioned; but was much more troublesome, being attended with very thick snow, and the cold intense. The wind abating shifted to the S.W.W. and N. W. whilst the ship passing east of Staten land, on the 26th was in the lat. of 34° and long. 32 and 30'. Here they fell in with winds at E. and S.E. which indeed are the brisas or general winds.

The slow progress of the voyage, and the heaviness of the frigate, which even in the most favourable weather, never went above seven miles an hour, gave room to apprehend, that it would be impossible to reach the coast of Spain, without putting in to some harbour for a fresh supply of provisions; the captain therefore represented to the supercargo, that no place could be more proper for such a purpose than Monte-Video, being a Spanish port; and that if they passed it, they should be obliged to make use of one belonging to some foreign power. But he, conformably to the precise order of the register against putting into any harbour, unless on the coast of Spain, could not be prevailed upon to comply with the captain's proposal: and accordingly the course was pursued without alteration.

The winds continued at S. E. E. sometimes at S. and S. W. with heavy rains, thunder and lightning, till the frigate came into 23° of lat. and 39 of longitude.

On the 12th of May, at one in the morning, they discovered a small frigate to leeward; and on the 19th being in 10° 30' S. latitude and 39 east longitude, saw three large ships: but both sides continued their respective course, without making any motion to avoid or approach each other.

On the 27th they crossed the line, 44° east of Valparaiso, or 30° 30' W. of Paris. As these parts abound in sharks, they caught several, and one of them, after opening it and taking out its intrails, heart and lungs, they threw it again into the water; and it being

being calm they saw it swim near the frigate above a quarter of an hour, till floating out of sight they could not see the death of the creature. The heart also of this and many others on which the same experiment was tried, was observed to have a motion on board the ship for above a quarter of an hour.

On the first of June, the frigate was in 4° 30' N. lat. the wind N. E. and S. E; and sometimes at S. and S. W. with heavy rains; but now the provisions, and particularly water growing short, the captain, with the approbation of his officers and passengers, determined to put in at Martinico, and accordingly the course was directed thither.

On the 11th in the morning, being in the latitude of 9° 30', and 39° east of Valparaiso, they had sight of three large ships which continued their course without standing for the frigate; and as their courses were directly opposite, they soon lost sight of each other.

On the 21st at night, they had a short squall rather of rain than wind, but the night being dark, they saw at the top-gallant-mast head, the meteor called by the sailors San Telmo, which lasted six hours. Some imagine this meteor to be a sign of fair weather; but this opinion is as little to be relied on as many others adopted without reflection, and justly called vulgar errors: it is only a natural phænomenon, more particularly seen in nitrous and damp places of the earth, in church yards and the like, and on the sea it proceeds from the same cause; and tho' it most commonly makes its appearance in stormy weather, the agitation of the waves sending forth a greater quantity of nitrous particles, and being more copiously carried up to a greater height, by the force of the winds, the luminous matter settles at the extremity of the masts or yards by a small part of it, whilst the remainder has the appearance of a flame

in

in the air: yet it is not very uncommon to see this meteor in fair easy weather: and this was the case here, it being quite calm; and in the Delivrance on the 9th of August, at half an hour after one in the morning, and in 28° 40' S. lat. we saw one of these kinds of lights, and on the same part of the mast; but ours only lasted an hour, the wind at that time was but faint; and this also had been preceeded by hard violent showers attended with some wind; and the atmosphere every where covered with a thick cloud. In both instances no tempest happened before or soon after; consequently they concurred to confute and explode the false notions of sailors, who are possessed with a belief of certain consequences being presaged by these lights, according to their situation, the part of the sea and the time; and may likewise undeceive those, who too easily swimming with the stream of vulgar opinions, are fond of turning the fortuitous effects and products of nature into ominous mysteries.

On the 15th, in the long. of 13° 30' they saw great numbers of birds, which in their opinion indicated that land was not far off, and accordingly lay to all that night, and the following: but fearing that some English privateers might be cruizing to windward of Martinico, in order to avoid them the Lys steered for the island of Tobago, intending to go directly from thence to Martinico. On the 28th the colour of the water become totally changed, so as to resemble that of a turbid river; which they attributed to the issue of the Oronoco, tho' the mouth of that river is betwixt sixty and seventy leagues distant; lying to in the night they sounded and found sixty fathom water, and a muddy bottom.

On the 29th, at half an hour after seven in the morning, they made the island of Tobago lying westward: and at noon saw the little island of San Gil, distant about two leagues from the N. E. from the

former:

former: it bore S. three leagues and a half or four leagues off: and the latitude obferved at the fame hour, was 11° 36'. According to the obfervations of longitude taken at Valparaifo and Martinico, deducting from them that of the ifland of Tobago, the error in Don George Juan's eftimate was only thirty five leagues, which may rather be termed an inaccuracy, being abundantly fufficient for, or at leaft, it was of a fufficient juftnefs in a voyage of fuch a length; and from it I conclude that they met with no currents about Cape Horn; tho' not above a month before, when the Delivrance failed round the cape, we found them very ftrong; and confequently they muft foon after ceafe. The fame change was obfervable in the weather, and this partly occafioned that of the currents, for tho' the wind was at S.E. during that part of our voyage, yet it was not conftantly there, nor had we any of thofe hard gales which the Lys met with: an evident proof that thofe winds already prevail'd there; and thus check'd the courfe of the waters, keeping them in their eaftern fituation.

From the ifland of Tobago, they continued their courfe to Martinico, and in order to this fteered all the night of the 20th betwixt the ifland of Barbadoes and St. Vincent. On the 30th, when they imagined themfelves betwixt thofe iflands, having fteered N. $\frac{1}{4}$ northerly, they had no fight of any land. On the 1ft of July they were in 14° 30' lat. and by eftimate a degree W. of Tobago: and thus the frigate fhould have been not far from the ifland and to windward of Martinico; but they ftill were out of fight of all land. So great a difference in the fhort time of two days fail was conjectured to proceed from currents; but the greateft perplexity was to determine whether they fet to the eaft or weft. This doubt, however, was removed by confidering that it was impoffible they could have paffed thro' the knot

of

of iſlands, from Granada to Martinico, without ſeeing at leaſt one of them, even if it had been in the night time, as beſides their magnitude, the great concern they were under of meeting the enemy, cauſed them to keep a very careful look-out. It was therefore concluded that the frigate could not be to the weſt of Martinico, but that the currents had drove her to the eaſtward. Accordingly they ſteered S. W. $\frac{1}{4}$ weſterly, in order to fall in with it; and after ſailing thus thirty leagues without making any land, other reflections aroſe, tho' ſtill with ſome apprehenſion that they were to the weſt of Martinico; and now the courſe was altered to N. without knowing the place where the ſhip actually was, in order to avoid the danger that if ſhe was on the weſt ſide, by ſteering as the day before ſhe would fall to leeward of the harbours of Puerto-Rico or St. Domingo; and thus find it extreamly difficult to reach any port. The wind was at E. N. E. and keeping as cloſe to it as poſſible, on the fourth at half an hour after three in the afternoon, they made the middle part of the iſland of Puerto-Rico. This was a tranſporting ſight to all, as having before their eyes a ſecure and plentiful port: and having happily eſcaped the dangers of the granadillas, a knot of iſlands where the greateſt channel is but three or four leagues broad, the currents having very providentially carried the ſhip thro' the midſt of them, clear of the rocks, which on both ſides have proved fatal to many veſſels: and they had not ſo much as any ſight of land. By don George Juan's eſtimate he found that they might when they ſteer'd betwixt the iſlands of Barbadoes and St. Vincent, the currents had carried them almoſt forty two leagues to the weſt: and tho' they all very well knew that the courſe of the waters in that part of the neighbourhood of Martinico ſets weſtward, they were at at a loſs to conceive how they had paſſed betwixt thofe iflands without having fight of any one, they lying fo near one another, the night being clear, and every one keeping a good look out.

On the night of the 4th day, they fometimes lay to, and fometimes made an eafy fail, in order to get into the channel betwixt the iflands of Puerto-Rico and St. Domingo, intending for Guarico, otherwife called cape Francois. On the 5th at fix in the morning, the S. W. point of the ifland of Puerto-Rico bore N. at about four leagues diftance: and ftanding towards it till within the diftance of only two leagues, they could very plainly fee the bottom, which was ftony; and on founding found feven fathom water. On this they tack'd to the W. and continuing in this direction about two hours, they had always the fame depth of feven fathom, but coming into twenty they returned to their former courfe.

At eleven in the forenoon they difcovered to leeward two large fhips: and apprehending they might belong to the enemy, the frigate tack'd: on which they alfo did the fame, and crowded fail. At noon the latitude by obfervation, was 8° 7'. And the ifland of Defecheo bore N. ¼ wefterly, diftant five leagues. The two privateers, for fuch it is believed they were, lay becalmed; and this enabled the Lys to keep at the fame diftance as when fhe firft difcovered them; and the wind frefhning to the N. about fun fet, fhe ftood E. N. E. in order to get clofe to the fhore, and thus avoid the two fuppofed privateers, determined however to make a ftout refiftance, if they fhould be obliged to come to that extremity. Afterwards the wind fhifted to E. N. E. and the privateers continuing S. W. the Lys fteered northward and weathered the ifland of Defecheo about two leagues. The wind afterwards frefhen'd, and at eleven at night the Lys fpread all the canvas poffible, fteering N. W. and by the 6th in the morning, had neither fight of the land nor the privateers.

On the 7th at fix in the morning they made old cape

Ch. VI.  SOUTH AMERICA.  355

cape Francois five leagues diſtance; they kept in with the coaſt, and at noon by obſervation found the latitude 19° 55′ from which they concluded that of the cape to be about 19° 40′, and tho' the land which projects into the ſea be low, the inland parts appear very mountainous.

On the 8th at ſix in the morning, cape la Grange bore S. diſtant five leagues; and by noon the frigate being within three leagues of cape Francois harbour, lay to with a ſignal for a pilot, who being come aboard, carried the Lys into the harbour, where ſhe anchor'd at two in the afternoon, in eight fathom water and a muddy bottom; about a quarter of a league diſtant from the town.

Variations of the needle obſerved during the whole courſe of the voyage, the longitude being taken from the meridian of Valparaiſo.

| Latitude. | | Longitude. | | Variations. | |
|---|---|---|---|---|---|
| D. | M. | D. | M. | D. | M. |
| 48 | 45 South | 10 | 30 Weſt | 14 | 30 E. |
| 57 | 15 | 9 | 30 Eaſt | 24 | 30 |
| 49 | 30 | 23 | 30 | 19 | 0 |
| 40 | 0 | 27 | 30 | 14 | 0 |
| 38 | 15 | 29 | 0 | 12 | 30 |
| 37 | 15 | 30 | 0 | 12 | 0 |
| 36 | 15 | 30 | 45 | 11 | 0 |
| 35 | 0 | 31 | 40 | 10 | 30 |
| 33 | 25 | 33 | 30 | 9 | 0 |
| 27 | 0 | 36 | 15 | 4 | 0 |
| 22 | 15 | 38 | 45 | 2 | 0 |
| 15 | 30 | 37 | 0 | 1 | 30 |
| 7 | 30 | 41 | 0 | 0 | 0 |
| 1 | 15 | 43 | 15 | 2 | 15 W. |
| 0 | 0 | 44 | 0 | 3 | 30 |
| 9 | 30 N. | 38 | 30 | 1 | 30 |
| 11 | 15 | 28 | 0 | 1 | 0 |
| 11 | 15 | 14 | 0 | 4 | 0 E. |
| In Cape Francois or Guarico | | | | 5 | 15 |

THE frigate arrived at the harbour of Guarico in the moſt favourable time, five men of war being then at Leogan, another harbour in that iſland belonging to the French, and expected there in order to convoy a fleet of merchantmen to Europe.

GUARICO lies on the N. W. ſide of the iſland of Saint Domingo in 19 deg. 45 min. 48 ſec. N. lat. and 73 deg. 0 min. 45 ſec. W. of the meridian of Paris, according to the obſervation of Don George Juan taken on the ſpot: the town is about one third of a league in length, and contains between thirteen and fifteen hundred inhabitants, who are a mixture of Europeans, white creols, negroes, mulattoes and caſts; but the laſt the moſt numerous. It is but a few years ſince that all the houſes in the town were of wood; but the greateſt part of them having been conſumed by the unextinguiſhable rapidity of a fire, the greateſt part of them have ſince been built of ſtone. They all have only a ground floor, except here and there one with a ſtory. Beſides the pariſh church, which adds an ornament to the ſquare where it ſtands, here is a college of Jeſuits, who have the care of the ſpiritual concerns of the inhabitants, and diſcharge it with exemplary affection and ſedulity. Indeed at the firſt ſettlement of the French here, the prieſts were capuchins; but the latter being either unable to bear the climate, or not bleſſed with a ſufficient ſtock of patience to reconcile themſelves to it, forſook the churches, on which the Jeſuits took charge of them. Here is alſo a nunnery of Urſelines recently founded, and a convent of religious of San Juan de Dios. About three quarters of a league from the town is an hoſpital, remarkably ſpacious and beautiful, and which receives all patients who apply for admittance. The pariſh church, though a handſome building, has not yet recovered the damages it ſuſtain'd at the fire. The college of Jeſuits is a moſt elegant ſtructure in every reſpect; and

tho'

tho' not large, is sufficient for the conveniency of the fathers generally residing in it, which never exceed six. The nunnery is of greater extent; but by the king's order that the increase of the town may not be obstructed, no young women natives of the country are allow'd to take the veil, so that it can only be considered as a place of genteel and regular education, till they are of age to enter on another state.

THE town lies open without any other defence than a single rampart, two batteries on the sea-side, and a little fort on the point of Puolet for defending the entrance of the harbour, at about two thirds of a league from the town. The regular garrison both for it and the place itself consists partly of French and partly Switzers, besides a numerous and complete body of militia formed of all the inhabitants capable of bearing arms, who are disciplined, and on the same footing as the regulars; jointly with whom, the better to fit them for service on any emergency, they mount guard and perform all other military duties. No country can be better cultivated than the neighbourhood of cape Francois. There is not a spot of ground capable of bearing any thing, but is sown with the most proper species of grain. And by these farms or habitations, as they are generally called, where the servile work is all done by negroes, the people subsist in comfort and even in affluence; being enabled to send vast returns to France for the European commodities brought hither. The grounds belong'ng to these habitations are laid out in plantations of sugar, indigo, tobacco, and coffee, the joint produce of which is so large that 30,000 tons are annually exported to France; and this vast quantity only from the territories of cape Francois; that it may be conceived how immense the produce wou'd be, were all the country which the French possess in this island cultivated. The contrast of this with the little advantage drawn from the remaining part of it, which tho' even more fertile, cannot maintain itself, a supply being every year sent for the subsistence of the garrison and ecclesiasticks, strongly shews the advantages accruing to a country from skill and industry.

The large fleet of ships which frequent the ports of this colony, are so plentifully supplied with European products and manufactures, that at all times, and especially in time of peace, they enjoy a plenty of every thing; excellent bread made of wheat brought from France, wines, distilled liquors and fruits of all kinds. The only article of provisions the inhabitants are obliged to procure from the Spaniards is meat, in return for which they supply them with linen, and other European goods. This commerce is indeed prohibited: but the want being reciprocal, it is carried on with as little secresy and disguise, as if it had the sanction of the laws. For as no register ship goes from Spain to St. Domingo, the island, for want of a due culture of the lands, being incapable of making any returns, the colony must necessarily perish, unless supplied with goods from the neighbouring plantations.

There cannot be a more convincing proof of the vast commerce carried on by France thro' the channel of this colony, than the number of ships which come annually to its different ports: no less than one hundred and sixty small and great, that is, from one hundred and fifty to four or five hundred tons, come to Guarico; and this may serve to give some idea of those destined to Leogane and Petit Guave, and others of less note: all these ships come loaded with goods and provisions, and every one returns with at least 30 or 40000 dollars, in silver or gold. Those only which go from Guarico, exclusive of the cargo which consists of the products of the colony, carry to France every year half a million of dollars; and the same computation, which is not in the least improbable, being made for each

of

CH. VI.   SOUTH AMERICA.   359

of the other two chief ports, and as much for all the other smaller ports, the total will be two millions of dollars per annum: and this was precisely the sum carried in the fleet which the Lys had the good fortune to join with in her return.

IT is easily conceived that not one fourth part of the cargo of so many ships can be consumed in this colony and its dependencies; and consequently it must find a vent among the Spanish settlements, as the Havanna, Caraca's, Santa Martha, Carthagena, Terra Firma, Nicaragua and Honduras. Accordingly Spanish barks put into the little bays and creeks near Guarico, and carry on this clandestine commerce, when by register they are authorized to go to the ports permitted.

THE climate of Guarico is extreamly hot, which equally proceeds from the country being every where mountainous, and from its proximity to the line; so that persons who come there only occasionally, on the least excess in diet or other circumstances, seldom escape being attacked by distempers, which in three or four days carry them off; particularly great numbers of the ships crews are swept away after extreme pains, the continual labour these unhappy people are obliged to go through in unloading and loading, taking in water and other necessary services of the ship, exposing them to all the violence of such distempers. The malignant fevers and dysenteries are of the same kind as those so fatal at Porto-bello: and a sufficient account being given of the temperature, the inconveniences accompanying it, and of the products of countries similar to this, I may here be excused from dwelling any farther on those subjects.

THE customs, genius and manners of the people here are no less different from the European French, than those of the Spanish Creoles in this part of America are from the real Spaniards. Here are

A a 4                                                       some

some persons of very great fortune, and all acquired from the cultivation and improvement of their lands: and all live in ease and happiness, labouring under very few inconveniences either natural or political; and this is not the least cause of its daily increase: besides, the people settled here are of themselves laborious, frugal, inventive, and continually exerting themselves in making new improvements; a turn of mind pregnant with so many advantages, that I wish it could raise a suitable imitation in the Spaniards, that by labour and industry they might attain that prosperity, they see their neighbours the French have done.

THE harbour, tho' open to the east and north winds, is very secure, being partly inclosed by a ridge of rocks which fence it against the impetuosity of the sea. The chief inconveniency is, that when the breeze blows strong, it is extreamly difficult and dangerous for boats to land; for those winds especially at E.N.E. sweep along the whole harbour.

AT the end of the month of August, the French squadron under Mr. Desturbier de l'Etanduere, which had been expected from Leogane, came into the harbour of Cape Francois; it consisted of the following five ships.

Le Juste, the commodore of — 70 guns
L'Alcide ——— 70
L'Ardent ——— 60
Le Caribou ——— 50
La Mutine ——— 26

SEVERAL merchant ships bound for Europe, took the advantage of sailing with this convoy; and on the 6th of September, the whole fleet put to sea to the number of fifty three sail, including the men of war, frigates, brigantines, and bilanders. At sun-set Picolet-point bore S. 5° W. distance four leagues and a half. The 7th they steered for Caycos, and not getting sight of these islands during the

the day, it was thought adviseable to lay to all night: but on the 8th at eight in the morning they saw the Cayco-grande, an island of sand three leagues in length, N. and S. but appears the more conspicuous from a few bushes growing on it. At noon its south point bore S. E. $\frac{1}{4}$ southerly distant two leagues and a half. By the latitude they observed, that of the island was set down at 21° 35′ and by the course its longitude determined to be the same with that of cape Francois, unless the current of the waters, which was perceived to set to the northward, may be supposed to have occasion'd some small error.

The frequent danger which the merchant ships were in of running foul of each other, and the retardment occasioned by such confusion, had induced them to divide themselves, some going to windward and others to leeward of the men of war. But this was a conveniency which they were not long permitted to enjoy, a privateer of the enemy appearing in sight to windward of the fleet: and on this the commodore ordered his squadron to form into a line; and the merchant ships to run to leeward of him, and keep at a proper distance. The currents towards the north continued with greater force on the 10th, 11th, and 12th; and during these days, the winds shifted from E.S.E. to N.

On the 13th, the fleet coming into lat. 27° 30′ the force of the currents, which had hitherto been observed, now entirely decreased; the privateer did not fail to come in sight of the fleet every morning; and towards night of drawing nearer, with a view of carrying off a prize: but in the day time she kept out of sight. On the 15th in the morning she was seen so near, that the commodore made a signal for two ships to chace. But being a ship very fit for the service she was employed in, the men of war soon lost sight of her. The winds continued at E. and S. E.

S. E. but no more currents were perceivable.

On the 17th, in 31° of lat. and 3° 14' E. of the meridian of Cape Francois, the wind shifted to N. and N. N. E. with fresh gales and showers; the fleet stood to the east; but the sea running high, they drove to 28° 44' lat. as was observed on the 23d, and 8° 40' long. Here the winds came about to the N. W. and they began to steer N. E. one quarter northerly.

On the 25th, the wind veered to the S. E. and S. with fair weather; and freshning veered to the S. S. W. S. W. and W. the course of the fleet was N. E. one quarter E. and E. N E. till the 27th of October, when they made Cape Prior on the coast of Gallicia; and at five in the evening Cape Ortegal, bearing S. S. E. distance 7 leagues.

Don George Juan, by his reckoning, concluded the difference of longitude betwixt Cape Francois and Cape Prior to be 59° 30' which is however considerably different from the real longitude: but this I attribute to the strong tendency of the currents eastward at the mouth of the Caycos channel.

When the weather permitted, he continued the observations of the variation of the needle; and taking his meridian from the point of departure, which was Cape Francois, they proved as follows:

| N. Latitude. | Longitude from Cape Francois. | Variations. |
| --- | --- | --- |
| D. M. | D. M. | D. M. |
| 30 00 | 2 00 | 1 30 E. |
| 29 00 | 6 40 | 1 00 |
| 29 00 | 9 15 | 0 00 |
| 33 00 | 11 40 | 1 30 W. |
| 36 22 | 18 30 | 7 00 |
| 40 00 | 26 00 | 11 00 |

On making Cape Ortegal, the course was altered to N. N. E. and on the 31st, at seven in the morning.

the

the squadron had again sight of land, which proved that of Brest bay; and at three in the afternoon, the whole fleet came to an anchor in that harbour.

Don George Juan, being thus landed in France, embraced with pleasure this opportunity of paying his respects to so illustrious a body as the royal academy of sciences; at the same time communicating several particulars relating to our operations in Peru; together with some observations concerning the aberration of light, and its effect on the fixed stars, according to his own accurate observations in the province of Quito. And that celebrated body were pleased to express their esteem of his application and knowledge, by admitting him a corresponding member. Having thus honourably terminated all his business at Paris, he set out for Madrid, in order to lay before the ministry the event and success of his commission; and at the same time sollicited that a report of it might be made to his majesty.

## CHAP. VII.

*Account of the harbour and town of* LOUISBOURG; *and the taking of it by the* ENGLISH; *together with some particulars relating to the* French *fishery, and the trade carried on there.*

LOuisbourg is in the latitude of 45° 50′ N. lat. and 61° W. of the meridian of Paris. It stands in the S. E. part of l'Isle Royale, and E. of Cape Breton. The town is of a middling size, the houses of wood on a foundation of stone to the height of two yards or two yards and a half from the ground. In some houses the whole ground floor is of stone, and the stories of wood. It is walled, and extreamly well fortified with all the modern works;

works: it is only in one place about 100 toifes in length, where the wall is difcontinued, as indeed unneceffary, this being filled up by the fea, and fufficiently defended by a pallifade. Here the water forms a kind of a large lake; but where the fmalleft barks cannot come, and the large fhips muft keep at a confiderable diftance, by reafon of rocks and fhoals; befides there are two collateral baftions, which flank this paffage to a very great advantage. Within the fort, and in the center of one of its chief baftions, is a ftrong building with a moat on the fide towards the town; and this is called the citadel, though it has neither artillery, nor is of a ftructure for receiving any; the entrance to it is indeed over a draw-bridge, on one fide of which is a corps de garde, and advanced centinels on the other. Within this building is the apartment for the governor, the barracks for the garrifon, an arfenal, and under the platform of the redoubt, a magazine, always well furnifhed with military ftores. The parifh church, or rather chapel which ferved as fuch, alfo ftood within this citadel, and without it was another belonging to the hofpital of St. Jean de Dieu, which is an elegant and fpacious ftructure all of ftone, though founded long fince.

THE harbour is large and fafe; but the entrance very narrow, being confined by an ifland called Goat ifland, on which ftands a pretty large fort; and on the oppofite fide is a very high tower which ferves as a light houfe. The coaft on this fide within forms a point, which advances towards the fhore till it faces the mouth of the harbour. Here alfo is a large fortification called the royal battery, being that which defends the entrance of the harbour, and the fort on that fide. From this fort the coaft winds inward, and forms a large bay, which ferves as an excellent careening place for veffels of any burden, having a good depth of water, and being in a great meafure

land-

land-lock'd: and as such the country vessels lay up here in winter. In summer they all come to an anchor before the town at about a quarter of a league distance; though the smaller vessels may come within a cable's length of the shore, where they lie quiet from all winds except the east, which blows right into the harbour's mouth, and causes some agitation; but without any danger to the ships at anchor in it.

BETWIXT the royal battery point and that of the lighthouse, but nearer to the former, lies a sand always above water; but every where else the harbour is clear, so that ships may tack with the greatest safety in going out or coming in when the wind is not fair. In winter, however, this harbour is totally impracticable, being entirely frozen so as to be walked over; that season begins here at the end of November, and lasts till May or June; sometimes the frosts sets in sooner, and are more intense, as in the year 1745; when, by the middle of October, a great part of the harbour was already frozen.

THE inhabitants of Louisbourg, which at that time was the only town in the island, consisted of French families, some Europeans and others Creoles, of the place itself, and from Placentia in the island of Newfoundland, from whence they removed hither on the ceding of that island to the crown of Great Britain. Their principal if not only trade is the cod-fishery, from which also large profits accrued to them, not only on account of the abundance of this fish, but that the neighbouring sea affords the best of any about Newfoundland. The wealth of the inhabitants consisted in their storehouses, some of which were within the fort, and others scattered along the shore, and in their number of fishing barks; and of these more than one inhabitant maintained forty or fifty, which daily went on this fishery, carrying three or four men each, who received a settled salary, but were at the same time obliged to deliver a certain

number

number of standard fish; so that the cod storehouses never failed of being filled against the time the ships resorted hither from most of the ports of France, laden with provisions and other goods, with which the inhabitants provided themselves in exchange for this fish; or consigned it to be sold in France on their own account; likewise vessels from the French colonies of St. Domingo and Martinico, brought sugar, tobacco, coffee, rum, &c. and returned loaded with cod; and any surplus, after Louisbourg was supplied found a vent in Canada, where the return was made in beavers skins and other kinds of fine furs. Thus Louisbourg, with no other fund than the fishery, carried on a continual and large commerce both with Europe and America. Louisbourg was not, however, the only port where the French vessels loaded with cod, greater numbers going themselves to fish at Newfoundland, off the coast of Petit Norde, and on the bank, as will be more particularly seen in the sequel. Besides the inhabitants of Louisbourg, great numbers of French were settled along the coast of the neighbouring islands, particularly that of St. John, where besides their dwellings they had storehouses and all the appurtenances of a fishery; which being the most profitable occupation, and the gain less uncertain, very few applied themselves to the cultivation of the country: indeed, its being in winter covered with snow, sometimes to the depth of three or four feet, and even not dissolved till summer was pretty far advanced, husbandry seemed to want a requisite time for the products to attain their proper maturity. Nor could any considerable graziery be followed here, being obliged for the support of the few cattle they had, to lay up a winter's stock of hay, and to keep them housed all that season, till the summer's heat had removed the snow from the pastures, the richness of which, in a great measure, compensated for this dreary season; and the quick growth of the corn and

other

Ch. VII. SOUTH AMERICA. 367

other products for the length and feverity of the winter.

In this and the adjacent iflands were a confiderable number of inhabitants, born in the country, or on the main land: and what is remarkable, thefe Indians not only refemble thofe of Peru in complexion and afpect; there is alfo a confiderable affinity in their manners and cuftoms; the only vifible difference is in ftature, and this advantage lies vifibly on the fide of the inhabitants of thefe northern climates.

These natives, whom the French term favages, were not abfolutely fubjects of the king of France, nor entirely independent of him. They acknowledged him lord of the country, but without any alteration in their way of living; or fubmitting themfelves to his laws; and fo far were they from paying any tribute, that they received annually from France a quantity of apparel, gun-powder, and mufkets, brandy, and feveral kinds of tools, in order to keep them quiet and attached to the French intereft: and this has alfo been the politick practice of that crown with regard to the favages of Canada. For the fame end priefts were fent among them to inftruct them in the chriftian religion, and performing divine fervice and all the other offices of the church, as baptifm, burial, &c. And as the end to be anfwered was of the higheft importance to the French commerce, the perfons chofen for thefe religious expeditions were men of parts, elocution, graceful carriage, and irreproachable lives: and accordingly they behaved with that prudence, condefcention, and gentlenefs towards the Indians under their care, that befides the univerfal veneration paid to their perfons, their converts looked upon them as their fathers; and, with all the tendernefs of filial affection, fhared with them what they caught in hunting, and the produce of their fields.

L'Ifle Royale had only one of thefe miffionaries who
was

was the Abbe Mallard; one affiduous perfon being fufficient for the few Indians which inhabit this and the adjacent iflands.

THESE Indians, like thofe of Canada, live in migrating companies; and though chriftians, and already formed into villages, ftay but a fmall time in one place: accordingly they run up their dwellings very flightly, knowing that they foon fhall leave them. Their firft bufinefs in a new place where they intend to fettle fome time, is to build a chapel and a dwelling for the prieft; afterwards every one builds himfelf a hut, and here they remain two, three, four, fix months, or more, according to the plenty of game in the neighbourhood; for this being their only fubfiftence, whenever it begins to grow fcarce, they remove, and the affectionate prieft follows them wherever they go. Many of them come voluntarily to the French fettlements, hiring themfelves for hufbandry or any other laborious work, and at the expiration of the time agreed on, return to their countrymen. Others repair to the French fettlements in order to difpofe of the fkins of the beafts they have killed, and furnifh themfelves with the neceffaries they want. Thus the French live in an entire fociality and repofe with them, little apprehenfive of any infurrection, or their inclination to any other government, as their own takes care to recommend itfelf to them by the moft ingratiating meafures; and the Indians as little harbour any fufpicions of a defign in the French to erect a tyranny over them, or of making any infringements on that liberty of which they are fo fond, or on that indolence to which they are fo remarkably addicted, that want alone can roufe them to action.

WHEN the favages have built their huts, their firft bufinefs is to fcour the country, and thus they continue hunting three or four days fucceffively, or till they judge they have a fufficiency to ferve them fome time; when they return to their huts, where they never fail

CH. VII. SOUTH AMERICA. 369

of carrying to the prieſt the full amount of his quota. The ſkins of quadrupeds they reſerve for ſale, having firſt made the due offering to the prieſt, who, on the produce of them, ſupplies his own neceſſities, and likewiſe furniſhes the chapel; but its ornaments, like the veſtments of the prieſt, are neither remarkable for their number or ſplendor; their ambulatory life, among other circumſtances, ſcarce admitting of either.

BESIDES Louiſbourg, the only fortified harbour of this iſland, it has other places of good anchorage, on the eaſtern coaſt, which terminates at Cape Nord; and on that running ſouthward fron E. to W. Of theſe the beſt for ſecurity and largeneſs are St. Anne's bay, with a narrow entrance like that of Louiſbourg, and Cabaru bay: but theſe are all uninhabited, the French having confined their views to the fortifying of Louiſbourg; as by means of it they hoped to maintain themſelves in the poſſeſſion of the whole iſland; which being ſo very woody, that on whatever part the enemy ſhould make a deſcent, there was no acceſs to it by land; and experience has demonſtrated that they thought very juſtly, it being impoſſible, without taking the fort, to become maſters of the iſland; nor had this fort ever been taken, if ſuccoured in due time; or if, from the opinion of its being impregnable, proper precautions had not been omitted.

MOST of the trees, of which the thick foreſts of this iſland conſiſt, are pines, though not of the ſame nature with thoſe of Europe. They are of two kinds: one very fit for boards and ſuch like uſes; the other, being ſhort and knotty, is uſed for fuel or making ſhort rafters; and this is called pruche. A decoction of the ſprigs, being mixed with a little moloſſes, and fermented, makes the ale generally drank at table; the water itſelf, being of ſo light and penetrating a nature, that the drinking of it always cauſes dyſenteries: but thus corrected and turned into pruche or ſprufs beer, is found very wholeſome, and of no diſagreeable taſte.

VOL. II. B b THUS

Thus the French of thefe parts live in the greateft tranquillity and comfort; and their happinefs might have ftill continued had they themfelves not occafioned the interruption of it. For though the two crowns of France and England were at war, and fome of the fubftantial inhabitants here, as well as the Englifh at Bofton, had fitted out privateers, the hoftilities were never carried beyond the act of privateering, without any thoughts at that time of higher enterprizes. It muft be obferved, that before the war betwixt the two powers, at the beginning of this century, France was poffeffed of that peninfula and the lands called Acadia, weft of l'Ifle Royale: but by the treaty of peace, in which France ceded to the crown of England, Placentia the capital of Newfoundland, and the whole ifland, this peninfula was alfo included, a fuggeftion which the court of England owed to its inhabitants, who being generally proteftants, reafonably promifed themfelves more freedom under a fovereign of their own religion. Many parts of that peninfula belonged to the inhabitants of Louifbourg, who became deprived of them by this treaty: and among them one, concerning which there feems to have been a difpute, whether it was to be included in Acadia or not. But the inhabitants ftrongly infifting on the affirmative, and the king of England fupporting their plea, France was obliged to give up the point, and confent to its being reckoned a part of the peninfula. The owner of this parcel of land, however, who was one of the moft confiderable inhabitants of Louifbourg, defirous of recovering fo valuable a part of his poffeffions, and availing himfelf of the prefent war, laid before the miniftry of France his fcheme for the conqueft of it, without any charge to the king, with the allowance only of a body of troops from the garrifon; fetting forth the great advantage which would refult from it to the French intereft in thefe parts. The miniftry entered into his views; a commiffion was fent him for

the

the expedition, accompanied with an order for furnishing him with the number of regulars he had required.

THE country in queſtion little apprehending any invaſion, was totally unprovided with the means of defence, ſo that after little or no reſiſtance, it was taken poſſeſſion of by the former owner, who, with the body of regulars and adventurers that had attended him, returned in triumph to Louiſbourg. In the mean time, the clamours not only of the ſufferers, who had been the immediate object of this act of violence, but of all the inhabitants of Acadia, reached the ears of the governor and other powerful perſons of Boſton, who, alarmed at the recent example, began to look upon their own welfare as in danger: accordingly they held conſultations on the means of preventing further miſchief, and taking ſatisfaction for the late inſult: they with reaſon apprehended, that the French muſt carry all before them in a country like theirs, every way open, without fortreſſes or troops; and they imagined that the French, from the facility of its execution, had really formed ſuch a deſign; and that the firſt ſucceſs ſo eaſily obtained, would naturally animate that ambitious nation to greater enterprizes. This colony had ever looked upon the neighbourhood of the French as dangerous; and in order to have them at a proper diſtance, the people of Boſton had made repeated ſolicitations to the court of England, that Acadia might be delivered up to that crown, in order to form a barrier betwixt the other dominions of the two powers.

THE reaſon that the colony of New-England, and its capital Boſton, is without any fortreſs or regular troops, is owing to the apprehenſion of its inhabitants, that they might be brought into ſubjection to the laws of England and acts of parliament, to the prejudice of thoſe liberties under which they have roſe to ſuch a height of proſperity. Thus the whole country lies open without any other defence than the great number of people it contains. The king of England fends over a governor, but with fuch a commiffion as is entirely compatible with its free conftitution. This defencelefs ftate of Bofton awakened in them a jealoufy of farther enterprizes from the French; that in a confultation, at which the governor and the chief perfons of the colony affifted, it was refolved that New England could not be fafe by land or fea, till the French were difpoffefs'd of Louifbourg; but that in order to fucceed, the defign muft be conducted with fuch impenetrably fecrecy, that the firft notice of it at Louifbourg muft be the arrival of the fleet before it; and in Europe the account of its furrender: that the former might be prevented from fending for fuccours to Canada, and that a force might not be fent from France fufficient either to fave or recover it. The governor of New-England at that time was Mr. Shirley, a gentleman of great abilities and merit; and the commodore of the men of war on that coaft, was Mr. Peter Warren, a perfon of the like character, befides his naval accomplifhments, and an ardent zeal for the glory of his nation; and who in this affair had the additional incentive of felf-intereft, being owner of lands and houfes to a confiderable amount; that he was looked upon as one of the moft opulent inhabitants of Bofton. Thefe two officers, in conjunction with the chief inhabitants, determined to undertake the fiege of Louifbourg, the governor offering to concur in it with a body of land-forces, provifions and other neceffaries; whilft the commodore, who had fignaliz'd his courage on feveral occafions, engaged with his fquadron, tho' confifting only of three or four large fhips and a fmall frigate, fo to block up the harbour, that no fuccours fhould be thrown into it; whilft the land forces befieged it in form. The greateft difficulty was the want of regular troops,

and

and experienced officers capable of conducting a siege; and the discipline of the soldiery, that there might be some probability of succeeding. This embarrassment was removed by an expedient of Mr. Shirley's, and to which chiefly was owing the happy event of the expedition. There was a gentleman of the name of Pepperel, one of the largest traders in Boston, who had a general correspondence among the country people of the colony, both Indians and Mestizos. He placed an entire confidence in them, and trusted them with whatever goods they wanted; and they were no less punctual in their payments at the time of their several harvests. These acts of kindness, and the open courtesy with which he always treated them, had endeared him to such a degree, that they looked upon him as their father; and so sensible are even the rudest minds of disinterested beneficence and affability, that they on all occasions expressed an unreserved devotion to him; and no doubt was made, but they would readily sacrifice themselves for him at his desire. On this confidence the governor of Boston, proposed to Mr. Pepperel, that he should go general of this expedition; as thus all the country people would offer themselves to go volunteers, and grudge no dangers or fatigues which they shou'd undergo in his presence. Mr. Pepperel was not ignorant of his interest, and saw all the weight of the proposal; but declined it, as being entirely destitute of that military knowledge required in much inferior posts. At length yielding to the instances of the governor, and the entreaties of his acquaintance, who seconded the proposal, he accepted of the post; and at once from merchant became a warrior. This was no sooner made public, than multitudes of the country people flocked from all parts, desiring to be enlisted, and impatient for the enterprize: rather from a zeal to accompany their chief protector, than for any concern about the conqueft of Louifbourg.

Such was the privacy of the enterprize, that even in England nothing of it was known till the execution. The governor had fent notice of it to his fovereign, but it went no further, left an enterprize undertaken with fo much fpirit, and of fuch importance, fhould be rendered abortive.

Thus the new-raifed troops with provifions and military ftores, but little fuitable to fuch an attempt, embarked at Bofton; and, in company with commodore Warren's fquadron, failed for Louifbourg; which received the firft notice of the defign from the appearance of the armament.

I have already mentioned that France every year fends a remittance to Louifbourg of money and provifions for the payment and fubfiftence of the garrifon; and for the repairs and improvement of the fortifications: at which the foldiers themfelves, when not on guard, very gladly work as being a comfortable addition to their pay. But through covetoufnefs, one of the general vices of mankind, thofe who were commiflioned with the payment of the foldiers, and even the very officers of the garrifon, befides wronging them in what they earned by their work, curtailed them even in their fubfiftence money. This was no recent evil; and on the death of the governor, the foregoing winter, the oppreffion of the rapacious paymafters and officers rofe to fuch an excefs, as twice to occafion a mutiny in the garrifon, and for want of timely lenitives, thefe refentments contributed not a little to the lofs of the place.

The garrifon of Louifbourg and all its forts, confifted only of fix hundred French and Swifs regulars, and eight hundred militia; formed of all the inhabitants capable of bearing arms. The governor of Canada, who was not ignorant of the difcontented

ftate

state of the garrison, and knowing that even with an unanimous zeal, it was not a sufficient number in time of war for a place of such consequence, had, without any knowledge of what was on the carpet, offered to send a reinforcement to Louisbourg. But the commandant, either apprehending that there would be no occasion for making use of those succours, or that he judged the usual force sufficient for its defence, or for some other secret reason, thanked the governor of Canada for his offer, and told him that on any appearance of danger he would embrace it. It was not long after before he saw himself surrounded by the enemy; and all the ways for applying for succour blocked up. Thus he became besieged in form, his forces unequal to the defence of the place; and without any probability of receiving a reinforcement either from Canada or Europe. This was the first, and not the least error to which his disgrace for the loss of Louisbourg may be imputed, as with the succours offered he would have found himself at the head of a body of men more than sufficient not only to defend himself; but to sally out and drive before them the raw undisciplin'd multitude which were come against him.

The design of the English having been to surprise the place when unprovided, they pushed the enterprize with the greatest dispatch and vigour, that they might prevent the arrival of the annual supply from France: and with this view it was no later than the end of April or beginning of May, when they appeared before the town, in hopes of the double advantage, that instead of its reaching the French, the ships that brought it would fall into their hands, as it indeed happened. Another accident equally unfortunate with the former, was, that a man of war and a frigate having been fitted out at Brest for carrying succours to this place, and loaded with all kinds of military stores, and ready to put to fea within two or three days, the man of war took fire, and was burnt to the water's edge. Nor was there at that time any other fhip fit to fupply her place, except the Vigilante, juft on the point of launching. The captain of the fhip which had been burnt, was the marquis de la Maifon Forte; who alfo was appointed to command the Vigilante: and get her ready with the utmoft expedition for the fame voyage. This delay however gave an opportunity to the Englifh of making themfelves mafters of the entrance of the harbour, and landing the troops for the fiege, tho' they did not venture to open the trenches for battering in breach.

WHEN the Vigilante arrived near the coaft of this ifland, the atmofphere was filled with fuch a thick fog, that to have attempted to approach fo near as to have a fight of it, would have been dangerous: accordingly the marquis flackened fail, and tack'd till the weather fhou'd clear up, that he might make the ifland without any danger. On the 30th of May, he difcovered near him a frigate of forty guns, which he immediately knew to belong to the enemy; and elevated with the hopes of fuch a capture, began to fire at the frigate, which, as had been concerted, feigned a flight; and, favoured by the fog, drew the Vigilante, which eagerly gave her chace to that part of the coaft where the other fhips of the Englifh fquadron lay: fo that when the fog, which hitherto intercepted the fight of diftant objects, became difperfed, the Vigilante found herfelf in the midft of Mr. Warren's fquadron. Then the frigate which had decoyed her into the fnare, together with two men of war, the one of fixty and the other of fifty guns, began about half an hour after one in the afternoon, to pour their fire into her, as a fhip, whofe fafe arrival would have fruftrated their enterprize. Another great difadvantage to the Vigilante, befides this fuperiority was, her being fo

deep

deep loaded with military ſtores, that ſhe could make no uſe of her lower tier. But neither this diſparity, nor the ſight of two other ſhips at a ſmall diſtance could intimidate the French from making a vigorous reſiſtance till nine o'clock at night, when the ſhip being battered in every part, full of water, and her rudder ſhot away, they ſurrendered; left their heroick courage might have been miſconſtrued to have proceeded only from a ſavage deſpair. To this misfortune France may attribute the loſs of that important place: for the ignorance of the beſiegers, whoſe conduct ſhewed them not to have a ſingle ray of military knowledge, the vigorous reſiſtance of the forts, which they now began more and more to think impregnable, the ſmall quantity of ammunition, and the proportion of the artillery to the deſign, together with the increaſing diſguſt of theſe new-levied ruſticks, at the fatigues and dangers of war, which had already laſted long beyond their expectations: theſe circumſtances, I ſay, had ſo diſcouraged the New-England men, that they began to repent of having left the repoſe of their plantations, for what ſome now called a romantick ſcheme; and the general inclination ſeemed to be for a return: and this being known from ſome of the Engliſh as bore none of the loweſt commiſſions, a reſolution was taken, that if they were not maſters of the place in a fortnight at fartheſt, the ſiege ſhould be raiſed. But the taking of the Vigilante, diffuſed a new ſpirit thro' the troops: and ſeeing that by this capture they had gained a conſiderable reinforcement, and that the fort was deprived of the aſſiſtance ſo long expected, their hopes of ſucceſs revived; and they puſhed the ſiege with more vigour than even at the commencement of it.

At the ſame time the Engliſh laid ſiege to the fort, they alſo threatned the royal battery, having a body of troops encamped on that ſide, tho' without ever rifking an affault. This battery, happened to be commanded by an officer of no competent experience, and very unfit for fuch a poft; the garrifon alfo was weak, and it was without any guns towards the land, which was the very place facing the enemy; and confequently the only one from whence they could be annoyed. In this exigence the commandant of the fort went over to view it and give directions; but as he could not fpare any men, he left orders, that in cafe of the approach of the enemy on that fide, they fhou'd remove thither the guns which pointed feaward; and ufe them to the beft advantage. But left the royal battery fhould fall into the hands of the enemy, who would certainly turn the cannon againft the fort, he left inftructions with the commandant, that if he found it abfolutely neceffary to capitulate, he fhould with all his men, pafs over to the fort, after nailing up the artillery, fo as to render it unferviceable to the enemy. But the poltroon commandant of the battery availed himfelf of this inftruction to haften his retreat: and, without ftaying till he had tried the fuccefs of his cannon on the enemy, who continued quiet in their camp; that very fame night embarked his men, and made over to the fort in a hurry, on pretence that the enemy had made an affault on the battery with a large force. But the falfity of this plea was foon difcovered, the French flag flying for fome time after; an evident fign that there was no perfon in the fort to lower it: which could not have been the cafe had the Englifh made the pretended attack.

THE enemy obferving from their camp, that no perfon appeared as ufual on the parapet of the royal battery, concluded that the garrifon were employ'd on fome fecret attempt, or on fome works within the fort, and therefore did not make any approaches, till queftioning whether the French might not privately have abandoned it, a Bofton Indian (for the Englifh
army

army was a medley of various kinds of people,) less fearful than the others, offered to clear up the difficulty. Accordingly without any arms, as if disordered in his senses, he went in a rambling manner towards the gate: where, forsaken as it was, he had no great difficulty of getting into the fort; and immediately gave notice of its condition by lowering the French flag. On this signal the English army advanced with great alacrity to take possession; and the artillery not having been well nailed up, was made fit for service; and proved a very great detriment to the town, which it batter'd in flank.

All the guns of the royal battery were from 36 to 40 pounders, the Vigilante also carried some of the same size; all which the English, on being masters of this fort, employed against the principal place; and under the shelter of these guns, which kept a very smart fire, they began their approaches, and raised forts for battering in breach. The place was bravely defended: but a large breach having been made, and every thing prepared for a storm, it was thought proper to capitulate on honourable terms; which were readily granted by the English, not less out of esteem for that valour which a concurrence of misfortunes had forced to yield, than from a desire of putting an advantageous period to a state of life, which had drawn them from their domestick concerns, and was not at all agreeable to their disposition. The officers of the besieged were not ignorant, that the most favourable opportunity of repelling the enemy, was to fall on them when they were beginning their works, in order to form their approaches: yet such was the mistrust from the too recent mutinies of the regular troops, that though they themselves made the offer, a sally was not judged adviseable, fearing that the soldiers in their present discontent, being once without the walls, would go over to the enemy, either from a dread of the punishments which they were conscious their disobedience deserved,

and

and would on some favourable opportunity be inflicted on them; or to be revenged for the oppreſſions which they had undergone from their commanders.

UNDER a combination of contrary events and with a weak garriſon, this place held out a ſiege of ſix weeks; not ſurrendering till the end of June. By this ſucceſs England made an acquiſition of new dominions, and the colony of Boſton acquired an increaſe of territory, proſperous before throughout its large inland extent, it only wanted this iſland to command the whole coaſt: and Louiſbourg being now annexed to it, a ſhort account of this colony will not perhaps be unacceptable.

## CHAP. VIII.

*Of the* ENGLISH COLONY *of* BOSTON, *its riſe, progreſs, and other particulars.*

THE firſt ſettlement of the colonies of New-England, the principal province of which bears that name, and has Boſton for its capital, was made in the year 1584 by Sir Water Raleigh, tho' the firſt diſcovery of theſe coaſts is not to be attributed to him; Juan Ponce de Leon, having many years before, namely in 1513, given them the name of Florida, from his diſcovery of them on palm ſunday; he was ſoon after followed by Lucas Vazques de Ayllon, a native of Toledo, who having been driven by a tempeſt on the eaſt coaſt of Florida, he afterwards employed an interval of fair weather, in coaſting, reconnoitring, and taking draughts of its capes, rivers, and bays; at the ſame time landing in ſeveral parts, and quietly trading with the natives.

RALEIGH took poſſeſſion of this country in the name of queen Elizabeth of England, and gave it the title of Virginia, a corruption as ſome think from that of

the

## CH. VIII. SOUTH AMERICA. 381

the chief Cacique of these parts, who was called Viginea; but others, and indeed the generality, will have it to have been in honour of his sovereign; and in allusion to that princess's invariable aversion to marriage, which would have brought her into a state of subordination; but to whoever the compliment was designed, whether to the Cacique or the queen, this is the name of that part of the coast which reaches from 38 to 45 deg. of N. latitude. Raleigh began to people it with his countrymen; and he found such great numbers ready to embrace his proposals, and second any further enterprizes, that the settlement he had made, increased beyond expectation, and the country was divided into several provinces, beginning with the most northward, which lies in 45 deg. by the names of New-England, New York, Pennsylvania, Maryland, and the most southern retained its original name of Virginia. This last was the chief object of the attention of Raleigh, and afterwards of England: no measures were neglected for the peopling and prosperity of it. Hither particularly fled the unfortunate friends of Charles I. as an asylum from the cruelties of Cromwell and his parliament, who, not satisfied with having embrued their hands in the blood of that monarch, by causing his head to be struck off on a publick scaffold, and by this action casting a shade over the honour of the nation; now endeavoured to wash off that horrid stain by the blood of others: and to palliate their tyranny, and give a colour of justice to their resolutions, they pretended that all who did not conform to their pleasure, were the king's adherents and malignants. In this dangerous situation, great numbers of honourable families were obliged to seek in other climates that security, which they could no longer enjoy in their native country.

THESE numerous emigrations not only enlarged the first towns in Virginia, but also occasioned the building of many others. The royalists had made choice of

Virginia

Virginia preferably to any other part, as being sure of the protection and countenance of Sir William Berkley, governor of that province, who abhorring the procedure against his sovereign, maintained his loyalty unshaken; refusing obedience to Cromwell, and immediately declaring for the son of the late unfortunate monarch, as his rightful sovereign: but though Virginia had received such large additions by several vast emigrations of people, and though companies were erected in England for the support of it, yet not receiving the necessaries wanted both for cultivation and defence, they had the mortification of seeing the province of New-York taken from them by the Dutch; who, desirous of a settlement on this coast, twice dislodged the English, reducing them within the limits of Virginia, till a peace was concluded betwixt these two nations on the 19th of February, 1674.

This was not the only disgrace attending the English in these parts: for as the Dutch had drove them from New-York, so they were dispossessed of other countries; of Florida by the Spaniards, and of Canada by the French: and tho' they still remained masters of a considerable extent of country, yet their settlements were not so secure, so well established, and placed on so good a footing as they have been since. This partly arose from the discovery of a tract of land betwixt New-York and Virginia; the soil so fertile, and the temperature so mild, that it was thought the peopling of it would be attended with greater advantages than that of any other of their colonies. This discovery with the particulars, was fortunately published in England at a time when severe persecutions were carrying on against the quakers, a sect newly sprung up, and which, like primitive christianity, increased the more it was persecuted, that now it numbered amongst its members several persons of a more elevated rank and greater abilities than its founders. Among these was one William Penn, who, both on account of his parents and

his

his perſonal qualities, was univerſally eſteemed. To him Charles II. made a grant of the province, that he might withdraw thither with all his ſect; as thus it would become totally extinguiſhed, and policy hoped to accompliſh that by indulgence, which it had in vain attempted by rigour.

This grant was made to William Penn in the year 1681; tho' others date it from the year 1682. However, he ſet out with a numerous and well-provided company; and began to people the province which had been granted him, calling it Pennſylvania, from his own name, and the woodineſs of the country. In order to increaſe his numbers, and ſecure their ſtay by the ſtrongeſt ties, he made one of the fundamental laws of his colony, a general toleration, by which all who followed the precepts of morality, ſhould enjoy the free exerciſe of their religion, without moleſtation; which, with other privileges and immunities granted to the ſettlers, had ſuch good conſequences, that induſtrious perſons flocked thither from ſeveral parts, particularly the French refugees from England. The number of families increaſed in a ſhort time to ſuch a ſurprizing degree, that the firſt territory not being ſufficient for them, they ſpread themſelves along the neighbouring colonies on the coaſt; where their deſcendants ſtill continue. To theſe are owing the commencement and riſe of the town of Boſton, which, by the deſcription I have from many who have been there, may, for extent, wealth, and handſome buildings, vie with ſome of the moſt flouriſhing in Europe: nor is this the only place in ſuch happy circumſtances. Beſides the many towns on the coaſts, the inland parts, to the diſtance of one hundred leagues and more, alſo make a chearful appearance, being diverſified with large towns, villages, ſeats, and plantations. Thus, from the exuberant fertility of the country and the induſtry of the people, the nation reaps an immenſe benefit.

The reſort of ſo many nations, which compoſe the

inhabitants of New-England and the other provinces, renders them so populous and wealthy, that a considerable kingdom might be formed of them: for though its extent along the coast be not very large in comparison of others in America, this deficiency is compensated by its inland distance, and the great number of people it contains. These inhabitants, though so different as to their native countries, are all subject to the same laws in respect of polity and civil government; and live in a quiet obedience to them and harmony with each other. As to religion, the original toleration still obtains; and one sees here all the sects of Old England, and even those of other protestant countries: but the roman catholicks, so far from being tolerated or connived at, are not admitted to settle in this colony.

ALL this country is of an extraordinary fertility, and particularly abounds in timber for ships; so that great numbers of vessels are every year built in these parts, though the timber is not accounted the fittest for this use, as not lasting above eight or ten years, and therefore is made use of only for sloops, bilanders, brigantines, and other vessels of small burden. These large and wealthy provinces, such as that of Boston and the others, are subject to the sovereign only, as agreeable to their own laws: the gentleness of the government to them secures their affection; and the governor sent over to them from England is looked upon by the others only as one of their eminent fellow citizens; and beloved for his care of the publick welfare and the tranquility and safety of the whole society. They allow him a competent salary: as they do also to the judges, for the more sedulous administration of justice, without any further impost, tax, or demand. In order to prevent the least encroachment on such a state of freedom, they allow of no fortifications or garrisons among them, that under pretence of security of their possessions their liberties may be in danger. Thus

these

these provinces, in reality, constitute a kind of republick, partly admitting the political laws of England as depending on it; but either amends or rejects those which may injure its immunities: the towns being the fortresses of the country, and the inhabitants the garrisons. Here is seen an universal concord, union, and friendship: the great do not despise or insult the mean, nor the rich distinguish himself from the poor, by luxury, pomp, and an imperious carriage. Here also is none of that pernicious, dishonest affectation of appearing above their circumstances: and what is still more admirable, that though five or six different sects are openly professed, we see none of those feuds which naturally arise among persons of different persuasions. Nor do the inhabitants, notwithstanding they are composed of such different kinds, as Europeans, Creoles, Mestizos, and natives or Indians, the latter of which are intractable and ferocious, ever offer to disturb the government; but imitate, in this particular, the peaceful behaviour of the others. This sociable conformity greatly contributes to the increase of these colonies; for as many of the causes of the decay of families do not subsist here, nor is there any thing to create private differences, the repose in which they live, naturally induces young persons to marry; and the rather, as there is no difficulty in providing a subsistence: a quantity of fertile land being allotted to every one who petitions for it. Thus the territories of the colony increase, and as they increase are cultivated.

The marquis de la Maison Forte having been carried to Boston after he was made prisoner, drew up an exact account of this colony; and was pleased whilst we were both prisoners at Fareham in England, to communicate it to me: and it is from thence I have chiefly extracted the foregoing account. The marquis is of opinion, that within a century, Boston, in extent and number of people, will form a kingdom superior to that of England; and will be able to give law to all the neighbouring countries. This conjecture he deduces, and not without probability, from its amazing progress since the time of its first establishment; nor can it well be doubted, when at its commencement, as I may say, it had a spirit sufficient to undertake the conquest of such a place as Louisbourg; and a conduct to accomplish it; so that it is reasonable to expect, that with the future increment of power and people, it will exert the same spirit and conduct to remove by force all obstacles to its greater aggrandizement: especially as they can meet with little resistance, the whole country being, as it were, destitute of inhabitants.

But it must be observed, that though these colonies are so large, fertile, well peopled, and flourishing, yet the current money is not of metal, but of paper, in the form of common coin, being two round pieces pasted together, and stampt on each side with the arms of the colony: and of this there are pieces of all values from the lowest to the highest; and with these they buy and sell without making use of any metallic coin whatever. But as these are liable to grow foul, or break with use, there is a particular house which may be called a kind of mint, this paper-money being made there; and another in every town for the distribution of it. To these houses are brought all such pieces as from any cause whatever can no longer pass current: and here others of like value are issued in the lieu of them. In this particular the disinterestedness and probity of the directors of this money are really admirable, as having it in their power to enrich themselves by causing great numbers of this specie to be struck, and putting them in their own purses.

The houses for distribution of this money receive remittances of new from the chief house at Boston, and pass accounts with the directors by sending those which have been brought for exchange. And such is the integrity of these judges, that even a slight suspicion of being capable of a fraud would be an injury to the high

high reputation in which they stand. But what seems strange and almost incredible is, that they, in whose power it is to give what value they please to the paper, by the stamps, of which they have the care, never have been known to abuse their trust: but the wonder ceases upon reflecting, that the former establishment of these colonies is in a manner owing to quakers; and that, to the laws which they and the first settlers compiled, the colonies chiefly owe that quiet and prosperity they still enjoy. The quakers are a kind of sectaries, who tho' zealously fond of several ridiculous and extravagant notions, cannot be sufficiently commended for their punctual observance of the laws of nature: sometimes they carry this strictness to superstition: and from this principle all the penalties laid on them in England could not bring them to take the oaths required by the government, so that at length they obtained from the parliament, that the simple affirmaation of a quaker should have the same force as an oath, except in capital cases. As they make such a strict profession of truth, and lay down as a fundamental article of their belief, the necessity of inviolably adhering to their affirmation, they also make profession of candour, justice and simplicity in all their dealings; and it is a thing well known, that all treaties, agreements and conventions made with quakers, tho' only on their bare word, prove better founded and fufilled, without any of that chicane and delay, which so often occurs in those with other people, tho' corroborated by bonds, witnesses and securities. Such persons as these having the direction, distribution and making of the money in the colony of Pensylvania, and others where it is current, the inhabitants are under no manner of concern with regard to any malversation; nor can it morally be expected, for such a breach of trust would be a total departure from their faith. This has been their uniform conduct: and as this sect has greatly increased in these colonies, they have always strictly adhered to their ceremonies and rules; and irreproachably obferved the maxims tranfmitted to them by their anceftors; and this probity has doubtlefs communicated itfelf to the members of other religions, that among thofe people to harbour the flighteft fufpicion concerning the difintereftednefs of their magiftrates, would be an injury; thofe virtues being as common here as they are rare among other nations.

The traders fell all their European goods in exchange for this money; and with it buy thofe of the country; and confign them to their correfpondents in other parts for vent: and having made up their gains in filver or gold they remit it to the bank in London: and as in their own country they ftand in no need of coined gold, or filver, they purchafe with the yearly returns of their gains fuch goods as they want: and thefe they fend to Bofton on their account. Thus the commerce is every where kept up; and the filver and gold fpecie remain in England. The wealthy inhabitants of Bofton have at the fame time two capitals; one in effects and paper-money; and the other returns from the bank, where the principal refts without any diminution.

Having given this fhort account of the happy ftate of thefe Englifh colonies; and the means by which they are maintained, I fhall add, as a conclufion of this fubject, that the unfortunate Delivrance was not the only fhip deceived by the falfe appearance of Louifbourg being ftill in the hands of the French. The fame fate befel the Charmonte and Heron, two homeward bound Eaft Indiamen; and who had orders to touch at no other port than Louifbourg, where they wou'd find a fquadron of men of war, under whofe convoy they might fafely reach Europe.

CHAP.

## CHAP. IX.

*Voyage from* LOUISBOURG *to* NEWFOUNDLAND; *account of that Island, and the Cod fishery: and also of our Voyage to* ENGLAND.

I Shall not trouble the reader with an account of the disagreeable circumstances of our captivity at Louisbourg; but justice and gratitude will not permit me to pass over the humanity of Mr. Warren, commodore of the English squadron; who, among many other instances of his kindness to us, besides the honour of his table, which I several times enjoyed, recommended my papers to the care, and myself to the good treatment of the captain of the ship who was to carry me to England.

On the 5th of October, arrived at Louisbourg a packet-boat, which had been dispatched for England with the news of the taking that place; and brought with her, grants from the king of England of the title of baronet to Mr. Warren, and to Mr. Pepperell; also two commissions for the former, appointing him governor of the island, and rear admiral of the blue; and to the latter a colonel's commission, accompanied with many gracious expressions, relating to the behaviour of these gentlemen. News at the same time arrived that a squadron of men of war was ready to sail with a convoy, having on board two thousand regular troops as a garrison to the new conquest, and six hundred persons of both sexes towards peopling it, with provisions, military stores, and every thing necessary to put it in a posture of defence, in case the French should attempt to recover it. The expectation of this squadron was the only thing that delay'd the other at Louisbourg, it being designed to convoy the Newfoundland fleet; and the time of its return to Europe now drew near. And as the arrival of the former could not be far off, preparations were making for our departure: and the prifoners of the three prizes, together with the few French families which remain'd difperfed in their dwellings on the ifland, and on that of St. John, were to be diftributed on board the fhips of the fquadron. I was ordered on board the Sunderland, commanded by captain John Brett, with whom my misfortune had before procured me fome acquaintance; as likewife the captain and officers of the Delivrance with others; one of thefe was Monfieur de Baubaftin, a perfon of great note in Louifbourg; and who, as captain of the militia, was the more able to acquaint me with feveral particulars relating to the fiege, in which I have reafon to believe he did not fpare himfelf.

On the 4th of October, we embarked on board our refpective fhips. The fquadron confifted of the Princefs Mary, commanded by captain Edwards, who as oldeft captain was commodore, the Sunderland, the Superbe, and the Canterbury: the three firft of fixty guns, and the laft of forty fix or fifty. The Heron and Charmante had alfo been fitted up as armed fhips: the only ones remaining in the harbour, being the Vigilante, now repaired from the damages fhe had received in the action, and the Chefter.

My papers, as I have before obferved, Sir Peter Warren delivered to captain Brett, with orders on his arrival in England to remit them to the admiralty. On the 19th of October, the fquadron put to fea, fteering for Newfoundland. On the 22d, in the evening we had fight of cape Raze. On the 23d the wind being at S. W. the fquadron tacked for the bay of Bulls, where it intended to anchor; but that being found impracticable, on the 24th it entered that of Ferryland, and remained there till all the merchant fhips, which were taking in their lading of cod in the other harbours of the ifland, had

ren-

rendezvous'd: the method of this fishery and commerce, as likewise the island itself being little known in Europe, I shall give as good an account of it, as my late situation will admit-of; the most innocent questions or undesigning remarks, being suspicious in a prisoner.

The capital of the island of Newfoundland, so famous for the cod-fishery along its coasts and the neighbouring seas, is Placentia. Its first discovery and peopling was owing to the Spaniards before the year 1550, as the very name of the capital, and several other capes and parts of it, as cape Buena Vista, Punta Rica, sufficiently demonstrate. But probably the settlement they made here was of little force; for in 1583, Humphry Girber an Englishman settled there; tho' he was afterwards obliged to evacuate it, and sail for England in the following year; but did not reach it, perishing in a storm.

In the year 1622, the English again returned to settle in this island, under the conduct of Mr. George Calvert, who, with more foresight than his predecessor, brought with him all kinds of seeds, grain, and pulse, and immediately set his followers to work in clearing those parts which seemed best adapted to culture; and accordingly the produce of his seeds contributed greatly to the comfortable subsistence of these new adventurers, besides affording a stock for the ensuing years.

The French had for a long time been in possession of Placentia, and with it of the principal part of this island, but without any molestation to the settlements of the English on the eastern coasts of it; and the vessels of both nations quietly fish'd together. The English, however, long entertain'd a desire of making themselves masters of Placentia, as the only fortified town in the island, as also of the whole southern part held by the French. They had

had tried force and negociations to compafs their ends; but all their endeavours ended in difappointment, till the peace of Utrecht, concluded betwixt that nation and Lewis XIV. of France; when they took advantage of the low ſtate to which that monarch was reduced, and infifted on the entire and abfolute ceſſion of Newfoundland; and ever fince that time no other nation has fettled there; tho' with a referve of the right of cod-fifhing both to the French and Spaniards; to the former by articles nine, ten and twelve of that ceffion; and to the Spaniards by the 15th article of the fame treaty.

THE country of this ifland is very unequal, and covered with hills and mountains; and thefe at a diftance appear much higher than thofe near the fea. They are alfo every where overgrown with pines or pruches, as the French call them, fo as to be practicable only in thofe parts, where the inhabitants have cut roads This fpecies of pine feldom exceed the height of two or three toifes in the open parts: but in valleys where they are fheltered from the froft and the piercing winds, they rife to a much greater height. In winter the cold is exceffive here, nothing but fnow and ice being feen; and the bays and harbours entirely frozen. This fevere weather fets in fo early, that tho' it was but the 21ſt of November when we were there, it froze to fuch a degree, that we were obliged to wait till the fun had begun to break the ice; and thus force a way thro' without waiting till the next day, left the froft fhould return; and then it would have been impoffible, and the fhips under the dreadful neceffity of wintering among the ice.

THIS is the more remarkable, as the latitude of Placentia is only 47 degr. 10 min. and the bay where we happened to be was but little more. The inhabitants of the ifland keep themfelves fhut up in their houfes during the winter, except in fair and
fun-

sun-shiny weather, when they go out with a great deal of pleasure to enjoy the enlivening rays of the sun.

The whole circuit of the island is full of bays and harbours, all so spacious and sheltered on all sides by the mountains except their entrance, that the vessels lie in perfect security; they all grow gradually narrower from their entrance, that at the end of them, there is scarce room for a single vessel to anchor. Some of these harbours are a league and a half or two leagues in length; and their greatest breadth about half a league. But there are also others much larger and some less; into them run several rivers and brooks, which besides the fineness of their water afford great quantities of trouts and other kinds of fresh water fish, seeming to vie with the sea in fœcundity. These harbours are complete anchoring places, being clear, and having a good bottom, that they may be safely sailed into without a pilot. Some there are with reefs of rocks, but these are generally visible; and those that are covered, are usually about the capes or points at the entrance of the harbours: and therefore by keeping in the middle all danger is avoided. These harbours are so near each other, as to be openly separated by a point of land, which seldom forms a distance of above two leagues; so that the whole coast of the island, is a succession of harbours. But it is not in all that the English have any town or village; and these, which are to be found only on the larger bays, and where the nature and disposition of the country are most convenient for a settlement, are small, and the inhabitants but few. Cod-fishing is the universal business; and besides their dwellings they have offices and storehouses for preparing and laying up their fish till the time arrives for sending it into Europe, on their own account, or selling it to vessels which come there to purchase it in exchange for

Euro-

European goods. None of thefe villages are without a fort or battery for their fecurity in time of war; but thefe are fo infignificant, that the moſt they could do would be to drive away fome petty privateer. The greateſt extent of this iſland is from N. to S. being ninety five leagues, that is, from cape St. Mary, in 46 degr. 55 min. to the north-cape which forms the ſtreights of Belifle in 51 degr. 20 min. And the diſtance from E. to W. that is, from cape Raze to cape Cod, is eighty leagues. But the fettlements of the Engliſh are only about the harbours and in the country near Placentia; and along its bays eaſtward towards cape Raze, and from thence to cape Buena Viſta: all the remainder both up the country and along the coaſt, northwards towards the ſtreights, and from thence weſtward, is entirely defart. This muſt however be imputed to the rigour of the climate, and the badnefs of the foil, more than to any negle&t of the proprietors, who feldom are wanting in induſtry, when they have a probability of fuitable advantages. The inhabitants relate, that it was formerly peopled by a race of favage Indians, who fince have retired to the continent; nor do they often vifit the iſland, and even when they do, they ſtay but a very fmall time, returning to the continent from whence they came. This was indeed their cuſtom before ever the names of French or Engliſh were known in the iſland, retiring from the feverity of the froſts at the approach of winter. Thefe Indians generally live by fiſhing and hunting; and both this iſland, the iſle royale and the adjacent parts of Canada, abound in buſtards and wild geefe. There are alfo found, tho' in no great numbers, the quadrupeds of this country, as foxes, bears, beavers and others: but the continual fearch after them for the fake of their ſkins has much leffened their numbers.

UNDER all the feverity of the climate, they are
not

not without some horned cattle; but these are preserved with no less care and difficulty than at Louisbourg. The inhabitants have also their little kitchen gardens for summer herbs: but all the other species of provisions, as flour, salt, meat, &c. they are supplied with from Boston, Penfylvania, and other colonies to the fouthward. With regard to the goods of other kinds, they are brought from England.

Having observed in chapter seven that the greatest part of the French ships employed in the cod-trade do not take in their lading at Louisbourg, it will be necessary to explain the nature of this trade; and in order to a more clear understanding of this traffick it is to be observed, that the ships both of that nation and those of England, have two methods of carrying it on; one is to go to the fishing villages, and there buy a cargo in barter for goods, or to load with cod on their owners account; the other is to employ the ship's company in fishing in the inhabited bays; and for this the French make use of the harbours on the west part of the island of Newfoundland, which as being desart, and likewise an article stipulated in the treaty of peace, no opposition is made to it: for this seems to me the meaning of the expression often occuring in the treaties, *That the English shall admit the French and Spaniards into the harbours of Newfoundland:* and not as some insist the harbours where the English have settlements, they having referved these for their own conveniency. This certainly is the most natural interpretation, for the latter being their dwelling and the best part of the island, it is not to be thought that they would give them away to others, the convenience of harbours, being the sole and chief advantage of this island: and this was the only point in view amidst the contests of nations for the possession of a country valuable only for the fishery; and where the inhabitants,

tants, at leaft two thirds of the year labour under all the inconveniences and hardfhips of deep fnows, hard frofts, and other rigours of winter.

THE weftern coaft of this ifland, diftinguifhed by the name of Petit Nord, and no lefs provided with bays and harbours than thofe inhabited by the Englifh, forms the department where the French veffels repair to fifh; as likewife north beyond the river of St. Laurence; and ftretching eaftward forms Belifle ftreight. In all thefe parts it is an inviolable rule, that the veffels which comes firft has the privilege of chufing her bay, and the beft part in it for fifhing; and likewife has the title of admiral of it: and as fuch not only all the timber works which happen to remain there belong to the mafter, but he alfo affigns to every veffel her particular birth, tho' herein he has always a regard to the date of their coming into the bay: and during the whole time of the fifhery, he carries a flag at his main-top-maft head. This diftinction and the advantage of chufing the ftation for fifhing, are fuch powerful incentives to expedition, that tho' the harbours are generally frozen in the months of March and April, fome fhips arrive there during thefe months, and fecure to themfelves the beft ftations, and build huts beforehand, by fending fome of their crew in their longboats, when the fhip is at the diftance of fifty leagues or more from the coaft, tho' it muft be acknowledged, that this ardor is often attended with fatal confequences; the boat during the darknefs of the nights running on the large iflands of ice common on the coaft; aud fometimes founder in ftorms, which are here very fudden and violent. But thefe dangers are all overlook'd by an attachment to gain and frivolous ambition. The fuccefs or failure of this fifhery depend indeed in a great meafure on the ftation of the fhip, and the conveniences for curing the fifh, Befides as the wages paid

by

## CH. IX. SOUTH AMERICA. 397

by the owners to the mafter, petty officers and men, is always one third part of the found fifh brought to Europe, the fhorter the time, the greater is the advantage to each man on board.

Though all the coafts of Newfoundland may be faid to abound in cod, yet in fome parts it is found in greater numbers than in others, and fome there are which produce few or none. This proceeds from the quality of the bottom; for thofe parts where the bottom is fandy are fuller of fifh than where it is rocky; but if the bottom be muddy, fifh are very fcarce: likewife in a great depth of water the fifh are not caught in that plenty as when it does not exceed thirty or forty fathom. For tho' cod be found at a greater or lefs depth, yet this feems to be that which the cod moft delight in.

Such are the motives for which the mafters of veffels in this trade are fo eager to be among the firft, that they may chufe their feveral conveniences, in order to finifh their fifhery with the greater difpatch; and returning early to Europe, may turn their cargo to a better account.

When a fhip has taken her ftation, fhe is immediately unrigg'd; and at the fame time a fit place chofen for fecuring the fifh, as it is prepared: huts are likewife run up for the men who work afhore, fo as to form a kind of village; and at the water's edge is alfo built a large ftage or fcaffold. Here the number of launches defigned for the fifhery is got ready, and when built are left there till the following year; when he who firft enters the bay, has the privilege of applying them to his own ufe. Every thing being ready, the whole fhip's company, officers included, without exception of any one, are divided into as many claffes as there are occupations: fome fifh, others cut off the heads, others gut the fifh, which the French call habiller; whilft others have the care of falting and laying them up.

The

The fiſhers ſet out very early in their boats, that they may be at their ſtation by break of day, and do not return till the evening, unleſs they happen to have caught their boat-load before. This fiſhery is all performed with the hook; and every boat is provided with a ſufficient quantity of all kinds of fiſhing-tackle, to be ready at hand in caſe of any accident, as breaking a line or the like. On their return the fiſh is delivered to thoſe who open them; and that this may be done with the greater diſpatch, a boy ſtands by to hand them to them and take them away when cured. This work is done in a methodical manner; for he who beheads them does nothing elſe. They are opened with one cut length-wiſe, their back bone, and all their entrails are taken out; and another immediately taken in hand, and the offals thrown into the ſea. While ſome open, others ſalt, and others again pile up; and all this is done with the greateſt care and regularity. The next day, or when the ſalt appears to have ſufficiently penetrated, they waſh them, and take them in pairs by the tails, then ſhake them in the water in order to carry off the ſcum extracted by the ſalt: afterwards, that the water may run off, they are piled up on little boards; then they are ſtretched out one by one, with the ſkin upwards, in order for drying, where they are turned three or four times. Being thus thoroughly dried, they are piled up in ſmall parcels that they may not entirely loſe the heat communicated to them by the firſt ſalt: and now being ſalted a ſecond time, they are laid up in regular heaps on the ſtage; and there they remain till the time of ſhipping them. As the boats go conſtantly every day, the work of the ſeveral claſſes may be imagined pretty hard and fatiguing. On the return of the boats they immediately begin with opening and ſalting the fiſh, which takes up the greater part of the night; and the ſucceeding parts

of

of the curing abovementioned neceſſarily keep them employed the following day, when the return of the barks calls upon them to renew their taſk; that thus they have very few hours left for ſleep and refreſhment. There are two kinds of cod, as to their quality; and of each three ſizes. Both have a line running from the gills to the tail; following the figure of the belly of the fiſh, and winds a little downwards from the head to the tail; but this is more diſtinct in one ſpecies than the other: and the whole fiſh from this line to the back is of a dark brown, whilſt the lower part is ſpotted with white. The connoiſſeurs in fiſh ſay that this is better than the other; the whole body of which is of a darkiſh white with reddiſh ſpots; but the belly and all its hinder parts the whiteſt. I ſhall not enter into an account of the diſproportion of its head comparatively to the other fiſhes, or the quantity of oil made from it and the livers, which are alſo very large. As to the ſpecies diſtinguiſhed by their ſize, the ſtandard cod is that which is two feet in length with the head off. The ſecond is ſmaller, called the middling: the third is the leaſt. The dealers in this commodity however ſubdivide it into ſeven or eight kinds: one of theſe is a fiſh in the opening of which, or in ſevering the head, ſome fault has been committed.

ANOTHER kind of fiſhery; but followed more by the French than any other nation, is that of the Mud-fiſh: and they cure it in the following manner. This fiſh is caught on the great bank of Newfoundland; and others as far as ſandy iſland ſouth of L'iſle royale: and as ſoon as it is caught it is opened, ſalted and laid in little piles in the hold of the ſhip, till it has ſufficiently purged; then they ſhift its place, and having ſalted it a ſecond time, ſtow it for the voyage. The ſhips intending for this fiſhery repair to the bank in the beginning of February;

bruary: as that caught in fummer, that is after June or July, on any of the banks, is inferior to that caught at the end of winter, thefe fhips finifh their fifhery and return to Europe with fuch difpatch, that fometimes they are known to make two voyages in a year. For 'tis the fouth part of the bank that this fifh chiefly haunts: and thefe likewife are accounted better than thofe taken on the north.

THE cod appears to be one of the moft prolifick kind of fifh. Of this there needs no other proof than the great number of fhips which annually load with it only from this ifland: and it is only known in thefe feas; for tho' the Britifh channel and the German ocean are not without this fifh, their numbers are fo inconfiderable comparatively to thofe of Newfoundland, that they may rather be looked upon as ftragglers. Some perfons of long experience in this fifhery, informed us that the cod fpawns twice a year; and befides the infinite number of their animalculæ, it is very feldom that any of them mifcarry; for they depofite them in the fand; and thus by a natural inftinct they are laid on thefe banks, to which they adhere; without being ever removed by any agitation of the waters, till impregnated with life. The cod alfo delights to continue at the bottom; at leaft is never feen on the furface of the water. But tho' their number is ftill immenfe, they are evidently diminifhed, a proof of this is that much fewer are now caught in the fame fpace of time, than there were twenty five or thirty years ago.

THE coaft of the continent oppofite to Newfoundland is inhabited by Indian favages; and tho' the crown of France keeps poffeffion of it for the conveniency of the fifhery; it has no proper fettlement: and was reprefented only by a perfon who follicited and obtained, without much difficulty, the title of governor of thefe countries. He kept up a
good

Cʜ. IX.   SOUTH AMERICA.   401

good correspondence with the Indians, and lived among them. The winters he spent solitarily with his wife and family; in summer time he enjoyed the company of the masters of the fishing vessels. Thus he spent many years, and as I have been informed, it was not till this present year 1745, or a little before, that he retired to Canada; and rather out of indulgence to his wife's fears of some misfortune in the present war, than from his own inclination. These Indians live very easily with the French; come to their huts, and bring them game in exchange for brandy, wine and toys: But are much addicted to theft, as many ships have experienced by the loss of their sails and other parts of their furniture when ashore; so that it has been found necessary to keep a constant guard; and for greater security, the tents and huts are so disposed, as entirely to environ on the land-side as in a fort the whole spot of ground where their other necessaries are kept. These precautions and the known alertness of the French on any sudden alarm, have disheartened the Indians, that of late, despairing of success, they seem to have desisted from their pilfering practices.

The manner of the English fishery on the bays of the east coast of Newfoundland, is carried on in the same manner as that of the French before described; and whether it be that the great bank lies nearest, or that its bottom is such as this fish most delights in; and where consequently it is more numerous than in the western parts, that nation chose these parts preferably to the others, as the French do not frequent the western parts so much as the Petit Nord.

The frosts being set in, laid our squadron under a necessity of hastening out of this bay, which it left on the 21st of November, with the vessels under its convoy; and in the offing was joined by many others, so as in the whole to form a fleet of

Vᴏʟ. II.                 D d                  betwixt

betwixt sixty and sixty five ships of all sizes: and among these were two frigates of forty guns, who had continued cruising in these parts to secure the fishery against any attempts of the French privateers. Our voyage to England afforded nothing remarkable; and on the morning of the 22d of December, the squadron anchored in Plymouth-sound, except the Sunderland, which kept on her course with a considerable part of the convoy, and at three in the afternoon came to an anchor in Dartmouth road.

WHILST our squadron lay at Newfoundland; and in the passage to England, it met with several storms, which I shall specify in order to convey some idea of what may be expected in these seas. On the 3d of November, the wind blowing fresh at W. and with all the appearances of a violent storm, the wind abated and the weather cleared up. But on the 10th of the same month we had a storm at N. W. lasting from two in the afternoon, till two the next morning; and on its decline snow and showers. On the 14th it began to blow fresh in the morning; and at noon came on a storm no less violent than the former, at N. E. and E. N. E. It continued in this point till the 15th, when in the morning it shifted to the north, tho' blowing still with the same force; but at four in the evening it began to abate. This was succeeded by thick snow: and on the 17th, and the days following, came on those frosts which obliged the squadron to hasten its departure from that island.

WHILST we were on our voyage, namely on the 22d of the same month of November, we had hard gales at east, which on the 23d increased to a direct storm, that lasted with all its violence till the 26th; when the wind came about to S. W. and the fog which had covered the whole atmosphere cleared up. On the 27th of the same month, it began to blow hard at S. W. and thus continued at

the

## Ch. IX.   SOUTH AMERICA.   403

the fame point and at S. and W. without abating in violence till the 4th of December; when fhifting to the N. W. we had fine weather. Afterwards the wind was at N.W. and N. and from thence veered to the N. E. and E. where it continued with fome violence till the 21ft of December; on the evening of which it came about to the S. and S. S. W. that the fleet was obliged to work up the channel. In 48 degr. 45 min. lat. the lead was hove, and found 78 fathom water, with a bottom of fine white fand, which is the particular mark of the entrance of the channel.

DARTMOUTH harbour is a kind of road or open bay, at the end of which ftands the town of that name. The country is delightfully interfperfed with feats and farm-houfes; which with the various cultivation of the hills and plains, the verdure of the paftures, and the hedges feparating the fields, make a moft agreeable appearance; and fhew the goodnefs of the foil, and the induftry of the inhabitants. We ftay'd here no longer than till the wind favour'd our proceeding to Portfmouth, which was the rendezvous of the whole fquadron; and on the 28th the wind veering to the S. W. and W. we got under fail; and on the 29th the fhip anchor'd at Spithead, where at that time lay feven three deck fhips carrying from 90 to 100 guns. From the fhip I was carried to Fareham, a pleafant village at the upper end of Portfmouth-harbour, and about three leagues by land from the town. This being appointed for the place of my captivity, and of thofe who had been included in the capitulation of Louifbourg: the fate of the others was to be confined in the common prifon at Portchefter caftle. The commiffaries indeed could not well take upon them to difpenfe with the ftrictnefs of their orders. I muft not here omit the courtefy and generofity of captain Brett of the Sunderland, to all the prifoners of any rank, whom he

D d 2   not

not only admitted to his table during the voyage; but prevailed on all the other officers to imitate this good example; and who seemed to vie in civilities towards us, and humanity towards the inferior fort; sparing for nothing to alleviate our misfortunes. And let this remain a monument of my gratitude to such a generous set of gentlemen.

WE arrived in England at the time when Charles Edward eldest son of the Chevalier de St. George landed in the north of the kingdom, among the Scots Highlanders; and was by their assistance endeavouring to recover the throne of his ancestors; tho' with how little success is now known to all the world. These commotions left little hopes of a favourable reception to us prisoners, whose long sufferings and hardships naturally caused more ardent longings after ease and liberty: and the jealousies, which in such cases are only a prudent care, together with the irregularity of some prisoners, who, contrary to the rules of honour, abuse any indulgence shewn them, and violate their parole, occasioned an order for abridging the prisoners of several privileges they had before enjoyed, and confining them with greater strictness. However, the favours which Mr. Brookes, commissary for the French prisoners, and Mr. Rickman, who acted in the same capacity for the Spaniards, were pleased to shew me, were accompanied with such politeness and cordiality, that I became entirely easy under my present condition, and even the reflection on my misfortunes grew less painful. Here I could expatiate in the praise of these two gentlemen; the former to his learning, abilities, and address in the conduct of affairs, added the most endearing humanity, of which all the prisoners in his department felt the good effects; but I shall not insist on a character, the brightness of which would be but obscured by the praises of my insufficient pen.

THE

THE commissary for the Spanish prisoners, was Mr. William Rickman, under whose care consequently I should have been, without the circumstance of having been taken in a French ship: yet my being a Spaniard recommended me to his kindness, which I with gratitude own he carried to a very great height; and I had a large share of those acts of goodness by which he has deserved the universal acknowledgement of the whole Spanish nation. For from the beginning of the war, and the taking of the Princessa, he exerted all possible care for the comfort of the common prisoners; and the chief officers he even lodged at his own seat, and many others at an adjacent farm-house, about a quarter of a league from Titchfield in the London-road, called Pesbrook, and about three miles from Fareham. He made public and private solicitations in their behalf; he treated all with affability, and used the greatest dispatch in their several affairs: he raised charitable contributions, which were chiefly laid out in apparel for those of the lower class; and the officers he in the most genteel manner furnished with money, that they might live in tolerable decency.

BOTH the abovemention'd gentlemen offered to join their interest in solliciting the admiralty for my papers, which was the thing I had most at heart; but I judged that Mr. Brookes, being the commissary to whom I belonged, it would come best from him to inclose my petition, with his recommendation to the duke of Bedford, and the admiralty, that they would be pleased to order my papers to be examined for their satisfaction, and then return them to me. The answer was entirely becoming the generosity of that nation among which the chance of war had brought me: this was, that the duke of Bedford, as first commissioner of the admiralty, and the other lords of that board unanimously, and with pleasure granted the contents of my memorial;

nobly adding that they were not at war with the arts and sciences or their professors; that the English nation cultivated them; and it was the glory of its ministers and great men to protect, and encourage them. In the same generous strain ran all the answers with which the admiralty were pleased to honour me with, by their secretary Mr. Corbet; and this condescension put into my hands an opportunity of solliciting several favours to the great relief of the Spanish prisoners who were in Fareham hospital, and the common prison, besides some personal favours for myself. The worthy Mr. Brookes, soon after my arrival, had offered to procure me a warrant for going over to France, in a packet-boat, which was to carry over to St. Malo the Louisbourg captives. But I could not think of going out of England and leaving my papers behind me.

THE insurrection in Scotland induced the admiralty to issue orders, that all prisoners who were upon leave in London, should immediately repair to some distant places; tho' in this no more was meant than their own security, left in the present commotions the people should rise upon them being Roman catholics, the sovereigns of which religion were judged to foment the rebellion. On this I laid aside all thoughts of solliciting leave to go to London, tho' I was not insensible that my affairs required my personal attendance there. Thus I was obliged to wait till the agitation of the court subsided; for as by their importance they necessarily took up the attention of all the persons at the helm, a considerable time naturally elapsed, before I had the pleasure of seeing the accomplishment of the admiralty's promises relating to my papers.

IT was not long before the scale was turned by the great levies of troops in England, and the transportation of others from Flanders to act against those of the pretender, whose son having sustained a defeat,

feat, and being deftitute of all refource, was obliged to withdraw from the kingdom. On this the perturbations in the minds of the people fubfided; and the miniftry feemed to be more at leifure for attending to private affairs.

This revived my thoughts of forwarding my affairs, by a perfonal follicitation at London. I found no difficulty in obtaining the ufual permiffion, and had the pleafure of performing the journey in company with Mr. Brookes, whom bufinefs called to that capital, where we arrived on the 12th of April.

On my firft attendance at the office for prifoners of war, an order was fhewn me from my lord Harrington, fecretary of ftate, for bringing me to his houfe. This nobleman having been ambaffador for fome years in Spain, among his other eminent qualities had a great affection for the Spaniards, which he was pleafed to extend to me in a moft obliging reception and affurances, that nothing fhould be wanting in him to procure me my papers, or do me any other good offices.

Martin Folkes, Efq; prefident of the royal fociety of London, a perfon equally diftinguifhed for his learning, politenefs and readinefs to do every good action in his power, being informed I was a prifoner at Fareham, and that my papers were lodged at the admiralty; and fearing they might fall into the hands of perfons entirely ignorant of their contents, and by that means be miflaid or abufed, had applied for having them delivered to him; alledging, that as the fubject of them related to the fciences, none could be fitter for them than the fociety. But as they were unhappily mingled with many others of a very different kind taken at the fame time, it was difficult to feparate them without the prefence of the author himfelf, to diftinguifh them by the hand and other marks. By his affiftance and the alacrity of Mr. Brookes, who was determined not to give himself

self any rest till the affair was ended to my satisfaction, an order of the admiralty was obtained to the secretary of the India company, to whom they had all been sent, that I might make a search for them, and those which I should separate were to be sent to the admiralty. This order met with such a punctual compliance, that it was executed the very day of its date.

THE president of the Royal society, for whom all the lords of the admiralty entertained an esteem suitable to his great merit, was again pleased to interest himself in behalf of my papers; and in regard to his sollicitations the examination of them was referred to him. This gentleman, who possessed in the highest degree all the social and intellectual qualities, affability without artifice, of a genius which nothing could escape, and an amiable deportment, and generous manners, had from my first arrival shewn me great kindness; he introduced me to the meetings of the society: and thus to him I owe the acquaintance of many persons of distinction, and the marks of friendship I received from them. He condescended to carry me to the most famous musæums, places of delight to a rational curiosity, where all nature is collected into a living history of the several products of the waters and earth, both in the mineral, vegetable and animal kingdoms. He further brought me acquainted with several of the most distinguished literati: and carried his friendship very far beyond any thing I could have expected.

THE recommendation of so distinguished a person, to whose judgment so much deference was paid in all things, together with the honour of having been one of the two appointed for measuring the degrees of the earth in Peru, had such an influence on the patrons of science, that I should wrong them did I not acknowledge, that I chiefly owe to them, the happiness of recovering my papers, my liberty, and the

## CH. IX.  SOUTH AMERICA.

the polite treatment several persons of rank and quality were pleased to shew me.

Actions like these convinced me of the sincerity of the English, their candor, their benevolence and disinterested complaisance. I observed the tempers, inclinations, particular customs, government, constitution and policy of this praise-worthy nation, which, in its œconomical conduct and social virtues, may be a pattern to those who boast of superior talents, to all the rest of mankind.

Mr. Folkes having gone thro' my papers, made his report to the admiralty; and so much in my favour, that did I insert it here, it would be the most honourable testimonial of our work; and that board being thoroughly satisfied, gave him leave, according to his desire, to deliver them up to me; which he did on the 25th of May. But as a more illustrious testimony of the great esteem with which he honoured me, he proposed to Earl Stanhope and several other gentlemen of the Royal Society, that I might be admitted a member of that learned body, rightly judging that such an honour could not fail of adding an ardour to my desire of contributing to the improvement of the sciences. Having thus happily finished my affairs, and obtained my liberty at the first sollicitation for it, I embarked at Falmouth in the Lisbon packet-boat; my predominant inclination now being to see my native country, after such a variety of adventures. On my safe arrival at Lisbon, I hastened to Madrid which I reached on the 25th of July 1746; eleven years and two months after my embarkation at Cadiz on this commission.

I found Spain in mourning for the loss of its late excellent sovereign Philip V. who had passed to a better state, on the 9th of the same month. My first care was to wait upon the marquis de la Ensenada,

nada, secretary of state, with my papers; that he might lay them before his majesty, whom God long preserve. His majesty was pleased to order that these papers should be published under his patronage: a declaration truly becoming a prince, who, to all the estimable qualities of a king and a man, added a love for the sciences.

Thus have we concluded a work, which has been long expected by all nations; its importance entitled it to the encouragement of the greatest monarchs: and the length of time employed in it, long kept in an impatient suspense, the learned of Europe.

*FINIS.*

# INDEX.

A.

ABYSSES, frightful ones, Vol. 1. 207
Aconcagua, Vol. 2. 264
Adobes, what Vol. 1. 269
Aji, defcribed Vol. 2. 140
Adventures, pleafant Vol.1.232
Aguacate, defcribed Vol. 1. 301
Alaufi, affiento of, Vol.1. 334
Alligators, defcribed Vol. 1. 194
—— manner of laying eggs 195
—— take little care of their young ibid.
—— their number, how diminifhed 196
—— deftroy great quantities of fifh ibid.
—— devour calves, colts, &c. 197
—— their great voracity ibid.
—— often fatal to the human fpecies ibid.
—— how catched ibid.
Alparupafca, fignal on, Vol. 1. 244
Amancaes, mountain of, its height Vol. 2. 31
Amatope, town of, defcribed, Vol. 2. 7
Amazons, account of Vol. 1. 393
—— river of, defcribed Vol. 1. 380
Amparaes, jurifdiction of Vol. 2. 150
Amula, fignal on Vol. 1. 261
Amufements of Carthagena Vol. 1. 39
Ananas, common at Carthagena Vol. 1. 71
——— defcribed ibid.
——— dimenfions of 72
Anchovies, great plenty of Vol. 2. 104

Andaguales, jurifdiction of, Vol. 2. 125
Andes, defcribed Vol. 1. 130
Angaraes, jurifdiction of, Vol. 2. 127
Anfon, lord, takes Paita Vol. 2. 198
—— a fhort account of his voyage 202
Antin, the marquis de, taken by the Englifh Vol. 2. 333
Antonio San, mountain of Vol. 1. 217
Apolo bamba, miffions of Vol. 2. 136
Aporama, a famous gold mine, Vol. 2. 135
Arauco, Indians of Vol. 2. 274
Archidona, city of Vol. 1. 369
Arequipa, city of defcribed Vol. 2. 136
——— diocefs of 138
Arica, juridiction of Vol. 2. 140
Armadillo, defcribed Vol. 1. 54
Afangaro, jurifdiction of Vol. 2. 135
Afilo, jurifdiction of Vol. 2.135
Affes, wild, account of Vol. 1. 316
Affiento, its import Vol. 1. 322
Afuay, defert of defcribed Vol. 1. 441
Ata-Hualpa, king of Quito Vol. 1. 264
—— puts his brother to death 265
—— put to death by Pizarro ibid.
Atacama, government of, defcribed Vol. 1. 302
—— jurifdiction of Vol. 2. 155
Atun-

# INDEX.

Atun-canar, described Vol. 1.
335
Avancay, jurisdiction of Vol. 2.
136
Audience of Panama Vol. 1.
130
—— of Quito Vol. 1. 272
—— of Lima Vol. 2. 43
Avila, city of Vol. 1. 370
Axes, copper ones Vol. 1. 483
—— of flint ibid.
Aymaraes, jurisdiction of Vol. 2.
134

B.

Baba, district of Vol. 1. 181
—— town of ibid.
—— river of ibid.
—— its course altered 182
Baeza, town of Vol. 1. 369
Bagre, a fish, Vol. 1. 194
Balza, described Vol. 1. 189
—— wood used in building it ibid.
—— how managed 192
—— how steered Vol. 1. 193
Banana, described Vol. 1. 72
Bannos, village of Vol. 1. 443
Barber an Indian, described Vol. 1. 280
Base for the series of triangles, how measured Vol. 1. 219
Bastimentos, what Vol. 1. 96
Bats of Carthagena, described Vol. 1. 58
Bay of Carthagena, described Vol. 1. 26
Bay of Manta Vol. 1. 174
Bay of Conception described Vol. 2. 246
Beasts, how slaughter'd in Chili Vol. 2. 241
Bejuco, snake described Vol. 1. 59
—— plant Vol. 1. 217
Bethlehem, order of our lady of, when founded Vol. 1. 271
—— great probity of the fathers 272

Biobio river of Vol. 2. 163
Birds near Carthagena Vol. 1. 56
—— vast flights of Vol. 2. 104
Biru, town of Vol. 2. 20
Boca chica, described Vol. 1. 22
Bongos, a sort of vessel Vol. 1. 108
Bannos, los, signal on, Vol. 1. 263
Borma, signal on Vol. 1. 243
Boston, account of Vol. 2. 380
Bridges, how constructed Vol. 1. 449
Bridge, a famous one over the Desaguadero Vol. 2. 162
Brisas, what Vol. 1. 85
Buenos Ayres described Vol. 2. 184
Bueran, signal on Vol. 1. 242
Building, how performed near Guayaquil Vol. 1. 187
Bulgados, described Vol. 2. 251
Burials at Carthagena Vol. 1. 39
—— at Quito Vol. 1. 289
Butterflies of Carthagena Vol. 1. 62

C.

Cacao, common at Carthagena Vol. 1. 38
—— at Guayaquil Vol. 1. 182
—— plantations, great numbers of Vol. 1. ibid.
—— tree described Vol. 1. 182
—— fruit of, how cured 183
—— soil proper for 184
—— manner of cultivating ibid.
Colcagua Vol. 2. 264
Calagula described Vol. 1. 454
Calcaylares, jurisdiction of Vol. 2. 133
Caldera, in Porto Bello harbour Vol. 1. 90
Cali, town of Vol. 1. 351
Callao, terrible earthquake at Vol. 2. 82
Callao, a palace of the Yncas Vol. 1. 214
—— another

# INDEX.

—— another Vol. 1. 487
Caloto bells, their origin Vol. 1. 358
Calves, frozen ones Vol. 2. 103
Caluma, account of Vol. 1. 174
—— temperature of Vol. 1. 205
Camana, jurisdiction of Vol. 2. 138
Camea, described Vol. 1. 303
Camini, herb Vol. 2. 173
Canals, great benefit of, in Peru Vol. 2. 28
Canas, or Canes described Vol. 1. 216
—— wonderful phænomena of ibid.
Calaguala, described Vol. 1. 454
Chancay, extraordinary manure used in that jurisdiction Vol. 2. 98
Canches, jurisdiction of Vol. 2. 133
Cancla, or cinnamon tree described Vol. 1. 361
Canete, town of Vol. 2. 115
Canta, jurisdiction of Vol. 2. 115
Campanario, signal on Vol. 1. 245
Cape Horn, passage round described Vol. 2. 296
—— remarks on the currents near Vol. 2. 306
Capiro, a celebrated mountain Vol. 1. 91
Capisayo, what Vol. 1. 280
Carabaya, jurisdiction of Vol. 2. 135
—— famous for gold mines ibid.
Carabura, signal on Vol. 1. 236
Caracol, account of Vol. 1. 180
Caracol solhado, described Vol. 1. 61
Carangas, jurisdiction of Vol. 2. 152
—— mines of 153
Cargadores, who so called Vol. 1. 79

Carguairaso, mountain Vol. 1. 214
—— eruption of Vol. 1. 324
Carthagena, described Vol. 1. 21
—— discovered, by whom ibid.
—— advantageously situated ibid.
—— often taken 22
—— fortifications of 23
—— houses, churches, &c. 24
—— extent of its jurisdiction 25
—— bay of described 26
—— account of its inhabitants 29
—— dress of the different classes 32
—— genius of the natives 33
—— customs of the inhabitants 37
—— amusements at 39
—— burials how performed ibid.
—— climate of 42
—— distempers, common at 47
—— country about, described ibid.
—— trees of different kinds 49
—— vegetables in the neighbourhood of 50
—— beasts, reptiles, insects, &c. 52
—— provisions used by the inhabitants 68
—— great fertility of the country 69
—— trade of 78
—— fair of 80
—— revenues of 82
Cascabele, described Vol. 1. 59
Cascade, a beautiful one Vol. 1. 205
Cascarilla, described Vol. 1. 340
Casms, large ones left by earthquakes Vol. 2. 87
Casonate, what Vol. 1. 197

Cassava

# INDEX.

Caffava bread, what Vol. 1. 68
Caftro Virreyna, jurifdiction of Vol. 2. 127
Cafts, or tribes, what Vol. 1. 29
Caxa mines, what Vol. 1. 470
Caxamarca, jurifd. of Vol. 2. 121
Caxamarquilla, jurifd. of Vol. 2. 122
Caxatambo, jurifdict. of Vol. 2. 117
Cayambe, plain of Vol. 1. 227
——— village of Vol. 1. 220
Cayamburo, mountain of Vol. 1. 319
——————— Vol. 1. 445
Cedar tree, defcribed Vol. 1. 48
Ceremonies at the public entrance of the viceroy Vol. 2. 46
Ceibo wooll, defcribed Vol. 1. 199
Chachapayas, jurifdiction of Vol. 2. 121
Chagre, river defcribed Vol. 1. 106
——— fort of 107
——— prodigious trees on its banks 108
——— taken by Morgan 113
Chalapu, fignal on Vol. 1. 240
Chancay, town of, defcribed Vol. 2. 26
Changalli, fignal on Vol. 1. 237
Chapotonada, what Vol. 1. 42
Chapetones, who Vol. 1. 29
Characters of feveral Englifhmen Vol. 2. 415 feq.
Charcas province of Vol. 2. 141
Chatas, a fort of veffel Vol. 1 108
Chayanta, province of Vol. 2. 151
Chicha, what Vol. 1. 279
Chichichoco, fignal on Vol. 1. 240
Ciacica, province of Vol. 2. 155

Chica, defcribed Vol. 1. 303
Chicas, jurifdiction of Vol. 2. 149
Chilan Vol. 2. 271
Chili, great fertility of Vol. 2. 240
——— part of the kingdom of, defcribed Vol. 2. 258
——— when conquered ibid.
——— governments in 260
——— commerce of Vol. 2. 268
——— mines of 277
Chiloas, jurifdiction of Vol. 2. 122
Chiloe, account of Vol. 2. 262
Chilques, jurifdiction of Vol. 2. 133
Chimbadores, who Vol. 2. 21
Chimbo, jurifdiction of Vol. 1. 331
Chimborazo, defert of Vol. 1. 213
——— mountain of, Vol. 1. 443
Chinan, fignal on Vol. 1. 244
Chincoulagua, fignal on Vol. 1. 249
——— mountain of Vol. 1. 445
Chiquitos, miffions of Vol. 2. 164
Chirimoya, defcribed Vol. 1. 300
Chocope, town of Vol. 2. 18
——— a remarkable occurrence there ibid.
——— obfervations of a furprizing rain there Vol. 2. 74
Choglos, what Vol. 1. 305
Cholos, what Vol. 1. 212
Chorrera, what fo called Vol. 1. 205
Chriftopher St. mountain of, its height Vol. 2. 31.
Chucha, defcribed Vol. 1. 241
Chucuito, jurifdiction of Vol. 2. 160

Chu-

# INDEX.

Chuchunga, town of Vol. 1. 377
Chulapu, signal on Vol. 1. 249
Churches of Lima, their astonishing riches Vol. 2. 38
Chusay, signal on Vol. 1. 242
Coca, a plant, described Vol. 1. 362
Cochabamba, province of Vol. 2. 152
Cochineal, account of the breeding of Vol. 1. 341
Coco nut, common near Carthagena Vol. 1. 74
——— description of 75
Cod-fishery, account of Vol. 2. 405
Colta lake of Vol. 1. 326
Comegan, an insect, described Vol. 1. 66
Commerce of Carthagena Vol. 1. 78
——— of Porto Bello, Vol. 1. 101
——— of Panama Vol. 1. 124
——— of Guayaquil Vol. 1. 198
——— of Quito Vol. 1. 307
——— of Lima Vol. 2. 106
——— of Chili Vol. 2. 268
Companario, signal on Vol. 1. 263
Conception, city of, described Vol. 2. 232
——— earthquakes at 233
——— government of 234
——— dress of the inhabitants 235
——— bay of, described 246
Canclon, described Vol. 1. 457
Cordesuyos, jurisdiction of Vol. 2. 139
Condor, described Vol. 1. 455
Contrayerva, described Vol. 1. 455
Convulsions, shocking ones at Lima. Vol. 2. 89
Cope, a mine of Vol. 2. 9.

Coquimbo, town of, described Vol. 2. 265
Coral snake, described Vol. 1. 59
Corazon, signal on Vol. 1. 239
Cordova, city of Vol. 2. 167
Corientes, city of Vol. 2. 186
Cosin, signal on Vol. 1. 245
Catopaxi, signal on Vol 1. 238
——— terrible eruption of Vol. 1. 324
Cottage on Pichincha, described Vol. 1. 224
Couplet M. death of Vol. 1. 220
Cow, sea, described Vol. 1. 414
Coya, or Coyba, a remarkable insect, described Vol. 1. 360
Cruz de Canos, temperature of Vol. 1. 211
Cuença, signal on the church of Vol. 1. 244
——— city of, described Vol. 1. 332
Cuichoca, lake of Vol. 1. 319
Culebrilla, what Vol. 1. 46
——— how cured ibid.
Currents on the coast of Carthagena Vol. 1. 85
——— of the Chagre, velocity of Vol. 1. 106
——— observations on Vol. 1. 139
——— of Guayaquil river Vol. 1. 186
——— a prodigious one Vol. 1. 389
——— near Cape Horn, curious remarks on Vol. 2. 306
Cusco, diocese of Vol. 2. 128
——— city of described ibid.
——— temple of 129
——— ruins of a famous fort ibid.
——— cathedral of 130
——— parishes of 130
——— government of 131
Cuyes,

# INDEX.

Cuyes, what      Vol. 1. 319
Caylloma, jurifd. of Vol. 2. 138
───── famous for silver mines
                          139

### D.

Dances of the Indians, Vol. 1.
                          275
Darien, mines of   Vol. 1. 129
───── province of, defcribed
                    Vol. 1. 135
Daule, lieutenancy of Vol. 1.
                          184
───── town and river of   185
Degree, length of, how determined      Vol. 1. 9
Delivrance, taken by the Englifh      Vol. 2. 346
Defaguadero, river of Vol. 2. 162
───── famous bridge of    ibid.
Dialects different in Quito Vol.
                       1. 289
Difeafes common at Porto Bello
                    Vol. 1. 94
───── at Carthagena, Vol. 1. 45
───── at Quito     Vol. 1. 295
───── at Lima      Vol. 2. 89
Difpertadores, defcribed Vol. 2.
                          242
Doctrina, what     Vol. 1. 135
Dominicos, defcribed Vol. 1. 72
Drake, Sir Francis takes Carthagena        Vol. 1. 22
Drefs at Carthagena, Vol. 1. 32
───── of the inhabitants of Panama         Vol. 1. 119
───── at Guayaquil  Vol. 1. 166
───── of the Spaniards at Quito
                    Vol. 1. 279
───── of the Meftizos    ibid.
───── of the Indians     ibid.
───── of the ladies of the firft
rank                      280
───── of the Meftizo women 281
───── of the Indian women 281
───── of the men at Lima Vol. 2.
                           56
───── of the women       ibid.

───── of the Indian women in
Valles             Vol. 2. 13

### E.

Earthquakes at Quito Vol. 1. 294
───── terrible at Latacunga
                    Vol. 1. 322
───── at Hambato   Vol. 1. 329
───── at Arequipa  Vol. 2. 137
───── at Santiago  Vol. 2. 255
Emeralds, their value fallen Vol.
                          1. 78
───── cut by the ancient Indians              Vol. 1. 485
───── mines of     Vol. 1. 494
Eminences, how defcended Vol.
                         1. 209
Entrance public of the viceroy
of Lima defcribed Vol. 2. 46
Eftancia, what     Vol. 1. 30
Exchequer of Quito Vol. 1. 272
Expedition to Louifbourg, account of       Vol. 2. 372

### F.

Fair of Carthagena   Vol. 1. 80
───── of Porto Bello, defcribed
                    Vol. 1. 102
Fandango, what      Vol. 1. 39
Feet, fmallnefs of, reckoned a
beauty at Lima     Vol. 2. 58
Feralones, what    Vol. 2. 190
Fernandes Juan, iflands of defcribed        Vol. 2. 217
Fertility of the foil at Quito
                    Vol. 1. 297
Feftivals, two extraordinary ones
                    Vol. 1. 275
Fevers at Guayaquil Vol. 1. 169
Field-tent how pitched Vol. 1.
                          228
Fifhery, pearl, defcribed Vol. 1.
                          126
───── at Newfoundland Vol. 2.
                          401
Fifhing of the Indians defcribed
                    Vol. 1. 175
───── on Guayaquil river defcribed          Vol. 1. 193
                          Fogs,

# INDEX.

Fog, a thick one generally at Lima Vol. 2. 65
Fogs, common in the South Sea Vol. 1. 159
Fords, dangerous ones Vol. 1. 204
Fortifications, Indian method of Vol. 1. 491
Fortresses of the Yncas, Vol. 1. 489
Fox of Carthagena, its artifice Vol. 1. 54
Franciscans, convent of at Quito, an elegant piece of architecture Vol. 1. 268
Francois, cape described Vol. 2. 357
—— value of to the French ibid.
Frutilla, described Vol. 1. 303
Fruits of various kinds in the country round Carthagena Vol. 1. 70

## G.

Gallinazo, a bird, described Vol. 1. 57
Gallinazos eat the alligator's eggs Vol. 1. 196
Gallinazo stone described Vol. 1. 482
Gamalote, a plant, described Vol. 1. 181
Garua, what Vol. 2. 69
Geese, wild, method of taking Vol. 1. 53
Gloria castle Vol. 1. 89
Godin, M. chosen professor of mathematics at Lima Vol. 2. 291
Gold, how extracted from the ore Vol. 1. 472
Granadilla, described Vol. 1. 300
Guabas, described Vol. 1. 302
Guacas, or graves of the antient Indians, described Vol. 1. 480
—— near Lima Vol. 2. 100

Guaca Tambo, described Vol. 2. 23
Guamac Vol. 1. 207
Guamalies, province of Vol. 2. 119
Guamanga, jurisd. of Vol. 2. 124
Guamani, signal on Vol. 1. 247
Guamanga, city of, described Vol. 2. 122
Guamanga, jurisdictions in the diocese of 124
Guanabana, described Vol. 1. 73
Guanaco, described Vol. 1. 459
Guanta, jurisdiction of Vol. 2. 124
Guanacauri, signal on Vol. 1. 244
Guanca-Belica, jurisd. of Vol. 2. 125
Guanoes, birds so called Vol. 2. 98
Guanuco, city of Vol. 2. 117
Guapulo, signal on Vol. 1. 245
Guaqueros, what Vol. 1. 483
Guaura, town of, described Vol. 2. 25
—— used in steering balzas, what Vol. 1. 192
Guarachiri, jurisdiction of, Vol. 2. 117
Guaranda, manner of entring Vol. 1. 212
Guarico, described Vol. 2. 356
Guarmey, town of Vol. 2. 24
Guasos, their dexterity Vol. 2. 241
Guayaba, described Vol. 1. 73
Guayaquil, described Vol. 1. 160
—— customs and dress of the inhabitants 164
—— its riches 166
—— temperature of the air at Vol. 1. 167
—— snakes and other poisonous reptiles ibid.
—— prodigious number of insects 168
—— diseases at 169
—— pro-

# INDEX.

—— provisions and manner of living 170
—— extent of its jurisd. 173
—— river of, described 185
—— commerce of 198
Guaylas, province of Vol. 2. 119
Guineos, described Vol. 1. 72
——— how eaten 73
Guinea pepper, described Vol. 2. 140

## H.
Habilla, at Carthagena described Vol. 1. 51
Hadley's Quadrant, described Vol. 1. 145
Hambato, assiento of Vol. 1. 329
Harbour of Porto Bello, described Vol. 1. 89
Harbour of Panama Vol. 1. 116
Hazianda, what Vol. 1. 31
Horn, cape, passage round Vol. 2. 296
—— remarks on the currents near 306
Horses, American described Vol. 1. 464
Houses, several forsaken on account of the number of Moschitos Vol. 1. 203
Hueyna-Capac, account of Vol. 1. 264
Humming bird, described Vol. 1. 458
Hunting, manner of at Quito Vol. 1. 463
Hut at Pichinca, described Vol. 1. 224
Hypothesis, a new one to account for the want of rain in Peru Vol. 2. 67
—— for earthquakes 84

## I.
Jaen government of Vol. 1. 375
Jauxa, jurisd. of Vol. 2. 118
Idols of the ancient Indians Vol. 1. 484

Jesuits, their missions in Paraguay described Vol. 2. 169
Illinisa, mountain of, Vol. 1. 445
Jivicatsu, signal on, 260
Indians, their manner of fishing on the sea Vol. 1. 175
—— on Guayaquil river Vol. 1. 193
—— their unfaithfulness, Vol. 1. 226
—— their dress Vol. 1. 279
Indians of Quito described Vol. 1. 418
—— their moderation 420
—— their remarkable sloth 422
—— their feasts 423
—— their funerals 425
—— their food ibid.
—— their huts 426
—— their language Vol. 1. 427
—— their superstition 428
—— their marriages 430
—— their insensibility 432
—— their intrepidity 434
—— their constitution 438
—— their diseases 439
—— their diversions ibid.
—— ancient, monuments of Vol. 1. 479
—— very ingenious Vol. 1. 484
—— wild, account of Vol. 1. 497
—— monuments of the ancient Vol. 2. 100
—— Arauco, account of Vol. 2. 273
Iguana, an amphibious creature, described Vol. 1. 121
—— eaten at Panama ibid.
—— lays great quantities of eggs 122
Inna Quito, plain of Vol. 1. 266
Inscription, an historical one Vol. 2. 196
Iron castle Vol. 1. 89
Ica, town of Vol. 2. 116
Islands of Juan Fernandes, described Vol. 2. 217

Ladies

# INDEX.

## L.

Ladies of Lima, their dress Vol. 2. 56
Lagarto, what Vol. 1. 198
Lalangufo, fignal on Vol. 1. 241
Lambayeque, town of Vol. 2. 16
Lampa, jurifd. of Vol. 2. 134
Lana de ceibo, defcribed Vol. 1. 199
Lard, its great ufe at Carthagena Vol. 1. 77
Laricaxas, jurifd. of Vol. 2. 159
—— famous gold mine of 160
Latacunga, affiento of Vol. 1. 322
Lavadero, famous one Vol. 2. 135
—— what Vol. 2. 270
Leprofy, common at Carthagena Vol. 1. 44
Lima, city of defcribed Vol. 2. 29
—— when founded 30
—— name, whence ibid.
—— delightful fituation of ibid.
—— river of 31
—— grand fquare of ibid.
—— dimenfions of 33
—— difpofition of the ftreets, &c. ibid.
—— houfes, how built 33
—— its parifhes 34
—— convents, &c, 35
—— hofpitals 36
—— churches 38
—— power of the Vice-roy of 40
—— tribunals of 42
—— how governed 43
—— Univerfity, colleges of 44
—— public entrance of the viceroy 46
—— inhabitants of 52
—— commerce of 54
—— drefs of the inhabitants 56
—— number of ornaments, worn by the ladies of Lima 59
—— dreffes of the lower clafs 62
—— temperature of the air 64
—— feafons, how divided at ibid.
Lima, never rains there, and why 67
—— not fubject to tempefts 77
—— inconveniences of 78
—— earthquakes at 79
—— diftempers at Vol. 2. 89
—— foil of, vitiated by an earthquake 94
—— monuments of antiquity near 100
—— different kind of provifions at 102
—— trade and commerce of 106
—— extent of its jurifdiction 112
Limes defcribed Vol. 1. 75
—— how ufed 76
Limpie pongo, fignal on Vol. 1. 248
Lions, fea, defcribed Vol. 2. 223
Lipes, jurifd. of Vol. 2. 149
—— mines of ibid.
Limpion, what Vol. 2. 108
Llama, defcribed Vol. 1. 459
Llulla, jurifd. of Vol. 2. 121
Log-line, error in marking it Vol. 1. 9
Loja, jurifd. of Vol. 1. 339
—— city of ibid.
Longitude, how found, by the variation Vol. 1. 14
—— of Panama, how determined Vol. 1. 115
Louis Erafme, taken by the Englifh Vol. 2. 333
Louifbourg, in cape Breton defcribed Vol. 2. 363
—— inhabitants of 367
—— account of its being taken by the Englifh 372
Lucanas, jurifd. of Vol. 2. 127

# INDEX.

Lunar rainbow Vol. 1. 62

## M.

Machangara, river of Vol. 1. 267
Macas, diftrict of Vol. 1. 372
Machala, town of Vol. 1. 178
Madera, river of Vol. 1. 384
Magdalena, fources of that river Vol. 1. 352
Maize how prepared by the Indians Vol. 1. 303
Matapalo, defcribed Vol. 1. 218
Mal de Valle, what Vol. 1. 295
Mamarumi, cafcade at Vol. 1. 205
Mameis, defcribed Vol. 1. 74
Mancora, breach of Vol. 2. 8
Mangrove tree, defcribed Vol. 1. 179
—— ufe of its wood ibid.
Mani, a fruit defcribed Vol. 1. 76
Manta, a fifh of an enormous fize defcribed Vol. 1. 128
Manta, bay of Vol. 1. 174
Manure, an extraordinary kind Vol. 2. 98
Manzanillo, defcribed Vol. 1. 48
Maranon river, defcribed Vol. 1. 381
Marimondas, a large fpecie of monkey, defcribed Vol. 1. 215
Marquis d'Antin taken by the Englifh Vol. 2. 333
Mofque Pacona, province of Vol. 2. 164
Mafques, jurifdiction of Vol. 2. 133
Mate, what Vol. 1. 286
Materials ufed in building near Guayaquil Vol. 1. 187
Maynas, government of Vol. 1. 380
Melilla Vol. 2. 264
Meftizos, who Vol. 1. 277

Meftizos apply themfelves to trade Vol. 1. 278
—— their drefs Vol. 1. 279
Micos, a fmall fpecies of monkeys Vol. 1. 54
Miguel de Santiago, a famous painter Vol. 1. 278
—— (fan) de Ibarra defcribed Vol. 1. 314
Milin, fignal on Vol. 1. 239
Mines in the kingdom of Terra Firma Vol. 1. 129
—— in the province of Quito Vol. 1. 469
—— in Popayan Vol. 1. ibid.
—— in the governments of Quijos and Macas Vol. 1. 477
—— of Quickfilver Vol. 1. 478
—— of fulphur Vol. 1. 495
—— of quickfilver in Peru Vol. 2. 125
—— of gold, famous ones Vol. 2. 135
—— of filver, in Caylloma Vol. 2. 139
—— of Potofi, how difcovered Vol. 2. 145
—— prodigious richnefs of 146
—— quantity of filver taken out of 148
—— of Porco Vol. 2. 149
—— of Lipes ibid.
—— of Oruro Vol. 2. 150
—— of Carangas Vol. 2. 152
—— of Pacajes Vol. 2. 159
—— of gold, famous Vol. 2. 160
—— of Chili Vol. 2. 269
Mira, fignal on Vol. 1. 245
Mirrours of ftone Vol. 1. 482
Miffions of Apolo-bamba Vol. 2. 136
—— of Chiquitos Vol. 2. 164
—— of Paraguay, defcribed Vol. 2. 169
—— how fettled 170
—— inhabitants of 171
—— temperature of the air 172
—— products of 173

Miffions,

# INDEX.

Missions, how governed 174
——— churches of 175
——— manufactures of 177
——— priests of 178
——— manners of the inhabitants 181
——— policy of the jesuits ibid.
——— on the Maranon Vol. 1. 409
Mocha, temperature of Vol. 1. 213
Monkeys, of various kinds Vol. 1. 109
Monquegua, jurisd. of Vol. 2. 139
Monsefu, town of Vol. 2. 17
Monte Christo, town of Vol. 1. 174
MonteVideo, city of Vol. 2. 186
Monuments of the ancient Indians Vol 1. 479
——— of antiquity near Lima Vol. 2. 100
Mopa-mopa, described Vol. 1. 362
Morgan, John, takes Porto-bello Vol. 1. 86
——— takes Panama Vol. 1. 113
Morrope, town of Vol. 2. 16
Moschitos at Carthagena Vol. 1. 62
——— different species of ibid.
——— their tortures Vol. 1. 202
Moths at Carthagena, their surprizing voracity Vol. 1. 66
Motives for the voyage to South America Vol. 1. 1
Mountain, an artificial one Vol. 1. 489
Muca muca, described Vol. 1. 460
Mulattoes, how distinguished Vol. 1. 286
Mules, a surprizing instance of their sagacity Vol. 1. 219

Mulmul, signal on Vol. 1. 240

N.

Napo, river of Vol. 1. 385
Naranjal, town of Vol. 1. 178
Newfoundland, account of Vol. 2. 391
——— manner of fishing there 395
Nigua, a surprizing insect, described Vol. 1. 63
——— very troublesome ibid.
——— how taken out of the flesh 64
——— kinds of it 65
Noises subterranean, whence Vol. 2. 87
Nomarelte, signal on Vol. 1. 263
Nombre de Dios, when founded Vol. 1. 86
Nopal, described Vol. 1. 342
Norona, Fernando de, island of described Vol. 2. 317
——— strongly fortified 320

O.

Oca, described Vol. 1. 303
Olive plantations Vol. 2. 94
Omaguas Indians, their odd customs Vol. 1. 412
Omasuyos, jurisd. of Vol. 2. 159
Oruro, jurisdiction of Vol. 2. 150
——— mines of ibid.
Otabalo, described Vol. 1. 318
Oyambaro, signal on Vol. 1. 236
Oysters, excellent ones Vol. 1. 117
——— produce pearls ibid.

P.

Pablo (San) lake of Vol. 1. 319
Pacaes, described Vol. 1. 302
Pacajes, jurisdiction of Vol. 2. 159
——— mine of ibid.

E e 3 Paccha,

# INDEX.

Paccha, what so called Vol. 1. 205
Pacific, why the south sea, called by that name Vol. 2. 211
Pajara Nino, described Vol. 2. 253
Painting practised at Quito Vol. 1. 278
Paita, course steered from Callao to Vol. 3. 191
—— town of, described Vol. 2. 193
—— taken by the English 198
Palace of the Yncas, described Vol. 1. 487
—————— another 489
Palm trees, described Vol. 1. 49
Palos, herb, described Vol. 2. 173
Pambamarca, signal on Vol. 1. 237
Panama, description of Vol. 1. 111
—— burnt by John Morgan 113
—— rebuilt 114
—— totally destroyed by fire 115
—— government of 116
—— harbour of ibid.
—— climate of 118
—— dress of the inhabitants 119
—— trade of 124
—— mines in its neighbourhood 128
—— extent of its audience 130
—— province of, described Vol. 1. 131
Panecillo, described Vol. 1. 267
Papa-urco, signal on Vol. 1. 239
Papas, described Vol. 1. 303
—— of silver, what Vol. 2. 152
———— how form'd ibid.
——————— magnitude of 159
Papayas, described Vol. 1. 73
Pucaguaico, signal on Vol. 1. 238

Paraguay, government of, described Vol. 2. 168
—— history of ibid.
Paraguay, towns of 169
—— missions of ibid.
—— herb described 172
Paramo, what Vol. 1. 441
Paria, province of Vol. 2. 151
Paria, lake of Vol. 2. 162
Parina Cocha, jurisd. of Vol. 2. 127
Parinnas, breach of Vol. 2. 8
Parties at Quito Vol. 1. 273
Paspaya, jurisd. of Vol. 2. 151
Passage between Callao and Paita Vol. 2. 191
Patavirca, town of, described Vol. 2. 24
Pataz, jurisd. of Vol. 2. 122
Paucartambo, jurisd. of Vol. 2. 132
Payjan, town of Vol. 2. 17
Paxla, city of Vol. 2. 156
—— magnitude of 157
—— prodigious lump of gold found at 158
—— jurisdiction of ibid.
Pearl fishery described Vol. 1. 126
Peasants of Chili, their remarkable dexterity Vol. 2. 236
Peckugueros, what Vol. 1. 296
Pedro St. town of Vol. 2. 17
Pensylvania, account of Vol. 2. 383
Perico ligero, a remarkable animal described Vol. 2. 98
Petrifactions, remarkable ones described Vol. 1. 495
—— attempt to explain that transmutation ibid.
Phænomena, curious ones, observed in the deserts Vol. 1. 461
Picaflores described Vol. 1. 458
Pichinca, great cold of Vol. 1. 222
—— height of ibid.

Pichinca,

# INDEX.

Pichinca, difficulty of afcending 222
—— ftrange manner of living on 226
Pichincha, commonly hid in clouds Vol. 1. 229
—— violence of the winds on ibid.
—— common food there 225
—— time fpent on 226
—— fignal on 236
—— famous for its riches and great height 265
—— eruptions of 267
Pie de Burro, defcribed Vol. 2. 251
Pignas, what Vol. 2.117
Pilaya, jurifdict. of Vol. 2. 151
Pillachiquir, fignal on Vol. 1. 244
Pine-apple at Carthagena defcribed Vol. 1. 71
Pifco, town of Vol. 2. 116
Piura, city of, defcribed Vol. 2. 10
Plain of Yaruqui defcribed Vol. 1. 219
—— of Cayambe Vol. 1. 220
—— of Turu-bamba Vol. 1. 266
—— of Inna Quito ibid.
Plata, Archbifhopric of, Vol. 2. 141
—— city of, defcribed 143
—— cathedral of ibid.
—— tribunals of 144
—— jurifdictions of 145
—— river of, its ufe Vol. 2. 164
Platanos, what Vol. 2. 22
Poetical conteft, what Vol 2. 50
Pointis, M. de takes Carthagena Vol. 1. 22
Pollera, what Vol. 1. 33
Pomallacta, fortrefs of Vol. 1. 491
Popayan, city of Vol. 1. 352

—— government of, defcribed Vol. 1. 350
—— abounds in gold mines, Vol. 1. 463
Porco, jurifd. of Vol. 2.149
—— mines of ibid.
Porto Bello, when difcovered Vol. 1. 86
—— defcribed 87
—— fuburb of called Guinea 88
—— harbour of defcribed 89
—— fortifications of ibid.
—— mountain near 91
—— climate of ibid.
—— beafts never procreate there 92
—— violent tempefts at 93
—— difeafes of 94
—— inhabitants of defcribed 96
—— provifions fcarce there 97
—— waters of, pernicious ibid.
—— forefts in the neighbourhood of ibid.
—— animals in the woods 98
—— ferpents of defcribed 99
—— trade of 101
—— fair of 102
Potofi, town of Vol. 2. 145
—— famous mountain and mines of ibid.
Preacher, a bird, defcribed Vol 1. 55
Precipices, frightful ones Vol. 1. 208
—— manner of defcending ibid.
Premadillas, what Vol. 1. 119
Pronunciation, fingular in America Vol. 1. 319
Profpects, elegant ones Vol. 1. 109
Pacara, what Vol. 1. 212

Puchugchu

# INDEX.

Puchugchu described Vol. 1. 453
Pucro, what Vol. 1. 189
Pugin, signal on Vol. 1. 244
Pulizones, who Vol. 1. 35
Puna, island of, described Vol. 1. 178
Pucaguaico, signal on 238
Puno, town of described Vol. 2. 163
Purple, the ancient, how extracted Vol. 1. 176
—— fish that produces it described ibid.

## Q.

Quadrant, Hadley's, described Vol. 1. 145
Quarries of stone, different ones Vol. 1. 493
Quebrantahuessas, described Vol. 2. 214
Quickfilver, mines of Vol. 1. 477
———— in Peru Vol. 2. 125
Quilotta Vol. 2. 264
Quinoa, a grain, described Vol. 1. 305
Quinoaloma, signal on Vol. 1. 262
Quinquina, account of Vol. 1. 339
Quispicanchi, government of Vol. 2. 132
Quito, city of, its foundation Vol. 1. 264
—— made a kingdom ibid.
—— situation of 265
—— described ibid.
—— how supplied with water 267
—— principal square of described 268
—— its houses described ibid.
—— divided into parishes 268
—— churches of 271
—— its convents, nunneries, &c 270

Quito, hospitals 271
—— courts of justice 272
—— corporation 273
—— chapter of the cathedral 274
—— full of people 276
—— class of the inhabitants 277
—— dresses used at 279
—— public schools 283
—— employment of the inhabitants 284
—— entertainments at 285
—— burials, how performed at 289
—— temperature of the air at 291
—— food of the inhabitants 297
—— commerce of 307
—— province of described 310
—— jurisdictions of 314
Quixos, government of Vol. 1. 368

## R.

Raft, see Balza Vol. 1. 190
Rain, why none in Peru Vol 2. 67
Rainbow, a lunar one Vol. 1. 361
Raneagua, country of Vol 2. 264
Rancherias, what Vol. 1. 132
Raspaduras, what Vol. 1. 306
Rats numerous at Guayaquil Vol. 1. 168
Rattle-snake described Vol. 1. 59
Riobamba described Vol. 1. 325
River of Guayaquil described Vol. 1. 185
———— how far navigable ibid.
—— of the Amazons Vol. 1. 380
Rivers, how passed Vol. 1. 450

Road

# INDEX.

Road from Caracol to Ojibar described Vol. 1. 204
—— a terrible one Vol. 1. 207
Roads near Guayaquil, dangerous Vol. 1. 160
—— shamefully neglected Vol. 1. 211
Robalo, a fish Vol. 1. 194
Robberies unknown in Peru Vol. 1. 45
Ruins of a famous fort Vol. 2. 12
Ruins of a palace of the Yncas Vol. 1. 213
—— of several of the ancient Indians Vol. 1. 487
Rumi-bamba, what Vol. 1. 267

S.

Salta de Tumbez descr Vol. 2. 4
—— de Frayle descr. Vol. 2. 24
Sangagua, what Vol. 1. 269
Sanguay, mountain of Vol. 1. 442
San Miguel de Ibarra described Vol. 1. 314
San Pablo, lake of Vol. 1. 319
Santa river, how forded Vol. 2. 21
—— prodigious current 22
Santa Cruz, province of Vol. 2. 164
—— city of, described Vol. 2. 165
—— government of Vol. 2. 167
—— when conquered 166
—— extent of ibid.
Santa Fé, account of Vol. 2. 186
Santiago de Nata de los Cavellos described Vol. 1. 131
Santiago, city of, described Vol. 2. 253
—— earthquakes at 254
—— its churches and convents 255

—— customs of the inhabitants 256
—— tribunals of ibid.
Sapatoes described Vol. 1. 74
Scolependra, account of Vol. 1. 60
Scorpion described Vol. 1. 60
—— kills itself 61
Sea-cow described Vol. 1. 413
Sea-lions described Vol. 2. 222
Sea-wolves described Vol. 2. 220
Sechura, town of Vol. 2. 12
—— desert of Vol. 2. 15
Senegualap, signal on Vol. 1. 261
Sensitive plant described Vol. 1. 50
Serpents near Porto-Bello Vol. 1. 99
—— an astonishing one Vol. 1. 415
Sesgum, signal on Vol. 1. 261
Sheep, Peruvian, described Vol. 1. 449
Shells, large strata of Vol. 2. 250
—— quarries of, in the tops of mountains 251
Shoal, a dangerous one, Vol. 2. 227
Signal, where erected on Pichincha Vol. 1. 227
—— on Pambamarca Vol. 1. 237
—— on Tanlagua Vol. 1. ibid.
—— on Carabara Vol. 1. ibid.
—— on Changalli Vol. 1. ibid.
—— on Oyambaro Vol. 1. 236
—— on Pucaguaico Vol. 1. 238
—— on Corazon 239
—— on Papa-urco ibid.
—— on the mountain of Milin ibid.
—— on the mountain of Vengotosin ibid.
—— on the mountain of Chalapu 240
—— on Chichichoco ibid.
—— on Mulmul ibid.

Signal

# INDEX.

Signal on Sifa-Pongo 241
—— on Lalangufo ibid.
—— on Chufay 242
—— on Tialoma ibid.
—— on Sinafaguani 262
—— on Bueran 242
—— on Yafuay 243
—— on Borma ibid.
—— on Pugin 244
—— on Pillachiquir ibid.
—— on Alparupafca ibid.
—— on Chinan ibid.
—— on Guanacauri ibid.
—— on the great church of Cuenca ibid.
—— on Guapulo 245
—— on Campanario ibid.
—— on Cofin ibid.
—— on Mira ibid.
—— on each extremity of the bafe of Yaruqui 246
—— on Pambamarca ibid.
—— on the mountain of Tanlagua ibid.
—— on the mountain of Guapulo 247
—— on Gumani ibid.
—— on Corazon 248
—— on Cotapaxi ibid.
—— on Chinchulagua 249
—— on Papa-urco ibid.
—— on the mountain of Milin ibid.
—— on Chulapu ibid.
—— on Jivigatfu 260
—— on Mulmul ibid.
—— on Guayama ibid.
—— on Amula 261
—— on Sifa-pongo ibid.
—— on Sefgum ibid.
—— on Senegualap ibid.
—— on Chufay ibid.
—— on Sinafaguan 262
—— on Quinoaloma ibid.
—— on Yafuay ibid.
—— on Namarelte 263
—— on Guanacauri ibid.
—— on los Bonnos ibid.

Signal on the great church of Cuenca ibid.
—— on Guapulo 263
—— on Pambamarca ibid.
—— on Campanario ibid.
—— on Cwicocha ibid.
—— on Mira ibid.
Sinafaguan, fignal on Vol. 1. 242
Sifa-Pongo, fignal on Vol. 1. 241
Snakes near Carthagena defcribed Vol. 1. 58
—— with two heads Vol. 1. 122
Snakes near Guayaquil Vol. 1. 167
Soldier Snail defcribed Vol. 1. 61
Sources of the Maranon Vol. 1. 381
Spaniards ridiculous pride of Vol. 1. 279
—— their drefs at Quito ibid.
Springs very common near Lima Vol. 2. 97
Strawberry of Peru, defcribed Vol. 1. 303
Storax-tree, defcribed Vol. 1. 374
Storms, terrible ones Vol. 2. 211
—— how prognofticated Vol. 2. 214
Sugar-canes, their quick growth at Carthagena Vol. 1. 69
Sulphur, mines of Vol. 1. 495
Sun, temple of, its grandeur Vol. 2. 128
Supay-Urco, famous mountain of Vol. 1. 338
Sures, or fouth winds Vol. 1. 157

T.

Tables of variation, fee Variation

Taburones,

# INDEX.

Taburones, an enormous fish, described Vol. 1. 127
Talcaguana, port of Vol. 2. 247
Tamarinds described Vol. 1. 76
Tanlagua, signal on Vol. 1. 237
Tarabita, what Vol. 1. 449
Tarija, jurisdict. of Vol. 2. 149
Tempests, terrible ones Vol. 1. 93
Temple of the Sun, grandeur of Vol. 2. 128
——— an ancient one Vol. 1. 486
Terra Firma, kingdom of, described Vol. 1. 130
Thread how dyed purple Vol. 1. 176
Tialoma, signal on Vol. 1. 242
Ticsan, village of Vol. 1. 336
Tides at Porto-Bello Vol. 1. 90
——— regular at Panama Vol. 1. 116
——— in Guayaquil river Vol. 1. 178
Tiempo muerto, what Vol. 1. 81
Tigers common in the forests of Porto-Bello Vol. 1. 97
——— manner of killing them 98
Timber, great quantities of Vol. 1. 199
Tintoreras, monstrous fish, described Vol. 1. 127
Tiopullo, plain of Vol. 1. 214
Titi-caca, famous lake of Vol. 2. 160
——— spendid temple of 161
Toads, great numbers at Porto-Bello Vol. 1. 99
Tolo, large fishery of Vol. 2. 156
Tolu, balsam of Vol. 1. 48
Tomina, jurisdiction of Vol. 2. 148
Tooth-ach, a strange remedy for Vol. 2. 224

Totumo, what Vol. 1. 286
Trade of Carthagena Vol. 1. 78
——— of Porto-Bello Vol. 1. 101
——— of Panama Vol. 1. 124
——— of Guayaquil Vol. 1. 198
——— of Quito Vol. 1. 307
——— of Lima Vol. 2. 53
Travelling, method of Vol. 2. 7
Travesia, what Vol. 2. 212
Truxillo, city of described, Vol. 2. 19
——— bishopric of Vol. 2. 120
Tulcar, a bird described Vol. 1. 55
Tumbez, town of Vol. 2. 5
Tunguragua, mountain of Vol. 1. 443
Tura-Bamba, plain of Vol. 1. 214
Turbonadoes, what Vol. 2. 208

V.

Valdivia described Vol. 2. 262
Valles, meaning of that word Vol. 2. 6
Valparaiso, town of, described Vol. 2. 280
——— bay of 283
Variation chart of Dr Hadley Vol. 1. 14
Variation, its use in finding the longitude Vol. 1. 16
Variations, tables of ibid.
——— how to be observed Vol. 1. 17
——— a table of, observed in the south-sea Vol. 1. 143
——— a table of Vol. 2. 229
——— table of Vol. 2. 314
——— table of Vol. 2. 341
——— 343
——— table of Vol. 2. 355
Vendabales, what Vol. 1. 88
Vengotasin, signal on Vol. 1. 239
Veraguas, province of, described Vol. 1. 134
Vernon takes Porto-Bello Vol. 1. 89

Vice-

# INDEX.

Vice-roy of Lima, his power Vol. 2. 40
——————— his public entrance described Vol. 2. 46
Vicho, what Vol. 1. 295
Vicuna, described Vol 1. 459
Vijahua, described Vol. 1. 217
Ujiba, account of Vol. 1. 180
Virgin, two miraculous images of Vol. 1. 276
University of Quito, account of Vol. 1. 270
——————— of Lima Vol. 2. 44
——————— of Cuſco Vol. 2. 132
Volcanoes, how formed Vol. 2. 85
——————— new ones, Vol. 2. 84
Vomito Prieto, or black vomit Vol. 1. 44

## W.

Water a remarkable tract of Vol. 1. 14
Whirlwinds, dreadful ones Vol. 1. 249
Wild Indians, account of Vol. 1. 497
Winds generally prevailing between Carthagena and Porto Bello Vol. 1. 84
——————— violent ones Vol. 1. 224
——————— in the south-seas, observations on Vol. 2. 27
Wolves, sea, described Vol. 2. 220

## Y.

Yaguache, lieutenancy of Vol. 1. 180
Yaguoche, town of ibid.
Yagarchoca, lake of Vol. 1. 315
Yerva de Gallo, or cocks herb, a fabulous account of Vol. 1. 123
Yaraqui, plain of Vol. 1. 219
——————— ſignals at Vol. 2. 146
Yuſuay, ſignal on Vol. 1. 243
Yauyos, palace of, described Vol. 1. 487
——————— another 501

## Z.

Zumbador, described Vol. 1. 457

*F I N I S.*

www.ingramcontent.com/pod-product-compliance
Lightning Source LLC
Chambersburg PA
CBHW032136010526
**44111CB00035B/593**